T. S. Eliot

THE POET AND HIS CRITICS

T. S. Eliot

THE POET AND HIS CRITICS

ROBERT H. CANARY

AMERICAN
LIBRARY
ASSOCIATION
CHICAGO
1982

THE POET AND HIS CRITICS

A series of volumes on the meaning of the critical writings on selected modern British and American poets.

Edited by CHARLES SANDERS, University of Illinois, Urbana

Robert Frost by Donald J. Greiner
William Carlos Williams by Paul L. Mariani
Dylan Thomas by R. B. Kershner, Jr.
Langston Hughes by Richard K. Barksdale
Wallace Stevens by Abbie F. Willard

LIBRARY OF CONGRESS CATALOGING IN PUBLICATION DATA
Canary, Robert H.
T. S. Eliot : the poet and his critics.

(The Poet and his critics)
Includes bibliographies and index.
1. Eliot, T. S. (Thomas Stearns), 1888–1965—Criticism and interpretation—History. I. Title. II. Series.
PS3509.L43Z6473 821′.912 81-20516
ISBN 0-8389-0355-X AACR2

Printed in the United States of America.

For Molly

Contents

Preface

T. S. Eliot (1888–1965) was one of the major poets and most influential literary critics of this century; some would argue, as well, that he is one of the most important modern dramatists in English. New books on his work appear each year, apparently justified by his intrinsic significance, even when the authors have little new to say. This book, however, is only secondarily about Eliot; its primary concern is with criticism of Eliot, and so some words of explanation may be in order. The principal justification for this survey of Eliot criticism is that readers interested in Eliot need some sort of guide to a body of criticism so massive that it threatens to overwhelm its subject and obscure its own major themes. One may add to this the hope that this assessment of the characteristic strengths and weaknesses of Eliot criticism will encourage others to build upon the strengths and remedy the weaknesses; this seems especially important because the strengths and weaknesses of Eliot criticism are, by and large, those of modern literary criticism in general.

We can fill one small shelf, perhaps, with the works of Thomas Stearns Eliot. The collected poetry makes a slim volume. Crowded together in its pages are poems which have deeply affected the sensibility of this century—"The Love Song of J. Alfred Prufrock," "Gerontion," *The Waste Land*, *Ash Wednesday*, and *Four Quartets*. Its companions will be a handful of plays and some volumes of literary and cultural criticism. Eliot's own literary criticism consists of brief essays, mostly written as book reviews or lectures. Modest about the possibilities of interpretation, Eliot's criticism works through apt quotations and suggestive generalizations; its occasional dogmatism and pedantry are redeemed by a vein of ironic self-deprecation which suggests that Eliot takes literature more seriously than he takes himself as a critic.

Critical works on Eliot will fill the rest of the shelves in a fair-size room. There will be thousands of items in English alone, and many other languages will be represented. There will be long books for specialists, devoted to particular topics, and general introductions intended for students. There will be a plethora of tiny notes, many of them calling attention to allusions to other works; if we were to add to the collection all the works to which Eliot has been said to refer, we might need several more rooms. Between the books and the notes we can place a mass of critical articles and monographs. In all this literary criticism and scholarship, we will find plenty of dogmatism and pedantry; modesty in interpretation will be rare and ironic self-deprecation even more so, for Eliot criticism is apt to take itself very seriously indeed.

The purpose of all these critical studies is to help us understand Eliot, his work, and its place in literary history, but it is easy to lose sight of the small shelf of Eliot's own work, surrounded by so many works of analysis. The best critics, of course, will send one back to the poetry, equipped to read it with fresh perceptions, but excellence is no less rare in literary criticism than in other literary forms or intellectual endeavors. Although Eliot has received relatively little attention from recent structuralist and poststructuralist critics, his prominence has meant that many, perhaps most, of the best modern critics have written about his work; less-well-known critics have also written well about Eliot. One fairly obvious purpose of a book like this is to call attention to valuable critical works that might otherwise be overlooked by readers disinclined to traverse the great deserts that lie between such oases.

The sheer bulk of Eliot criticism also tends to obscure its major themes. Literary criticism is, or should be, a cooperative enterprise. A complex body of work like Eliot's presents a series of problems; in the course of time, some of these problems are resolved and others, more intractable, are at least more clearly defined. Even lesser critics can contribute to this process. Like other forms of intellectual enterprise, literary scholarship advances, when it does, partly through the patient accumulation of understanding of matters less important in themselves than in what they ultimately contribute to the whole. In Eliot criticism, this process, which requires dialogue, is difficult even for specialists; some discoveries have been made several times over, presumably because the bibliography is out of hand. This seems to me a more serious problem than simply separating the wheat from the chaff, which is a task to be met by anthologies and checklists as much as by books. This book tries to assess the progress and current state of Eliot criticism in addressing the central issues raised by his work.

Because my concern is with those central issues, this book is organized on a topical basis, rather than around particular works of Eliot or the chronological development of Eliot criticism. Chapter 1 deals with efforts to connect the man and his work through biographical or psychological criticism. Chapter 2 takes up studies of Eliot's "impersonal" theory of poetry and his use of personae in his work. Chapter 3 is concerned with the critics of Eliot's social and cultural views as reflected in his prose and poetry. Chapter 4 surveys critics who stress the religious dimensions of Eliot's work. Chapter 5 discusses critics who deal with Eliot's interpretation and use of the Western literary tradition, and chapter 6 discusses efforts to characterize Eliot's position as a "modern" poet. Within this topical framework, I have made some effort to group together discussions of particular works, so that most studies of Eliot's early poems are dealt with in chapter 1 and most studies of his plays are dealt with in chapters 4 and 5. A poem like *The Waste Land*, however, has been subjected to such a variety of approaches that it is referred to in every chapter.

As a guide to Eliot criticism, this book is selective and representative rather than comprehensive. Many works are discussed only briefly, and the list of references at the end of each chapter may seem long, but many times more works are not included. Some of the principles of selection are relatively objective: I have generally confined myself to criticism published in English, and I have given more space to criticism published in the last two decades than its merits and relation to the whole might suggest. To the extent that I have tried to separate the wheat from the chaff, the selection reflects my own prejudices and fallibility; I have, however, tried to take into account works regarded favorably by others, even when I think them of little worth. Some works of interest or value appear only in the list of additional references appended to each chapter, but readers familiar with Eliot criticism will no doubt find some items omitted completely which they would have included. I apologize in advance for such omissions and assure such critics that by the time this has reached print I will probably regret some omissions myself. But I am less concerned with whether or not particular items should have been mentioned than with whether those I discuss fairly represent the strengths and weaknesses of Eliot criticism.

The weaknesses of Eliot criticism are as important as its

strengths. Despite the volume of criticism on Eliot that has been published, there still are areas which seem remarkably weak. In at least some cases (e.g., biographical criticism or technical analysis), the weaknesses of Eliot criticism represent general deficiencies in modern Anglo-American criticism. Typical, too, is the all too common failure to do justice to the complex experience offered by the poetry. In some cases this failure results from reductive readings, which are encouraged by our literary culture's cult of originality. In other cases the failure results from the critic's insistence that his or her private associations (legitimate enough when acknowledged as such) are objectively present in the poem. This, too, seems not untypical of much modern criticism, though it seems in some recent critics to be replaced by an assumption that the critic's private associations are of greater interest than the poem. Such failures help justify the current interest in literary theory and the current dissatisfaction with interpretive procedures sometimes called the "New Criticism"; at any rate, Eliot criticism displays the New Criticism at both its best and its worst. The focus of this book must be on Eliot criticism itself, and there is little time to draw or argue for such parallels with criticism in general, but I hope that some readers find that it leads them to general reflections on criticism in the "Age of Eliot."

My own views on particular issues in Eliot criticism are necessarily (perhaps obtrusively) on display in this volume, and I need not recite them here. Given the present theoretical climate, it may be only fair to say that while I share some of the current suspicion of interpretation, I believe that one can judge whether particular interpretations are more or less adequate in accounting for historical data or the language of a poem. Not accepting the author's intent as a final authority, I base such judgments on general canons of probability (which are not scientific laws) and on the conventions of language (which are never fully determinate). Such assumptions do not allow one to identify a particular interpretation as representing ultimate truth, and the judgments they allow one to make remain subjective except to the extent that they accurately reflect an intersubjective consensus. Readers whose sense of probability or language differs greatly from my own will presumably find themselves at variance with my judgments, and readers who hold very different theoretical positions may question my right to make them. I can do no more here than indicate my position by giving fair warning.

Assuming that one can judge the adequacy of interpretations, I have tried to express such judgments as forthrightly as possible, if only because considerations of space have not allowed me room for the endless qualifications called for by my academic background and by simple prudence. Where the judgments are harsh, injustice may be done. Like good lines in a bad poem, valuable insights may be found in some works I have dismissed as mostly pointless nonsense. Some works are discussed mainly as exemplifying common faults, with less attention to their individual merits. Some critics whose work I generally admire seem to me at their very worst in writing about Eliot. It is possible, too, that I have been overgenerous in some cases, listing as a four-star attraction in the strange country of Eliot criticism items that a better guidebook would give but one star. I can only say that I prefer guidebooks to have opinions; that half of the pleasure in reading them is disagreeing with them; and that no one should confuse them with gospels.

Reading my way through Eliot criticism while working on this book, I have sometimes been bored or infuriated, or moved to laughter, but I have also learned a great deal. More than ever, I feel a great respect for Eliot, his work, and those special critics who can help one see long-familiar words with fresh eyes. I owe such critics special acknowledgments, and I hope I have done them justice in the text.

No text can record the debt I owe to Henry Kozicki, my coeditor of *Clio*, who has borne extra burdens at times when my immersion in Eliot criticism has rendered me more or less useless as an editor. I owe a special debt, too, to my wife Molly, who has always been my most acute critic. Finally, I want to thank my editor, Charles Sanders, for his criticism, his understanding, and his patience.

ROBERT H. CANARY

CHAPTER 1

The Personal Poet

It was the Age of Eliot. Born in 1888, Thomas Stearns Eliot died in 1965, leaving behind a slender body of work which has inspired an enormous body of criticism and scholarship. In 1915, when the lyric fragments of "The Love Song of J. Alfred Prufrock" puzzled the readers of *Poetry* magazine, Eliot was an unknown young American poet and student of philosophy. When he died, Eliot was a distinguished elder statesman of British letters, the gracious recipient of such honors as the Nobel Prize for Literature (1948). In the intervening half century, his poetry had helped shape the poetic style of a generation, and his criticism had helped form its taste. Since those years were also an Age of Criticism, his work has been as much studied as admired. This book offers itself as a guide to Eliot criticism; as such, it also reflects the strengths and weaknesses of contemporary literary studies.

Eliot's status as a modern "classic" and the overabundance of critical studies of his work pose problems in themselves. The major poems of Eliot have become public monuments, landmarks in the literary history of our century. We visit them frequently, sometimes conducting tours for the less instructed, to whom we point out details of craftsmanship and nuances of symbolism. The later, more overtly religious poems are like old cathedrals where worshipers are outnumbered by curious tourists. It is hard to recall our first encounter with these poems, to summon up again the sense of having entered a private world of feeling, dense with allusions we may not grasp, made up of fragments whose connections may escape us. We would not return to these poems if the feelings they express were, in the end, merely private; Eliot's *Waste Land* must be, in some sense, our own, if it is to have any power over us. Eliot himself stressed the impersonal character of poetry. In one of his earliest and most influential essays, "Tradition and the Individual Talent" (1919), he argues that poetry is "not the expression of personality, but an escape from personality"; his very next sentence, however, is a reminder that "only those who have personality and emotions know what it means to want to escape from these things." For many years, Eliot criticism was apt to stress the impersonal achievement of the poetry. Recent decades have seen a renewed interest in its personal sources. It is to this biographical and psychological criticism that we turn in this chapter.

Despite the existence of many useful studies, Eliot criticism does not yet offer us a coherent picture of the man; we are still in a world of fragments. There is a New England Eliot, an American Eliot, and a British Eliot. There is a spiritual seeker, whose apparently irreligious early verses can be seen as steps along a sacred way. There is a neurotic young man, who made a bad marriage and made the worst of it. These and other versions of Eliot can find some justification in the external facts of his biography, and we may add to them various psychological interpretations of his poetry, some of which are remarkably cavalier in their use of facts, biographical and literary. These fragments have not yet been brought together in a way which would do justice to the complexity of the man. Too many critics write as though the fragment which concerns them might represent the whole or its essence; too few are sensitive to the complexity of the relationship between a poet and his poem. Our age has some outstanding literary biographers but biographical criticism is not one of its strengths, and too much of our psychological criticism remains at the level of parlor Freudianism. It is, perhaps, understandable that the achievements of Eliot criticism in these areas are not yet impressive. The poet of "Prufrock" puzzles us yet.

Autobiographical Sources

If our age is weak in biographical and psychological criticism, the influence of Eliot's resistance to such criticism may be partly to blame. He was by nature a reticent man, and his earliest critical writings were partly a reaction against previous critics whose attention to biography suggested more interest in poets than in poetry. Although prepared, particularly in his later criti[illegible], to admit that biographies of poets are inevitable and even

2nd Floor

W.B. Eerdmans

PS3509.L43 Z6444

PS3509.L43 Z677

PS3509.L43 Z7854

PS509.L43 Z868
3

Z64924

Z68148

PS3509.L43 Z818

PS3509.L43 Z68455

PS3509.L43 Z69136

PS3509.L43 Z598

PS3509.L43 Z6185

Odyssey

PA 4167 . S44

. H48

. C54

desirable, Eliot surrounds such concessions with a host of reservations, warnings that "a knowledge of the springs which released a poem is not necessarily a help toward understanding the poem" ("The Frontiers of Criticism," 1956). Such remarks mingle oddly in his criticism with almost equally numerous hints about the personal nature of his works, particularly *The Waste Land;* Leonard Unger has brought together such remarks in his useful "T. S. E. on *The Waste Land*" (1971). Aware though he may have been of the personal sources of his poetry, Eliot did little to make life easier for critics and scholars interested in exploring them.

During his lifetime, Eliot did his best to preserve his privacy by denying to would-be biographers all access to his private papers and correspondence. A memorandum attached to his will requested that there be no biography of him. So far as they could, his widow and some of his friends discouraged serious biographical studies of Eliot for several years after his death. A number of works written in the biographical mode, therefore, are based almost entirely on published sources, yielding more information on his intellectual development as a poet and man of letters than on his personal life; and some such studies will be dealt with in later chapters. Experience with unauthorized biographies and unrestrained biographical speculation, however, has evidently convinced Mrs. Eliot that there should be an authorized biography; moreover, she will edit an edition of Eliot's letters. We may hope that these will improve our understanding of the man behind the poetry.

In the meantime, Eliot's widow has made available some previously unpublished material, mostly poetic. As materials for a biography, unpublished poems are no easier to use than published ones, but anything that contributes to our understanding of the development of Eliot's themes and techniques is useful. The first such offering was *Poems Written in Early Youth* (1967). Strictly speaking, this volume reproduces a collection made by John Hayward in 1950, but since it was published in an edition limited to twelve copies, the 1967 volume is the first to make some of its contents generally available to scholars. Poems from Eliot's Harvard days appear in more accurate texts than in a *Harvard Advocate* pamphlet, *The Undergraduate Poems of T. S. Eliot* (1948), and two new poems are included. One of these, "The Death of Saint Narcissus," was set in type at *Poetry* but never published. Some lines from the poem made their way into *The Waste Land*, but it is a powerful and disturbing poem in its own right. If Hayward was correct in dating its composition to 1915, its fascinated depiction of the sensual martyrdom of Narcissus is bound to affect our views of Eliot's development.

Much more important was the publication in 1971 of Valerie Eliot's edition of *The Waste Land: A Facsimile and Transcript of the Original Drafts including the Annotations of Ezra Pound.* The manuscript had long been thought lost, and Eliot's widow herself did not learn of its existence until 1968. Quite aside from the light it casts on Eliot's (and Pound's) craftsmanship, her edition has great biographical value, because of the excluded poetic material it includes and because of the biographical material in her introduction and comments. Facsimile and transcript pages are provided for the complete manuscript, for poems which contributed lines to it (including two versions of "The Death of Saint Narcissus"), and for some shorter poems which Eliot considered publishing with *The Waste Land*, until advised against it by Pound. In addition to Pound's annotations, we find comments by Eliot's first wife, Vivien (or Vivienne) Haigh-Wood, who seems to have suggested two lines that were incorporated in the final version. Most of the previously unpublished material is of interest primarily for what it says about the themes with which Eliot was wrestling while writing the poem.

The material with which Valerie Eliot surrounds the reproduced manuscript also has biographical interest, and the epigraph certainly points us in this direction. Eliot is quoted as saying that the poem was not meant as social criticism but as "the relief of a personal and wholly insignificant grouse against life; it is just a piece of rhythmical grumbling" (p. 1). In evaluating such remarks, not infrequent in Eliot's later work, we need to recall the ambivalence many writers feel toward their first successes. Mrs. Eliot's annotations also cite a number of personal sources for the poem: for the opening passage, a conversation with Countess Marie Larisch (whose memoirs had already been suggested as a possible source); for the cockney passages, a maid employed by the Eliots. Her introduction is basically biographical and draws heavily on letters to John Quinn and others from Eliot and Pound, emphasizing those which convey the financial difficulties facing Eliot, the fear that his poetic inspiration was drying up, and the increasing tensions in his marriage.

The sort of material Valerie Eliot provides in her introduction is the very sort that Eliot, in his lifetime, steadfastly refused to give, albeit with his usual courtesy. When asked about his poetry, he was sometimes elaborately evasive, sometimes helpful in ways which do not, in the end, tell us very much. Reading his interviews and letters to scholars, one is reminded of his notes to *The Waste Land*. A possible allusion may be acknowledged; a few comments on structure may be given. And one sometimes suspects that the inquirer's leg is being pulled.

Of the various published interviews with Eliot, the most useful are one with John Lehmann ("T. S. Eliot Talks about Himself and the Drive to Create," 1953) and the *Paris Review* interview conducted by Donald Hall (in *Writers at Work*, 1963). The Lehmann interview includes useful information on the origin of *Four Quartets*. The Hall interview, longer and wider ranging, can serve as an example of Eliot's method in such forums. In the portion of the interview concerned with *The Waste Land*, for example, Eliot is asked whether Pound's cuts in the manuscript affected "the intellectual structure of the poem"; Eliot responds, "I think it was just as structureless, only in a more futile way, in the longer version" (p. 96). This, while amusing, effectively cuts off any further discussion of the poem's structure, intellectual or otherwise. Asked about the poem's intent, Eliot speaks at greater length: "One wants to get something off one's chest. One doesn't know quite what it is that one wants to get off the chest until one's got it off. But I couldn't apply the word 'intention' positively to any of my poems. Or to any poems" (p. 97). This may, of course, be a completely accurate description of how the poem was written. It also has the effect of affirming the poem's personal nature while saying nothing at all about it. As such, it is a not unfair example of Eliot's way of being reticent without being unresponsive.

Although Eliot is characteristically evasive when faced with direct inquiries, a number of autobiographical statements are scattered through his criticism and miscellaneous prose. Less certainly, there are many occasions on which we may suspect that comments about other writers have some autobiographical content. The best guide to such fugitive pieces is Donald Gallup's *T. S. Eliot: A Bibliography* (rev. ed., 1969), an exemplary bibliography in all respects. Since Eliot's letters to his friends often contain useful information, Gallup's section on "Books Containing Letters" is a particularly useful guide to Eliot letters in out-of-the-way places. The section "Contributions to Periodicals" includes letters which respond to published comments on Eliot's life and work. Anyone embarking on a serious study of Eliot will need to refer frequently to Gallup's volume.

Of Eliot's miscellaneous prose pieces, the one with the highest autobiographical content may be his 1953 address at Washington University, a St. Louis institution which his grandfather had served as chancellor. This talk was published as *American Literature and the American Language* (1953), with an appendix, "The Eliot Family and St. Louis," prepared by the members of the university's Department of English; the talk also appears in *To Criticize the Critic* (1965). His introductory remarks include some reminiscences of his boyhood in St. Louis, the most useful being a passage about having been raised in the shadow of his grandfather's commitment to public service. The general mode of these remarks is "public speaker pays gracious tribute," and it is difficult to say how seriously one should take, for example, Eliot's suggestion that he was lucky to have been born in St. Louis rather than Boston or New York. The body of the talk, concerned with the relationship between localism and universal value in national literatures, has some obvious relevance to Eliot's career; but though Eliot draws some illustrations from his own time, reticence and judiciousness combine to make his remarks less than revealing.

How much is missing in Eliot's Washington University address —and, by extension, in most of his published autobiographical remarks—can be seen by comparing its careful prose with a 1928 letter preserved by Herbert Read ("On T.S.E.—A Memoir," in Tate, *T. S. Eliot: The Man and His Work*, 1966): "Some day I want to write an essay about the point of view of an American who wasn't an American, because he was born in the South and went to school in New England as a small boy with a nigger drawl, but who wasn't a southerner in the South because his people were northerners in a border state and looked down on all southerners and Virginians, and who was never anything anywhere and who therefore felt himself to be more a Frenchman than an American and more an Englishman than a Frenchman and yet felt that the U.S.A. up to a hundred years ago was a family extension" (p. 15). The Faulkneresque sprawl of this letter is not typical of the Eliot letters published so far, but its verve, so in contrast with his magisterial public prose, is often duplicated. It suggests that we may gain much of value when Eliot's letters and private papers become more generally available. It also suggests, of course, that even Eliot's national identity might be a complex question.

An Eliot in America

Eliot may sometimes have seen himself as an eternal outsider, but by conventional standards he certainly began as an American. He was born in St. Louis, Missouri, and its Mississippi River is presumably the "strong brown god" which flows in the opening lines of "The Dry Salvages." But even that poem takes its title from a group of rocks off the coast of Cape Ann in Massachusetts, where his family maintained a summer home. Although Eliot's grandfather had come west to spread the light of civilization and Unitarianism, the Eliots remained conscious that they were part of the Eliot family that had taken a prominent role in New England from the beginning. Eliot conformed to family tradition in attending Harvard. He was an undergraduate student there when he first found his voice as a poet, and he went on to be one of its more promising doctoral students in philosophy, even as he was writing his first major poems. We may assume that his family and its tradition and his experiences as a young man in Cambridge did much to form his character. It is remarkable, however, how few clear traces all this has left in his mature poetry. In the end, Eliot rejected New England for old England.

Howard Howarth's *Notes on Some Figures behind T. S. Eliot* (1964) covers all of Eliot's life, but it is most useful on his years in America. Howarth's coverage of Eliot's later life in England is based primarily on published sources. Posing no threat to Eliot's desire for privacy, Howarth's book is primarily an account of Eliot's intellectual development; Eliot's first wife does not even appear in the index. For portions of Eliot's earlier life, however, Howarth gives us the results of research that will not easily be duplicated. In reconstructing the flavor of Eliot's undergraduate courses at Harvard, for example, Howarth obtained information from a good number of Eliot's classmates. Some unpublished and relatively inaccessible material also informs his account of Eliot's family. Howarth attaches particular importance to the influence of Eliot's mother, professing to see in her poetry, mostly published in religious journals, "the qualities of a true poet" (p. 28). Eliot himself, he notes, had Charlotte Eliot's long poem *Savonarola* published in 1926 by the printers for the *Criterion* and wrote an introduction for it. Howarth recognizes Charlotte Eliot's very real limitations as a poet but suggests that her ambitions as a poet made her more sympathetic to her son's than male Eliots, committed to the stern course of duty, could be. Most subsequent biographic studies of Eliot have made use of Howarth.

Presenting itself as a study of background figures, Howarth's volume inevitably includes material with little direct relevance to Eliot—one feels this, for example, about his description of the political and cultural life of St. Louis in the poet's youth. One feels this, as well, about much of the information John J. Soldo offers in "The American Foreground of T. S. Eliot" (1972). Eliot was sufficiently interested in his ancestry to have written "East Coker" about the Somerset village from which Andrew Eliot left for the Massachusetts Bay Colony in 1667—and to have chosen to be buried in the parish church there. Even so, it is hard to say just what Eliot derived from the long line of Eliots who flourished in New England before his grandfather set out to bring Unitarianism and other fruits of Bostonian civilization to St. Louis. Soldo's view is that Eliot acquired from his family tree a certain elitism and the moralism sometimes called his "Calvinist heritage"; on the latter, Soldo notes that such Calvinism as Eliot inherited was more a matter of work ethic than of predestinarian theology. Theologically, "Eliot's Unitarian heritage could justly be characterized as Puritanism without Calvinisim" (p. 364). We may assume that such effect as this heritage had in forming Eliot's character came through his living relatives; there does not seem to be a gene for high-mindedness. If we may judge by his early poems, Eliot sometimes viewed his Boston relatives and their genteel friends with more than a little irony.

Our most useful witness for Eliot's days at Harvard is Conrad Aiken, a friend who knew him both as an undergraduate and a graduate student. Many valuable reminiscences of Eliot are in the flowing prose of Aiken's autobiographical *Ushant* (1952), where Eliot appears under the ambiguous name of "the Tsetse." Aiken has contributed, as well, to a number of symposia concerned with Eliot. Although Aiken is himself a poet of merit, the great value of his reminiscences is that they give us a more variegated portrait of Eliot than we might derive from the poems alone. In "King Bolo and Others" (in *T. S. Eliot*, ed. March and Tambimuttu, 1948), which takes its title from a long, evidently obscene poem which Eliot added to over a period of years, Eliot appears sipping tea with the lady (Adelaide Moffat) of "Portrait of a Lady," but also as taking boxing lessons from an Irish ex-pugilist. In this essay and elsewhere, Aiken also tells how he took to England typed copies of some Eliot poems and that only Ezra Pound recognized the value of "The Love Song of J. Alfred Prufrock."

Another friend of Eliot's from his last days at Harvard was

Emily Hale, who may have been the model for the woman in "La Figlia che Piange," the closest thing to a love poem in Eliot's early canon. Information on that relationship is the most useful contribution of T. S. Matthews' biography of Eliot, *Great Tom* (1974), which is in other respects no more than a journalistic biography, of interest mainly for original interpretations of fairly familiar points. Matthews is, for example, unusually unsympathetic toward Eliot's mother, whom he pictures as "one of those admirable women who have strict standards of conduct and no intimate friends, and who are admired, disliked, and feared by all who know them" (p. 8). He also suggests that, far from suffering from lack of passion, Eliot found that marriage unlocked strong desires that shocked his tidy Puritan soul to its foundations. In trying to get at the truth of Eliot's relationship with Emily Hale, Matthews seems to have gone to some effort to talk with people who knew her, and this may make his book of continuing use.

Although Eliot married and settled in England, he continued to correspond frequently with Emily Hale (their correspondence, sequestered until 2020, is in the Princeton University Library). They saw each other only when he was in America for lectures and readings or when she was in England on visits. It was Emily Hale with whom he walked in the garden at Burnt Norton, and she may be the one addressed in its opening lines, which speak of "the passage we did not take" and "the door we never opened." Matthews sees Emily in *The Family Reunion* as Agatha, the favorite aunt, loved by the father of the play's protagonist but left to "a life of scholarly spinsterhood as head of a woman's college" (p. 143). Matthews notes that Emily Hale never married and taught at a number of girls' schools and colleges. He reports that Eliot often sent her his works in manuscript and she would read them aloud to selected favorites. Matthews believes that their long relationship was "more than a friendship, definitely not a flirtation, something a little less than a love affair but very like a long engagement" (p. 139). By the time he walked with Emily Hale at Burnt Norton, Eliot had ceased to live with his first wife, but religious scruples would have kept him from divorce. After Vivien Eliot's death in 1947, Eliot did not marry his old friend; ten years later, he married Valerie Fletcher, his thirty-year-old secretary—a marriage that was to bring him much happiness in his last years. Matthews speculates that the news of the second marriage crushed Emily Hale. We may suspect that the relationship had long been more important to her than to Eliot, but all such speculations will be guesses until we have their letters.

Aside from Emily Hale and the Boston ladies of early verses, Eliot's American heritage is chiefly felt in his poetry through a handful of landscapes, most of them from New England. "The Dry Salvages" is the most obvious example. Howarth notes Eliot's connection with the Cape Ann area, and additional details can be found in Samuel Eliot Morison, "The Dry Salvages and the Thatcher Shipwreck" (1965). The best essay on the landscape of the poem is John D. Boyd's "*The Dry Salvages:* Topography as Symbol" (1968), although his efforts at symbolic interpretation are less valuable than his presentation of the biographical facts and his attempts to identify features of the area referred to in the poem.

The five lyrics of the Landscapes series, written in the mid-thirties, seem like finger exercises. Three of them have American settings—"Cape Ann," "New Hampshire," and "Virginia." The best treatment of them is in Nancy Duvall Hargrove's *Landscape as Symbol in the Poetry of T. S. Eliot* (1978). Her chapter on them may be Hargrove's most valuable contribution, although in other chapters she discusses the use of scenes in the full range of Eliot's poetry, even where the original cannot be explicitly identified. Readers not interested in the "landscapes" should still find this book a useful compendium of possible identifications. Hargrove also provides nearly fifty photographs, some unnecessary (e.g., a photograph of London Bridge) and others very useful (two photographs of the area which inspired "Rannoch, by Glencoe" and one of the "landscapes").

Hargrove places Eliot's use of landscape within the meditative tradition of landscape poetry in English. In the same vein, J. M. Reibetanz tells us that "*Four Quartets* stands squarely in the tradition of English romantic landscape poetry" ("*Four Quartets* as Poetry of Place," 1976, p. 527). Hargrove adds to this the influence of Baudelaire and the French Symbolists, from whom Eliot may have learned to concentrate on a few significant details. It is, of course, the paucity of scenic detail in Eliot's landscapes which makes one wonder whether Reibetanz and Hargrove should be quite so confident in placing Eliot in the English tradition. To the extent that their arguments are persuasive, the traditions that helped shape Eliot's use of landscape seem more significant than the scenes he uses. If we accept the conclusions of David W. Evans in "The Penny World of T. S. Eliot" (1958), Eliot's use of children in his poetry may owe more to Wordsworth than to Eliot's childhood memories. The surface of Eliot's poetry, at least, offers few reminders that Eliot was by birth an American poet and heir to a long New England tradition.

The Expatriate American Poet

In his Washington University address, Eliot says he is uncertain whether W. H. Auden should be counted as an English or an American poet, given his residence in both countries, but that "whichever Auden is, I suppose I must be the other." The connections between English and American literature are so close that it seems pointless to insist on labels in cases like those of Eliot and Auden. Nor is this phenomenon peculiar to our cosmopolitan age; the bust of Henry Wadsworth Longfellow in the Poets' Corner at Westminster Abbey does not seem out of place. Eliot was neither the first nor the last American writer to become an expatriate and to identify himself primarily with the English literary tradition. The efforts of some critics to tie him more closely to his native American tradition have not been convincing.

For a young doctoral student, study abroad was very desirable, as Harvard recognized when it gave Eliot a fellowship for the purpose. For someone with ambitions as a poet, staying in England was a logical decision. London was still the cultural capital of the English-speaking world in Eliot's youth, attracting not only genteel figures like Henry James and cosmopolitans like Pound but less obviously Anglophile writers, like Mark Twain, Stephen Crane, and Harold Frederic. Eliot was one of several generations of expatriate Americans. He was also one of a number of young American poets (including Robert Frost) whose merits were quickly discerned by Ezra Pound and praised by him to editors on both sides of the Atlantic. Eliot differed from the others mainly in being more loyal to the obligations thus incurred, though in the early days he sometimes chafed under Pound's proprietarial air. Stanley Weintraub's *The London Yankees* (1979) captures the ambience of this milieu. Although it provides little new information on Eliot himself, it is useful as an account of the Anglo-American literary scene which Eliot found on his arrival in England and as a guide to the ways in which Eliot's path resembled and differed from those of his fellow expatriates.

It may be excessively dramatic, then, to speak, as Doris L. Eder does, of "The Exile of T. S. Eliot" (1977). Eder's essay stresses some of the personal factors in Eliot's expatriation, particularly his marriage. Noting that this was hardly the act of the dedicated young careerist some have pictured, Eder speculates that "guilt at rebelling against an overprotective mother led to a masochistic marriage to an overdependent girl" (p. 104). She thinks it significant that both of Eliot's marriages were to women slightly below him on the social scale, though one wonders what Eliot's social position was at the time of his first marriage. Eder's conclusion also stresses cultural factors: Eliot, she believes, could never have felt at home in a democratic, rapidly changing America, and England simply suited him better. One may concede that there is truth in this, but surely England has also undergone dramatic social changes.

To be an expatriate is to expose oneself to condescension from both sides. Although the Atlantic looks less wide in these days of jet planes and television, it is still possible to denounce Eliot as a "renegade" American. The classical expression of this approach is by Van Wyck Brooks in *Opinions of Oliver Allston* (1941). A more recent version appears in Alan Holder's *Three Voyagers in Search of Europe: A Study of Henry James, Ezra Pound, and T. S. Eliot* (1966), a product of diligent research and simplistic thinking. One interesting product of the research is a 1908 Eliot review in the *Harvard Advocate* of Van Wyck Brooks' *The Wine of the Puritans.* Holder observes that Eliot's review is sympathetic to Brooks' picture of Americans alienated from their country, without mentioning Brooks' conclusion that Americans should nevertheless stay home and write out of their native consciousness. Holder sides with Brooks. Like Brooks, he has no sympathy for Eliot's religious views, which he identifies with authoritarianism: "Few American writers today would be willing to follow" Eliot's expatriate example (p. 360), at a time when democratic values, etc., are in peril. Any essays by Eliot critical of England or Europe are, for Holder, evidence of the deep disillusionment Eliot brought upon himself by leaving America. Eliot's handful of American landscapes are evidently insufficient for Holder, whose sensibility suggests that Eliot could have pleased him only by remaining in America and re-creating himself in the image of Carl Sandburg, hymning her prairies, perhaps, and the pluralism of her cities.

One may agree that there were personal sacrifices in Eliot's cutting himself off from his family and taking up permanent residence in a country in which he would remain an outsider, even when he had become part of its cultural establishment. But it is not at all clear that such sacrifices are of the kind which inhibit rather than nourish creativity. In attaching himself to the English literary tradition, which he had, after all, been raised on, Eliot gained much that he could hardly have found in American literature. Efforts have been made, however, to place Eliot's work within a native American literary tradition. Such efforts have heuristic value at best, especially when one considers the surprisingly frequent efforts to link Eliot with Walt Whitman.

Eliot's most obvious link would seem to be with a fellow expatriate like Henry James, another New Englander, born elsewhere, who became a British citizen, though one would hardly say of Eliot, as he said of James, that he "had a mind so fine that no idea could violate it." Grover Smith has suggested the influence of James on "The Ghosts in T. S. Eliot's 'The Elder Statesman' " (1960), and perhaps on *The Family Reunion* as well, but he adds that such influence was probably "neither very extensive nor very specific" (p. 234). Larger claims for James "as a significant early source for Eliot of method, approach, and theme" are made in Sara deSaussure Davis's study, "Two Portraits of a Lady: Henry James and T. S. Eliot" (1976, p. 367). Her argument depends on the assertion that Eliot's poem more closely resembles James's novel than it does Pound's poem, "Portrait d'une Femme." Like many who propose influences unacknowledged by Eliot, Davis believes that his failure to acknowledge this influence is deliberate and disingenuous. In fact, she establishes little more than a certain affinity in social attitudes and use of irony, and these seem more a matter of temperament than cultural origin.

Eliot's philosophic idealism is close enough to that of the New England Transcendentalists to allow Jack L. Davis to present it as their heir ("Transcendental Vision in 'The Dry Salvages,' " 1971), but the differences are too great to make the presentation convincing. The use Eliot makes of Emerson in "Sweeney Erect" hardly suggests great respect for the Transcendental tradition, as Charles Peake makes clear in some detail in his study " 'Sweeney Erect' and the Emersonian Hero" (1960). As with other nineteenth-century figures, one may consider that Eliot resembles Emerson in more ways than he might admit, and John Clendenning's comparative essay, "Time, Doubt and Vision: Notes on Emerson and T. S. Eliot" (1967), makes some useful points. But one cannot fit Eliot into the American literary tradition by making him a modern Transcendentalist.

If there is a distinctively American poetic tradition, it is the vernacular tradition which stems from Whitman. Poets in this century, consciously working within the Whitman tradition, have generally regarded Eliot and those influenced by him as their natural enemies. As James E. Miller, Jr., points out in "Whitman and Eliot: The Poetry of Mysticism" (1967), Eliot's *Four Quartets* share with Whitman's "Song of Myself" a focus on mystical transcendence. But the doctrinal differences, important to Eliot, at least, are sufficient to account for Eliot's continued low opinion of Whitman. Eliot was reluctant to consider Whitman a poet at all, and he did little to encourage one to find Whitman's influences in his work. Sholom J. Kahn reports that Eliot replied to a draft version of Kahn's "Eliot's 'Polyphiloprogenitive': Another Whitman Link?" (1959) by writing that "it seems to me that you are wasting your time" (p. 54n). All this has not kept critics from finding in Eliot the influence of Whitman, either unconscious or deliberately concealed.

The best and most thorough attempt to demonstrate the influence of Whitman on Eliot remains that of Sydney Musgrove's monograph, *T. S. Eliot and Walt Whitman* (1952). Some of the tricks of style to which Musgrove points do not suggest direct influence so much as a common acquaintance with biblical and liturgical language, but others are suggestive, for example, "their habitual use of the definite article" (p. 29). In the same way, it seems likely that at least some of the many verbal echoes cited by Musgrove are genuine. Musgrove devotes little attention to structural parallels, but these assume a major role in James E. Miller's chapter on *The Waste Land* in *The American Quest for a Supreme Fiction* (1979). Giving roughly the same interpretation of Eliot's poem as in his book on it (discussed below), Miller sees *The Waste Land* as part of an American tradition of "the personal epic" and maintains that it would not "have been possible without the precedence of Whitman's own experiments in similar forms" (p. 125). This rather free use of "epic" is bothersome though not uncommon, but Eliot could certainly have found precedents in Whitman for his extended lyric sequences.

One way to explain Eliot's similarities to Whitman, despite his distaste for Whitman, would be through Pound. Whitman's influence on Pound is somewhat clearer, despite Eliot's insistence (duly noted by Miller) that Pound was not influenced by Whitman. Although Miller is one who believes that Pound's excisions made *The Waste Land* less personal, it is possible that certain Whitmanesque qualities in Eliot's style came to him through Pound. This sort of explanation would fit well with the argument offered by Philip Hobsbaum in "Eliot, Whitman, and the American Tradition" (1969): "Whitman, Eliot, Pound, Stevens—our great 'modernists,' so wrongly called; in fact a fine flowering of a great culture" (p. 263). If Modernism in general is simply Americanism by another name, it certainly makes more sense to think of Eliot as an American poet, however much he and Pound may have laid claim to the European tradition. This approach suits the neo-Georgianism of some recent English critics and the cultural imperialism of some American critics, though it neglects the extent to which Modernism extended across national boundaries and through more than one form of art.

An alternative approach may be implicit in Musgrove's repeated invocations of Tennyson. "Both Whitman and Tennyson," says Musgrove, "are men of an older generation who have, each in a different way, fascinated the awakening poet in Eliot. Both he has come to distrust; but fragments from the poetry of each have remained embedded in his memory, to work their way to the surface when a common subject or a common situation calls them forth" (1952, p. 47). To this we may add that, like Whitman, Tennyson could have provided Eliot with examples of extended lyric sequences; Miller, for example, reads *The Waste Land* as a kind of *In Memoriam.* It is not surprising to find a poet simultaneously engaged in reacting against and learning from his predecessors. One may still doubt whether Whitman was, in fact, one of the significant predecessors from whom Eliot learned. To the extent that he was significant, we may well believe that it was as part of a larger Romantic tradition. There are, perhaps, elements in Whitman which mark him as distinctively American, but Eliot's debts to Whitman, such as they may be, do not make such national categories more useful in discussing his works.

The British Man of Letters

If Eliot was an expatriate American, he was, by most standards, an extraordinarily successful one. He came to England in

1914 for a year of study at Oxford, though he brought with him some poems and an introduction to Pound from Aiken. He stayed to become one of the leading figures of the English literary world. It was a remarkable feat, one that bemused even his admiring contemporaries. His first steps were aided by Pound, and his rise owed much to the gradual recognition accorded his poetry, and even more to the virtues of his criticism. At least as important were the personal qualities he displayed, both as a struggling young critic and as a successful editor and publisher, qualities which allowed him to escape much, though not all, of the jealousies success normally engenders in literary circles. This side of Eliot has been less extensively chronicled than most, perhaps because it is hard to relate to his poetry. Its chief value for us is as a warning against constructing our picture of the man entirely on the basis of his creative work. We are used to discovering that poets whose work is warm and passionate, or folksy and genial, were, in their private lives, grasping and selfish. Eliot's poetry often shows us the darker side of his emotional life, but that is not necessarily more fundamental to the man than the more genial characteristics recalled in reminiscences by his contemporaries and younger associates.

The most important of Eliot's contemporaries for his literary development was Ezra Pound, and works that are primarily concerned with Pound often provide useful information about his relationship with Eliot. Most biographical accounts of Eliot make use of such basic sources as *The Letters of Ezra Pound, 1907–1941* (1950), edited by D. D. Paige. This book includes Pound's letters nagging Harriet Monroe of *Poetry* and other editors into printing Eliot, as well as some letters of advice to Eliot about *The Waste Land* drafts. One of the best accounts of the relationship is Donald Gallup's little pamphlet, *T. S. Eliot and Ezra Pound* (1970), which reprints an article from the *Atlantic Monthly* (Jan. 1970). This is based mainly on letters and reminiscences by the two men themselves; most, but not all, of the quoted Pound letters are in the Paige collection. Having compiled the standard bibliographies of both men, Gallup knows their work well. He covers their changing relationship sympathetically, from the days when Pound was Eliot's sponsor to the days when Eliot was a harried publisher of Pound's libel-ridden prose. He touches on their continuing disagreements, high opinions of each other, and efforts to boost each other's reputation. B. L. Reid's *The Man from New York* (1968) is a valuable biography of John Quinn, the most important of the patrons to whose attention Pound called Eliot and others. Quinn later received *The Waste Land* manuscript from Eliot as a gift.

One of the first employments in literary journalism which Pound helped Eliot secure was as an assistant editor of Harriet Shaw Wheeler's *The Egoist*, a post in which Eliot replaced Richard Aldington, who was leaving to join the British army. Later, Aldington introduced Eliot to the editor of the *Times Literary Supplement*. Aldington's autobiography, *Life for Life's Sake* (1941), observes that Eliot "by merit, tact, prudence and pertinacity . . . succeeded in doing what no other American had ever done–imposing his personality, taste, and even many of his opinions on literary England" (p. 199). In other writings, Aldington, who had a habit of quarreling with people he admired, provides some of the few examples of genuine malice toward Eliot among those who had known him once as a friend. "Richard Aldington's Letters to Herbert Read" (ed. David S. Thatcher, *Malahat Review*, 1970) allows us to watch the process whereby Aldington's respect for Eliot's poetic powers is moderated by jealousy and fancied resentments. Aldington's short novel *Stepping Heavenward* (1931) is full of animus against Eliot's religious views and speculations about the failure of his marriage. Eliot appears as Jeremy Cibber, later the sainted Father Cibber, whose wife (like Eliot's) is a hysteric. The fault is Cibber's cold careerism and piety: "It must be rather a shock to think you are marrying a nice young American and then to discover that you have bedded with an angel unawares" (1931, p. 47). The satire is too broad to make this a useful source. One of Aldington's wives, Brigit Patmore, has also left an autobiography, *My Friends when Young* (1968), which provides a much less grim picture of Eliot's social life and first marriage.

Eliot is apt to play a role in most memoirs of English literary life in the between-wars period, though few of these contribute significant new information. He moved, for example, in the literary and social circles of the Bloomsbury Group, and Leonard and Virginia Woolf printed his *Poems* (1919) at their Hogarth Press. Of the Bloomsburyites, he was probably closest to Virginia Woolf; of their various memoirs, the most useful for readers interested in Eliot is probably Leonard Woolf's *Downhill All the Way* (1967). Many of them seem to have found Eliot's seriousness a bit wearing and his preciseness a bit ridiculous; it is conceivable that he found them a bit shallow.

Several symposia devoted to Eliot include memoirs by friends and professional acquaintances, as well as critical studies. The best of these is probably a symposium edited by Allen Tate for the *Sewanee Review* after Eliot's death, which was then published in book form as *T. S. Eliot: The Man and His Work* (1966). An earlier symposium, *T. S. Eliot* (1948), was edited by Richard March and Tambimuttu in honor of Eliot's sixtieth birthday. Eliot's seventieth birthday was also marked by the publication of a symposium, *T. S. Eliot* (1958), edited by Neville Braybrooke. Essays collected on such occasions are hardly apt to present fully objective portraits. Nevertheless, one is struck in reading such collections by the degree to which Eliot's high moral and aesthetic standards, applied quite coolly in public, did not prevent his displaying in private a fierce loyalty to his friends, whatever their morals, and genuine sympathy for his fellow writers, whatever his opinion of their merits. One learns, too, that he could be a competent man of business. Such impressions do not add much to our understanding of Eliot's poetry, but they round out our picture of the man. His success as an editor of *Criterion* and his usefulness to the publishers Faber and Faber was probably based in good part on qualities not much displayed in his poetry.

Frank Morley's essay "T. S. Eliot as a Publisher" (in March and Tambimuttu, 1948) is a fair example of what such essays have to contribute. Morley suggests that Eliot's literary reputation was still confined to the elite when he was taken into Geoffrey Faber's publishing firm (then Faber & Gwyer). Eliot's prime qualifications were that he was both a gentleman and "a man of business" (p. 62). Within the firm, Eliot proved himself "conscientious, scrupulous, careful, attentive" and "a willing workhorse" (p. 67, 68). His tact meant that he was given more than his share of the troublesome authors to work with. Morley also gives some examples of Eliot's fondness for elaborate practical jokes.

Eliot's reputation as a sound man of business had been made in several years' labor at Lloyd's Bank, undertaken at a time when his literary work and lecturing produced far too little to support himself and his new wife. We have no full account of Eliot's work there, but I. A. Richards' contribution to the Tate volume (1966) reports an accidental meeting with a banking colleague of Eliot, inclined to view Eliot's poetry writing as an acceptable hobby for a young banker. The man said that "if he goes on as he's been doing, I don't see why—in time, of course, in time—he mightn't even become a Branch Manager" (p. 5). It is true that in this period Eliot's nerves collapsed under the strain of his multiple responsibilities and anxieties, and that we may owe *The Waste Land* to that collapse, but he returned to the bank after a rest cure. Had Faber's offer not come along, it is quite possible that the qualities which helped make him successful in publishing would have brought him success in banking. Any portrait of Eliot as a young man should make some place for the promising young banker, alongside the neurasthenic author of *The Waste Land.*

Another memoirist, Sir Herbert Read, tells us that Eliot was "a serious but not necessarily a solemn man, a severe man never lacking in kindness and sympathy" (in Tate, 1966, p. 32). One should be able to find those qualities in the poetry and prose, but some critics have found therein nothing but solemnity and a lack of sympathy. He was particularly generous in offering advice and encouragement to younger poets. Stephen Spender, who was one of them, says in "Remembering Eliot" (in Tate, 1966) that Eliot "was the most approached by younger poets—and the most helpful to them—of any poet of his generation" (p. 48). Spender draws a contrast between Eliot's policy toward younger poets in the *Criterion* and the harshness shown by *Scrutiny*, the other major literary journal of the period. Philip Mairet's "Memories of T. S. E." (in Braybrooke, 1958) shows that similar generosity could be extended to younger editors as well; as editor of *New English Weekly*, Mairet was given the right to publish the last three *Quartets.* In the years of his greatest fame, Eliot continued to make himself available to younger poets. Donald Hall's chapter on Eliot in *Remembering Poets* (1978) is an amusing record of Hall's encounters with the elder poet. Few of the younger men he befriended became intimate friends of Eliot, and we do not find dramatic revelations in their accounts of meetings with him. But his kindness and openness to them needs to be part of any picture of the man.

The Spiritual Seeker

If the later Eliot was given to displays of kindness and shows of modesty, one element was certainly his effort to live up to the religious commitments he accepted when he joined the Church of England in 1927. Like his decision to become a British citizen, this can be seen as a way of marking his change of identity, from American expatriate to British man of letters. However, it was not taken to advance his career. It alienated old friends like Aiken and Aldington, and has alienated many critics since. It was obviously a decision to meet personal needs. Particularly after his separation from Vivien Eliot, much of Eliot's personal life was lived through his new church. He served for twenty-five years as senior warden of St. Stephen's parish in South Kensington, and during the late thirties he roomed at its clergy house. The relevance of his religious commitment to his later poetry is hardly in question, and some critics have been tempted in retrospect to see his entire life and work as a spiritual quest.

Pending publication of work based more extensively on his private papers, our understanding of Eliot's spiritual life depends mainly on his published prose and poetry. His clerical friends have been less prolific in providing memoirs than his literary friends. William Turner Levy may not count as an exception, since he began as a graduate student of literature, only later becoming a Protestant Episcopal priest. Levy's memoir, written with Victor Scherle, appeared in 1968 as *Affectionately, T. S. Eliot* (1968). It is based on very infrequent contact (Levy lived in New York) and is mainly useful as a picture of Eliot's manner with those who shared his High Church Anglican faith and love for cats. Such matters need to be included in our picture of the man, but if our interest is primarily in the poetry, it is with Eliot the spiritual seeker, rather than Eliot the churchman, that we will be concerned.

An interpretation of Eliot as a spiritual seeker from the beginning governs Lyndall Gordon's critical biography, *Eliot's Early Years* (1977), which sees his poetry and his life as "complementary parts of one design, a consuming search for salvation" (p. 2). This design is Gordon's rather than Eliot's, and it cannot accommodate his full complexity. The sensual man appears as a counterfoil to the aspiring saint; many of Eliot's friends receive only passing mention; and verses which do not fit the pattern are dismissed as temporary aberrations. This is, however, the best biography for the period it covers, the best researched and the most objectively written. One may feel that the early Eliot is explained too much in terms of what he later became, but our attention is called to characteristics which made that development possible.

Gordon's treatment of Eliot's family background is fairly conventional, though dressed in new vestments. His mother is seen as especially important, with her poetry using many of the same images (albeit less freshly) and dwelling on many of the same topics (albeit with less irony and doubt) as Eliot's own. Gordon says "Eliot must have known all the crucial questions and answers before he left his mother's side, but it was to be many years before he made them his own" (p. 6). The Unitarianism of his father's family, ethical rather than spiritual, stressed social duty and gave no place to the mysteries of the Incarnation or man's depravity, and so it could not understand his poetic impulse, satisfy his spiritual hunger, or fit him for survival in an America which had passed them by. For Gordon, the correct way lay through Eliot's mother's Emersonian emphasis on the individual's private spiritual experience; and searching for God, Eliot was bound to be alienated from the Eliot "family norms, Harvard cliches, and Boston manners" (p. 15). All this is a bit hard on the Eliots, Unitarianism, Harvard, and Boston, but it may have been true, at least for Eliot.

Gordon suggests that Eliot's first strong spiritual experience was about the time of his graduation from Harvard, a "timeless moment" in which "he saw the streets suddenly shrink and divide" (p. 14) and which he recorded in an unpublished poem, "Silence" (1910). On similar evidence, she believes that he had a like experience during his stay in Paris in 1910 and 1911. The visionary passages of the last section of *The Waste Land*, though deriving in part from earlier fragments, are also seen as reflections of immediate experience: "I am sure that before Eliot could have written this section he must himself have had some 'sign' " (p. 114). At such points, the poetry is used to illuminate the life, never an easy task, but we may find Gordon's evidence for at least one vision of nothingness (in 1910) persuasive.

As Eliot recognized, perhaps more strongly than Gordon, such experiences are open to a variety of interpretations. Gordon sees Eliot's intellectual and poetic development determined by the need to work out the implications of his experiences. An appendix lists forty books on which Eliot's student notes appear on cards; as Gordon notes, "The majority of the cards show his interest in mysticism and the psychology of religious experience" (p. 141). A number of manuscript poems from this period reinforce her picture: "The First Debate between Body and Soul" (1910), "The Little Passion" (1911/14), and "The Second Debate between Body and Soul" (1911). Also relevant are the poems with *The Waste Land* manuscript and some others, probably dating from 1914 and 1915—"The Burnt Dancer" and "The Love Song of Saint Sebastian." In this last poem Gordon sees a new version of the body and soul debate. In the first stanza, the saint deliberately flogs himself to attract the woman's sympathy; in the second, he becomes a Sweeney-like figure, strangling the woman with a towel. In this and the Narcissus poem, the attractions of asceticism and self-chosen martyrdom are undercut by the poet's ironic tone. "Eliot had moved too fast," says Gordon, but later, "by immersing himself in the metropolis of a foreign country and by marrying a terrifying, haunted woman he found, during this very period, the genuine trials against which he might refine his soul" (p. 64). Long before then, his vision of the void had been drawing him toward sainthood.

As her reference to Eliot's marriage may suggest, Gordon sometimes belongs with those who see Eliot's first marriage as a kind of heaven-sent trial to spur Eliot to poetry and faith. For a rather blatant secular version, we can cite Donald Hall's view of Vivien as "a death-muse" whom Eliot married "in order to be impotent, to suffer, and to write poems" (*Remembering Poets*, 1978, p. 100). Gordon, however, is fairer to Vivien Eliot than some and inclined to see Eliot as partly to blame for the failure of their marriage. Despite his knowledge of spirited and intelligent women (e.g., his mother and Vivien), Eliot freely indulges in stereotypes of women as mindless, the basic forms being the dark and dangerous enchantress and the pale, spiritual ideal. Such literary stereotypes, suggests Gordon, help protect Eliot from shame over his sexual instincts and inhibitions. Adelaide Moffat is caricatured in several Eliot poems from 1909 to 1911, but remains "elusive . . . because he does not strive to elicit her character . . . but immediately fits her to a variety of female stereotypes" (1977, p. 26). Gordon believes that Eliot was in love with Emily Hale, but she appears in the poetry as the idealized garden lady "hidden under the heron's wing," "La Figlia che Piange," the "hyacinth girl" of *The Waste Land*, and perhaps the pure ladies of the Saint Sebastian poem and *Ash Wednesday*.

Eliot's involvement with Emily Hale, however, is dealt with only in passing, as an interlude in years spent in studying comparative religion and Idealist philosophy and writing poems on the attractions of martyrdom. His failure to find in such exercises a way to "awaken his religious emotions" led to the "sudden impulse" of his marriage; in any case, "he was ready for women to fall in love, he told Aiken, and naively expected shyness to vanish with virginity" (p. 72). Gordon's tendency to see the marriage as a false step for an aspiring saint is reflected in the use of "recognizes" in this passage: "He goes on to say that both sexual and religious passion offer possibilities of 'escape' into feeling, but already he recognizes–he was twenty-eight when he wrote these words–that religion promised a more durable satisfaction" (p. 72).

A curious feature of Gordon's book is that it explains Eliot's unpublished poems better than his published ones, *The Waste Land* manuscript better than *The Waste Land* itself. Gordon complains that Pound could not understand Eliot's religious impulse and "convinced him to return to the social satire of 'Prufrock' " (p. 69). For Gordon, "the witty, satiric poems Eliot wrote between 1917 and 1919 seem like a digression from his poetic career" (pp. 90–91). The original *Waste Land* was a failed "spiritual autobiography" of a poet "who saw himself as a potential candidate for the religious life but was constrained by his own nature and distracted by domestic claims" (p. 118). If the published version does not give that impression, it is because Pound encouraged the suppression of religious, meditative, and confessional elements and encouraged the introduction of new, satiric fragments. This seems unfair when one recalls that Pound helped cut such satiric passages as the original opening and the couplets in imitation of Pope. Gordon's discussion of the poem, however, has the great virtue of convincingly relating it to such earlier efforts as "The Death of Saint Narcissus." Her sympathetic grasp of Eliot's spiritual development is always illuminating; her book's defect is its exclusive concentration on that development.

Gordon is by no means alone in reading Eliot's early life and poetry in the light of his later religious commitments, though most other attempts are not backed by much biographical research. Generalizing his interpretation of *The Waste Land*, Cleanth Brooks has written that "Eliot's poetry, from the very beginning, is conceived in terms of the following problem: how is revealed truth to be mediated to the gentiles" (*The Hidden God*, 1963, p. 71), though Brooks is aware that Eliot "was not always a Christian" (p. 68). An extreme case of this reading is Ruby K. Ferrell's *T. S. Eliot and the Tongues of Fire* (1972), which regards all his work as part of one religious epic. In "Burbank with a Baedeker: Bleistein with a Cigar," Ferrell sees Bleistein as a Christ figure, whose sagging knees and outturned palms indicate that he is on a crucifix. The poem is grouped with "Portrait of a Lady" and "Gerontion" as one of three "Cathedral Poems."

Much of Eliot's poetry, of course, is open to religious interpretation, and such interpretations will be discussed in a later chapter. What concerns us here are efforts to force into the context of spiritual autobiography poems with no obvious connection with it. Gordon, for example, cites anticlerical poems, like "Mr. Eliot's Sunday Morning Service" and "The Hippopotamus," as evidence that Eliot continued to brood about religious matters and the state of the Church. She recognizes that these may be "blasphemous poems," though she notes that Eliot "explained later that genuine blasphemy stemmed from the 'partial belief' of a mind in a peculiar and unusual state of spiritual sickness" (1977, p. 71). Unless one shares Eliot's religious commitment, however, his explanation reduces to the truism that someone concerned enough to engage in blasphemy is at least emotionally involved with religion. Blasphemy, in any case, seems a strong word for a playful poem like "The Hippopotamus." Such considerations have not deterred the Christian revisionists.

For "The Hippopotamus," for example, Herbert Marshall McLuhan suggested a Lancelot Andrewes sermon as a source ("Eliot's 'The Hippopotamus,' " 1944). "And verily," preached Andrewes, "He will not have us worship Him like elephants, as if we had no joints in our knees." The hippo's "hoarse" voice "at mating time" in the poem, says McLuhan, echoes Andrewes' argument that "as our joints are stiff to bow, so our voices are hoarse to confess." The hippopotamus is thus an instrument of satire against the Broad Church party, to be identified with the lukewarm Laodiceans of the second epigraph, while Eliot's sympathies are with the High Church ascetics, apparently satirized as the "True Church."

Even more fanciful sources are used to justify the religious readings in Christine Meyer's two short notes on this poem. In one, she uses Frazer and other sources to suggest that the mango, which the hippopotamus cannot reach, is the same as the pomegranate which the True Church receives, both being emblems of spiritual truth ("Eliot's 'The Hippopotamus,' " 1949). In "Some Unnoticed Religious Allusions in T. S. Eliot's 'The Hippopotamus' " (1951), Meyer identifies the hippo with Job's behemoth and tries to identify the hymnals used in a series of alleged allusions. Her investigations lead her to a Unitarian

hymnal as the source for the first part of the poem and, (
sillier, a Methodist hymnal for the last part. Since Meyer is w
ing to regard "at being one with God" as an allusion to a hymn with a similar thought, not much significance can be attached to her findings.

In the poem, the hippopotamus "is merely flesh and blood" but ends "among the saints." As portrayed by some critics, Eliot, the spiritual seeker, began as mere flesh and blood but soon rejected its transient satisfactions for the True Church, which, in the poem, "remains below / wrapt in the old miasmal mist." It seems easier to read the poem as a reminder that the spiritual Eliot is not all of Eliot—that there was more to his life and work than the spiritual quest.

The Imperfect Lover

For those who read Eliot's poetry in the light of his religious commitments, the sterility of *The Waste Land* may be primarily sexual. The sexual aridity of Eliot's poetry has often been noted. In "The Woman Who Wasn't There: Lacuna in T. S. Eliot" (1968), Arthur Sampley lists the unattractive or shadowy young women in Eliot's work, allowing only Monica of *The Elder Statesman* as an exception. Sampley implies that Eliot's unhappy first marriage explains the absence of attractive women in his earlier work, and that his happy second marriage explains Monica. He is willing to accept this pattern as the price paid for other kinds of insight: "Grateful though we may be for the belated appearance of Monica, an earlier entrance would have altered the poet's perspective, and what his work might have gained in balance and perspective, it might well have lost in poetic power" (pp. 609–10). Other critics have been more certain about the biographical sources of this characteristic of Eliot's poetry and less willing to accept it.

For sheer certainty the prize must go to D. J. Lake, who asserts that Eliot's collected poetry "is essentially a single poem . . . whose argument is the poet's life" ("T. S. Eliot's 'Vita Nuova' and 'Mi Chemin': 'The Sensus Historicus,' " 1975, p. 57). The figure of the betrayed hyacinth girl, an adolescent mistress, "appears as a *main* character in 'La Figlia Che Piange' (1911), 'Dans le Restaurant' (1916–17), 'A Cooking Egg' (1918-19), *Gerontion* (1919), *The Waste Land* (1921), *Ash Wednesday* (1927–1930), *Marina* (1930), *Burnt Norton* (1935),

The Family Reunion (1939), *The Elder Statesman* (1958)" (p. 48). The theme of betrayal is common in Eliot, but the arguments for a single biographical source are of a kind one would not accept in a historical study, or even in a detective novel, and there is no reason to adopt lower standards for literary criticism.

A more common theme in biographical criticism of Eliot is his first marriage. It does not take much reading in the biographical sources to see echoes of that marriage in at least the "Game of Chess" section of *The Waste Land.* At the moment, our best source on the marriage is probably *The Autobiography of Bertrand Russell, 1914–1944* (1968). Neither Eliot nor his wife plays a very large part in this volume of Russell's autobiography, but Russell played a large part in their early married life, and the volume contains a number of letters from Eliot to Russell and references to the Eliots in letters by Russell to others. Russell had met Eliot while serving as a visiting professor of philosophy at Harvard, where he found Eliot the most civilized of his students; Eliot's picture of Russell at that time appears in "Mr. Apollinax." Russell met Eliot again in England, dined with the young couple soon after their marriage, and took them into his apartment in September 1915. Fond of both, he thought Eliot "ashamed of his marriage" and a bit dull for the lively Vivien, who impressed Russell as "a person who lives on a knife edge, and will end as a criminal or a saint" (pp. 54, 62). His observations have been widely used.

Given Russell's reputation as one of the great rakes of his time, their ménage has attracted a certain prurient interest. When Vivien was ill and Eliot was unable to get away from his job, Russell took her on a brief holiday to Torquay. It has been assumed by some that this was a love affair, although that makes Eliot's expressions of gratitude to Russell, then and later, read rather oddly. Russell seems to have been emotionally involved with Vivien, though perhaps only as a would-be therapist. Ronald Clark's massive *Life of Bertrand Russell* quotes unpublished letters in which Russell insists to his onetime mistress Lady Ottoline Morrell that he does not find Vivien attractive and (after the jaunt to Torquay) that "I shall never have a physical relation with her" (1976, p. 312). Given the shocking candor of his letters to Lady Ottoline, one may want to take this assertion at face value.

Biographers concerned with Eliot's first marriage have also used the Aldington and Patmore materials, already discussed, and Vivien's diaries, now at the Bodleian Library at Oxford. Lyndall Gordon, however, reports that the latter are "not as significant as one might hope, for all but one were written before and after she lived with Eliot" (1977, p. 165). One diary, written just before she met Eliot, is taken up with a previous romance. The diary written during their marriage is "in a more sensible vein, after four years of marriage, which shows a physically attractive woman, an enthusiastic bather, and ball-room dancer" (p. 79). Among the letters published with the manuscript edition of *The Waste Land* is one of September 16, 1916, from Eliot to his brother Henry, in which Eliot says that "the present year has been, in some respects, the most awful nightmare of anxiety that the mind of man could conceive, but at least it is not dull, and it has its compensations" (1971, p. xi). In context, it is not clear whether Vivien is part of the nightmare or of the compensations; perhaps both.

Robert Sencourt's memoir, *T. S. Eliot* (1971), is primarily of interest for the light it claims to cast upon Eliot's marriage. Unfortunately, Sencourt's acquaintance with Eliot appears to have been slight, and the reliability of his book is brought into question by his tendency to exaggerate that acquaintance. Sencourt met the Eliots in 1927, when he and Vivien were taking treatment for similar nervous disorders at the same place in Switzerland–treatments "from which Tom profited more than Vivienne" (p. 124). Sencourt was an ardent Anglo-Catholic, while Eliot was on the brink of becoming one, and Sencourt seems thereafter to have been among those acquaintances with whom Eliot discussed religious matters. In 1930 Sencourt stayed for a few days with the Eliots in their London flat, and he contributes a few anecdotes of the marriage in its last years. This small handful of observations is the only personal contribution of any value made by this memoir.

One might think that this array of sources would make it difficult to say anything about the Eliots' marriage, except that it seems to have made them very unhappy and that its failure seems to have been harder on the wife than on the husband. Incompatibility of temperament is apparent, but many marriages survive it. Certain poems may suggest sexual incompatibility as well, but that is often as much effect as cause in the failure of a marriage. Even when one has heard both sides of a story at excruciating length, it is hard to judge other people's relationships, but with little to go on, some critics have been quite confident in diagnosing the failure of Eliot's marriage. Often enough, the principal cause is seen as Eliot's sexual squeamishness, a revulsion from the flesh, caused by his early training and religious aspirations. This is sometimes generalized into an incapacity for love.

That Eliot's alleged inability to love in a proper, healthy-minded way is the great weakness of his poetry is one of the perennial negative themes of Eliot criticism, and we may expect to encounter versions of it throughout this book, though it is not always linked to seeing his work in terms of its personal sources. When it is so linked, one sometimes feels that the critic feels betrayed, as when Ian Hamilton complains of *The Waste Land* that its technique "is to proffer personal disabilities as impersonal talents, to allow emotional weaknesses to masquerade as moral strengths" ("*The Waste Land*," in *Eliot in Perspective*, ed. Graham Martin, 1970, p. 109). One cannot help feeling that this complaint would more legitimately be directed against Eliot criticism, since Eliot never claimed that the poem exhibited either impersonal talent or moral strength. Nor is it entirely clear why Hamilton is so certain that "Eliot wanted the poem to be difficult" (p. 102). One supposes that there is poetic justice in Eliot's being judged wanting by standards he helped promote, but this and other examples of the moralism of the "healthy minded" make one marvel at the purity such critics apparently find when they explore their own deepest motives and the candor with which they would expose themselves.

Bernard Bergonzi's critical biography, *T. S. Eliot* (1972), responds directly to Hamilton's essay at one point by arguing that there is great value in exploring disordered sexuality, as *The Waste Land* does. In effect, Bergonzi accepts the view that Eliot is incapable of love, but praises him for writing about his incapacity. Like most of those who see Eliot as deficient in love, Bergonzi is unable to see love as involved in Eliot's religious poetry; he speaks of "Eliot's cruelly bleak mode of Christian belief" (p. 109). Based entirely on published sources, Bergonzi's volume is more a critical synthesis than a biography, and not very original on either score. His sympathies make him more favorable toward and more useful on the early rather than the later Eliot. Even Eliot's prose style is seen as having worsened with age. Bergonzi blames this on the *Criterion* editing, which encouraged Eliot to pontificate on cultural questions. Bergonzi compares the *Criterion* unfavorably to *Scrutiny* in terms of critical influence, though the former's much greater openness to younger writers might allow a contrary judgment. On the earlier Eliot, however, Bergonzi is often worth reading. None of Hamilton's sense of betrayal infects Bergonzi's persuasive argument that "the historical and cultural dimension" of *The Waste Land* is metaphorical, that the mythic references are scaffolding, and that the "true underlying themes" are "sexual disorder; and the lack, and need, of religious belief" (pp. 93, 95).

Hamilton and Bergonzi are among the critics in Martin Scofield's useful survey of critics who accuse Eliot of lacking loving warmth and other good things (" 'A gesture and a pose': T. S. Eliot's Images of Love," 1976). Scofield admits that "a direct treatment of relations between the sexes is not within his scope, except in the early poems of failure," but says that Eliot moves toward "a highly personal sense of love," one which "does not lose its humanity while moving toward a religious realization" (p. 25). Scofield's chief evidence is "Marina," but Eliot critics who equate "love" with direct relationships between the sexes will hardly be satisfied by this argument. Scofield's essay has, at least, the merit of focusing on the poet's ability to portray love in verse, rather than speculating, on the basis of insufficient data, on the man's ability to love. Most assertions about Eliot's ability to love are not serious biographical statements but value judgments, based on personal reactions to the poetry, simplistic theories of poetic creation, and, quite often, sympathy—or lack of it—for Eliot's religious position.

Phlebas and Narcissus

A willingness to indulge in biographical speculation on the basis of very slim evidence is especially marked in studies which argue that much of Eliot's early poetry reflects a deep emotional attachment to Jean Verdenal, a young French medical student whom Eliot met during a year in Paris and who died in World War I. *Prufrock and Other Observations* (1917) was dedicated "to Jean Verdenal, 1889–1915," and the same dedication appears with the fuller *Poems* (1920—the American edition of *Ara Vos Prec*, also 1920) and heads the poems included therein in all subsequent collections. Verdenal may be the friend referred to in an April 1934 "Commentary" for *Criterion* as "coming across the Luxembourg Gardens in the late afternoon, waving a branch of lilac, a friend who was later (so far as I could find out) to be mixed with the mud of Gallipoli." In the manuscript edition of *The Waste Land* is a letter from Eliot to Aiken in early 1916, commenting on the troubles of 1915. Verdenal's death, Vivien's health, and financial worries are among the reasons given for Eliot's not getting much work done—"but I am having a wonderful time nevertheless. I have *lived* through enough material for a score of long poems in the last six months" (1971, p. x). Out of this slender body of evidence, a great deal has been made.

The "Verdenal interpretation" began with John Peter's "A New Interpretation of *The Waste Land*" (1952). In this essay, Peter sees the poem as not unlike Tennyson's *In Memoriam*, a bleak meditation inspired by the death by drowning of a young man the poet loved. Although Madame Sosostris identifies the card of the drowned Phoenician sailor with the speaker of the poem, Peters argues that Phlebas is Verdenal, who also appears as the hyacinth girl. The corpse in the garden of the speaker's past is a secret he would not have resurrected by memories stirred up in spring. The speaker's love is echoed in lines which respond to the thunder's demand for "control." The identification of the speaker with the bisexual Tiresias is seen as significant, and love for the dead Verdenal "explains" the rejection of sex in "A Game of Chess" and "The Fire Sermon."

Eliot responded to this interpretation by repudiating it and demanding, through his lawyers, that all undistributed copies of the offending issue be destroyed. Moreover, he refused permission to have the offending essay reprinted when a reprint firm reissued the first sixteen volumes of the journal. The story of Eliot's reaction may be found in Peter's "Postscript" to an April 1969 reprinting of the 1952 essay, again in *Essays in Criticism.* Announcing that republication in his January 1969 "Editorial Commentary," F. W. Bateson adds some details on the suppression, along with an extraordinary explanation for his acceptance of the original essay: Eliot "had come to typify the Enemy for me, though with two provisos to the hostility: what I said or encouraged others to say had to be true (as far as the evidence was available), and it had to be expressed with the respect due to a great writer" (p. 3). Eliot's stern reaction to the Peter essay was thus a response to an avowedly hostile act. Nor is it easy to agree with Bateson that the essay met his two conditions.

The 1969 "Postscript" by Peter is more overtly biographical in its implications, though touched by a tendency to argue through innuendo. On the identification of Phlebas with the hyacinth girl, Peter cites the puzzling note to line 126 of *The Waste Land*, which seems to refer "those are pearls that were his eyes" back to the hyacinth girl passage. This may seem less puzzling now that the original drafts have shown that the hyacinth girl was originally part of that line, though Peter's argument is not thereby rendered entirely invalid. More tentatively, Peter cites Eliot's frequent use of lines from Dante's canto XXVI of the *Purgatorio*, lines which refer to the lustful whose sins were "hermaphroditic." More convincingly, Peter suggests that Eliot may have incorporated his reaction to the 1952 essay into *The Elder Statesman*, where we find "the parallel situation of a distinguished public man confronted with various reminders out of his past, and obliged to vindicate himself against the unfounded extensions common report might lend to them" (p. 174).

Although Peter received little credit for it, his line of interpretation was revived in the *Times Literary Supplement* review of *The Waste Land* manuscript edition and in the controversy it led to in the *TLS* letter columns. G. Wilson Knight's letter (Jan. 14, 1972b) suggests that the manuscript supports a reading that makes the hyacinth girl "apparently male" (p. 40). Knight then amplified his "Thoughts on *The Waste Land*" for the *Denver Quarterly* (1972a). His arguments are mainly convincing if one accepts his view that "poetry *is* bisexual" (p. 8) and that much of the best of English poetry pays tribute to the "seraphic" vision of the beautiful boy. Actions may not be involved, nor would Eliot necessarily be conscious of his own vision. "Eliot might have repudiated the interpretations here advanced," admits Knight, "having perhaps forgotten the meanings, which came only under poetic inspiration. Or through caution. But this is not to say that he would repudiate them now. What appears necessary on this plane may assume different proportions on the next. Granted this key of the seraphic, Eliot becomes a great poet wrestling with the ultimates of human culture" (p. 13). It is this sort of confidence in his interpretation that has made Knight a major critic. How few of us would think, lacking earthly evidence, to call in a dead poet's ghost to ratify our reading!

The controversy over Verdenal was of sufficient interest to send George Watson on a "Quest for a Frenchman" (1976). It is not clear whether Watson had access to the seven Verdenal letters to Eliot at Harvard, but he describes them as "full of the friendship and the passion for literature and music which the two young men had shared" (p. 465). In France, Watson was not able to find a great deal of information on Verdenal, and what he found gives little support to the identification of Verdenal with Phlebas the Phoenician sailor. Verdenal, it seems, was neither tall nor particularly handsome, and he did not die at sea but on land, as Eliot may have known—Eliot's reference to "the mud of Gallipoli" suggesting death by land more than death by water. Watson is not much taken with homoerotic interpretations of the relationship—"reductive . . . unproven . . . trivial" (p. 475). Watson sees the Mr. Eugenides reference in *The Waste Land* as illustrating the decadence of the scene, and Eliot's sympathy (sometimes cited) for a homosexual friend as simple decency. The Statius-Dante parallel in the epigraph, eventually attached to the dedication, Watson would explain by suggesting that Verdenal had the right contacts to introduce Eliot into the literary and social circles of Charles Maurras' Action Française, the royalist Catholicism of which certainly appealed to Eliot later. If a mere passing friendship of this sort seems inadequate to explain the large gesture of the dedication and the epigraph which later accompanied it, Watson asks, "How else are we to honor the dead, unless by exaggeration?" (p. 473).

Those who prefer other forms of exaggeration and find Watson something of a spoilsport may want to consult Robert F. Fleissner's "Anent J. Alfred Prufrock" (1977), which argues that Prufrock's first name is "Jean" for Verdenal—concealed by Prufrock "because it had feminine or girlish implications" (p. 207). Fleissner's fancy would reinforce the Tennyson-Hallam parallel as well. Not only does he see Prufrock's middle name as taken from Tennyson but he sees Prufrock's identification of himself as "an attendent lord" as an appropriation of Tennyson's "middle name . . . Alfred *Lord* Tennyson" (p. 210)! The mention of Verdenal's death in the dedication also inspires Fleissner: "Would not Eliot, in his far-ranging poetic mind (and having composed *Prufrock* when William James's theories of mental associations were dominant at Harvard), have linked death and the Dardenelles with death and the Hellespont, hence with the drowning of Hero and Leander in the same straits? That the most famous lyric about this mythic love affair was written by an avowed homosexual, Christopher Marlowe, from whose *The Jew of Malta* Eliot quoted elsewhere in a headnote, would not have escaped his attention" (p. 212n). A far-ranging mind is certainly at work here, but it would seem to be Fleissner's, regrettably unrestrained by common sense.

More obviously relevant to the identification of Verdenal with Phlebas is the poem in French in which the "Death by Water" passage first appeared; this is discussed in George Whiteside's "T. S. Eliot's *Dans le restaurant*" (1976). Whiteside accepts both Grover Smith's suggestion that the Phlebas passage began as an imitation of a Greek cenotaph and John Peter's Verdenal identification. He suggests that the French poem was originally two poems, which Eliot has tried, perhaps not altogether effectively, to fuse together—both to increase the private meaning for himself and to help conceal his meaning from the reader. Whiteside's suggestion that Eliot's writer's block in this period was linked to Verdenal might help explain why he was able to free himself by writing poems in French. The rest of the essay is somewhat marred by Whiteside's inability to believe that a poet can ever imagine an experience or use someone else's experience in a poem. He thus assumes that Eliot must have had a sexual experience like that described by the waiter in the poem. Whiteside wants to date this experience at age five or six, the evidence being that Eliot's 1929 Dante essay suggests that the experience of the *Vita Nuova* might have occurred at that age rather than at nine, the age given by Dante. Whiteside would also distinguish this experience from an assumed adolescent boy/girl experience with the proto hyacinth girl. More cautious than some in speculating on the exact nature of the Verdenal relationship, Whiteside is content to assert that Eliot's caution in treating it was due to a recognition that it could be regarded by others as homoerotic.

Caution is not a critical virtue much practiced in James E. Miller's *T. S. Eliot's Personal Waste Land* (1977), the most detailed rendering of the Verdenal hypothesis, though like most reductive works it warns against reductive interpretation. Miller's book rests on points made by Peter, Knight, and Whiteside, and only readers already convinced of the identification of Phlebas and the hyacinth girl with Verdenal are likely to be persuaded by the additional arguments and identifications supplied by Miller. A characteristic ploy is to assert that some aspect of Eliot's life and work is inexplicable except in light of the Verdenal interpretation, a form of argument which ought always to arouse our distrust. When Miller maintains that Eliot's hasty and unsuccessful marriage must be explained as a reaction to Verdenal's death, he is actually offering one not very plausible explanation out of the many which are possible. When he argues that Eliot's praise of *In Memoriam* can only be explained by fascination with the Tennyson-Hallam relationship, he assumes a rather outdated view of Eliot's relationship to the Victorians. Miller's neglect of the religious dimension of Eliot's work is suggested by his description of "The Death of Saint Narcissus" as "a sympathetic treatment of an invert who 'could not live men's ways' " (p. 32)—a summary which hardly does justice to the cited line, which reads in full: "He could not live men's ways, but became a dancer before God." The great merit of Miller's book is that he is generally willing to put his interpretations to the test of a detailed, passage-by-passage reading of the poems, particularly *The Waste Land*. It cannot be said, though, that the results are convincing. In the Emmaus passage of *The Waste Land V*, for example, Miller hears the voice of Vivien Eliot, asking whether the third party to their marriage is a man or a woman. Such insights do little to persuade one that the Verdenal hypothesis provides a useful key to *The Waste Land*.

Miller's book provides interpretations of poems which have received little critical attention, notably "The Death of Saint Narcissus" and "Ode," a poem from the British *Ara Vos Prec* (1920) which was replaced by "Hysteria" in the American *Poems* (1920) and all subsequent collections. Eliot's virtual suppression of both poems seems significant to Miller, and both are assimilated to the Verdenal hypothesis. For "The Death of Saint Narcissus" he supplies a reading which balances Gordon's concentration on Narcissus as a would-be saint by stressing the sensual content of his martyrdoms. Homoerotic elements are certainly present, as when Narcissus becomes a young girl, raped in the woods, but Miller's brief treatment underrates the poem's irony and neglects Narcissus' search for sainthood. His reading of "Ode," which is more detailed, interprets it as presenting a loss of poetic inspiration, direct transcriptions of Eliot's disastrous honeymoon, and regret over the lost Verdenal. The least convincing portion of this argument is the presence of Verdenal, which requires that we shift our focus from the poet-husband in lines like "the cheap extinction of his taking-off." To be fair, the closing strophe of the poem is very difficult. In an earlier (1968) essay that makes some of the same points as Miller, though without the addition of Verdenal, E. P. Bollier concluded that the final strophe's "incoherence seems genuine" ("Eliot's 'Lost' Ode of Dejection," p. 14).

A more balanced and convincing discussion of both poems

appears in Vicki Mahaffey's 1979 article in *American Literature*, " 'The Death of Saint Narcissus' and 'Ode': Two Suppressed Poems by T. S. Eliot." Mahaffey stresses the confessional nature of the poems but avoids reductive readings. Moreover, she offers a reasonably convincing explanation for their suppression: "Eliot was attempting to emphasize in his collected poetry the rational aesthetic attitude that he so appreciated in Jonson, Gautier, and Laforgue" (p. 612). The two poems were banished, then, because they failed to attain sufficient aesthetic distance from their subjects. Some such explanation seems called for, if only because the poem which replaced "Ode," "Hysteria," seems to be confessional in origin.

Mahaffey's reading of "The Death of Saint Narcissus" is not unlike that of Lyndall Gordon and is close to that of Lillian Feder ("Narcissus as Saint and Dancer," 1976). The autoerotic elements ("writhing in his own clutch") and homoerotic elements are given the recognition they deserve, but Mahaffey sees the poem's structure as determined by Narcissus' death wish. For Mahaffey, Eliot appears to be trying to place ironic distance between himself and Narcissus, but failing to do so; the lines from the poem which finally appeared in *The Waste Land*, she argues, are placed in an ironic perspective. Mahaffey's reading of "Ode" follows Miller for much of the first two strophes. Her reading of the third strophe is superior to Miller's, mainly because she convincingly argues that its main source is not Ovid but Laforgue's "Persée and Andromède." Bollier's essay recognized this source, but Mahaffey uses it to show how the final section "represents and attempts to gain perspective on the horrifying experience described in the first two stanzas by establishing an ironic mythology which will encompass and explain the weariness and pain described earlier" (p. 610). Mahaffey's readings of these two early poems display a rare ability to connect the various strands of Eliot's life and work—the imperfect lover, the spiritual searcher, and the traditional poet whose sources are as much in previous poetry as in his own life.

Mahaffey's essay makes no use of the Verdenal hypothesis, and that hypothesis has not yet proved itself useful in considering Eliot's work as a whole. There is too little evidence at present to establish its likelihood as biographical speculation; as a critical hypothesis, it has produced as many distortions as insights. Those critics who have explored it have called attention to androgynous features in the sexuality expressed in Eliot's poetry, such as we may expect to find in any poetry which evokes the deepest recesses of the self. They have also called attention to the elegiac qualities of *The Waste Land*; but acknowledging such qualities does not require one to accept the Verdenal hypothesis. William Empson, for example, makes a convincing argument that guilt over the death of his father was the source of both Eliot's nervous breakdown and many lines in *The Waste Land* ("My God Man There's Bears on It," 1972). Whatever biographical hypothesis we accept, we must distinguish between the personal sources of the poem and what emerges from the poet's struggle with his material.

Eliot on the Couch

Psychoanalytic studies of Eliot and his work offer another way of getting at the personal sources of his poetry, but there are, of course, certain problems in conducting analysis without a patient. A minor one is that the poet, being dead, gains little from having an analyst expose the fantasies embedded in the poetry. A major problem is that there is no check on the analyst's fantasies. Such problems are compounded in Eliot's case by the paucity of useful biographical material. Only one psychoanalytic study makes a real biographical contribution, and many focus almost entirely on the poetry, so that it is not always clear whether the poet or the characters in the poems are being analyzed.

The only study to make a contribution to our quest for biographical facts is Harry Trosman's 1974 essay, "T. S. Eliot and *The Waste Land*," in which Trosman provides some details on the treatment practiced by Roger Vittoz, the Swiss psychologist who treated Eliot at the time *The Waste Land* manuscript was being completed. Though Vittoz diagnosed patients by feeling their "brain vibrations" with his hands through their forehead, Trosman nevertheless suggests why Vittoz and his treatment may have done Eliot some good. Trosman's account of Eliot's problems stresses alienation from the father and need for maternal support—an Oedipal triangle reproduced in his and Vivien's relationship with Russell. The death of his father in 1919 activated feelings of guilt, and a visit from his mother in 1921 led to intense depression after her departure, which was the immediate cause of Eliot's breakdown. The underlying cause was the threatened collapse of the defenses with which he kept at bay the threat to his ego control posed by his sexual desires. Vittoz and Pound served as father figures, giving Eliot acceptance and strength in this crisis. For Trosman, *The Waste Land* is an important act of reintegration, in which Eliot used "the content of his narcissistic regression for creative purposes," making "narcissistic fragmentation a basis for poetic form and alienation of self legitimate content" (p. 717). Trosman's analysis of Eliot's problems parallels that of the literary biographers on whom he draws; the psychiatrist, however, is more willing than some critics to see *The Waste Land* as a partial answer to, rather than simply an expression of, such problems.

The same sense of therapeutic possibilities of creativity is seen in Gregory Siomoupoulos' remarks on Eliot in his "Poetry as Affective Communication" (1977). Siomoupoulos' sample analysis of a portion of *The Waste Land* is not especially insightful, for example: "The third stanza contains the systematic probability assessment of the hope for the re-establishment of a sense of well-being" (p. 505). But his description of the effect of such poetry seems sensible: "When they meet in the poetic experience, poet and reader bring together all active elements from their psychological past. In such an atmosphere, which is not necessarily regressive, they share in the present a sense of mastery that extends from the present to their most remote psychological past" (p. 512). This reminder that making poetry out of psychic problems can be healing for the poet and his reader is useful, because psychoanalytic analyses of poetry often have a reductive and debunking air.

Most psychoanalytic studies of Eliot and his work find constellations of imagery in line with those suggested by Trosman's study. Spratt, for example, argues that "all through the early poems, i.e., those published before 1930, the father-son conflict is emphasized in one way or another" ("Eliot and Freud," 1960, p. 64). *Ash Wednesday* includes the other major element of Oedipal conflicts, love for the mother (the Lady), but the poet reconciles with the father by leaving behind such maternal symbols as the "slotted window bellied like a fig's fruit." In the later poems, the quiet center of the turning world "probably stands for the womb or the sex organs" (p. 66), though elsewhere Spratt thinks (in "Coriolan") it may represent castration. Spratt is not convincing in showing that the symbols he identifies function in the poems in ways congruent with his identifications. His emphasis on reconciliation with the father as a motif in the later work, however, has intuitive appeal. John D. Mitchell, for example, has found this pattern in *The Confidential Clerk* ("Applied Psychoanalysis in the Drama," 1957).

Oedipal difficulties are also seen as basic by Arthur Wormhoudt in "A Psychoanalytic Interpretation of 'The Love Song of J. Alfred Prufrock,'" (1949). In this reading, Prufrock's Oedipal problems lead to "an oscillation between passive and aggressive attitudes toward the mother image with masochistic submission as the basic thesis and sadistic violence as the defensive antithesis" (p. 117). It is not clear whether this oscillation is the poet's or his character's. One's confidence in its relevance is not increased when Wormhoudt finds aggressive tendencies in such lines as "I have measured out my life with coffee spoons."

Critics who see Eliot's work as filled with Oedipal imagery often stress associated fears of castration. For George Whiteside, such fears provide the key to "A Freudian Dream Analysis of 'Sweeney among the Nightingales' " (1978). The poem is said to be open to such analysis because of its dreamlike atmosphere. Whiteside thinks it significant that Sweeney, with his knees spread, and the sprawling, silent man of the poem are both "vulnerable to castration" (p. 15), and the silent man apparently suspects this and leaves. He and Sweeney represent the dreamer's active and passive sides. The women are also paired: the "person in the Spanish cape" is sexually alluring, while Rachel is orally aggressive, ripping at grapes that represent male testicles. The silent man displays his active character by appearing, framed in the window, as "a vivid image of sexual penetration," the window, with its borders of wistaria, representing a woman's vulva with its pubic hair "Circumscrib[ing] the entered phallus" (p. 16). This symbolic penetration makes the scene change "in a way to make him feel caught guilty in the act" (p. 16). The dreamer thus wakes, as the last stanza comments on the episode as a whole. The nightingales sing of men's violence to women and of women's retaliatory violence to men. In guarding the horned gate, Sweeney keeps the truth of the dream from the dreamer's waking consciousness. Whiteside's interpretation is consistent, but some of the invoked associations are so hard to follow that one is unsure whether the analysis applies to the poem or simply to one reader's response.

Castration appears as an even more general key to Eliot's work in Whiteside's earlier essay, "T. S. Eliot: The Psychobiographical Approach" (1973), where Whiteside suggests that

Eliot was one of those "men so filled with castration fear that they cannot regard a woman as desirable unless they convince themselves she is uncastrated (i.e., has a phallus). Perhaps for this reason Eliot had to see flowers—particularly stalklike ones such as lilacs and hyacinths—in a woman's hands in order to feel desire for her" (p. 7). In this passage, Whiteside converts an extremely speculative suggestion into a "reason" capable of explaining another speculative interpretation. Whiteside goes on to define Eliot as a "schizoid" personality, a diagnosis which depends in part on the assumption that doubts about the reality of the unified self and the world are clinically schizoid, an assumption which dismisses the sort of continuing philosophic problems Eliot wrestled with in his dissertation.

Whiteside's essay brought a response from Philip Waldron in his "T. S. Eliot, Mr. Whiteside and the Psychobiographical Approach" (1973). Waldron dismantles some of Whiteside's peculiar notions—Eliot's "Buddhist" view of sexuality, for example—but he may overstate the case against psychological criticism: "The speculation is unnecessary because there is nothing particularly strange in Eliot's personality" (p. 147). This can be said of so few of us that it is pressing matters to assert it of Eliot.

Perhaps the fullest inventory of castration imagery in Eliot can be found in Reginald Fitz's article, "The Meaning of Impotence in Hemingway and Eliot" (1971). The Fisher King of *The Waste Land*—or its notes—is the chief impotent, but Fitz finds many suggestive images elsewhere: threatening mouths in "Sweeney among the Nightingales," "Hysteria," and "Prufrock" ("Do I dare to eat a peach?"); threatening animals in "Gerontion" ("Christ the tiger") and *Ash Wednesday* (the leopards); and references to castrates like Origen ("Mr. Eliot's Sunday Morning Service"). Fitz, who is vague on the sources for the imagery he finds in such profusion, is content to take it as evidence for self-alienation of some sort. The depersonalization of modern society means that the artist's self-alienation can speak to others. Fitz sees Eliot as eventually submitting to the dissolution Hemingway resisted. Whether one calls Hemingway's resistance intellectual strength or rigidity, says Fitz, it kept him from finding (or succumbing to) the kind of affirmation that was Eliot's way out.

Despite all the references to alleged castration imagery, Fitz ends with a very conventional interpretation of the major themes of Eliot's poetry. If we allow for the peculiarities of psychoanalytic terminology, the same can be said of most of the studies considered thus far in this section. Although published in *Psychoanalysis* (1954), Marie Baldridge's "Some Psychological Patterns in the Poetry of T. S. Eliot" is remarkably light on jargon. The patterns she finds in Eliot's poetry are described as variations of a "conflict between the demands of the physical and spiritual in man's nature" (p. 20), leading to "desire, guilt, renunciation, punishment and salvation" (p. 21). Like many critics, Baldridge prefers those poems which embody the conflict to those which express its religious resolution. Her preferences are sometimes expressed in terms which seem objective;—that is, Eliot's views on sexuality (in the Baudelaire essay) demonstrate "his misconception of the meaning of psychosexual integration" (p. 43)—but such comments reflect opposing value commitments more than scientific judgment.

A similar point can be made about Richard P. Hovey's "Psychiatrist and Saint in *The Cocktail Party*" (1959). Hovey's point is that Eliot's psychiatrist in that play does not treat his patients according to the enlightened dictates of depth psychology in diagnosing sin rather than alleviating their sense of guilt. As Norman Holland points out in his commentary on Hovey's paper, Sir Harcourt-Reilly is not intended to function in the play like a real psychiatrist, having enough other functions to perform. If he "is to be Hercules, Pheres, priest, theologian, angel, Christ, and soul healer, is it just to demand of him that he also be a literally correct psychiatrist?" ("Realism and the Psychological Critic; or, How Many Complexes Had Lady Macbeth?" 1962, p. 7). Hovey's assertion that depth psychology demonstrates Eliot's misconception of the nature of love is an objection to the contrast between sacred and profane love which Hovey sees in Eliot's play. Like Baldridge's, Hovey's objections to Eliot's views of love are no more scientifically based than those of literary critics who voice similar objections, and his use of depth psychology adds little to what critics have said more straightforwardly in other contexts.

John Johnson's " 'Prufrock' as Mimetic Portrait: A Psychological Reading" (1976) uses another version of analytic theory —humanistic psychology, mainly that of Ernest Schachtel and Karen Horney. The jargon is different ("embeddedness effects") but the conclusions are familiar. Like Hovey, Johnson treats a fictional character as a real person. Johnson's praise of Eliot's psychological realism amounts to little more than saying that Johnson is able to slap labels on Prufrock's responses.

Pigeon holing of this sort adds nothing to our understanding of Eliot's work.

Similar cavils apply to the more original form of pigeon holing in Chester G. Anderson's "On the Sublime and Its Anal-Urethral Sources in Pope, Eliot, and Joyce" (1972). Anderson's starting point is a passage from the rejected portion of *The Waste Land* in which "Fresca slips softly to the needful stool," and his focus is on anal imagery, though he acknowledges a wider field of possibilities—Eliot's early poems being "filled with oedipal guilt, impotence, decapitation, castration, and anal regression" (p. 240). The Fresca passage was an imitation of Pope—appropriately so, since Anderson believes that both "*The Rape of the Lock* and *The Waste Land* are stylizations of anal fantasies" (p. 232). The passages he cites to support this amusing notion are not very numerous, and we gain no new insights into the "infantile" sources of Eliot's famous reserve and control.

If psychoanalytic studies have so far told us little that is new about the sources of Eliot's work, we might hope that they could explain its effect upon the reader. In such efforts, Anglo-American critics have often turned to the theories of Jung, finding in literature's presentation of certain archetypes the source of its power over us. An early example is Maud Bodkin's *Archetypal Patterns in Poetry* (1934), which devotes a few pages to *The Waste Land*'s initiation themes (the Grail quest) as exemplifying the rebirth pattern. The argument is very sketchy, amounting to little more than an assertion that the poem's inner unity conforms to an archetypal pattern.

A more original, though almost certainly misguided, Jungian reading appeared in 1935 in M. Esther Harding's *Woman's Mysteries*. Harding's book is mainly concerned with the Moon Goddess and the cult of the Magna Mater. As such, it represents a cross-breeding of Cambridge anthropology and Jungian psychology. Examples are cited with little regard for context, an underlying unity being both asserted and assumed. Eliot appears in terms that would better fit the later Robert Graves. *The Waste Land*'s barrenness is a result of the modern neglect of the feminine principle represented by the Moon Goddess. For Harding, this explains both the poem's meaning and its contemporary relevance; it also, of course, serves as another datum supporting the author's theory. No real argument from the text is made to support this interpretation, which is, in many ways, a better diagnosis of Eliot's problems than of his poem.

Surprisingly, Harding's interpretation was revived in 1945 by Genevieve Foster in "The Archetypal Imagery of T. S. Eliot," who tells us that "the reader's attention is turned back to a historical period when certain 'feminine' values—represented by the image of the Magna Mater—had an importance currently denied to them" (p. 578). Its very shape makes the Grail a female symbol and thus an equivalent of the Lady (a Jungian *anima*) celebrated in *Ash Wednesday*. These symbols, like the eye, rose, and star of "The Hollow Men," represent "the unconscious part of the psyche . . . those lost qualities of feeling and intuition so much needed in our civilization," while the figure of the "redeemer or hero" represents "the principle of integration" (p. 584). The connection with Eliot's lament over "dissociation of sensibility" is suggestive, but Foster's insistence on the feminine principle, as well as the Magna Mater, seems alien to Eliot's thought. One has the sense that one symbol system is being translated into another quite unlike it, with no gain in meaning and perhaps some loss.

The best-known Jungian interpretation of Eliot's poetry is Elizabeth Drew's *T. S. Eliot: The Design of His Poetry* (1949). Drew begins under the influence of Foster, but the Magna Mater is mercifully dropped—not much, in fact, remains. Drew's book is primarily a short introduction to Eliot's work, sensitive to the poetry in a conventional and uncritical way. Its Jungian pretensions are recalled by an occasional footnote or a few pages on the relevance of Jung's theories, but no new insights can be attributed to the use of Jung. Identification of *The Waste Land* as concerned with Jung's "archetype of transformation" seems separate from Drew's reading of the poem, as does identification of the Lady of *Ash Wednesday* as a Jungian *anima*. These archetypal identifications serve mainly as ways of giving Eliot's use of religious symbols and myths a secular, even "scientific" legitimation. "Jung's theory," says Drew, "is that just as the personal dream is a message from the unconscious of the personal needs of the individual, so the great artist experiences and then creates in his particular art-form those archetypes of which his whole age is most in need" (p. 210). Suddenly we are back in the nineteenth century—poetry as prophecy, poetry as religion. Since Jung's theory is in no sense empirical, it is hard to see that Drew's invocation of Jung to praise Eliot is more useful than others' invocation of Freud to criticize him.

Jungian psychology also dominates Johannes Fabricus' study, *The Unconscious and Mr. Eliot* (1967). Subtitled "A Study in Expressionism," this book links Eliot with other developments in modern art, such as the cross-cutting techniques of film, which allegedly represent "an eruption of the collective unconscious into the conscious strata of modern civilization" (p. 7). Fabricus quotes an inordinate amount of material without saying anything very specific about anything.

If we believe Freud, the Oedipal complex is nearly universal; it is not surprising, then, to hear that it can be found in Eliot's work. If we believe Jung, the collective unconscious is everywhere; surely, then, it will manifest itself in Eliot. But what counts, surely, is what the poet makes of our common problems and shared symbols. The Holland essay (cited earlier) suggests that the proper role for the psychological critic is not to focus on the author or his characters but on the work as a whole and its effect on its readers. An example of such criticism is Leon Waldoff's "Prufrock's Defenses and Our Responses" (1969), in which Waldoff lists Prufrock's major defenses as "regression, a masochistic turning on the self, and passivity as reaction formation" (p. 192). Although Prufrock cannot face the anxiety of loving others, he finds ways to love himself by gaining a fragile "sense of mastery" (p. 193) over his desires, a feeling that can last only "till human voices wake us, and we drown." The reader, says Waldoff, is led to gain a similar feeling of mastery through understanding Prufrock.

The general weakness of psychoanalytic studies of Eliot's work is insufficient recognition of the kind of integrative function of art pointed to in Trosman's article. This is clearly related to Eliot's distinction between the origins of a work and what the poet makes of them, a distinction too often neglected in the biographical studies discussed earlier in this chapter. Even the best of the biographical and psychoanalytic studies of Eliot give us only fragments of the man; what we need are studies that are themselves integrative, bringing together the life and the work without confusing them. Whether Eliot would have welcomed even such ideal works is doubtful; he certainly did nothing to encourage them. His impersonal theory of poetry may well have been born of his efforts to escape his personal demons, but it has been widely influential. In our next chapter, we turn to studies which explore that theory and its implications.

References

Aiken, Conrad

1952. *Ushant, an Essay*. New York: Duell, Sloan and Pearce.

Aldington, Richard

1931. *Stepping Heavenward*. London: Chatto and Windus. Reprinted in *Soft Answers*. London: Chatto and Windus, 1932.

1941. *Life for Life's Sake*. New York: Viking Pr.

Anderson, Chester G.

1972. "On the Sublime and Its Anal-Urethral Sources in Pope, Eliot, and Joyce," in *Modern Irish Literature*, ed. Raymond J. Porter and James D. Brophy, pp. 235–49. New York: Iona College Pr. and Twayne Publishers.

Baldridge, Marie

1954. "Some Psychological Patterns in the Poetry of T. S. Eliot," *Psychoanalysis* Fall, pp. 19–47.

Bateson, F. W.

1969. "Editorial Commentary," *Essays in Criticism* Jan., pp. 1–5.

Bergonzi, Bernard

1972. *T. S. Eliot*. New York: Macmillan.

Bollier, E. P.

1968. "T. S. Eliot's 'Lost' Ode of Dejection," *Bucknell Review* Mar., pp. 1–17.

Bodkin, Maud

1934. *Archetypal Patterns in Poetry*, pp. 308–14. London: Oxford Pr.

Boyd, John D.

1968. "*The Dry Salvages:* Topography as Symbol," *Renascence* Spring, pp. 119–33.

Braybrooke, Neville

1958. (editor) *T. S. Eliot, a Symposium for His Seventieth Birthday*. New York: Farrar, Straus and Cudahy.

Brooks, Cleanth

1963. *The Hidden God*, pp. 68–97. New Haven: Yale Univ. Pr.

Brooks, Van Wyck

1941. *Opinions of Oliver Allston*. New York: E.P. Dutton.

Clark, Ronald W.

1976. *The Life of Bertrand Russell*. New York: Knopf.

Clendenning, John

1967. "Time, Doubt and Vision: Notes on Emerson and Eliot," *American Scholar* Winter, pp. 125–32.

Davis, Jack L.

1971. "Transcendental Vision in 'The Dry Salvages,'" *Emerson Society Quarterly* Winter, pp. 38–44.

Davis, Sara deSaussure

1976. "Two Portraits of a Lady: Henry James and T. S. Eliot," *Arizona Quarterly* Winter, pp. 38–44.

Drew, Elizabeth
1949. *T. S. Eliot: The Design of His Poetry*. London: Routledge and Kegan Paul.

Eder, Doris L.
1977. "The Exile of T. S. Eliot," *Denver Quarterly* Winter, pp. 95–111.

Eliot, T. S.
1953. *American Literature and the American Language*. St. Louis: Washington Univ. Main contents reprinted in *To Criticize the Critic* (New York: Farrar, Straus and Giroux, 1965), pp. 43–60.
1957. "The Frontiers of Criticism" (1956), in *On Poetry and Poets*, pp. 113–31. New York: Farrar, Straus and Cudahy.
1971. *The Waste Land: A Facsimile and Transcript of the Original Drafts including the Annotations of Ezra Pound*, ed. Valerie Eliot. New York: Harcourt Brace Jovanovich.

Empson, William
1972. "My God Man There's Bears on It," *Essays in Criticism* Oct., pp. 417–29.

Evans, David W.
1958. "The Penny World of T. S. Eliot," *Renascence* Spring, pp. 121–28.

Fabricus, Johannes
1967. *The Unconscious and Mr. Eliot: A Study in Expressionism*. Copenhagen: Nyt Nordisk Forlar Arnold Busck.

Feder, Lillian
1976. "Narcissus as Saint and Dancer," *T. S. Eliot Review*, pp. 13–19.

Ferrell, Ruby K.
1972. *T. S. Eliot and the Tongues of Fire*. New York: Exposition Pr.

Fitz, Reginald
1971. "The Meaning of Impotence in Hemingway and Eliot," *Connecticut Review* Apr., pp. 16–22.

Fleissner, Robert F.
1977. "Anent J. Alfred Prufrock," *Names: Journal of the American Name Society*, pp. 206–12.

Foster, Genevieve W.
1945. "The Archetypal Patterns of T. S. Eliot," *PMLA* June, pp. 567–85.

Gallup, Donald
1969. *T. S. Eliot: A Bibliography*. Rev. ed. New York: Harcourt, Brace and World.
1970. *T. S. Eliot and Ezra Pound: Collaborators in Letters*. New Haven: Henry W. Wenning/C. A. Stonehill.

Gordon, Lyndall
1977. *Eliot's Early Years*. Oxford: Oxford Univ. Pr.

Hall, Donald

1963. "T. S. Eliot," interview in *Writers at Work: The* Paris Review *Interviews (2d Series)*, ed. George Plimpton, pp. 89–110. New York: Viking Pr.

1978. *Remembering Poets*, pp. 77–110. New York: Harper and Row.

Hamilton, Ian

1970. "*The Waste Land*," in *Eliot in Perspective*, ed. Graham Martin, pp. 102–11. New York: Humanities Pr.

Harding, M. Esther

1935. *Woman's Mysteries*, pp. 297–99. London: Longmans, Green.

Hargrove, Nancy

1978. *Landscape as Symbol in the Poetry of T. S. Eliot*. Jackson: Univ. Pr. of Mississippi.

Hobsbaum, Philip

1969. "Eliot, Whitman, and the American Tradition," *Journal of American Studies*, pp. 239–64.

Holder, Alan

1966. *Three Voyagers in Search of Europe: A Study of Henry James, Ezra Pound, and T. S. Eliot*. Philadelphia: Univ. of Pennsylvania Pr.

Holland, Norman N.

1962. "Realism and the Psychological Critic; or, How Many Complexes Had Lady Macbeth?" *Literature and Psychology* Winter, pp. 5–8.

Hovey, Richard P.

1959. "Psychiatrist and Saint in *The Cocktail Party*," *Literature and Psychology* Summer and Fall, pp. 51–55.

Howarth, Howard

1964. *Notes on Some Figures behind T. S. Eliot*. Boston: Houghton Mifflin.

Johnson, John

1976. " 'Prufrock' as Mimetic Portrait: A Psychological Reading," *Gypsy Scholar*, pp. 96–110.

Kahn, Sholom J.

1959. "Eliot's 'Polyphiloprogenitive': Another Whitman Link?" *Walt Whitman Review* June, pp. 52–54.

Knight, G. Wilson

1972a. "Thoughts on *The Waste Land*," *Denver Quarterly* Summer, pp. 1–13.

1972b. "*The Waste Land*," letter in *Times Literary Supplement* Jan. 14, p. 40.

Lake, D. J.

1975. "T. S. Eliot's 'Vita Nuova' and 'Mi Chemin': 'The Sensus Historicus,' " *Ariel* Jan., pp. 43–57.

Lehmann, John
1953. "T. S. Eliot Talks about Himself and the Drive to Create," *New York Times* Nov. 29, pp. 5, 44.
Levy, William Turner, and Victor Scherle
1968. *Affectionately, T. S. Eliot: The Story of a Friendship, 1947–1965*. Philadelphia: Lippincott.
Mahaffey, Vicki
1979. " 'The Death of Saint Narcissus' and 'Ode': Two Suppressed Poems by T. S. Eliot," *American Literature* Jan., pp. 604–612.
March, Richard, and Tambimuttu
1948. (editors) *T. S. Eliot: A Symposium.* London: Editions Poetry.
Matthews, T. S.
1974. *Great Tom: Notes toward the Definition of T. S. Eliot.* New York: Harper and Row.
McLuhan, Herbert Marshall
1944. "Eliot's 'The Hippopotamus,' " *Explicator* May, item 50.
Meyer, Christine
1949. "Eliot's 'The Hippopotamus,' " *Explicator* Oct., item 6.
1951. "Some Unnoticed Religious Allusions in T. S. Eliot's 'The Hippopotamus,' " *Modern Language Notes* Apr., pp. 241–45.
Miller, James E., Jr.
1967. *Quests Surd and Absurd*, pp. 112–36. Chicago: Univ. of Chicago Pr.
1977. *T. S. Eliot's Personal Waste Land: Exorcism of the Demons.* University Park: Pennsylvania State Univ. Pr.
1979. *The American Quest for a Supreme Fiction: Whitman's Legacy in the Personal Epic*, pp. 100–125. Chicago: Univ. of Chicago Pr.
Mitchell, John D.
1957. "Applied Psychoanalysis in the Drama," *American Imago* Fall, pp. 263–80.
Morison, Samuel Eliot
1965. "The Dry Salvages and the Thatcher Shipwreck," *American Neptune* Oct., pp. 233–47.
Musgrove, Sydney
1952. *T. S. Eliot and Walt Whitman.* Wellington: Univ. of New Zealand Pr.
Patmore, Brigit
1968. *My Friends when Young.* London: William Heinemann.
Peake, Charles
1960. " 'Sweeney Erect' and the Emersonian Hero," *Neophilogus*, pp. 54–61.
Peter, John
1952. "A New Interpretation of *The Waste Land*," *Essays in Criticism* July, pp. 242–66.

1969. "A New Interpretation of *The Waste Land* (1952), with a Postscript (1969)," *Essays in Criticism* Apr., pp. 140–175.

Pound, Ezra
1950. *The Letters of Ezra Pound, 1907–1941*, ed. D. D. Paige. New York: Harcourt Brace and Co.

Reibetanz, J. M.
1976. "*Four Quartets* as Poetry of Place," *Dalhousie Review* Autumn, pp. 526–41.

Reid, B. L.
1968. *The Man from New York: John Quinn and His Friends.* New York: Oxford Univ. Pr.

Russell, Bertrand
1968. *The Autobiography of Bertrand Russell, 1914–1944.* Boston: Little, Brown.

Sampley, Arthur
1968. "The Woman Who Wasn't There: Lacuna in T. S. Eliot," *South Atlantic Quarterly* Autumn, pp. 603–10.

Scofield, Martin
1976. "'A gesture and a pose': T. S. Eliot's Images of Love," *Critical Quarterly* Autumn, pp. 5–26.

Sencourt, Robert
1971. *T. S. Eliot, A Memoir*, ed. Donald Adamson. New York: Dodd, Mead.

Siomoupoulos, Gregory
1977. "Poetry as Affective Communication," *Psychoanalytic Quarterly* July, pp. 499–513.

Smith, Grover
1960. "The Ghosts in T. S. Eliot's 'The Elder Statesman,'" *Notes and Queries* June, pp. 233–35.

Soldo, John J.
1972. "The American Foreground of T. S. Eliot," *New England Quarterly* Sept., pp. 355–72.

Spratt, P.
1960. "Eliot and Freud," *Literary Half Yearly* (Bangladore), pp. 55–68.

Tate, Allen
1966. (editor) *T. S. Eliot: The Man and His Work.* New York: Delacorte.

Thatcher, David S.
1970. (editor) "Richard Aldington's Letters to Herbert Read," *Malahat Review* July, pp. 5–44.

Trosman, Harry
1974. "T. S. Eliot and *The Waste Land:* Psychopathological Antecedents and Transformations," *Archives of General Psychiatry* May, pp. 709–17.

Unger, Leonard
1971. "T. S. E. on *The Waste Land*," *Mosaic* Fall, pp. 157–65.
Waldoff, Leon
1969. "Prufrock's Defenses and Our Responses," *American Imago*, pp. 182–93.
Waldron, Philip
1973. "T. S. Eliot, Mr. Whiteside and 'The Psychobiographical Approach,' " *Southern Review* (Australia) June, pp. 138–47.
Watson, George
1976. "Quest for a Frenchman," *Sewanee Review* Summer, pp. 465–75.
Weintraub, Stanley
1979. *The London Yankees: Portraits of American Writers and Artists in England*. New York: Harcourt Brace Jovanovich.
Whiteside, George
1973. "T. S. Eliot: The Psychobiographical Approach," *Southern Review* (Australia) Mar., pp. 3–26.
1976. "T. S. Eliot's *Dans le Restaurant*," *American Imago* Summer, pp. 155–73.
1978. "A Freudian Dream Analysis of 'Sweeney among the Nightingales,' " *Yeats-Eliot Review*, pp. 14–17.
Woolf, Leonard
1967. *Downhill All the Way*. New York: Harcourt, Brace and World.
Wormhoudt, Arthur
1949. "A Psychoanalytic Interpretation of 'The Love Song of J. Alfred Prufrock,' " *Perspective* Winter, pp. 109–17.

Selected Additional Readings

Aldington, Richard
(1954). *Ezra Pound and T. S. Eliot*. New York: Oriole Editions.
Christian, Henry
1960. "Thematic Development in T. S. Eliot's 'Hysteria,' " *Twentieth Century Literature* July, pp. 76–80.
Cuddy, Lois A.
1976. "Eliot and *Huck Finn:* River and Sea in 'The Dry Salvages,' " *T. S. Eliot Review*, pp. 3–12.
Fraser, Keith
1977. "*Stepping Heavenward:* The Canonization of T. S. Eliot," *Univ. of Windsor Review* Fall–Winter, pp. 5–17.
Gardner, Helen
1968. "The Landscapes of Eliot's Poetry," *Critical Quarterly* Winter, pp. 313–30.

Giannone, Richard J.
1959. "Eliot's 'Portrait of a Lady' and Pound's 'Portrait d'une Femme,'" *Twentieth Century Literature* Oct., pp. 131–34.
Joost, Nicholas, and Ann Risdon
1976. "Sketches and Preludes: T. S. Eliot's 'London Letters' in the *Dial*," *Papers in Language and Literature*, Fall, pp. 366–83.
Knapp, James F.
1974. "Eliot's 'Prufrock' and the Form of Modern Poetry," *Arizona Quarterly* Spring, pp. 5–14.
Profitt, Edward
1978. "Bald Narcissus: The Drowning of J. Alfred Prufrock," *Notes on Contemporary Literature*, issue 5, pp. 3–4.
Regnery, Henry
1972. "Eliot, Pound and Lewis: A Creative Friendship," *Modern Age* Spring, pp. 146–60.
Seferis, George
1967. "T.S.E. (Pages from a Diary)," *Quarterly Review of Literature*, pp. 209–26.
Stanford, Derek
1965. "Concealment and Revelation in T. S. Eliot," *Southwest Review*, pp. 243–51.
Stravinsky, Igor
1965. "Memories of T. S. Eliot," *Esquire* Aug., pp. 92–93.
Utley, Francis Lee
1944. "Eliot 'The Hippopotamus,'" *Explicator* Nov., item 10.
Vickery, John B.
1960. "Comment on Two Phrases in *The Waste Land*," *Literature and Psychology* Winter, pp. 3–4.

CHAPTER 2

The Impersonal Poet

Eliot's distaste for efforts to pry into the private lives of poets may reflect his personal reticence, but it is part of a coherent set of attitudes about poetry which first finds expression in the critical writings collected in *The Sacred Wood* (1920). Most of these essays began as book reviews, and the volume as a whole is more concerned with critical practice than literary theory. "Tradition and the Individual Talent," however, speaks of an "impersonal theory of poetry," and the arguments advanced in this essay are consistent with the thrust of Eliot's early criticism as a whole. The artist, we are told, must escape the merely personal by surrendering to the work at hand and to the tradition he is trying to affect. The resulting work will not express his "personality," for he is only a medium, a catalyst in the process of creation. It follows that the critic must direct his attention to the poem rather than the poet. The good critic will seek a certain objectivity, concentrating on the work rather than using it as an occasion for expressing his purely personal impressions or ideological preoccupations. Eliot was consciously reacting against Impressionistic and didactic tendencies in the criticism of his time; intentionally or not, he was also educating an audience for his poetry, in which the direct personal voice of traditional lyrics conceals itself behind masks and half-identified voices.

The intellectual rigor of Eliot's early criticism and the quality of his poetry have meant that his criticism has been widely read and discussed. There is, however, no real consensus on the nature and value of Eliot's "impersonal theory." Some of Eliot's most suggestive critical generalizations and widely quoted phrases occur in essays devoted to particular topics, and the critical studies discussed in this chapter take varying views on how and whether such phrases might be applied in other contexts. The language of Eliot's early criticism is elusive in ways which point to the influence of his philosophic training, and the last two decades have seen considerable advances in our understanding of the philosophic bases of his criticism. Misunderstandings persist, of course, partly because Eliot's philosophical work is not easy to follow, and partly because Eliot found it hard to deal with questions like the relationship between poetry and belief within the usual assumptions of his critical approach. But there is reason to hope there will be a gradual reduction in the number of essays which indulge in mere source hunting or which overstress the Romantic elements in Eliot's early criticism.

Eliot's dissertation in philosophy was much concerned with the possibility of interweaving individual points of view, and his early criticism suggests that the author is no longer present in the poem. Critics have taken the "impersonal theory" as a charter for speaking of "personae" in Eliot's poetry, sharply distinguishing between the poet and the speaker of the poem. On occasion, this distinction is useful and necessary, certainly in the case of dramatic monologues like "The Love Song of J. Alfred Prufrock." In other cases, insisting on using the speaker instead of the poet seems like a harmless critical tic. But the pursuit of personae in Eliot's poetry has led to an exaggerated emphasis on Tiresias in *The Waste Land* (encouraged by Eliot himself) and, on occasion, to unnecessary fragmentation of the *Four Quartets.* As changing critical fashions make Eliot's "impersonal theory" seem less salient, it is possible that the criticism of some of his poems will benefit from the change.

The Doctoral Student

The everyday use of terms like "emotion" and "object" varies widely, and interpretations of key passages in Eliot's early criticism reflect this variation. There is good reason to believe, however, that Eliot's use of such terms should be seen in light of his professional training as a doctoral student in philosophy, culminating in his doctoral dissertation on the British Idealist F. H. Bradley.

George Whiteside has provided a useful description in "T. S. Eliot's Doctoral Studies" (1973), based on the Harvard transcripts of Eliot's doctoral work. For each course, Whiteside identifies the teacher, mostly philosophical Idealists of one stripe or another, and indicates the general content. For Eliot's Indic studies, Whiteside notes the texts he read. He also cites courses Eliot may have audited, notes for lectures he may have heard, and gives Eliot's reasons for avoiding Santayana's graduate courses. Eliot's Indic studies ended in 1913, as his commitment to Bradley deepened; so Whiteside's summary is very useful. One would like to have similar information about Eliot's studies while he was in Germany and England.

For one of Eliot's Harvard courses we have more detailed information. Harry Todd Costello, the official secretary for the *Josiah Royce's Seminar, 1913–1914,* kept careful notes, which were published (edited by Grover Smith) in 1963. This volume includes Costello's rough notes and the formal summaries he wrote to be read aloud at the next meeting. Also included are an introductory essay on Bradley by Richard Hocking, a paper on the seminar which Costello gave in 1955, and an introduction and annotations by Smith. Costello's notes on Eliot's participation in the seminar show Eliot already concerned with issues like those which dominate his early literary criticism. Several of his contributions to the seminar, including his major paper, are concerned with the difficulty of separating description from explanation, fact from belief. His use of examples from primitive religion and ritual shows that he was already embarked upon reading which was to give him (from Sir James Frazer) the title *The Sacred Wood* and the Grail themes of *The Waste Land.* Although he does not deal with literary examples, his handling of the issues looks forward to his later skepticism about arriving at a definitive interpretation of a literary work and to the problems he experienced in talking about poetry and belief. Eliot's concern in this seminar with reconciling points of view, and his references to philosophers like Bradley and Alexius Meinong, may indicate that he was working on lines that would lead to his dissertation.

Eliot's dissertation is naturally the most useful document for the study of his philosophical background. It was published in 1964 as *Knowledge and Experience in the Philosophy of F. H. Bradley*, having originally appeared in 1916 as *Experience and the Objects of Knowledge in the Philosophy of F. H. Bradley.* An earlier edition was printed (and partially bound) in 1963 but proved too full of errors; the 1964 edition was edited with the assistance of Anne Bolgan. The last few pages of the dissertation have been lost but, by way of recompense, the 1964 edition reprints two philosophical articles by Eliot which were first published in the *Monist* in 1916, one on Leibniz's monadism and another comparing his monads with Bradley's "finite centers." Eliot's preface to the 1964 edition gives a brief account of his philosophic career and makes some typically self-deprecatory remarks about the dissertation: he can no longer understand it, and it is "a curiosity of biographical interest" (1964, p. 10). Readers who are seriously concerned with the philosophic bases of Eliot's early criticism must master the dissertation. This is not easy, and probably requires further reading in Bradley and the other philosophers Eliot uses.

Before its publication, the dissertation was available for inspection (but not quotation) by scholars. Bradley's influence on Eliot still attracted interest, but scholars who were unable to journey to Harvard to inspect it for themselves had to rely on Eliot's later essay, "Francis Herbert Bradley" (in *For Lancelot Andrewes*, 1928—originally a *TLS* review of Bradley's *Ethical Studies*, 1876), and on published summaries of the dissertation. Probably the most widely used of these summaries was R. W. Church's "Eliot on Bradley's Metaphysics" (1938). This is very brief and concentrates on the dissertation's metaphysical dimensions. For Church, the chief point of the dissertation is its defense of Bradley's position that both ideality and reality arise out of immediate experience—that is, both are later constructs from experience. Eliot's differences with Bradley are not mentioned, nor are such important terms in the dissertation as "point of view." Church indicates that the dissertation is relevant to Eliot's literary criticism, but it is not part of his purpose to argue that point. Church's summary is of interest because of its influence on some Eliot critics, but more adequate accounts of the dissertation are now available.

George Whiteside's account, "T. S. Eliot's Dissertation" (1967), presents itself modestly as a summary but includes a fair amount of interpretation. Whiteside, for example, is inclined to stress Eliot's differences with Bradley, perhaps to exaggerate them. He also likes to find psychological explanations for philosophical arguments. He believes, for example, that Eliot would like to share in the sense of wholeness which lies behind Bradley's system but is unable to do so, perhaps because of the sense of separation which made Bradley's philosophy seem to answer a personal need. Both Eliot and Bradley were aware of the extent to which predispositions enter into philosophic choice—Eliot was fond of Bradley's characterization of metaphysics as "the finding of bad reasons for what we believe on instinct"—but neither despaired of distinguishing between good and bad reasons, and explaining philosophical positions in terms of their instinctual sources contributes little to our understanding of them. In this case, Whiteside may assign too much importance to Eliot's rejection of the timeless Absolute, which holds together Bradley's world of finite centers. As Whiteside notes, Eliot ascribes timelessness to the flux of immediate experience. Whiteside argues that this makes it more difficult to say how our worlds cohere, but one wonders whether Bradley's rather shadowy Absolute makes it easier (a mystery does not become less a mystery when we have given it a name). At such points, Whiteside does less than justice to the "uncynical disillusion" of Bradley, to the unity posited in Eliot's views, and to the substantial agreement of Eliot's position with that of Bradley. Much of what Whiteside says about the relationship between Eliot's dissertation and his criticism is of interest, but he is not an ideal guide.

Richard Wollheim is a philosopher who has written a book on Bradley; so his comments on Eliot's dissertation are especially welcome. His first (and less useful) essay on this topic is "Eliot, Bradley and Immediate Experience," a review of the dissertation and of the Costello book for the *New Statesman* (1964). Wollheim welcomes both publications for the light they cast on Eliot's poetry and criticism, but he does not attach great importance to the influence of Bradley on Eliot. He suggests that Eliot's monism is the sort of feeling which precedes philosophical study as often as it follows from it. What is unusual in Eliot's monism "is the peculiar relations into which it enters with his taste for the fragmentary," so that one finds Eliot relatively unconcerned about the unity of particular works of art while "unrealistically" insisting "on the unity of art as a whole" (p. 402). To the extent that this is meant to apply to Eliot's criticism, it seems to underrate his concern for the unity of individual works on a practical level; to the extent to which his criticism depends on philosophic assumptions, the unity of art as a whole has an objective status equivalent to any idea. Wollheim sees some connection between Bradley's views and Eliot's "objective correlative" and "dissociation of sensibility," but considers that the former doctrine oversimplifies the relation between object and emotion in a way which is well beneath Bradley's standards of argument and understanding.

Much more detailed is Wollheim's "Eliot and F. H. Bradley"

in *Eliot in Perspective* (1970), which includes the best short treatment of the dissertation. Like Whiteside, Wollheim notes that Eliot is less optimistic about reassembling finite centers into a higher unity than is Bradley. Their differing treatment of ideas is seen as a facet of the problem of unity. Eliot's ideas exist because they point toward their references, an extreme position owing less to Bradley than to Meinong. The problem is that ideas now imply their objects, including false and self-contradictory ideas. Bradley had hoped to avoid this consequence, first by allowing for floating ideas (unattached to objects) and later by insisting that all internal contradictions are eventually resolved in a higher unity. In this case, Eliot sides with those who say that the resolution achieved in higher unity is a resolution achieved by changing our point of view; the unreal object remains. A more radical solution, and one Eliot adopts, is to deny that there is an external world of objects which is somehow *the* reality. One can then speak of degrees of reality, based on the extent of relations into which the object enters. This is consistent, in that it reinforces the priority of immediate experience over subject-object relations, but insisting on the virtual identity of ideas and their referents makes it even more difficult to explain how we may "unite the different points of view into a single world" (p. 183), an objection also raised by Whiteside. The doctrine that we are trapped in our own point of view is the form of solipsism Eliot attacks in his dissertation. One answer is that we seek a common reference, just as in our individual selves we seek to reconcile the various points of view which compose the self. Alternatively—Wollheim finds Eliot not entirely consistent on this issue—we may admit that the intention of a common reference is not the same as its achievement, and that its commonality is based on faith. Wollheim notes that the notion of commonality of points of view is related to Eliot's theory of tradition, but he says that the latter has "many other roots as well" (p. 184).

Wollheim remains rather skeptical about the degree to which Eliot's study of Bradley is reflected in his poetry and criticism. The Bradley passage appended to *The Waste Land* strikes most readers as solipsistic, as do the lines to which it refers; yet Bradley was not a solipsist, as Eliot knew. Wollheim considers that certain trends in Eliot's thought were probably reinforced, at least, by his study of Bradley. The first is a tendency to see the mind, its feelings and thoughts, as closely tied to objects. Wollheim sees a problem here, in that the philosophical theory seems to assume that the self is nonexistent, while the critical theory seems to assume that it is something to be escaped. It may be that here, as with the "solipsistic" lines of *The Waste Land*, Wollheim helps create the problem by accepting conventional interpretations of Eliot's literary output. Wollheim sees a possible answer in the dissertation's claim that one can transcend one's point of view by realizing that it is only a point of view; the impersonal poet is thus one who achieves a higher order of consciousness by transcending the merely personal. This answer does not, however, resolve the question of whether Eliot's theory is meant to be descriptive or normative.

A similar problem arises with "dissociation of sensibility," for the union of word and sensation, proposed as a norm, appears in the philosophy as a condition of language. Again, the poet appears to be one who expresses an ideal tendency inhering in the nature of consciousness. A third item Wollheim sees in Eliot is, of course, the "objective correlative," which appears closely related to the other two. Although recognizing the Bradleyan coloring of Eliot's early critical writings, Wollheim observes that Eliot fed on less and less substantial fare, so that second-rate theology and middle-brow books (like J. W. Dunne's *Experiment with Time*) may have much more to do with the metaphysics of the *Four Quartets* than Bradley or any philosopher.

The Philosophical Critic

It seems reasonably clear that Eliot's early criticism was at least partly influenced by his study of Bradley. Given the difficulties of Eliot's critical language, any aid to understanding has been welcome, though critics have not found the subtle Bradley an easy guide to the elusive Eliot. The chapter on Bradley in Hugh Kenner's *The Invisible Poet* (1959) helped spread interest in Bradley's influence, although we should note that the original Norwegian edition (1949) of Kristian Smidt's *Poetry and Belief in the Work of T. S. Eliot* (rev. ed., 1961) was earlier. Even before the dissertation's publication, then, some students of Eliot's criticism were using Bradley as the key to its meaning. Its appearance has naturally added to their number.

Although he did not have access to the dissertation, Ernest

P. Bollier gives a very sensible account of "T. S. Eliot and F. H. Bradley: A Question of Influence" (1963). Bollier's key text is Eliot's comment in his Bradley essay that "scepticism and uncynical disillusion are a useful equipment for religious understanding." Inability to accept this hard saying has led many critics of Eliot to see his development as moving from despairing skepticism to uncritical affirmation. Bradley's metaphysics is certainly skeptical in some ways; locating reality in immediate experience, it undermines both the objective reality of empiricism and the subjective reality of idealism. Such a position may indeed make one despair of attaining knowledge through rational metaphysics, but it is that sort of despair which makes it possible for a man like Eliot to accept the testimony of faith. Although Bradley did not take this step, he recognized that men might need a practical creed to live by, even if philosophy could not supply it, and he did not deny the reality of religious experience. Bradley's skepticism thus helped lead Eliot to the Christianity which was "a higher level of doubt" (p. 107). Bollier's portrait of Eliot's development thus bears some resemblance to the "existentialist" Eliot sketched in A. G. George's *T. S. Eliot: His Mind and Art* (1962, rev. 1969). Bollier also provides useful hints on the relationship between Bradley's views and specific aspects of Eliot's critical thought, particularly on the way in which Eliot's view of "impersonality" resembles the "self-transcendence" by which Bradley would have the self rise to a higher level of reality.

In *T. S. Eliot: Aesthetics and History* (1962), Lewis Freed also maintains that Eliot's "impersonal" theory of poetry derives from Bradley. Freed covers, as well, other philosophers, including Aristotle, the Scholastics, and, at greater length than his influence on Eliot would seem to justify, Kant; but Freed says that "when Eliot takes things from others, his general practice is to interpret them in terms of Bradley" (p. 140). Eliot's concept of tradition is related to Bradley's insistence on memory as a present experience from which we construct an ideal past. From Bradley, too, comes Eliot's insistence on sensuous apprehension as the initial step in both the critical and the poetic process. The distinction between emotions and feelings owes something to Bradley's conception of emotions as universals. The "impersonal" theory as a whole "is a theory of poetry as transcendence" (p. 164).

Useful as such studies as Bollier's and Freed's are, they are incomplete in that they do not take account of the valuable evidence provided by the dissertation, which shows Eliot wrestling with the philosophy of Bradley. Before the dissertation was published, the most thorough survey that took the dissertation into account was Eric Thompson's *T. S. Eliot: The Metaphysical Perspective* (1963). Thompson makes a number of important points. On the relation between the philosophy and the criticism of Eliot, Thompson notes that we must "be sensitive to the philosophical nuances of words like 'object,' 'feeling,' 'ideas,' 'point of view' as Eliot uses them" (p. 52). On the relation between the philosophy and the poetry, Thompson notes that "the metaphysical standpoint" is already present in poems written before Eliot began his doctoral studies; "so Eliot's philosophical studies between 1911 and 1915 are, not the finding of a point of view, but the testing and justifying of one" (p. xx). The likelihood of this assertion is not much impaired by the cloudiness of Thompson's description of what he means by "the" metaphysical standpoint. Thompson's summary of the dissertation is serviceable; some of his attempts to translate Eliot's prose into Shelley's images seem more confusing than clarifying, but he also offers such felicitous summaries as this, of Eliot's way of escaping from solipsism: "Though all our experiences are private, all of our ideas are common" (p. 45). Introducing R. G. Collingwood into the discussion of Eliot's criticism, however, is a bit confusing, as the reader is kept moving from Collingwood to Eliot to Bradley and back. Thompson also includes rather conventional readings of "Burnt Norton" and *The Waste Land;* the first is read as "a defense of poetry" (p. 80) and the second as a drama, with Tiresias as a combination stage manager and Greek chorus.

Of the studies to appear since the publication of the dissertation, the most detailed attempt to relate Eliot's criticism and his philosophy is probably Lewis Freed's *T. S. Eliot: The Critic as Philosopher* (1979), a better book than Freed's 1962 volume, though much less clearly written. Freed has obviously immersed himself in the prose of Eliot and Bradley, and the reader must likewise swim through the murky waters of extensive quotations. Freed says he is doing his best "to show the use that Eliot makes of his philosophy, without attempting to expound the philosophy" (p. xvii), but his closing sentence typifies the resulting organizational problems: "And here we find ourselves turning in a double circle" (p. 218). Standing alone, without clear connection to the enterprise as a whole, are discussions of other critical approaches to Bradley and Eliot. One such chapter, "Eliot and Bradley: A Brief Review," reprints a review article published in the *T. S. Eliot Review* (1976); sometimes acute and sometimes curiously inconclusive, it is certainly useful in itself. Another chapter is devoted to a critique of Kenner's remarks on Bradley's influence.

Freed maintains that Eliot's critical language must be interpreted in terms of a consistent philosophy, largely derived from Bradley and expressed in the early philosophical essays. Since Freed does not give a systematic account of the dissertation, it is difficult to compare his assessment of Eliot's relation to Bradley directly with, say, Wollheim's. Nevertheless, he makes a good case that Eliot was, or felt himself to be, in agreement with Bradley on major points. This does not necessarily imply that Eliot understood Bradley correctly. While Freed is probably correct to maintain that Eliot agreed with Bradley as Eliot understood Bradley, Whiteside and Wollheim, interpreting Bradley differently, may be justified in finding important differences. Freed interprets Eliot consistently in terms of Bradley; he also reads Bradley very much in Eliot's fashion. Since the main issue is influence, this is presumably appropriate.

Whether Eliot may be said to have consistently held to the position outlined in his early philosophical writings is far less certain. At one point or another, Freed makes a number of valid arguments to this effect: Eliot never repudiated his earlier philosophic work; he held to sharp distinctions between philosophy and theology which would keep his later theological speculations from being incompatible with his philosophy; and he often uses language derived from his philosophical training in discussing religious and cultural matters later in life. But in pursuing references to Eliot's philosophy, Freed sometimes adopts an almost cryptographic approach, suggesting that Eliot's determination to conceal the Greek sources of his dramas is paralleled by a determination to conceal the philosophic sources of "the origin of the literary theory" (p. 150). The result is that Eliot's "critical prose is marked by hints, suggestions, analogies, ambiguities, indirections, and misdirections" (p. 85). Freed sometimes seems unduly sure that all the ambiguities can be resolved and all the misdirections identified by appeal to Bradley. Particularly when the later prose is under discussion, one feels that Bradley is much more salient to the mind of Freed as a reader than it was to Eliot as a writer.

That we can reduce Eliot's language, particularly in the later works, to Bradleyan doctrine seems very unlikely; but certain terms and characteristic doctrines are obviously clearer if read in the light of Eliot's philosophic views, and it is Freed's great merit that he insists upon this. The "objective correlative," he says, "*is* the doctrine of immediate experience, in its aesthetic aspect" (p. 67). We cannot know immediate experience without objectifying it, abstracting from its flux some mental construct. These constructs are "objects" in a philosophical rather than an everyday sense. Emotions, insofar as we can know them, are objects, which is why Eliot speaks of Hamlet's inability to "understand" his emotion as an inability to "objectify" it. Such constructs need not be mere names, and we need not think of reason and imagination working in distinctly different ways. At its best, poetic language stands close to its object, *is* the objectified emotion, rather than an effort to create that emotion in the reader or a mere sign that the emotion is somehow present. The doctrine is thus descriptive of the conditions for understanding, aesthetic or otherwise, and prescriptive, in that it implies a criterion for measuring the efficacy of the work of art. Although he is forced to admit that Eliot sometimes employs words like "feeling" in inconsistent ways, Freed is able to show that many of Eliot's scattered remarks about feelings, thought, emotions, and objects fit together as part of a coherent set of notions about the operation of the mind.

Freed also demonstrates a certain consistency of thought in Eliot's comments on the autonomy of various artistic and intellectual disciplines, the unity of art, and the logic of imagination. Whether or not they are valid, Eliot's remarks are seldom silly, and his most difficult contentions often seem less inexplicable if proper attention is given to their language. If Freed seems to overstate his case at some points, his emphasis on this point is fully justified.

Anne Bolgan's role in editing the dissertation for Eliot makes her remarks on its import especially interesting. Her *What the Thunder Really Said* (1973) is disappointing in this respect, though what she has to say about *The Waste Land* is of sufficient interest to occupy us later in this chapter. The book's treatment of Bradley contributes little that is not already implicit in Bolgan's 1971 essay, "The Philosophy of F. H. Bradley and the Mind and Art of T. S. Eliot." Both works make large claims for the influence of Bradley, which contrast with the more tentative appraisal of Wollheim and resemble those of Freed. One wonders if this reflects the value systems of the two academic fields—literary critics are encouraged to make excessive claims by a publication system which stresses originality, while philosophers are expected to be more circumspect. Bolgan's 1973 book goes even further than Freed's, claiming that "it is in Bradley's philosophy that we shall find the source not only for every major critical concept appearing in Eliot's literary criticism but also for that informing ideology which gives rise to the controlling images and symbols of his poetry" (p. 178). The 1971 essay says "it is Bradley's mind that lies behind the structuring principles of Eliot's poetry, as well as behind every major theoretical concept appearing in his literary criticism" (p. 252). One can't help supposing, instead, that it is Eliot's mind which lies behind Eliot's poetry and criticism, however great the impact of Bradley upon it. Nor can one agree that all criticism which does not acknowledge the central role of Bradley in Eliot's thought is "doomed from the start either to irrelevance or ineptitude" (1971, p. 257). Neither of Bolgan's studies does much to justify such extreme statements.

To say that Bolgan sometimes overstates her case is not to deny that she offers useful insights, but only to say that one needs to use her work with care. Because it focuses more on the influence of Bradley, her 1971 essay is the more relevant at this point. It begins with the assertion that it was the study of philosophy which transformed Eliot from the young man whose high school graduate ode contained such forgettable lines as "Then with a song upon our lips, sail we" into the poet who, only five years later, wrote "The Love Song of J. Alfred Prufrock." This is certainly an impressive tribute to the virtues of philosophic study; but since Eliot took only three undergraduate philosophy courses in the intervening years, it seems almost as likely that the transformation of the poet led to the study of philosophy. As Thompson (1963) suggests, Eliot was a philosophic poet before he was a philosopher.

Bolgan then argues that such inconsistencies as people have found in Eliot's criticism arise from taking remarks out of context and failing to understand the doctrinal framework he shared with Bradley. This argument has limited merit when applied to the early criticism, but Bolgan's assumption, shared with Freed, that Eliot underwent no change at all in later years seems a bit restrictive. Bolgan admits that Eliot's criticism does not provide a full system in itself, but argues that, together with his dissertation, it provides hints toward a theory for "the counter-romantic movement" (1971, p. 265)—the very phrase reminds one of the way in which Bolgan ignores the influence of Irving Babbitt, who helped make Eliot a classicist and who probably influenced his decision to do graduate work in philosophy and Indic studies.

Bolgan's Eliot is counter-Romantic because he is opposed to Romantic notions of "personality" and to expressionist theories of art. Like several other students of Bradley's impact on Eliot's art, Bolgan sees the doctrine of impersonality as derived from Bradley's notion of self-transcendence. Bolgan often uses Keats' phrase "Soul-making" for this process, perhaps because it suggests the way in which creation itself is one of the ways in which the artist discovers his true self, even while losing it in the transcendent self. It also suggests, of course, how slippery are such terms as Romantic and counter-Romantic. In both the 1971 essay and the book, Bolgan interprets *Four Quartets* as a philosophical poem based on a mandala, a "circle of the Absolute," within which the descending dove creates four quadrants by its intersection with linear time. This "structure merely images in a concrete, visible form each of the pivotal doctrines within post-Kantian Absolute Idealism on which the wheel of that philosophy finally turns" (1971, p. 268). This metaphor leaves the living poem well behind, making us feel that literary critics should shun mandalas as vampires shun the cross. One also demurs at being told that the *Four Quartets* are a Bradleyan vision, when the few examples represent a Christian view of history which long antedates Bradley. One of the features Eliot may have taken from Bradley's thought is a certain skepticism about interpretation as a vehicle to truth, and one can see why.

Bolgan, in fact, overstresses the religious implications of Bradley's Absolute, which he did not (like some other Idealists) identify clearly with God; she also underrates the doubts expressed about the Absolute by Eliot. This allows her to find intimations of the Absolute in strange places—one of the less likely being Prufrock's "streets that follow like a tedious argument." One may agree with Bolgan that Eliot found ideas in Bradley which fascinated him, and a problem (self-transcendence) which meant a great deal to him. At the same time, one cannot help feeling that Bolgan's view that *Ash Wednesday* and *Four Quartets* are more successful in achieving this vision suggests that, while Bradley provided the terms, Christianity provided the solution. Bollier's analysis of Bradley's impact on Eliot's religious development seems much more believable.

Whatever the relationship between Bradley's metaphysics and Eliot's later theological position, it is less striking than the parallels between Bradley's thought and Eliot's early criticism. If we take such parallels as establishing influence, we may be justified in sharing John J. Soldo's judgment that Eliot's dissertation is "the single most important document in understanding his theoretical criticism" ("Knowledge and Experience in the Criticism of T. S. Eliot," 1968, p. 308). For Soldo, the key point is Eliot's rejection of even the possibility of our knowing anything about immediate experience without an admixture of consciousness. He sees Eliot's solution to the subjectivity produced by this position as represented by his use of "point of view" to denote what Bradley calls the "finite center," for Eliot's term suggests that there are other points of view, of the same reality, with which a given point of view may be connected. Prufrock may be a Bradleyan finite center, trapped in himself, but Tiresias, of *The Waste Land*, has been able to incorporate many points of view in himself. The ultimate unity of such points of view would be reality itself, that common reference of multiple centers of consciousness. Soldo is describing a process of transcendence, a feature derived from Bradley but certainly important in Eliot's view of consciousness. Soldo points out that the doctrine of "Tradition and the Individual Talent" is also based on the inadequacy of the single finite center as an interpreter of reality. The past to which it appeals can no more be known directly than can immediate experience; our experience of the past, as our experience of all things, is mediated through our consciousness of it. To attain unity is to attain a unity of such relations; "dissociation of sensibility" can lead only to false unity, for thought and feeling cannot be separated in the end. The metaphysicals are praised by Eliot because they have found their way to a relational unity which unites diverse points of view. It is in this sense, says Soldo, that we must take Eliot's "sensuous apprehension of thought." Soldo's Bradleyan interpretation of this term, because of its emphasis on relations, is more complex than those who would see "sensuous apprehension of thought" as closer to immediate experience rather than transcendent in nature. Soldo is also perceptive in his treatment of Eliot on objects; we can know reality only by turning it into objects, making them, insofar as possible, parts of a relational whole. In this view, Soldo sees the origin of the "objective correlative."

Armin Paul Frank has advanced a similar thesis on the relationship in "T. S. Eliot's Objective Correlative and the Philosophy of F. H. Bradley" (1972), but concentrates on Bradley's essay "On Our Knowledge of Immediate Experience," rather than on Eliot's dissertation. In the Bradley essay, Frank sees the key passage as one in which Bradley holds that "a feeling becomes an object of knowledge by projection onto an object—of which the observer knows through sense perception—and thereby becomes part of that object" (p. 315). Frank sees Eliot's use of Bradley's doctrine as implicitly Expressionistic—but not in conflict with the ideal of an impersonal poetry so long as Eliot maintains the distinction between the man who has the emotions and the poet who transforms them into art.

The Secret Subjectivist

It is possible, of course, to see Eliot's early criticism as surreptitiously expressionist and to make his overall position consistent by interpreting his dissertation in terms of subjective Idealism, as J. Hillis Miller does in his chapter on Eliot in *Poets of Reality* (1966). This is unfair to Bradley, for placing the ground of reality in immediate experience is an attempt to escape the problems raised by subjective Idealism. It is not really accurate as applied to Eliot, who argues in his dissertation (perhaps unconvincingly) that it is possible to interweave points of view. Ascribing subjective Idealism to Eliot, Miller makes intersubjectivity sound like a problem different in kind from the problem one faces as an individual in making a unity out of one's own diverse points of view. Common sense may be on Miller's side in this, but Eliot's dissertation is a work of philosophy, a discipline which advances by examining critically the assumptions of common sense. Miller recognizes the problematic character of the self in Eliot's dissertation, but he does not seem to realize the full implications of maintaining that the self is a secondary construct.

Miller's misreading of the dissertation is connected with a very stimulating interpretation of "The Love Song of J. Alfred Prufrock." He draws an interesting contrast between the novel as an intersubjective form and the dramatic monologue, in which one is enclosed within a single frame of reference—a process more advanced, he observes, in Eliot than in Browning. Prufrock, projecting his feelings onto the world around him, is swallowed up in "an all-inclusive subjective realm" (p. 138), which saps his will and traps him in a timeless present from which there is no escape. This is a bit abstract, but we may agree that Prufrock's excessive self-consciousness is related, at least by analogy, to Romanticism and subjective Idealism. Both the poem and the dissertation may be concerned with such dangers, but that does not mean that Prufrock's state of mind is the same as his creator's philosophic position.

Miller's interpretation of the dissertation also leads him to find more dramatic changes in Eliot's philosophic development than are plausible. Miller recognizes that some form of transcendence of the self is allowed for by the dissertation, and that its viewpoint is found in "Tradition and the Individual Talent." He even calls attention to the ease with which Eliot moves from mind to mind in such early poems as "Preludes" and *The Waste Land.* Miller claims that such transcendence "is really defeat" (p. 178) since the universal mind remains as fragmentary and self-enclosed as the individual consciousness. This is a fair criticism of both the poems and the philosophy, but it obscures the differences between Eliot's philosophy and subjective Idealism.

Eliot's acceptance of Christianity, which implies self-transcendence, thus seems to Miller a real break with Eliot's previous position. Miller makes the break seem even sharper by arguing that acceptance of the physical world is basic to Christianity because of the Incarnation. Christianity, however, has assigned a variety of meanings to the Incarnation, and Eliot's rather ascetic Christianity does not seem to have led him to a fervent embrace of the world and the flesh. Miller sees him doing so in *Ash Wednesday*, but the very lines Miller uses to establish the acceptance of physicality seem to be identified with "the empty forms between the ivory gates." As we have seen in the last chapter, some critics argue that Eliot's religious position entailed a positive rejection of the physical world; but arguments that Christianity necessarily entails particular philosophic positions are of little use in talking about individual figures. We may assume that Eliot's conversion had an effect on his views, but the sharp separation Miller makes between the immediate experience and the "still point" implies that more has changed in Eliot's thought than one can feel sure of.

Harry T. Antrim's monograph on development, *T. S. Eliot's Concept of Language* (1971), echoes Miller's misreading of the dissertation and Eliot's development but lacks Miller's redeeming quality of providing challenging interpretations of particular poems. Antrim's first chapter, "The Romantic Inheritance," identifies the Classicist Eliot of "The Love Song of J. Alfred Prufrock" with a Romantic tradition he consciously rejected. This confusion begins with identification of the persona of "Prufrock" with Eliot, and it is compounded by a solipsistic reading of Bradley. In this reading, language can only reveal "the agonizingly private nature of each experience" (p. 5). Antrim echoes Miller's critique of the notion of transcendence implied in "Tradition and the Individual Talent," saying "any escape from one's private personality into the reaches of the mind of tradition is but a substitution of a larger for a small world of experience" (p. 27), which echoes, as well, Eliot's criticism of Bradley's version of "transcendence of error" (1964, p. 119). But Antrim is at fault in seeing both the private and the larger world of experience as finally closed. Antrim recognizes that, in Eliot's early criticism, "words and feelings and emotions appear to be interchangeable" (1971, p. 28), but he fails to note the relevance of this to the objective correlative and errs in assuming that this is because Eliot has solved the subject-object problem by rendering everything subjective.

Like Miller, Antrim seems determined to make Eliot's conversion a more dramatic break than need be, and does so by imposing his own notions of Christianity on Eliot. Antrim says Eliot's conversion necessitated a change in philosophical stance on language, for "to be a Christian is to deny epistemological idealisms of any sort" (p. 44), which would certainly startle many theologians. Antrim's "proof" of the change is that Eliot was enabled to overcome his Romantic inheritance—that is, to cease to hold ideas which Antrim incorrectly imputed to him. Eliot's final doctrine in *Four Quartets*, says Antrim, is that language "can describe immediate experience and it can be ordered so as to suggest that that experience is a proper analogue to the experience of 'things unseen' " (p. 75). The use of "immediate experience" here is loose and misleading, bearing no resemblance to the meaning of the term in Bradley and in Eliot's dissertation. Antrim's summary, in any case, sounds so much like the "objective correlative" that one is left wondering where Eliot's philosophy of language can be said to have undergone any real development.

The version of Eliot's development advanced by Miller and elaborated by Antrim has the virtue of appearing to reconcile Romantic criticism and Bradleyan philosophy, the two most convincing sources suggested for Eliot's "objective correlative" and, by extension, for the rest of his early criticism. It does not work well, however, because "subjective Idealism" is not a fair term for Bradley's thought or Eliot's dissertation. A more convincing attempt is Mowbray Allan's study, *T. S. Eliot's Impersonal Theory of Poetry* (1974). Allan considers Miller's book the best attempt to relate Eliot's criticism to his poetry, but Allan's careful study is a more accurate guide to Eliot's poetics. The virtue of Allan's book is that he distinguishes between Idealism as a general movement in philosophy and subjective Idealism as a particular form of that movement. He sees Eliot linked to the Romantic critics by a shared acceptance of an Idealist theory of knowledge, an acceptance which need not be taken to imply more than strictly philosophical assent.

Rejecting philosophical (and literary) realism, Eliot also shared some of the metaphysical assumptions of the Romantics. DeLaura is thus justified in saying that Eliot could have found a model for the "objective correlative" in Pater, but, says Allan, Eliot could also have found such a model in Hegel, or in even earlier Idealists, for the implied relationship is part of the general inheritance of Idealism. But just as Bradley's emphasis on experience is meant to correct the subjectivity of nineteenth-century Idealism, Eliot's impersonal theory of art is meant to correct the excessive subjectivity of Romantic aesthetics. One might observe at this point that, in theory at least, Bradley's philosophy eliminates both ideality and the subject as categories of the real, just as Eliot's philosophy and criticism eliminate the self. However, Allan is probably safe in placing both Bradley and Eliot in the Idealist tradition on other grounds. Allan explains Eliot's admiration for Remy de Gourmont, despite the latter's subjective Idealism and emphasis on personality, by citing the French critic's complementary stress on physical experience. It is Eliot's resistance to the subjective side of Idealism which, in Allan's view, makes plausible Miller's claim that Eliot ended in a form of Christian realism. But Allan regards the question of this shift as unresolvable (and perhaps irrelevant) since, "before reaching the point at which (in Miller's view) Eliot should have succeeded in rejecting idealism, an even more fundamental change had occurred in his critical approach; he had purified his critical vocabulary of metaphysical assumptions . . . at least well enough that it does not imply any one philosophical position" (p. 43).

Allan is less concerned than many critics of the dissertation with transcending individual points of view. Instead, he stresses Bradley's doctrine of self-consistency. Along with doubts about our ability to know the external world, the notion of self-consistency may have encouraged Eliot's emphasis on making the work of art a self-subsistent world, with its truth dependent on the intensity of its internal relations rather than on its representation of external reality. Allan sees Eliot's doubts about direct communication between points of view as leading to his later rejection of "interpretation" and his comments on the need to find an "objective correlative." Allan argues that Eliot sees both a false "impersonality" (submission to the social world) and a desirable "impersonality" (submission to reality). There is even a desirable form of "personality," self-critical and aware of the tenuousness of the "self"; this is needed to avoid confusing the opinion of society with the realities of experience. Both poet and critic inevitably start with themselves; false "personality" consists in failing to move beyond the self, in confusing the self with the world.

Allan's version of Eliot's doctrine of impersonality smooths out many of the apparent contradictions in Eliot's various statements about personality and impersonality. The result is, perhaps, a bit more consistent and systematic than Eliot is himself, and it may be that Allan sometimes gives us the most defensible statement of Eliot's position rather than the most "Eliotic." Allan's book is distinguished, however, by its balance and modesty. He recognizes multiple influences on Eliot, by philosophers and literary critics, and he does not make large claims for specific influences. Allan's willingness to recognize that there may be a difference between one's philosophical arguments and one's operative beliefs is admirable, and his willingness to leave unsolved problems for which there is insufficient evidence is refreshing. Wollheim and Whiteside probably provide better summaries of the dissertation, and Freed is more thorough on its significance, but Allan provides a useful start in our effort to understand the philosophic bases of Eliot's critical but real relationship to the traditions of Romantic Idealism.

The Poet and the Believer

The difficulties in dealing with Eliot's early criticism are not all caused by misapprehensions by his critics. The very strategies Eliot used to avoid Romantic subjectivism brought him close to Romantic claims for the autonomy of art—claims he was not, in the end, prepared to accept in full. The preface to the 1928 edition of *The Sacred Wood* describes its essays as linked by "the problem of the integrity of poetry, with the repeated assertion that when we are considering poetry we must consider it primarily as poetry and not another thing." Poetry is "a superior amusement," not to be confused with "the inculcation of morals, or the direction of politics." Although by 1928 Eliot was a professed Anglican, he continued to assume that poetry had an integrity of its own and that purely aesthetic responses to it were possible. The "impersonal theory" had also aimed at divorcing poetry from the poet's personal beliefs and values, except insofar as these were part of the felt experience of the poem or were involved in its ordering of experience. Without repudiating that theory, Eliot ends his 1928 preface with an admission that poetry has "something to do with morals, and with religion, and even with politics perhaps," though in discussing such matters "we appear already to be leaving the domain of criticism of 'poetry.' " This is not an altogether satisfactory position, and the difficulties to which it leads are generally known as the "problem of poetry and belief."

Eliot returned to this question repeatedly, and James Noonan has provided a useful survey of Eliot's comments in "Poetry and Belief in the Criticism of T. S. Eliot" (1972). As Noonan observes, there are two problems, one connected with the poet's beliefs and the other with the reader's. Eliot's early criticism, says Noonan, deals mainly with the first; the later criticism, mainly with the second. In Noonan's interpretation of the impersonal theory of poetry, a poet who expresses a tradition may hold certain feelings and beliefs which find no place in his poetry. At the same time, the fusion of thought and feeling will make fully felt beliefs implicit in the poem. Noonan takes it that the essay "Shakespeare and the Stoicism of Seneca" (1927) shows Eliot prepared to doubt that belief need be involved in the works of a great poet; the 1929 essay on Dante shows Eliot still separating the poet's beliefs from his poetry, while admitting that in practice one could hardly imagine an unbeliever writing the *Divine Comedy*. We might note that in each case Eliot appears to be discussing "belief" as assent to some systematic set of ideas, rather than belief as felt experience.

On the second issue, the reader's beliefs and response to the poem, the 1929 essay on Dante seems to present Eliot's initial position, which distinguished between understanding (necessary for poetic assent) and belief, a position very close to Eliot's position on belief and the poet. But Eliot seems to take it all back, adding a note that indicates that full understanding may require belief. That such a view strikes a blow against even a limited idea of poetry as autonomous is indicated by Eliot's conclusion to this note: "It would appear that 'literary appreciation' is an abstraction, and pure poetry a phantom; and that both in creation and enjoyment much always enters which is, from the point of view of 'Art,' irrelevant."

Despite the implications of this note, the essays in *The Use of Poetry and the Use of Criticism* (1934) retain the distinction between understanding and belief. Eliot now maintains that understanding does not require one to accept immature views of life or low intellectual standards. Noonan, whose purpose is descriptive rather than critical, fails to note how easily this permits one to readmit important matters of belief back into one's criticism, under the guise of mature reflection; one could maintain, perhaps, that immature and irrational beliefs are symptoms of sensibilities incapable of creating self-consistent worlds of art. A more persuasive formulation occurs in Eliot's 1934 essay "Religion and Literature," in which the distinction between literary and religious standards is maintained, with extraliterary standards entering to determine our final evaluation of greatness. Noonan objects to this on the ground that we should be able to say that Shakespeare is a great writer without appealing to religious sanctions, but this is not really a problem so long as Eliot maintains the existence of distinctively literary standards. The real problem is Eliot's failure to specify more exactly what literary standards would be and how they might be set off from nonliterary standards. Noonan might have noted here the parallel with the approach in Eliot's *After Strange Gods*, in which Eliot professedly operates as a moralist rather than as a literary critic.

Noonan's final example is Eliot's 1935 lecture "Goethe as a Sage," which Noonan ranks higher than many Eliot critics do. Eliot uses "wisdom" as a transcendent way of reconciling understanding and belief: we may recognize Goethe's wisdom while disagreeing strongly with some of his beliefs. The reader who shares beliefs can identify with the poet as an aid to understanding; the reader who does not must try to put himself in the believer's place, moving from his initial position of detachment. Eliot says that their readings of a poem should eventually coincide, and Noonan takes this to mean that both identification and detachment have their problems, but in context it looks like the nonbeliever has much the harder job. Noonan claims that our view of Eliot's long and not very successful struggle with the problem of belief is useful to our understanding of the problem, but he does not say exactly how. Other critics have been less generous.

Victor H. Brombert's short study, *The Criticism of T. S. Eliot: Problems of an "Impersonal Theory" of Poetry*, was published in 1949 as a Yale Undergraduate Prize Essay and remains an interesting attempt at evaluation. Brombert gives much of his attention to the problem of belief, which he defines as "the relation of the goodness of the poem to the truth or falsity of what it seems to assert" (p. 32). Brombert's review of Eliot's position begins with "Theism and Humanism," a 1916 book review which sharply separates aesthetic and other values. By the time of his 1926 *Criterion* essay, "The Idea of a Literary Review," Eliot is willing to admit that literature inevitably includes nonliterary matters, while continuing to make a sharp distinction between intrinsic and extrinsic elements. Brombert is not happy with the emphasis on the poet's turning thought into emotion, in "Shakespeare and the Stoicism of Seneca" (1927); he sees this as an unworkable attempt to enable the literary critic to forego "any value judgments of thought content" (1949, p. 21). This judgment of Brombert's seems harsh; the view in question certainly flows naturally from other aspects of Eliot's "impersonal theory." Brombert endorses the view of Cleanth Brooks in *The Well-wrought Urn*—that a structurally coherent poem assimilates beliefs in such a way that the question does not arise for the reader—although Brombert admits that such a critical norm leaves us unable to deal with many works. Brombert does not seem to realize that Brooks' position is fundamentally the same as Eliot's in "Shakespeare and the Stoicism of Seneca," a position implicit in the doctrine of the objective correlative (which Brombert rather neglects). Brombert's objection to Eliot's comparison with Dante in that essay suggests why Brooks' position does not cover some works —and thus why Eliot was not fully satisfied with it. Brombert says that Eliot neglects the difference between dramatic and epic poetry—a fair criticism. Eliot's early position is best suited to drama and dramatistic lyrics. One is reminded that much in the "impersonal theory" seems to make the self-effacement of the dramatist the norm for poetry, even lyric poetry.

William Joseph Rooney's chapter on Eliot in *The Problem of "Poetry and Belief" in Contemporary Criticism* (1949) also sees Eliot's consideration of this problem as one of the weakest portions of his criticism. Rooney sees no reason why Eliot should regard his distaste for portions of Shelley or Goethe as requiring explanation in terms of extraliterary standards; the "immature" view of life expressed in, say, *Wilhelm Meister* results in artistic deficiencies in construction. As we have seen earlier, such a view can be derived from Eliot's early criticism, but Eliot does not seem to have consistently held to it. To do so may require dogmatic certainty in the truth of one's belief system—easier, perhaps, for Rooney's Romanism than Eliot's Anglicanism. For Rooney, the problem lies in Eliot's refusal to give his criticism an explicit metaphysical base; he notes that Eliot's admiration for Aristotle might have led Eliot in that direction, and he is probably right about this. Eliot's insistence on dealing with poetry *as* poetry is consistent enough, but within such a framework it is hard to see how he could have dealt with the relationship between poetry and external belief systems, except insofar as the latter are fully embodied in the poetry.

There are many good ideas in Vincent Buckley's chapters on Eliot in *Poetry and Morality* (1959). Most of them are Eliot's, for Buckley quotes extensively, but some of them are from other critics. When Buckley ends one chapter with a complaint that Eliot uses mechanical images to discuss the nature of poetry, he is echoing Leavis; when he ends another chapter with the observation that the modesty of Eliot's claims for the moral value of poetry "confers additional dignity on its subject" (p. 157), Buckley is echoing Blackmur (1951). Buckley is inclined to minimize the changes in Eliot's thought on the issues of poetry and morality and poetry and belief. This is a defensible position, but Buckley arrives at it partly by overemphasizing the rigidity of the tradition appealed to in Eliot's early criticism. To be fair, Buckley is encouraged in this by Eliot's later entangling of "tradition" and "orthodoxy," but Buckley is to blame for refusing to accept Eliot's warning that *After Strange Gods* is not meant as literary criticism. Buckley sees Eliot's role in that book, and other later criticism, as "pastoral," even protective, in its relation to readers. The valuable part in Buckley's emphasis on the continuity of Eliot's thought is his recognition that Eliot's assumption of a pastoral role in his criticism does not involve insistence that art can or should do more than create an ordered reality. The later criticism does not, therefore, repudiate the antididactic assumptions of the early criticism.

Kristian Smidt's *Poetry and Belief in the Work of T. S. Eliot*

(1949, rev. 1961) is more general in its coverage than its title might suggest. On the influence of Bradley, Smidt is sensible, although brief and a bit inclined to exaggerate the despair of metaphysics into metaphysical despair. On the influence of Bergson, Smidt is the most reasonable of those who see any influence here, recognizing that Eliot eventually repudiated Bergson. Smidt was one of the first to call attention to the influence of J. W. Dunne's *Experiments with Time* (1927). On many of the issues dealt with in this section, Smidt offers a balanced if not especially stimulating treatment, recognizing, for example, that Eliot's criticism is both traditional and individualistic and that Eliot's "impersonal" theory never becomes mere aestheticism. Smidt believes that "Eliot's views on poetic belief are more definite and consistent than his opinions on a great many other matters" (p. 68)—which may overstate the case a bit. Smidt sees the central principle as the reader's "poetic assent," an assent we can give to many philosophies we do not share, though not to all. One may agree, at least, that this is the most consistent view in Eliot's criticism. It is when Eliot (or his critics) attempts to specify the basis on which one can give this assent that inconsistencies and confusions seem to result.

The Romantic Critic

Behind many of the issues discussed so far in this chapter lies the question of Eliot's relationship to the Romantic tradition in poetry and criticism. Readers who identify Eliot's philosophy as subjectivist often link him explicitly with literary Romanticism. Those who identify his position on the relationship between poetry and belief as a form of aestheticism are also apt to place Eliot in the Romantic tradition. It may seem paradoxical to label as Romantic a critic who proclaimed himself a Classicist and was sharply critical of his Romantic predecessors, but there is evidence that Eliot felt the intellectual and aesthetic attractions of the subjectivism and Romanticism he criticized. Difficulties arise, however, when Eliot's intellectual position is distorted, either by the "discovery" of implausible sources for his criticism or by exaggerating the extent to which he shared the critical assumptions of Romanticism.

The reckless pursuit of previously unpublished sources is common in Eliot criticism; for the moment, we will confine ourselves to sources posited for the notion of an "objective correlative." As with many of Eliot's other critical generalizations, the argument that Hamlet's emotions are insufficiently motivated by the situations has a perfectly obvious source in the book Eliot was reviewing in the essay, so that looking further afield seems unnecessary. The book was *The Problem of Hamlet* by J. M. Robertson, whose general impact on Eliot has been explored by Leo Storm ("J. M. Robertson and T. S. Eliot: A Note on the Genesis of Modern Critical Theory," 1976). Terms like "object" and "correlative" are common in philosophical writing, and there seems no mystery about Eliot's having them in his critical vocabulary. Indeed, complaints about emotions' exceeding the facts are common in literary criticism; so it is only in applying them to *Hamlet* that Robertson and Eliot are distinctive. Unfortunately, the familiarity of the argument and terms has made it easier for later critics to find "sources," which give a false picture of Eliot's intellectual development.

The best known of those sources which have been alleged on the basis of verbal echoes is from a nineteenth-century American Romantic painter, Washington Allston. Eliot's preface to his *Essays in Elizabethan Drama* (1960) mentions Allston's use of "objective correlative." Robert Stallman had earlier printed the relevant passage from Allston in *The Critic's Notebook* (1950), but Allston's use of the phrase is not much like Eliot's and casts no light on Eliot's meaning; moreover, no one has given any reason to believe that Eliot ever read Allston. Given its previous publication by Eliot and Stallman, it is surprising to find Nathalia Wright "discovering" the Allston source anew in 1970 ("A Source for T. S. Eliot's Objective Correlative"). Wright's use of this source is modest, however, compared to what John Duffy makes of it in his "T. S. Eliot's Objective Correlative: A New England Commonplace" (1969). In addition to citing the Allston source, Duffy draws an unconvincing parallel between Eliot's objective correlative and Emerson's doctrine of correspondences, as advanced in *Nature*. Duffy also points to the use of "subjective correlative" and "objective correlative" in a set of lectures on psychology by a university president from Vermont. Since the lectures were never published, it is hard to see their relevance. On the basis of such parallels, Duffy argues that Eliot's failure to acknowledge his New England sources was part of a conscious effort to suppress his debt to Romanticism. But if Eliot *did* imbibe Romantic commonplaces, it does not seem likely that he had to find them in New England.

Although he was evidently not an admirer of Santayana's philosophy, Eliot probably read some of his works, which gives a possible point to the verbal echo in Santayana's *Poetry and Religion* (1900) which says of the poet that "the glorious emotions with which he bubbles over must at all hazards find or feign their correlative objects." This was noted in Stallman (1950) and by Bruce R. McElderry, Jr. ("Santayana and Eliot's 'Objective Correlative,' " 1957). There is further evidence that Eliot read Santayana's works if one accepts Henry Wasser's argument that the closing lines of "The Hollow Men" echo Santayana's *Three Philosophical Poets* ("A Note on Eliot and Santayana," 1960). Much less convincing as a philosophic source is Edmund Husserl, though Husserl used the term *objectives Korrelat*. Husserl has been suggested by both John M. Steadman ("Eliot and Husserl: The Origin of the 'Objective Correlative,' " 1958) and Jitendra Kumar ("Consciousness and Its Correlates: Eliot and Husserl," 1968). Kumar's essay is superior, because more modest in its claims; reading it suggests that such common features as Eliot and Husserl share derive from Alexius Meinong, whom Eliot used frequently in his dissertation as a corrective to Bradley. Even less persuasive is F. N. Lees' "T. S. Eliot and Nietzsche" (1964), which makes too much of a passage in *The Birth of Tragedy* where Nietzsche remarks: "The myth does not at all find its adequate objectification in the spoken word" (translation available to Eliot). This proves only that Eliot was not the first to speak of objectification—hardly a startling discovery. If Eliot needed to learn about such terms and concepts, he did not need to go so far afield.

Some of the essays that place Eliot in the English Romantic tradition also rely in part on verbal echoes. Pasquale di Pasquale, Jr., for example, draws unwarranted parallels in "Coleridge's Framework of Objectivity and Eliot's Objective Correlative" (1968). Coleridge used "framework of objectivity" in a set of obscure lectures, "correlative" by itself several times, and "objective correlative" not at all. Such agreement as is found between Coleridge and Eliot will surprise only those with simplistic notions about Coleridge's Romanticism or Eliot's Classicism. Only slightly more impressive is David DeLaura's "Pater and Eliot: The Origin of the 'Objective Correlative' " (1965); but the verbal parallels it offers are worse—between Eliot's comment that Hamlet's emotion is "in *excess* of the facts as they appear" and some remarks in Pater's essay on Botticelli (in *The Renaissance*), for example, "a passion greater than any known issue of them explains." On the general significance of Pater for Eliot, DeLaura follows lines laid down by William Blissett ("Pater and Eliot," 1953), who argues that Eliot's later denigration of Pater is a reaction against an earlier enthusiasm for Pater. DeLaura notes that the sin Eliot attributes to Impressionistic critics like Pater and Symons—excessive subjectivity which obscures the objects of their criticism—is analogous to the flaw Eliot finds in *Hamlet.* To DeLaura, this suggests that Pater's Botticelli essay helped Eliot find the terms in which to denounce Romantic critics like Pater. This would be an amusing irony, but no student of Irving Babbitt would need to learn about the dangers of Romantic subjectivism from Pater.

Similar objections apply to most efforts to derive Eliot's position from particular critics, whether or not the effort depends upon tenuous verbal echoes. Certain issues recur in English criticism among critics of a variety of persuasions, and critics who disagree on many issues can find common ground on others; but influence cannot be proved by such agreements. A case in point is Murray Krieger's "The Critical Legacy of Matthew Arnold; or, The Strange Brotherhood of T. S. Eliot, I. A. Richards, and Northrop Frye" (1969). Krieger claims that "Arnold may be seen as ultimately responsible not only for Eliot's (as well as Richards') ideas on poetry and belief, but also for such other central doctrines in Eliot as the objective correlative and the unity of sensibility" (1969, p. 458). Arnold's condemnation of his own "Empedocles" for having dealt with a situation "in which the suffering finds no vent in action" is presented as a source for Eliot's remarks about "emotion which can find no outlet in action." Arnold's admiration for medieval unity, shared with many Romantics and Victorians, is presented as a source for Eliot's admiration of the unified sensibility of the Metaphysicals. Such commonplaces can hardly demonstrate Eliot's debt to Arnold in particular, for they belong to a tradition older than either—and, we might note, are more intelligent than Krieger sometimes admits.

But it is possible to argue that Eliot shares more profound affinities with the Romantic tradition. One of the best-known arguments to that effect is by C. K. Stead, developed in his essay " 'Classical Authority' and 'The Dark Embryo': A Dichotomy in T. S. Eliot's Criticism" (1964a) and his book *The New Poetic: Yeats to Eliot* (1964b). Stead stresses the expressive and emotive elements in Eliot's account of the poetic process, both in the early criticism and in such later pieces as "The

Three Voices of Poetry" (in *On Poets and Poetry*, 1957). Eliot's "impersonality" is described as an escape from the conscious self to an unconscious self and as akin to Keats' "negative capability." In effect, immediate experience is equated with the unconscious, a procedure which involves translating Eliot (and perhaps the Romantics) into an alien idiom. Stead argues that Eliot termed himself a Classicist because only a Classicist ordering of life could ensure that poems written by the "First Voice" were not merely beautiful but true. Some may think this a common reason for adopting a Classicist aesthetic—and for calling Eliot a Classicist if that was his position.

It is possible, moreover, that Stead and those who agree with him are guilty of exaggerating the emotive aspects of the "impersonal theory." If we look at Eliot's dissertation and at "Tradition and the Individual Talent," "emotion" is treated in a rather special way. Objectification becomes the route to knowledge, and the poet's feelings may remain unclear to him until he has ordered them through art. The emotions in the poem need not be those of the poet, and Eliot's skepticism about interpretation suggests that the emotions aroused by successful objectification may differ from those felt by the poet, rather as men differ in their responses to the world of objects. As stated in "Hamlet and His Problems," however, the notion of an objective correlative can be taken to imply that the poet is engaged in a conscious search for an objective equivalent of an emotional state already fully known. Such are the views attacked by Eliseo Vivas, on the assumption that they constitute "The Objective Correlative of T. S. Eliot" (1944). Vivas' essay has been widely used, even by defenders of Eliot. William Wimsatt and Cleanth Brooks, for example, know that Vivas' attack does not hold good for Eliot's general approach as a critic, but they believe he may be right about the account of the poetic process in the Hamlet essay ("Eliot and Pound: An Impersonal Art," *Literary Criticism: A Short History*, 1962). But it seems likelier that Eliot was being unclear than that he was being inconsistent.

The apparent inconsistency in "Hamlet and His Problems" is less a problem if we understand that the failure to find an objective correlative is a failure in the internal construction of the drama. R. P. Blackmur made this observation some years ago in "In the Hope of Straightening Things Out" (1951). Allen Austin also insists on this point in his treatment of the objective correlative in his *T. S. Eliot: The Literary and Social*

Criticism (1971). The excessive emotion Eliot finds in *Hamlet* is Hamlet's own emotion, which is not, according to Eliot, fully motivated by the dramatic situation in which he is placed. Shakespeare's inability to order the plot is likened to Hamlet's inability to order his emotions; but Shakespeare's problems need not be the same as Hamlet's. Austin would like to see "objective correlative" restricted to discussions of the relationship between the objective situation in the work and the emotion it expresses. Long-standing critical use may prevent this, and the notion of objectification is surely somehow related to another element in Eliot's view of the poetic process—"that one of the ways in which poetry achieves intensity is through the embodiment of an emotion in a concrete object" (1971, p. 19). Successful objectification will embody itself in the kind of self-consistent reality Eliot finds lacking in *Hamlet.* The relationship between the emotion and its objectification, however, remains more complex than in a simple expressive theory.

There is, of course, an expressive, emotive element in the "impersonal theory" in "Tradition and the Individual Talent." Poetry is certainly spoken of as having its origins in emotions and feelings, that is, fragments of immediate experience. It is this which gives plausibility to Murray Krieger's argument that Eliot is inconsistent, seeking both an "objective" impersonality and an expressive "correlative." But there is a potential problem here, even if we ignore Krieger's assumption (following Vivas) that Eliot has the poet express preexisting, disembodied emotions. The problem, as raised by Krieger, is that the expressive origins assigned to the poem may seem at war with Eliot's demand for a unified sensibility in which thought and feeling are mingled. Eliot's position is, however, at least defensible; first, because thought and feeling need not be conceived of as separable at the level of immediate experience, and second, because thought is a condition of the objectification of emotion. Whether or not we agree that he satisfactorily resolved the problems he set himself, Eliot took a consistent approach to the difficulties raised by his critical relationship to a Romantic tradition he could not entirely escape.

How one conceives of Eliot's relation to that tradition depends partly on what one sees as Eliot's intentions. It is quite possible that the distinctions which separate Eliot from his Romantic predecessors will come to seem unimportant—though that will never justify misstating those distinctions—and that all of the moderns will be seen at last as late Romantics. Any such view will represent a reevaluation of what is essential in the Romantic critical tradition, and Eliot will still deserve some honor for opposing the Impressionistic and personalistic criticism that represented itself as heir to the Romantic tradition. Eliot will not, in that case, figure as a major theorist, but he never claimed to be one. In his later years, he was inclined to stress the close relationship between his early critical essays and his own work and literary tastes.

Such a view seems more likely to prevail than Rene Wellek's assertion that "Eliot has constantly been working at a general theory and, from the beginning of his writings, has had a theory in the back of his mind" ("The Criticism of T. S. Eliot," 1956, p. 400). This misstates Eliot's purpose and leads to the juxtaposition of statements made over many years as if they were part of a connected argument. Even a relatively consistent man must be allowed to change his mind occasionally. Wellek's approach, however, allows him to work his way through to the consistencies when they are really there. It also means that Wellek's discussion of Eliot has a desirable coherence. By way of contrast, Jyoti Prakrash Sen's *The Progress of T. S. Eliot as Poet and Critic* (1971), lacking any informing principle of its own, bogs down in a welter of details and is further obscured by extensive quotations from various critics of Eliot. Even Allen Austin's book (cited above), though much better than Sen's, tends to fall apart, into a series of essays, to which one can give individual marks: good on the objective correlative, satisfactory on the impersonal theory (overstresses expressive elements), usefully critical on essays on Marlowe and Marvell, below average on poetry and belief, unsatisfactory on the social criticism. If Eliot's critical work is not so consistently theoretical as Wellek suggests, it is more coherent as a body of work than these books manage to convey.

Much of the coherence of Eliot's critical work derives from his efforts to come to terms with the Romantic critical tradition. His Classicism lacks the assurance of more settled ages. It is, instead, a delicate balancing act, in which Romantic elements are paired with other, equally valid claims; hence the dualism of the "objective correlative" or the title "Tradition and the Individual Talent." Brian Lee's *Theory and Personality* (1979) stresses the lack of confidence implied by this dualism. Lee is a sensitive reader of Eliot's critical prose, which he finds much like Eliot's poetry in its fragmentary character and its efforts to express, and conceal, Eliot's personal dilemmas. Lee believes that Eliot's criticism is representative of the modern intellectual situation and that its weaknesses are closely tied to its strengths. It is possible that Lee overstates the extent to which Eliot leaves all issues unresolved and the sharpness of Eliot's dualisms; Lee's conclusion, that "true personality and true impersonality are the same thing," is fully consistent with some of Eliot's formulations of the question.

Eliot's balancing act can be seen in more positive terms as a kind of dialectic, as in Fei-Pai Lu's *T. S. Eliot: The Dialectical Structure of His Theory of Poetry* (1966). Lu cites a number of previous writers who have shown how Eliot's criticism works through a resolution of opposites, the most valuable being Ants Oras (*The Critical Ideas of T. S. Eliot*, 1932) and Charles Moorman ("Order and Mr. Eliot," 1953). Lu's treatment is more thorough, though marred by the introduction of more new terms into the discussion than seems strictly necessary. In Lu's view, Eliot's Classicism is the product of a dialectic which includes Romanticism, the completion of the Romantic in the Classic being an instance of the particular yielding, at last, a general truth. False "personality" is false because it is confined to the particular; a false "impersonality" would fail to ground itself in the particular. The dialectic of objectification allows the good "personality" (e.g., Shakespeare) to achieve impersonal order. The dialectic involves the transmutation of appearance and reality into each other, the organization of parts into wholes, and the reconciliation of opposites—processes which Lu labels with terms from Eliot's dissertation: correspondence, coherence, and comprehensiveness. Lu says that Eliot's changes through the years have been largely changes of emphasis, the major change being from advocacy of a centripetal poetry of concentration to a centrifugal poetry of exploration. Lu's work is dense but suggestive. One can find merit in his account of Eliot's dialectic without agreeing that Eliot is as systematic as Lu suggests. The truth of Eliot's relation to the Romantic tradition of "personality" may well lie somewhere between Lee and Lu.

Persona and Points of View

Although the term "persona" is not part of the vocabulary of Eliot's early criticism, his "impersonal" theory is a major source of the modern tendency to distinguish sharply between the poet and the "speaker" of a poem. Eliot's use of poetic masks may be connected, as well, to concerns expressed in his philosophic writings. A number of critics have attempted to relate the personae of the poems to Eliot's critical and philosophic writings.

One rather curious attempt to do this is Stanley J. Scott's "Beyond Modern Subjectivism: T. S. Eliot and American Philosophy" (1976). Scott argues that Eliot's poetic development is "strikingly parallel to the central developments in the golden age of American philosophy, especially if we regard the achievements of the empirical idealists, Josiah Royce and William Ernest Hocking, as complementary to those of the radical empiricists, William James and John Dewey" (p. 409). James and Dewey seem unpromising subjects for comparison with Eliot, and Scott does not prove them otherwise. Even Hocking and Royce seem less obviously relevant than Bradley; though Scott's comparison of the role of Tiresias in *The Waste Land* to Hocking's approach to intersubjective awareness is interesting, comparisons that carry no implication of influence do not seem helpful. Even Scott's reading of the direction of Eliot's poetry is open to question; if a universal center of consciousness is present in any poem, as one may doubt, it would presumably be Tiresias, while the speaking voice of the *Four Quartets* seems closest to the private Eliot. Scott's view of Prufrock as a "comic solipsist" (p. 413) is defensible, but his apparent equation with solipsism of the "finite centers" of Eliot's dissertation is not.

A more sensitive reading of the poems is found in Thomas J. Morrissey's " 'Intimate and Unidentifiable': The Voices of Fragmented Reality in the Poetry of T. S. Eliot" (1978). To Morrissey, these voices suggest that Eliot "never fully abandoned his early beliefs in the fragmentary nature of human experience or in the deficiencies of language as a means of expressing experience" (p. 2), though the last two *Quartets* express an acceptance of the necessity "of rendering imperfectible consciousness through an imperfect art" (p. 3). Morrissey may exaggerate the degree to which Eliot's latter-day Christian assurance that "there is a complete and unfragmented reality" (p. 27) is a new departure. Even in the dissertation, there is unity at the level of immediate experience; and it is our knowledge of that experience which is inevitably limited and subjective. To say, then, that "for the speaker of the 'Preludes' there is no objective reality beyond the limits of his subjective mind" (p. 17) may be to read into the poems an unduly subjectivist reading of the philosophy. Even to speak of a "subjective mind" is to maintain a subject-object distinction which does not exist at the level of immediate experience. But since our knowledge of external reality is problematic in Eliot's philosophy, Morrissey's general readings of these and other poems are not invalidated by the possible inaccuracy of his summary of the philosophy behind them.

Probably the best early treatment of the relationship of Bradley to Eliot's creative work can be found in Hugh Kenner's *The Invisible Poet* (1959). As his title suggests, Kenner is especially sensitive to the "Possum" side of Eliot, the poet's delight in his masks. Kenner, not much inclined to see Bradley's influence in Eliot's criticism, probably underrates its presence. Of Bradley, Kenner says that "it is as a coloring, not as a body of doctrine, that he stays in the mind; partly because such doctrines as he professes are so little detachable from their dry and scrupulous expression" (p. 45); hence he prefers to speak of "deposits of Bradleyism in Eliot's sensibility" (p. 47). Whether this approach does justice to Bradley's effect on Eliot's critical doctrines, it results in a number of useful observations on the way in which Eliot's sensibility expresses itself in various forms, as in an amusing passage explaining why drama (immediate experience of transitory selves, manipulating a world of pure appearance) is "the perfect Bradleyan form" (p. 301). Kenner is one of a handful of Eliot critics with a genuinely attractive prose style (often a useful sign of the quality of the sensibility at work). Although the following decades have kept us well supplied with general introductions to Eliot's work, Kenner's work remains fresh and stimulating.

George T. Wright's chapter on Eliot in *The Poet in the Poem* (1960) reviews Eliot's statements on the poet and his poem and comments on Eliot's treatment of the personae in his poems. Wright believes that Eliot, as a poet, is separate from the speakers in all his poems, both early poems like "Prufrock" and later poems like the *Four Quartets*. Eliot's persona can be identified by the tone of voice which underlies the poem, giving it unity even in the quick character changes of *The Waste Land*. The basic Eliot tone is conversational, but Eliot is able to modulate into other tones, always returning to the base. The reader is lured into tentative identification with the persona, but he must move beyond this to experience the poem as a whole. These general points are both conventional and questionable, and it is unlikely that readers familiar with Eliot's poetry and criticism will get much that is new from Wright, save, perhaps, whatever is gained from seeing this matter explored in Eliot side by side with other poets.

A more stimulating general survey is Kristian Smidt's "Point of View in Eliot's Poetry," a chapter added to the 1961 edition of *Poetry and Belief in the Work of T. S. Eliot*. Smidt points to the difficulty we experience in identifying the point of view in Eliot's early poetry. Who is the speaker of *The Waste Land*? Who is the "you" whom Gerontion would meet honestly, or the "you" whom Prufrock invites to accompany him? On the Prufrock question, Smidt prints a letter from Eliot to Smidt, saying that, as best as he could remember, "the 'you' in THE LOVE SONG is merely some friend or companion, presumably of the male sex, whom the speaker is at that moment addressing, and that it has no emotional content whatever" (p. 85). But even if we take Eliot's answer as authoritative—ignoring his critical principles—our knowledge of his intention does not help us answer the question in our reading of the poem or such related questions as whether Prufrock is to be thought of as continuing to address such an interlocutor. Smidt notes that the masks and evasions of the early poems fade in the later religious poems, so that the voice which confronts us in *Four Quartets* seems closely identified with the poet. Smidt thus seems to differ from Wright, though some of the differences may be products of the difference between Wright's persona-as-tone-of-voice and Smidt's persona-as-identifiable-point-of-view. To the extent that the difference is real, Smidt's sense of a narrowing gap between the persona and the poet seems a more useful insight.

Prufrock as Persona

The *locus classicus* for discussions of Eliot's use of personae is probably "The Love Song of J. Alfred Prufrock." Although some of the psychological interpretations of the poem discussed in the last chapter identify Eliot with his persona, both title and poem suggest at least an attempt to construct a separate persona. "Prufrock" is one of Eliot's most discussed poems, and its various interpretations illustrate the many ways in which critics have attempted to apply Eliot's criticism in the poems—and the degree to which others have felt free to ignore it.

There is, it happens, a generally recognized "standard" or "traditional" interpretation of "The Love Song of J. Alfred Prufrock" in Cleanth Brooks and Robert Penn Warren, *Understanding Poetry* (1938), a text whose many editions educated a generation of English professors and (probably) many of their students. In the clear separation they make between the poet and his protagonist, and in their claim that Prufrock's condition achieves a general, representative character, Brooks and Warren may be said to work on assumptions shared, in part, with Eliot's "impersonal theory." In their confident generalizations about what Eliot and the poem mean, Brooks and Warren typify those modern critics who have failed to share Eliot's oft repeated doubts about the possibilities of arriving at a single, correct interpretation. The question of whom is addressed as "you" presents itself to Brooks and Warren as a problem to be resolved, rather than an ambiguity left unresolved in the poem. They have an answer ready: "You" is the reader, damned to Prufrock's condition, just as Guido, in the epigraph, assumes that Dante is damned. Their skill at identifying allusions and showing their relevance made Brooks and Warren an eminently teachable text. Their tendency to reduce such allusions to direct statements is less desirable but was equally influential, encouraging a tendency to equate close reading with paraphrase.

Another 1938 reading, more complete but more dogmatic and reductive, appeared in the special December issue of the *Harvard Advocate* devoted to Eliot's work, "Observations on 'Prufrock' " by Roberta Morgan and Albert Wohlstetter. Morgan and Wohlstetter agree with Brooks and Warren in stressing the poem's "ironic" qualities, but they go even further in their arbitrary resolution of the poem's difficulties: the "you" is Prufrock himself (possibly a symptom of schizophrenia) and the "overwhelming question" is a declaration of love, which he does not make (p. 27). Morgan and Wohlstetter also deserve mention for being among the first to characterize Eliot's methods as "cinematic" and for anticipating much later criticism in laying special stress on Prufrock's denial that he is like Hamlet.

One of the few essays on "The Love Song of J. Alfred Prufrock" that Eliot himself commented on is that by Joseph Margolis in *Interpretations* (1955). In "The Frontiers of Criticism," Eliot cited this volume as an example of "the lemon-squeezer school of criticism" (1957, p. 126) and used it as an occasion for warning against assuming that a single, correct interpretation exists or that even a valid interpretation must necessarily also be an account of the author's intentions. Eliot, however, expressed gratitude that Margolis' essay is not an attempt to discover the poem's origins (through source hunting) but "to find out what the poem really meant—whether that was what I had meant it to mean or not" (p. 126). Eliot expressed polite interest in Margolis' reading and polite surprise at finding the fog in the drawing room.

The strength of Margolis' essay is its line-by-line analysis and its recognition of the way in which the poem's meaning rests in our cumulative understanding: he keeps his attention fixed on the poem in front of him. Margolis is too careful a reader to impose his own order on the poem, and this allows him to deal sensitively with many of the poem's uncertainties. Unfortunately, Margolis settles one uncertainty too quickly and it mars his entire reading of the poem: he assumes that the first introduction of the Michelangelo couplet is not an anticipation of the scene which awaits Prufrock but a sign that Prufrock has already arrived at the salon. This leads him to the odd introduction of the fog into the drawing room and an even odder explication of "time to turn back and descend the stair," as concerned with whether Prufrock will " 'descend' once again into the illusions of the salon, having pierced through to a clear vision of his career" (1955, p. 188). It seems much more likely that Prufrock arrives—if at all—much later in the poem, perhaps during the break before "the afternoon, the evening, sleeps so peacefully." J. Hillis Miller is probably right in saying that "one of the chief puzzles of the poem is the question as to whether Prufrock ever leaves his room" (*Poets of Reality*, 1966, p. 139).

There is also a more systematic problem with the Margolis reading. Margolis tends to identify Prufrock with the intelligence at work in the construction of the poem. This is to confuse the sensibility which is expressed (or observed) with the sensibility which expresses it and, ultimately, to dissolve the distinction between poet and persona, a distinction which most critics take as especially operative in this poem. As the passage quoted earlier may suggest, Margolis is more apt than most critics to credit Prufrock with "clear vision." Prufrock thus becomes less a figure of satire, and his habit of self-comparisons "—with John the Baptist, Lazarus, with Hamlet—seems quite proper now and not at all as ludicrous as Prufrock would have us believe" (1955,

p. 191). Just as we are to take Prufrock more seriously, Margolis encourages us to take other features of the poem with a high seriousness rather at odds with its mock-heroic style: "The fog is a kind of Grail, ambiguously characterized as corrupting but actually providing the occasion and the test of spiritual regeneration" (p. 187).

Generalizations of this sort may be distinguished from those which reduce a poem to its allusions by being grounded in Margolis' developing experience of the poem as poem. If one accepts the possibility of many valid interpretations, one cannot rule out Margolis' reading simply because it conflicts with a certain playfulness of tone other readers experience as part of the poem. Even so, there is something almost disturbing about the progression in solemnity from Brooks and Warren, rather didactic in approach, to Margolis, and one wonders whether "The Love Song of J. Alfred Prufrock" is not in danger of being read more as a sacred text than as a poem.

If a critic has his eye on the poem rather than on something else, his generalizations will emerge from his attempts to order his perceptions of the poem. The utility of such criticism, however, depends on the degree to which the process is reversible, on whether the critic's general statements help readers experience the poem anew or simply substitute the critic's ordering of experience for their own. An abstract but useful essay is Elisabeth Schneider's "Prufrock and After: The Theme of Change" (1972). Schneider sees Eliot preoccupied (though not exclusively, of course) with the problem of subjective change. In "Prufrock," change is impossible; in *The Waste Land*, it may be possible; and in the later poems the possibility of change is positively affirmed. This observation, perhaps not very remarkable in itself, allows Schneider to present a unified essay on the pattern of Eliot's development, marred only by rather conventional misunderstandings of his criticism. In her treatment of "Prufrock," Schneider makes a number of interesting points, as when she notes the dominance of the subjunctive mood in the latter parts of the poem or when she draws a contrast between the poem's two sorts of images, "the limited and literal details of Prufrock's daily concern" (p. 1105) and the more violent and extravagant images that keep breaking into the poem.

The danger of thematic studies like Schneider's is that, by focusing on relevant passages in individual poems, they may tend to fragment our experience of the poems. This problem is even more apparent in source studies, which too often have the effect of removing allusions from the context of relations which constitute the poem. Source studies are also subject to the objection raised to some of the psychoanalytic studies cited in the last chapter: they risk confusing the poem with its origins. Source studies often tell us more about the poet than about the poetry, a legitimate aim if recognized for what it is. Studies which focus on the ways in which a poem differs from another poem it echoes may also be useful in helping us understand a poet's complex relationship to his predecessors; this is the approach taken in Robert Novak, " 'Prufrock' and Arnold's 'Buried Life' " (1973), and in W. K. Wimsatt's "*Prufrock* and *Maud:* From Plot to Symbol" (1965; earlier version in *Yale French Studies,* Spring 1952). Eliot himself made effective critical use of similar juxtapositions, though generally without discussion of sources. Of the two essays, Novak's is the less valuable, because the resemblances between the two poems are not very striking and because Novak's discussion of their differences does not take us much beyond the conventional wisdom on the differences between Eliot and the Victorians. Wimsatt, who also notes echoes of the Tennyson poem elsewhere in Eliot, is more stimulating in arguing that the differences between "Maud" and "Prufrock" are a result of a modern tendency to unite the story and symbol, the tenor and vehicle, so that the literal level of a poem like "Prufrock" can hardly be distinguished from its symbolic structure.

Failure to attend to significant differences is one of several faults in Robert G. Cook's "Emerson's 'Self Reliance,' 'Sweeney,' and 'Prufrock' " (1970). It is true that Prufrock is somehow the natural opposite of the animal-like Sweeney of "Sweeney Erect," the poem in which Eliot refers to Emerson's essay. But Cook's claim that "it is likely that Prufrock, no less than Sweeney, was affected by Eliot's reading of 'Self Reliance' " (p. 224) marks his essay as belonging to the American imperialist school of Eliot criticism. The argument is that Prufrock is very much like the sort of man Emerson was preaching against, and that Eliot was rebuking Emerson by presenting his own version of what an adult sensibility was likely to look like in practice. Since Prufrock is inadequate by almost any ideal standard, this sort of argument could be used to establish almost any source one would like. Cook has little feeling for the special characteristics of consciousness in Eliot and little regard for the kind of evidence needed to establish influence.

Eliot's allusive method and the flood of source studies it has encouraged will be discussed at greater length in a later chapter; many of the source studies on "Prufrock," however, are at least potentially relevant to such matters as the nature of Prufrock's self-image and the relationship between Eliot and his persona, for the passages most often commented upon are Eliot's epigraph to the poem and Prufrock's various self-descriptions.

The epigraph raises the question whether Prufrock is to be identified with Guido de Montefeltro, the doomed spirit who speaks in the Dante passage, and, if so, which elements of Guido's situation are relevant. The standard interpretation has been generally confined to the words quoted, probably the safest course, for it does not take us so far outside Eliot's poem. In this view, found in Brooks and Warren, Prufrock is speaking to someone (perhaps the reader) who is damned, like Prufrock himself, and thus cannot betray Prufrock. Robert White ("Eliot's 'The Love Song of J. Alfred Prufrock,' " 1961) argues that more of the context in Dante is relevant, but his consideration does not lead us much beyond the usual view, for he concludes that "it is in his double desire to tell his story and not give himself away that Prufrock most resembles Guido." Somewhat lost in both views is the general issue of whether the epigraph is to be considered an integral part of the poem or whether it is simply a comment by Eliot on the poem.

William Stuckey finds Dante built into the poem's very structure, in "Eliot's 'The Love Song of J. Alfred Prufrock' " (1961). As we are led into a "sinister" part of the city, we enter an Inferno; we climb Purgatorial stairs; and we end (figuratively, at least) by water. Whereas Dante swims the Lethe and reaches the nymphs, the sirens in "Prufrock" sing only to each other; their voices are only "human," so Prufrock lingers and drowns. The poem is thus "a dramatization of the vital differences between Dante's world and Prufrock's." The equation of the mermaids' voices with the "human voices," which wake us, seems unlikely—as, for that matter, does the rest of Stuckey's interpretation.

A more specific Dantean parallel has been independently noted by Eugene Arden in "The Echo of Hell in 'Prufrock' " (1958) and by Eugene Hollahan in "A Structural Dantean Parallel in Eliot's 'The Love Song of J. Alfred Prufrock' " (1970). In the *Inferno* (2.32), Dante, hesitating to embark on his journey, protests to Virgil that he is neither Aeneas nor

Paul, two heroic predecessors in visiting Hades. The parallel is with Prufrock's denial that he is like Hamlet—but a large number of such protestations must exist in literature. Even if we take the epigraph as indicating that it is possible that this particular parallel was in Eliot's mind, nothing would justify our saying, with Hollahan, that "the dramatic structure and thematic conflict" of Eliot's poem "owe much" to this parallel (p. 91), nor in accepting Arden's argument that the verbal parallel somehow proves that Prufrock is no more damned than Dante. Prufrock is not Dante either, nor was meant to be.

Of clearer relevance, because raised by the poem itself, is whether it would have been worth it for Prufrock to announce that he was "Lazarus, come back from the dead, / come back to tell you all." There are two biblical Lazaruses, and the reader may remember either or both: the brother of Mary and Martha, whom John reports that Jesus raised from the dead, and the beggar of the parable in Luke 16. Both references are noted by Brooks and Warren, who do not suggest that we must choose between them or that all details in either story are relevant. Not citing Brooks and Warren, Clifford J. Fish ("Eliot's 'The Love Song of J. Alfred Prufrock,' " 1950) argues that the beggar in Luke is the more important. The rich man in hell, seeing Lazarus in heaven, begs Abraham that Lazarus be permitted to return and testify to the rich man's relatives, lest they share his fate, but Abraham says that if Moses and the prophets have proved insufficient, even the testimony of one returned from the dead will not persuade them. Prufrock is thus right in fearing that the rich dilettantes, among whom he finds himself, would receive no cosmic message from his hands. Daniel N. Dwyer agrees with Brooks and Warren that both are relevant, but goes beyond them in the course of defending the Lazarus of John against Fish's article ("Eliot's 'The Love Song of J. Alfred Prufrock,' " 1951). Dwyer suggests that the negative response of Jewish authorities to the raising of Lazarus, Jesus' last miracle, also is relevant to Prufrock's fears. Eugene Arden, apparently unfamiliar with these earlier contributions, gives the same arguments as Fish for the importance of the Luke passage in his "The 'Other' Lazarus in 'Prufrock' " (1960). That even one who had returned from the dead might find no hearing is sufficiently implicit in the poem that such biblical associations, beyond that of both Lazaruses with returning from the dead, add little to our understanding of Prufrock. This is true even for those who, like Margolis (1955), ignore the hypothetical mode of Prufrock's statement and treat his identification with Lazarus as a simple assertion.

John C. Pope's identification ("Prufrock and Raskolnikov," 1945) argues that Prufrock's character owes much to Dostoyevsky's *Crime and Punishment*. To the extent that Pope's argument depends on verbal parallels with the Garnett translation of 1914, it would seem to be destroyed by the earlier composition date of "Prufrock," pointed out in a letter from Eliot published later by Pope ("Prufrock and Raskolnikov Again: A Letter from Eliot," 1947). The possibility that Raskolnikov's character played a part in the origin of Prufrock's remains, for Eliot says in the same letter that he read a French translation of *Crime and Punishment* in 1910–11; but Eliot also says that his model was not the Hamlet-like Raskolnikov but the Hamlet of Jules Laforgue's "Hamlet or the Consequence of Filial Piety." Since Raskolnikov does not appear in the poem in any recognizable fashion, the question is purely one of origins for the general reader, whatever private associations the poem may conjure up for Pope. It is hard to see what effect Pope's essays could have on our reading of the poem.

The relevance of Laforgue's Hamlet to the character of Prufrock is traced by George Fortenberry in "Prufrock and the Fool Song" (1967). At issue is not simply our reading of Prufrock's statement that he is not Hamlet, but the meaning we assign to his statement that, instead, he is "almost, at times, the Fool." Brooks and Warren say that there is no fool in Hamlet, that Eliot must intend the generic fool of Elizabethan drama. Margaret Morton Blum has pointed out that there is the dead fool, Yorick, in *Hamlet* ("The Fool in 'The Love Song of J. Alfred Prufrock,' " 1957). Blum's argument for the relevance of Yorick—that it is too late for Prufrock, too—seems weak so long as one confines oneself to Shakespeare's *Hamlet*. But Fortenberry points out that Laforgue's Hamlet is the brother of Yorick. For readers familiar enough with Laforgue's work to recognize its echoes in Eliot, Laforgue's Hamlet is certainly a legitimate association to make with Prufrock, even without Eliot's statement that Laforgue was involved in the origins of "Prufrock." This association may even justify Fortenberry's identification of the closing lines of "Prufrock" as a "Fool Song," parallel to the sonnet which "Laforgue has his Fool compose . . . after he has made the discovery that he is of little importance in the universe" (1967, p. 53).

For most readers, even those familiar with Laforgue, Shakespeare's Hamlet and Shakespeare's fools are likely to be the most immediate associations called to mind by Eliot's references, even if Eliot's view of Hamlet was affected by Laforgue. Thus Prufrock's "No! I am not Prince Hamlet" is generally read as a refusal by Prufrock to take satisfaction in making his hesitations those of a tragic hero. Robert Seiler's note, "Prufrock and Hamlet" (1972), suggests that the fundamental difference is that Hamlet can articulate his questions and finally act, while Prufrock proves unable to do either. No doubt there are many other differences between Prufrock and Hamlet worthy of such exploring; as a student, for example, Hamlet was probably not even slightly bald.

Prufrock's insistence that he is no Hamlet is a key passage for another source study, bearing (not very convincingly) on Prufrock's understanding of himself: Robert F. Fleissner's " 'Prufrock,' Pater, and *Richard II:* Retracing a Denial of Princeship" (1966). Fleissner's source is Walter Pater's "Shakespeare's English Kings" (*Appreciations*, 1890), a passage famous for its reference to the "irony of kingship." Fleissner suggests that Pater's denial of greatness to Richard II has somehow attached itself to Prufrock, who shares with Richard self-pity, a split personality, excessive self-consciousness, and final resignation. Fleissner also believes that the Christ symbolism attached to Shakespeare's Richard may have influenced the Lazarus passage, that a reference to Shakespeare's "embalming pages" may have influenced the opening metaphor of "Prufrock," and that Pater's *Renaissance* may have induced the Michelangelo reference. None of these suggestions is at all persuasive, though they are interesting as clues to the private associations of Fleissner's well-stocked mind. Fleissner concludes that "evidence is available from one crucial line ('No! Shakespeare's kings are not, nor are meant to be, great men') to point to Eliot's indebtedness to Pater, to show that Prufrock's concern about religion may reflect and refract the qualms that Pater had himself" (p. 123). Although the verbal echo is enticing, the conclusions drawn from it are excessive, especially in the absence of any argument for them.

Prufrock's statement that he "should have been a pair of ragged claws" has also proved unexpectedly difficult. The line conveys a tone of self-disgust, but critics have offered different views on whether the image is a grotesque exaggeration of Prufrock as he is now (or may appear to be, to the men leaning out of the windows above) or an emblem of the animal vitality

Prufrock lacks. About the only item critics are agreed on is that the "ragged claws" are those of a crab; but this identification detracts from the sharpness of the visual image. Gerald Smith, who suggests that the crab is a perfect symbol for Prufrock's sideways approach to life (in "Eliot's 'The Love Song of J. Alfred Prufrock,' " 1962), cites a passage from a biologist on the role of the male claw in crab courtship. Crustacean courtship aside, the image seems best construed as a picture of Prufrock now, "scuttling" his way through life.

Literary sources for Eliot's crab, if it *is* a crab, have been found in a number of places. Robert Fleissner ("Prufrock's 'Ragged Claws,' " 1972) has again proved especially ingenious. Fleissner is not satisfied with the most commonly cited literary source, Hamlet's remark that Polonius "shall grow old as I am, if like a crab you could go backward" (II. ii. 200). Fleissner's arguments against a *Hamlet* allusion are not, in themselves, convincing. He believes that such an allusion is ruled out by Eliot's negative statements on *Hamlet* and Prufrock's statement that he is "not Prince Hamlet." The first is hardly incompatible with Eliot's having read *Hamlet* carefully and even often, and the second is an argument for Prufrock's having remembered the *Hamlet* passage. More persuasive are the other sources identifying crabs with age. Fleissner notes a crab reference in Webster's *Duchess of Malfi* but advances a poem by Lydgate, "So as the Crabbe goth Forward," as a possible source for Eliot (and Shakespeare and Webster). One concludes from this that *if* Eliot's lines imply a crab, and *if* the crab is going forward or backward (rather than sideways, as in Smith), Eliot may have picked up the notion from one of several Elizabethans—or, of course, elsewhere.

One other possible source for the "ragged claws" passage appears in George Spangler's "*The Education of Henry Adams* as a Source for 'The Love Song of J. Alfred Prufrock' " (1968). Spangler notes that chapters 26 and 30 of Adams' book end with passages in which the horseshoe crab, the *Limulus*, appears as an emblem of things unchanged and beyond change, a role it first is given in chapter 15. Adams deals in chapter 30 with the stifling of healthy sexuality, a theme in "Prufrock," and ends by identifying his position with that of the crab. Eliot quoted one of the crab passages in his review of the 1919 publication of Adams' book; and he may, according to Spangler, have read them earlier in the 1907 private edition, circulated in Cambridge during Eliot's Harvard days. But the verbal echoes Spangler can cite are not very impressive. This source, even if it is that, tells us little about the poem.

Elderly crabs appear again in Darrel Abel, "R.L.S. and 'Prufrock' " (1953). Abel maintains that "resemblances in theme, treatment, and expression suggest that T. S. Eliot's 'Love Song of J. Alfred Prufrock' contains reminiscences of Robert Louis Stevenson's 'Crabbed Age and Youth' " (pp. 37–38). No evidence is provided that Eliot had read Stevenson's essay, and the thematic resemblances are not striking; Stevenson was arguing against mere prudence as a guide to life and in favor of striking out on the sea of adventure. Abel's most interesting find is Stevenson's remark: "We have heard the mermaidens singing, and know that we shall never see dry land any more" (p. 38). This echo may be a source, but can hardly be intended as an allusion, and thus has little effect on our understanding of the poem.

Concentration on sources and allusions in the poem sometimes skews one's sense of the poem, leaving some passages relatively untouched by most critics. Arthur Waterman's note, "Eliot's 'The Love Song of J. Alfred Prufrock,' 15–22" (1959), takes up lines which are puzzling. Their portrait of the catlike fog seems self-contained and obtrusively poetic, overdeveloped for a mere piece of scene setting. Waterman relates this passage to the poem as a whole by arguing that the fog, which "rubs, licks, lingers, lets, slips, curls, and sleeps," represents the same world of natural freedom as do the mermaids later in the poem, a world from which Prufrock is excluded by his nature. An effort to incorporate another often neglected element, the street imagery, is the chief claim to originality of Vereen M. Bell's "A Reading of 'Prufrock' " (1969). Bell sees Prufrock as trying to find some kind of relationship among three worlds —the world of the streets, the effete world of the salon, and his private world of self. Beyond these is an ideal world, represented by the mermaids. It is his vision of the street which enables Prufrock to see through the world through which he moves, but he is unable to break through to any real communication and falls back, at last, into subjectivity and "the oppressive actuality of the unreal" (p. lxxiv). Of these two essays, Waterman's is probably the more persuasive, being more modest in its claims and less schematic in approach.

In "The Frontiers of Criticism," Eliot opened his last paragraph with an observation which helps explain some of the defects of the criticism reviewed in the last pages: "If in literary criticism, we place all the emphasis upon *understanding*, we are in danger of slipping from understanding to mere explanation. We are in danger even of pursuing criticism as if it was a science, which it never can be. If, on the other hand, we over-emphasize *enjoyment*, we will tend to fall into the subjective and impressionistic, and our enjoyment will profit us no more than mere amusement and pastime."

When Eliot began his career as a critic, overly impressionistic criticism was more common than today, when paraphrase and explanation are the order of the day. Once one goes beyond identification of the obvious allusions in the poem, the discussion of sources—as in many essays on "Prufrock"—can result in focusing attention on the relations between a passage and objects outside the poem, at the expense of its relation with other material in the poem. Criticism of this sort achieves only false impersonality, for in practice it often elevates the private associations of the critic into a generalized statement about the poem.

One of the virtues of Hugh Kenner's work is that it preserves the balance between understanding and enjoyment, analysis and impressionistic response. His sensitivity to the interplay between sound and sense is apparent in many of Kenner's remarks on "Prufrock." Understanding how much of the effect of the lines depends more on tone than on reference, Kenner sharpens his readers' ears for Eliot's tone. Kenner very sensibly rejects attempts to find single meanings for lines whose medium is their message: "To say that Prufrock is contemplating a young blade's gesture, or alternatively an old castoff's, rolling up his trousers because he either hasn't learnt to care for dignity or has outgrown its claim, is to substitute for the poetic effect a formula that fails to exhaust it because it is incapable of touching it" (1959, p. 6).

Kenner calls our attention to the presence in "Prufrock" and other Eliot poems of Jacobean rhetoric, Tennysonian melody, Laforguian irony, but he rarely reduces such presences to mechanical "sources" or "influences." Instead, Kenner helps us hear the way in which such voices are adapted and blended in Eliot's voice, to achieve Eliot's effects. Kenner also calls attention to the way in which Prufrock, as a character, anticipates the even vaguer personae of "Gerontion" and *The Waste Land:* Prufrock is not a "character" but "a name plus a Voice"; he is "strangely boundless," so that one cannot say where

Prufrock is speaking for himself and where another sensibility is expressing greater understanding than Prufrock himself could show (p. 40).

"Prufrock" has been so often anthologized, so often written about, that a fresh reading would seem almost impossible. But Barbara Everett's essay, "In Search of Prufrock" (1974), gives a reading which is not merely fresh in itself but communicates something of the eternal freshness of the poem. Her purpose is to rescue the poem from overrigid interpretations, though one wonders why she accepts the view that Prufrock decides to walk in the city *rather* than go to the party he is apparently bound for. For Everett, the poem is a process of discovery, a dynamic rather than a static work of art; in this, she is close to Margolis' insistence on cumulative meaning. Unlike Margolis, however, Everett knows that she is dealing with a poem rather than sacred writ. One of her strong points is the way in which she shifts the nature of the tradition against which "Prufrock" is to be read.

Beside the serious sources that have been suggested, Everett places other sources which correspond to Eliot's long interest in the mock-heroic: for the fog, Dickens; for the title, Turgenev's "Diary of a Superfluous Man," a popular *Punch* series collected as *The Diary of Nobody*, and H. G. Wells' *Love and Mr. Lewisham* and *The History of Mr. Polly* (Christian name, Alfred); for the opening line, Walt Whitman (*Allons . . .*); for the closing lines, Dante's Ulysses; and for some of the incidental foolery, W. S. Gilbert. To these we might add Kenner's suggestion of Edward Lear, as an earlier master of comic Tennysonian verse. The effect of reading the poem with such sources and analogues in mind is to make its effect less tragic and satiric; Prufrock's reluctance to pose as a hero is not necessarily base. There is no danger, these days, of reducing the poem to light verse, and Everett does not do so, but her reading helps us recover the lightness of touch that is in the poem.

Tiresias as Persona

After Prufrock, the most discussed persona in Eliot's work is probably Tiresias of *The Waste Land*, though there is reason to doubt whether he can properly be termed a persona at all. While the problem in reading "Prufrock" is to estimate where, at any given point in the poem, the poet stands in relation to his protagonist, in *The Waste Land* we have difficulty locating any protagonist, even in singling out one voice as somehow the master voice of the poem, capable of containing by quotation and imitation the many voices of the poem. Critics have therefore been attracted by the help Eliot seems to offer in the note to line 218, where he asserts that "Tiresias, although a mere spectator and not indeed a 'character,' is yet the most important personage in the poem, uniting all the rest."

The difficulties involved in taking Tiresias as the poem's persona are obvious. If Prufrock is, as Kenner says, a name and a voice, Tiresias is only a name, for the voice which speaks in the passage beginning "I, Tiresias," is only one voice among many, not the unifying voice of the poem, and Tiresias makes no other appearance in the poem. The notes themselves are a problem. In "The Frontiers of Criticism," Eliot says he has "sometimes thought of getting rid of these notes" and calls them a "remarkable exposition of bogus scholarship" (1957, p. 121). They did not appear with the poem's first published versions. Kenner suggests that the Tiresias note is "an afterthought, a token placation, say, of the ghost of Bradley" (1959, p. 150). The passage quoted in the note (from Ovid, in Latin) is funny enough to make one suspect irony in Eliot's description of it as "of great anthropological interest."

Even so, critics have generally followed this note and identified Tiresias with the speaker of the poem, its comprehensive comprehending consciousness. It may be that critics, though better able than most readers to tolerate a poem's initial obscurities, have a greater stake in seeing them resolved. The notion that Tiresias is the poem's persona is part of the conventional wisdom about the poem, passed along to students and other first-time readers in brief study guides like Helen Williams' *T. S. Eliot: The Waste Land* (1968): "The single subsuming figure of Tiresias serves, as does the Sanscrit in the poem, as a final unifying factor behind the fragmented races and languages, forming as it were, the apex of a pyramid structure whose base is multiple but which is refined backwards in time to a single unity" (p. 31). We may suppose that anyone whose experience of the poem finds that the use of Sanscrit lends it unity may feel the same about Tiresias.

The difficulty is that it is hard to make any concrete use of this identification in reading the poem. If Tiresias unites all the characters of the poem, if what he sees *is* the poem, then Tiresias has the unity ascribed to immediate experience and is, like immediate experience, ultimately unknowable. Denis Donoghue's "The American 'Waste Land' at Fifty" (1972) thus makes Tiresias a name for the transcendent, all-embracing experience but succeeds only in demonstrating the vacuity of such a label. To use Tiresias in this way is to do little more than assert that the poem is a unity because experience has ultimate unity. It is hard to imagine a poem for which such a Tiresias would not be a suitable speaker; positing him, therefore, tells us little about this poem in particular. In practice, most of the many critics who accept Tiresias as the persona use him mainly for more local associations (to explain the scene he seems to narrate, to cast light on the sexual element in the poem) or as a meaningless label.

Another discussion of the results of our fifty-year experience of the poem, Helen Gardner's *The Waste Land 1972* (1972), seems more to the point in saying that making Tiresias the hero of the poem requires "the most extraordinary exegetical feats" (p. 11). Making the fairly obvious point that the poem we read today "is a different poem from the poem that was printed in October 1922 in *The Criterion*" (p. 1), because of our familiarity with the poem and its critics, Gardner's Adamson lecture displays a useful skepticism about interpretations which take the notes with undue seriousness, whether in exalting the role of Tiresias or in finding Grail motifs strewn about its landscape.

The publication of the manuscript draft did little to promote Tiresias as a persona. D. E. S. Maxwell's essay, " 'He Do the Police in Different Voices,' " (1972), takes its title from a working title Eliot gave two sections in the draft. As Maxwell notes, the allusion is to the newspaper-reading Sloppy in Dickens' *Our Mutual Friend.* Maxwell is willing to accept Tiresias as the one doing the voices, citing the note as possible authority, but he notes that "it is not Tiresias that is important. It is the speaking parts into which he fragments, or which through him speak in chorus" (p. 179). Since Tiresias is identified in the poem with one of those speaking parts, it seems unnecessary to burden the poem as a whole with the specific associations his name conjures up. Maxwell's reference to the dissertation's concern with the way in which the various finite centers find a common reference in one consistent world seems a more promising angle of approach to a poem he presents as a mosaic.

Eliot was, of course, under no obligation to be consistent in his poetry with his philosophical writings, but a Tiresias like that suggested by the note is particularly hard to reconcile with his Bradleyesque views. Michael Hancher has suggested that Eliot may have had, somewhere in his mind, Anatole France's observation that "we cannot, like Tiresias, be a man and have recollections of having been a woman. We are shut up in our own personality as if in a perpetual prison" ("The Adventures of Tiresias: France, Gourmont, Eliot," 1973, p. 29). This connection of Tiresias with the problems of solipsism and skepticism may help explain Tiresias' presence in the poem and note, but does not, as Hancher seems to assume, require that Tiresias be the protagonist.

In line-by-line readings of the poem, the alternative to using Tiresias as a label for the poet is to ignore him. A. J. Wilks' *A Critical Commentary on T. S. Eliot's "The Waste Land"* (1971) takes the latter course. Aiming, like Williams, at students and the general reader, Wilks assumes that the presiding consciousness of the poem is, in the end, Eliot's, and he does not even mention the great to-do over Tiresias. What Wilks says on the poem's persona(e) is very sensible: "Although I have suggested that the whole of Part III can be read as if it were a series of reflections passing through the mind of a single person, this is a convenient rather than a necessary interpretation. It lends Part III a coherence that might be reassuring on early readings. What the part certainly does consist of is a succession of connected states of feeling or 'emotions,' the product of one consciousness presented in various poetic and dramatic guises" (p. 66). One could say the same, of course, of the other parts of the poem. Since the consciousness which produces the various "guises" is outside the poem itself, Wilks' position amounts to saying that the poem can be read in dramatistic terms—one poet's realizing himself through many characters, with our attention properly directed at the interaction of the voices in the poem rather than at the poet who devises them.

The issue is whether the poem can be said to be objectified in a coherent set of relations without there being a single persona. In drama, no one would think of requiring such a persona, unless we use that name for the intelligence implied in the arrangement of the action; in the lyric, we are used to a single voice which we can identify as the author's, and, failing that, we may expect a coherent persona as a substitute. Eliot's approach to consciousness can be seen as calling for unification of the sort which his note on Tiresias attributes to the poem. It is on the basis of the failure to achieve a single voice that Anne C. Bolgan can call *The Waste Land* an artistic failure (*What the Thunder Really Said*, 1973). Bolgan does not mean that *The Waste Land* is not a major poem, only that it is a failure by the kind of high standards Eliot himself applied in calling *Hamlet* an artistic failure, and probably for reasons like those Eliot gives for Shakespeare's failure in *Hamlet*. Bolgan believes that she is applying not merely the standards of Eliot's criticism but a standard which the poem sets for itself in its impulse to become a kind of epic of the inner life.

For Bolgan, there are at least two main voices speaking in *The Waste Land*, a private voice and a public voice. The public voice we may identify with Tiresias, but he cannot be the poem's protagonist because he is outside its action. The private voice is at once the Quester Hero and the Fisher King, but Eliot seems to accept this figure only reluctantly. The two voices resemble the first two voices in Eliot's "The Three Voices of Poetry" (1953) in *On Poetry and Poets;* Bolgan also identifies them with the reference in "Tradition and the Individual Talent" to "the man who suffers" and "the mind which creates." The dialectical and cinematic method of the poem is part of an impulse toward soul making, forging a unity out of the individual's multiple points of view. No such unity is finally achieved in the poem. The Quester Hero remains grounded in time and experience and does not unite with the timeless and transcendent Tiresias. Their failure to unite leaves the poem without final resolution; it may be related to another conflict implicit in the poem, between Romantic and Bradleyan philosophical assumptions. In later poems, Eliot was to attain the kind of unity *The Waste Land* lacks.

Bolgan's is an interesting attempt to understand *The Waste Land* in terms taken from Eliot's criticism and, even more, his philosophical studies. Her emphasis on his dialectical method, though marred by digressions into cinema and Modernism generally, is useful and recalls Lu's use of the dialectic as a key to Eliot's criticism. But Bolgan tends to hypostatize heuristic categories; we take a crucial and probably unjustified step when we move, from the two kinds of voices found in the poem, to speaking as if all those passages which seem to issue from some private recess could be ascribed to a Quester Hero and all those hich seem to address the reader directly could be ascribed to esias. One could argue for placing, say, the Son of Man ge with either; such questions matter if the two figures y Bolgan are not to be almost as vacuous in effect as the single protagonist, Tiresias, seen by other critics. In "The Three Voices of Poetry," Eliot indicates that the private and public voices often appear in the same poem, but in "Tradition and the Individual Talent" Eliot urges a sharp separation between "the man who suffers" and "the mind which creates." The contrast may suggest less that Eliot changed his mind than that Bolgan is wrong to identify the two. The task of the mind which creates is to objectify and transmute the experience of the man who suffers; the poet thus disappears behind the poem, which gives us not the poet's suffering but images of suffering. Where the poem which is left speaks in a single voice, as in "Prufrock," we are justified in speaking of a persona; to use such terms for a many-voiced poetic world like *The Waste Land* is to indulge in an odd sort of pantheistic anthropomorphism. The note on Tiresias suggests that Eliot himself was bothered by the apparent lack of a unifying persona, but there is no requirement that we take the notes as authoritative.

Stephen Kirk goes even further than Bolgan in dissolving the unity of *The Waste Land* and in regarding it as a failure ("The Structural Weakness of T. S. Eliot's *The Waste Land*," 1975). Like Bolgan, Kirk describes Eliot's method, in terms drawn from Bradley, as presenting "a collage of finite centres of experience" (p. 217). From this collage, certain fragments emerge, internally unified by concentration on particular objects, but these fragments are not connected to each other and their objects differ. Unlike most recent critics, Kirk believes that Pound's excisions made the poem even more fragmented than it was to begin with, by cutting out connecting links. Kirk argues that the unity posited for the poem by various analysts is external and rather unsatisfactory; the Grail quest, for example, is not a part of the poem, and critical constructs which make use of the Grail quest to unify the poem are artifacts of criticism, with only a tangential relationship to the poem. Kirk will not accept expressive disunity as a structural justification, since such formulations merely evade the question of what the poem expresses. Brilliant though the poem may be in parts, Kirk judges it less successful formally than the *Four Quartets*. Kirk's criticism of various efforts to ascribe formal unity to *The Waste Land* are telling, but his conclusion is unsatisfactory. Although criticism cannot advance beyond impressionism without employing general notions about structure, the failure of our concepts of unity to account for our experience of a work should not be charged against the work; great works should alter our view of the nature of art. At best, criticism plays Virgil to the Dante of our responses; it may expose what is false in our response and purge us of what is inappropriate, but it is obedient to a call it can describe but cannot meet itself.

If our task is to account for our experience of *The Waste Land* in ways which impose no external form upon it, C. B. Cox has made a useful beginning in "T. S. Eliot at the Cross-Roads" (1970). Cox rejects any notion of a unifying persona in *The Waste Land,* stressing instead the poem's shifting viewpoints. Eliot's images commonly strike readers in contradictory ways, Cox notes, and it is just as common for critics "either to ignore these contradictions, or to impose on them some false logical coherence" (p. 307): his example is the passage beginning "Who is the third who walks always beside you?" Critics have found contradictory implications in this hooded figure—the positive Christ of the road to Emmaus, and the sinister overtones of some other possible references and of the words themselves. For Cox, attempts to solve the riddle by insisting on one primary meaning are violations of the poem's Symbolist method, making "clear" what was deliberately left unclear. Sometimes Eliot's contradictions are matters of connotation, as in the contrast between the negative "ragged claws" and the strange richness of "the floors of silent seas," in "Prufrock." Sometimes the epigraph, like that to "Marina," may appear to contradict the thrust of the poem. Sections of a poem may contradict each other, so that, according to Cox, *The Waste Land* "offers two contradictory views of history, and is not interested in reconciling them: (1) certain periods in history reflect a beauty and heroism lacking in the twentieth century; (2) the same periods were just as horrid as the present" (p. 310). Even contradiction may be a misnomer in such cases, for no balance is drawn; as for the protagonist, "it is doubtful whether such a creature exists" (p. 312). The early poems explore consciousness, searching for a cohesion they do not find and which Eliot is too honest to impose. The voices shift and blend, so that we are unsure of who is speaking and how seriously to take them. *The Waste Land* begins with a parody of Chaucer, proceeds like a lyrical set-piece, shades into apparent quotation, and leaves us, throughout the opening lines, uncertain about who may be "us," surprised by summer, and whether they are the same as those kept warm by winter or those who stopped in the colonnade. The poem "is alive with the possibility of form. . . . But all of these possible structures break down" (pp. 318–19). The vitality and fascination of the poem derive from its willingness to play with opposed ideas and feelings and, thus, to comprehend them. Cox may sometimes overstate the extent and the virtues of the poem's incoherence, but he is surely right in saying that "the way to read *The Waste Land* is to examine how the words work together, and not to fight desperately to find an ordered narrative" (p. 308).

Barbara Everett follows somewhat similar lines: "*The Waste Land* has neither 'story' nor 'narrator' nor 'protagonist' nor 'myth' nor 'themes' nor 'music' nor 'locale': these are exact and technical terms deriving from conventions which the poem includes only to fragment and deny" ("Eliot in and out of '*The Waste Land*,' " 1975, p. 14). What Everett *does* allow the poem is its distinctive style, a "pseudoist" or even mannerist style, audible in the poem's many voices and individual enough that other poets enter only through quotation and conscious emulation. In effect, Everett affirms that the reader recognizes a single sensibility at work in the various private and public voices of the poem, though that sensibility has no name (except Eliot) and no voice of its own which we can label as the "persona." This "travesty style" (p. 20) is the crowning achievement of Eliot's early poetry, so that his later work can be seen as an effort to achieve a different, more sincere style. In some respects, this is close to George Wright's view that Eliot's personae are identified by a characteristic tone. Everett's reading of the poem is a bit fragmented, concentrating on love and isolation and devoting too much time to refuting a bizarre Wagnerian interpretation given wide circulation in a popular textbook. But Everett offers sensible readings of particular points and occasional generalizations that are very suggestive, for example, that *The Waste Land* "charts points of no return" (p. 30). Everett's work shows that what counts is the sensibility with which the reader approaches the poem, not the alleged presence of a unifying sensibility (like Tiresias) within the poem.

Eliot in Various Voices

To the extent that Eliot's "impersonal" theory has encouraged readers to concentrate on the poem rather than on the author, its effect on criticism has probably been healthy, and there can be no real reason to object to the use of terms like "persona" and "speaker" as devices for talking about the poem without seeming to draw inferences about the poet. When such terms lead us to expect that there will be an identifiable persona within the poem and clearly distinct from its implied author, the terminology may become misleading. A dramatic monologue like "The Love Song of J. Alfred Prufrock" is not necessarily a good model to look to in discussing *The Waste Land*. The latter poem speaks in many voices; if it achieves unity through the intensity of its internal relations, we do not understand that unity any better by naming it Tiresias. The same caveat applies to many of Eliot's other early poems. It applies even more forcefully to Eliot's later poetry. The creation of personae is, in the end, only a technique. Even if we accept the "impersonal theory," the poet can aim for and attain a kind of impersonality without speaking through personae.

Of Eliot's poems, "Gerontion" is, after "Prufrock," the one which is most often read as a dramatic monologue, though thematically the poem is closer to *The Waste Land*—close enough that Eliot considered prefixing "Gerontion" to *The Waste Land* as an aid (probably doubtful) to readers. The opening lines of "Gerontion" certainly encourage readers to see the "old man" as the speaker of the entire poem, a persona clearly distinct from the poet. The poem allows one to read it this way, and most of the readings discussed in later chapters of this book do so. Although the poem may feature a persona, it threatens to fall into disconnected fragments, and the search for a unifying sensibility should not blind us to its fragmentary character.

The fragmentary character of "Gerontion" is stressed in Jewel Spears Brooker's valuable essay "The Structure of Eliot's 'Gerontion': An Interpretation Based on Bradley's Doctrine of the Systematic Nature of Truth" (1979). " 'Gerontion' does literally and really consist of fragments," says Brooker, "and an acceptance of these fragments as fragments is preliminary to understanding the poem" (p. 338). Of the relevant Bradley doctrines, Brooker emphasizes Bradley's distrust of discursive reason and the notion that the fragmentary experiences find their context in larger fragments, with the final context being an absolute experiential reality. The value of these points goes beyond her specific analysis of "Gerontion," for they are, of course, relevant to much of Eliot's early poetry. In "Gerontion," Brooker sees a nonlinear series of expanding contexts, most of which can be seen as "houses" superimposed on Gerontion's own—the house of Israel, the house of the church, and the house of history (with its "corridors" and "passages"). Although the poem gains from rereading, insistence on its nonlinear character seems unnecessary, given the linear character of our experience in any given reading of the poem. The eventual reading is not, in fact, terribly different from many others: Gerontion's error, which is that of modern man, is overreliance on discursive reason, which threatens the very possibility of belief. Signs are given, but we do not see them, and Christ is not recognized in our Jewish landlord. In all the fragments of experience is the possibility of self-transcendence. The poem itself is a unity which comprehends its fragments without violating their individual character, though Gerontion's experience may remain fragmentary.

Bradley and the "impersonal" theory of poetry do not cease to be relevant as we move toward the later poems, though the notion of "persona" or "speakers" seems to become less so. C. J. Jahagirdar has even claimed that "it is in *Four Quartets*, more than anywhere else, that Eliot practises his doctrine of impersonality with an amazing degree of adherence" ("T. S. Eliot's *Four Quartets:* The Rhetoric of Impersonality," 1970, p. 67). It is hard to say just what Jahagirdar means by this, since he seems to believe that Eliot's theory requires Eliot to find adequate living symbols for the mystical experience, and since, in the absence of such "symbolic equivalents" (p. 68), Jahagirdar finds the poem something of a failure.

The *Four Quartets* does not present us with clearly identified personae, and most readers have little trouble identifying the presiding consciousness of the poem as Eliot. That consciousness speaks with several voices, of course, in ways that Andrew Kennedy has discussed in his essay "The Speaking 'I' in *Four Quartets*" (1979): "There is the 'I' that authenticates personal experience as well as a state reaching beyond personality; there is the editorial 'I' of the poet entering his own poem self-consciously, or as the empirical Eliot, and at the same time neutralising the personal tone; and there is the masked and compound Doppelganger 'I' of *Little Gidding*, reaching toward confessional poetry through a seeming loss of identity" (p. 166). Most critics note these various voices, and in some critical readings the voices come close to being true personae, obscuring the basic unity of the speaker of the poem. The voices should probably be seen as reflecting internal shifts in mood and purpose, not as a set of competing lecturers on a common platform. Part of the problem is noted by William T. Moynihan: "Although

Eliot's *Four Quartets* is essentially a dramatic meditation, it is more often discussed as though it were a didactic poem" ("Character and Action in 'The Four Quartets,' " 1972, p. 203). But one suspects that another part of the problem is the tendency to find personae throughout Eliot's poetry. For *Four Quartets*, Moynihan's single speaker, speaking to a single audience in ways which mirror changes in his thought and moods, is more convincing than Donoghue's collection of voices that offer us a single wisdom.

Although we may not find personae in the *Four Quartets*, there is a sense in which the *Quartets* provide a clearer exemplification of the "impersonal theory" than *The Waste Land*. We are not, at any rate, locked in a private world of fragments to the same extent; although the structure of *Four Quartets* remains more fragmentary than some would admit, a degree of order has been imposed upon experience, and one is less inclined to apply to these poems than to *The Waste Land*, Eliot's complaints about the unmotivated emotion in *Hamlet*. For at least some critics, the self-transcendence aimed at in the *Quartets* is a logical development of that implied by the "impersonal theory" and by Eliot's earlier study of Bradley. Among those critics who focus on the later poems, one of the more convincing exponents of this view is Ronald Moore, in his *Metaphysical Symbolism in T. S. Eliot's "Four Quartets"* (1965). Moore's monograph presents Eliot's later views as "a form of Christianized Bradleyan idealism" (p. 5). He sees the surrender of the poet to the poem in the "impersonal theory" as an anticipation of and parallel to the soul's submission to God. Although this suggests an unduly mystical reading of the early criticism, the parallel reflects the influence of Bradley on Eliot's criticism and religious convictions. Rather similar arguments are advanced in Peter G. Ellis, "T. S. Eliot, F. H. Bradley, and 'Four Quartets' " (1969), and, very unclearly, in C. O. Gardner, "Some Reflections on the Opening of *Burnt Norton*" (1970). As with the Bolgan book (cited earlier), one is a bit uncomfortable in seeing Bradley cited as a source for Christian positions of considerable antiquity, but there is certainly a substantial amount of continuity in Eliot's concerns.

Another obvious connection between the *Four Quartets* and Eliot's early criticism is that, in the *Quartets*, Eliot makes poetry (of a sort) out of his thoughts on such questions as the nature of the poetic process and the relationship between poetry and belief. Many studies of Eliot's criticism note this relationship;

of those mentioned in this chapter, those by Morrissey and Antrim have particularly interesting comments. A somewhat mystical account of the connection is given by R. L. Brett in his article "Mysticism and Incarnation in *Four Quartets*" (1966) and, in very similar language, in his chapter on the *Quartets* for his earlier book, *Reason and Imagination* (1960). Brett is useful in pointing to the way in which the structure of the *Quartets* reflects Eliot's belief that "the poet cannot *state* the truth; he can only point towards it by returning again and again to those places where the truth becomes manifest, beyond words" (1960, p. 127). Judgments of how successful Eliot is in this striving for self-transcendence will vary. It seems clear that the *Four Quartets*, more personal in style, are less private in content than *The Waste Land*, an achievement which is very much in keeping with the "impersonal theory" and its insistence that the poet may realize true personality by striving for impersonality and submitting himself to ordering principles. The next two chapters will take us to those places where Eliot thought the truth becomes manifest, as mapped by his critics, who have proposed many different locations.

References

Abel, Darrel
1953. "R.L.S. and 'Prufrock,'" *Notes and Queries* Jan., pp. 37–38.

Allan, Mowbray
1974. *T. S. Eliot's Impersonal Theory of Poetry*. Lewisburg, Pa.: Bucknell Univ. Pr.

Antrim, Harry T.
1971. *T. S. Eliot's Concept of Language*. Gainesville: Univ. of Florida Pr.

Arden, Eugene
1958. "The Echo of Hell in 'Prufrock,'" *Notes and Queries* Aug., pp. 363–64.
1960. "The 'Other' Lazarus in 'Prufrock,'" *Notes and Queries* Jan., pp. 33, 40.

Austin, Allen
1971. *T. S. Eliot: The Literary and Social Criticism*. Bloomington: Indiana Univ. Pr.

Bell, Vereen M.
1969. "A Reading of 'Prufrock,'" *English Studies*, Anglo-American Supplement, pp. lxviii–lxxiv.

Blackmur, R. P.
1951. "In the Hope of Straightening Things Out," *Kenyon Review* Spring, pp. 303–14.
Blisset, William
1953. "Pater and Eliot," *University of Toronto Quarterly*, pp. 261–68.
Blum, Margaret Morton
1957. "The Fool in 'The Love Song of J. Alfred Prufrock,'" *Modern Language Notes* June, pp. 424–26.
Bolgan, Anne C.
1971. "The Philosophy of F. H. Bradley and the Mind and Art of T. S. Eliot: An Introduction," in *English Literature and British Philosophy*, ed. S. P. Rosenbaum, pp. 251–77. Chicago: Univ. of Chicago Pr.
1973. *What the Thunder Really Said: A Retrospective Essay on the Making of* The Waste Land. Montreal: McGill-Queen's Univ. Pr.
Bollier, Ernest P.
1963. "T. S. Eliot and F. H. Bradley: A Question of Influence," *Tulane Studies in English*, pp. 87–111.
Brett, R. L.
1960. "T. S. Eliot's *Four Quartets*," in *Reason and Imagination*, pp. 108–35. London: Oxford Univ. Pr.
1966. "Mysticism and Incarnation in *Four Quartets*," *English* Autumn, pp. 94–99.
Brombert, Victor H.
1949. *The Criticism of T. S. Eliot: Problems of an Impersonal Theory of Poetry*. New Haven: Yale Univ. Pr.
Brooker, Jewel Spears
1979. "The Structure of Eliot's 'Gerontion': An Interpretation Based on Bradley's Doctrine of the Systematic Nature of Truth," *ELH* Summer, pp. 314–40.
Brooks, Cleanth, and Robert Penn Warren
1938. "The Love Song of J. Alfred Prufrock," in *Understanding Poetry*, pp. 589–96. New York: Holt.
Buckley, Vincent
1959. *Poetry and Morality*, pp. 87–157. London: Chatto and Windus.
Church, R. W.
1938. "Eliot on Bradley's Metaphysics," *Harvard Advocate* Dec., pp. 24–26.
Cook, Robert G.
1970. "Emerson's 'Self-Reliance,' 'Sweeney' and 'Prufrock,'" *American Literature* May, pp. 221–26.
Cox, C. B.
1970. "T. S. Eliot at the Cross-Roads," *Critical Quarterly* Winter, pp. 307–20.

DeLaura, David J.
1965. "Pater and Eliot: The Origin of the 'Objective Correlative,'" *Modern Language Quarterly* Sept., pp. 426–31.

Donoghue, Denis
1965. "T. S. Eliot's *Four Quartets:* A New Reading," *Studies* Spring, pp. 41–62.
1972. "The American 'Waste Land' at Fifty," *Art International* May 20, pp. 61–64, 67.

Duffy, John J.
1969. "T. S. Eliot's Objective Correlative: A New England Commonplace," *New England Quarterly* Mar., pp. 108–15.

Dwyer, Daniel N.
1951. "Eliot's 'The Love Song of J. Alfred Prufrock,'" *Explicator* Mar., item 38.

Eliot, T. S.
1957. "The Frontiers of Criticism," in *On Poets and Poetry*, pp. 113–34. New York: Farrar, Straus and Cudahy.
1960. "Preface," *Essays in Elizabethan Drama*, pp. vii–x. New York: Harcourt Brace Jovanovich.
1964. "Preface," *Knowledge and Experience in the Philosophy of F. H. Bradley*, pp. 9–11. New York: Farrar, Straus.
1965. "To Criticize the Critic," in *To Criticize the Critic*, pp. 11–26. New York: Farrar, Straus and Giroux.

Ellis, Peter G.
1969. "T. S. Eliot, F. H. Bradley, and 'Four Quartets,'" *Research Studies* (Washington State Univ.) June, pp. 93–111.

Everett, Barbara
1974. "In Search of Prufrock," *Critical Quarterly* Summer, pp. 101–21.
1975. "Eliot in and out of *The Waste Land*," *Critical Quarterly* Spring, pp. 7–30.

Fish, Clifford
1950. "Eliot's 'The Love Song of J. Alfred Prufrock,'" *Explicator* June, item 62.

Fleissner, Robert F.
1966. "'Prufrock,' Pater and *Richard II:* Retracing a Denial of Princeship," *American Literature* Mar., pp. 120–23.
1972. "Prufrock's 'Ragged Claws,'" *English Studies* June, pp. 247–48.

Fortenberry, George
1967. "Prufrock and the Fool Song," *Ball State University Forum* Winter, pp. 51–54.

Frank, Armin Paul
1972. "T. S. Eliot's Objective Correlative and the Philosophy of F. H. Bradley, *Journal of Aesthetics and Art Criticism*, pp. 311–17.

Freed, Lewis
1962. *T. S. Eliot: Aesthetics and History*. LaSalle, Ill.: Open Court.

1976. "Eliot and Bradley: A Brief Review," *T. S. Eliot Review*, pp. 29–58.
1979. *T. S. Eliot: The Critic as Philosopher*. West Lafayette, Ind.: Purdue Univ. Pr.

Gardner, C. O.
1970. "Some Reflections on the Opening of *Burnt Norton*," *Critical Quarterly* Winter, pp. 326–35.

Gardner, Helen
1972. *The Waste Land 1972*. Manchester: Manchester Univ. Pr.

George, A. G.
1969. *T. S. Eliot: His Mind and Art*. Rev. ed. New York: Asia Publishing House.

Hancher, Michael
1973. "The Adventures of Tiresias: France, Gourmont, Eliot," *Modern Language Review* Jan., pp. 29–37.

Hollahan, Eugene
1970. "A Structural Dantean Parallel in Eliot's 'The Love Song of J. Alfred Prufrock,' " *American Literature* Mar., pp. 91–93.

Jahagirdar, C. J.
1970. "T. S. Eliot's *Four Quartets:* The Rhetoric of Impersonality," *Literary Criterion*, pp. 65–69.

Kennedy, Andrew
1979. "The Speaking 'I' in *Four Quartets*," *English Studies* Apr., pp. 166–75.

Kenner, Hugh
1959. *The Invisible Poet: T. S. Eliot*. New York: McDowell, McDowell, Obolensky.

Kirk, Stephen
1975. "The Structural Weakness of T. S. Eliot's *The Waste Land*," *Yearbook of English Studies*, pp. 214–24.

Krieger, Murray
1956. *The New Apologists for Poetry*, pp. 46–56. Minneapolis: Univ. of Minnesota Pr.
1969. "The Critical Legacy of Matthew Arnold; or, The Strange Brotherhood of T. S. Eliot, I. A. Richards, and Northrop Frye," *Southern Review* Spring, pp. 457–74.

Kumar, Jitendra
1968. "Consciousness and Its Correlates: Eliot and Husserl," *Philosophy and Phenomenological Research* Mar., pp. 332–52.

Lee, Brian
1979. *Theory and Personality: The Significance of T. S. Eliot's Criticism*. London: Athlone.

Lees, F. N.
1964. "T. S. Eliot and Nietzsche," *Notes and Queries* Oct., pp. 386–87.

Lu, Fei-Pai
1966. *T. S. Eliot: The Dialectical Structure of His Theory of Poetry*. Chicago: Univ. of Chicago Pr.

Margolis, Joseph
1955. "The Love Song of J. Alfred Prufrock," in *Interpretations*, ed. John Wain, pp. 179–93. London: Routledge and Kegan Paul.

Maxwell, D. E. S.
1972. " 'He Do the Police in Different Voices,' " *Mosaic* Fall, pp. 167–80.

McElderry, Bruce R., Jr.
1957. "Santayana and Eliot's 'Objective Correlative,' " *Boston University Studies in English* Autumn, pp. 179–91.

Miller, J. Hillis
1966. *Poets of Reality*, pp. 131–89. Cambridge: Harvard Univ. Pr.

Moore, Ronald
1965. *Metaphysical Symbolism in T. S. Eliot's "Four Quartets."* Stanford: Stanford Honors Essays in Humanities (no. 9), Stanford Univ.

Moorman, Charles
1953. "Order and Mr. Eliot," *South Atlantic Quarterly* Jan., pp. 73–87.

Morgan, Roberta, and Albert Wohlstetter
1938. "Observations on 'Prufrock,' " *Harvard Advocate* Dec., pp. 27–30, 33–40.

Morrissey, Thomas J.
1978. "Intimate and Unidentifiable: The Voices of Fragmented Reality in the Poetry of T. S. Eliot," *Centennial Review* Winter, pp. 1–27.

Moynihan, William T.
1972. "Character and Action in the *Four Quartets*," *Mosaic* Winter, pp. 203–28.

Noonan, James
1972. "Poetry and Belief in the Criticism of T. S. Eliot," *Queen's Quarterly* Autumn, pp. 388–96.

Novak, Robert
1973. " 'Prufrock' and Arnold's 'Buried Life,' " *Windless Orchard*, pp. 23–26.

Oras, Ants
1932. *The Critical Ideas of T. S. Eliot.* Tartu: Tartu Univ.

Pasquale, Pasquale di, Jr.
1968. "Coleridge's Framework of Objectivity and Eliot's Objective Correlative," *Journal of Aesthetics and Art Criticism* Summer, pp. 488–500.

Pope, John C.
1945. "Prufrock and Raskolnikov," *American Literature* Nov., pp. 213–30.
1947. "Prufrock and Raskolnikov Again: A Letter from Eliot," *American Literature* Jan., pp. 319–21.

Rooney, William Joseph
1949. *The Problem of "Poetry and Belief" in Contemporary Criticism*, pp. 88–146. Washington: Catholic Univ. of America Pr.

Schneider, Elisabeth
1972. "Prufrock and After: The Theme of Change," *PMLA* Oct., pp. 1103–18.

Scott, Stanley J.
1976. "Beyond Modern Subjectivism: T. S. Eliot and American Philosophy," *Thought* Dec., pp. 409–27.

Seiler, Robert
1972. "Prufrock and Hamlet," *English* Summer, pp. 41–43.

Sen, Jyoti Prakash
1971. *The Progress of T. S. Eliot as Poet and Critic.* New Delhi: Orient Longman.

Smidt, Kristian
1961. *Poetry and Belief in the Work of T. S. Eliot.* Rev. ed. London: Routledge and Kegan Paul.

Smith, Gerald
1962. "Eliot's 'The Love Song of J. Alfred Prufrock,'" *Explicator* Oct., item 17.

Smith, Grover
1963. (editor) *Josiah Royce's Seminar, 1913–1914: As Recorded in the Notebooks of Harry T. Costello.* New Brunswick, N.J.: Rutgers Univ. Pr.

Soldo, John J.
1968. "Knowledge and Experience in the Criticism of T. S. Eliot," *ELH* June, pp. 284–308.

Spangler, George M.
1968. "*The Education of Henry Adams* as a Source for 'The Love Song of J. Alfred Prufrock,'" *Notes and Queries* Aug., pp. 295–96.

Stallman, Robert W.
1950. (editor) *The Critic's Notebook*, pp. 116–18. Minneapolis: Univ. of Minnesota Pr.

Stead, C. K.
1964a. "'Classical Authority' and 'The Dark Embryo': A Dichotomy in T. S. Eliot's Criticism," *Journal of the Australian Universities Language and Literature Association*, pp. 200–207.
1964b. *The New Poetic: Yeats to Eliot*, pp. 125–87. London: Penguin.

Steadman, John M.
1958. "Eliot and Husserl: The Origin of the 'Objective Correlative,'" *Notes and Queries* July, pp. 261–62.

Storm, Leo
1976. "J. M. Robertson and T. S. Eliot: A Note on the Genesis of Modern Critical Theory," *Journal of Modern Literature* Apr., pp. 315–21.

Stuckey, William
1961. "Eliot's 'The Love Song of J. Alfred Prufrock,'" *Explicator* Sept., item 10.

Thompson, Eric
1963. *T. S. Eliot: The Metaphysical Perspective.* Carbondale: Southern Illinois Univ. Pr.
Vivas, Eliseo
1944. "The Objective Correlative of T. S. Eliot," *American Bookman* Winter, pp. 7–18.
Wasser, Henry
1960. "A Note on Eliot and Santayana," *Boston University Studies in English* Summer, pp. 125–26.
Waterman, Arthur E.
1959. "Eliot's 'The Love Song of J. Alfred Prufrock,' 15–22," *Explicator* June, item 67.
Wellek, Rene
1956. "The Criticism of T. S. Eliot," *Sewanee Review* Summer, pp. 398–443.
White, Robert
1961. "Eliot's 'The Love Song of J. Alfred Prufrock,'" *Explicator* Nov., item 19.
Whiteside, George
1967. "T. S. Eliot's Dissertation," *ELH* Sept., pp. 400–424.
1973. "T. S. Eliot's Doctoral Studies," *American Notes and Queries* Feb., pp. 83–86.
Wilks, A. John
1971. *A Critical Commentary on T. S. Eliot's "The Waste Land."* London: Macmillan.
Williams, Helen
1968. *T. S. Eliot: The Waste Land.* Woodbury, N.Y.: Barron's Educational Series.
Wimsatt, W. K.
1965. "*Prufrock* and *Maud:* From Plot to Symbol," in *Hateful Contraries*, pp. 201–12. Lexington: Univ. of Kentucky Pr.
Wimsatt, W. K., and Cleanth Brooks
1962. "Eliot and Pound: An Impersonal Art," *Literary Criticism: A Short History*, pp. 657–78. New York: Knopf.
Wollheim, Richard
1964. "Eliot, Bradley and Immediate Experience," *New Statesman* Mar. 13, pp. 401–2.
1970. "Eliot and F. H. Bradley: An Account," in *Eliot in Perspective*, ed. Graham Martin, pp. 169–93. New York: Humanities Pr.
Wright, George T.
1960. *The Poet in the Poem*, pp. 60–87. Berkeley: Univ. of California Pr.
Wright, Nathalia
1970. "A Source for T. S. Eliot's 'Objective Correlative,'" *American Literature* Jan., pp. 589–91.

Selected Additional Readings

Bollier, E. P.
1960. "T. S. Eliot and the Sacred Wood," *Colorado Quarterly* Spring, pp. 308–17.

Child, Ruth C.
1951. "The Early Critical Work of T. S. Eliot: An Assessment," *College English* Feb., pp. 269–75.

Donoghue, Denis
1977. "On the Limits of Language," *Sewanee Review* July–Sept., pp. 371–91.

Fergusson, Francis
1927. "T. S. Eliot and His Impersonal Theory of Art," in *American Caravan*, ed. Van Wyck Brooks et al., pp. 446–53, New York: Macaulay.

Frank, Armin Paul
1973. *Die Sehnsucht nach dem unteilbaren Sein: Motive und Motivation in der Literaturkritik T. S. Eliots.* Munich: Wilhelm Fink.

Gomme, Andre
1966. *Attitudes toward Criticism*, pp. 145–52. Carbondale: Southern Illinois Univ. Pr.

Goodheart, Eugene
1978. *The Failure of Criticism*, pp. 51–68. Cambridge: Harvard Univ. Pr.

Jackson, John E.
1978. *La Question du Moi: Un Aspect de la Modernité Poetique Européenne*, pp. 45–142. Neuchatel: Editions de la Baconnière.

LaChance, Paul R.
1971. "The Function of Voice in *The Waste Land*," *Style* Spring pp. 101–18.

Lobb, Edward
1981. *T. S. Eliot and the Romantic Critical Tradition.* London: Routledge and Kegan Paul.

Oberg, Arthur K.
1968. "*The Cocktail Party* and the Illusion of Autonomy," *Modern Drama* Sept., pp. 187–94.

Rajnath
1980. *T. S. Eliot's Theory of Poetry*. Atlantic Highlands, N.J.: Humanities Pr.

Righter, William
1977. "The Philosophical Critic," in *The Literary Criticism of T. S. Eliot*, ed. David Newton-DeMolina, pp. 111–38. London: Athlone.

Schneider, Elisabeth
1975. *T. S. Eliot: The Pattern in the Carpet.* Berkeley: Univ. of California Pr.

Sen, Mihir Kumar
1967. *Inter-War English Poetry, With Special Reference to Eliot's "Objective Correlative" Theory*. Burdwan: Univ. of Burdwan.
Stanford, Donald E.
1969. "Classicism and the Modern Poet," *Southern Review* Spring, pp. 475–500.

CHAPTER 3

The Social Critic

In the introduction to *The Sacred Wood* (1920), Eliot chided Matthew Arnold for having been tempted into social and political criticism, work that might well have been left to lesser men. Eliot himself was to succumb to the same temptation. If his later literary criticism seems to lack the bite of his earlier work, it may be partly because the times had forced him to devote a major share of his intellectual energies to critical reflections on society and its problems. His growing interest in political issues was mirrored in the articles he chose to print in the *Criterion* (1922–39), and in his own editorial comments, as the conflict between fascism and communism replaced the conflict between Classicism and Romanticism. The *Criterion's* last issue appeared in January 1939, and later that year Eliot published a major statement of his position, *The Idea of a Christian Society*. Many of his postwar essays and lectures touched on social issues: *To Criticize the Critic* (1965) includes two especially important items, "The Aims of Education" (1950) and "The Literature of Politics" (1955). His most important piece of postwar social criticism was, of course, *Notes towards the Definition of Culture* (1948). The tentativeness of the title was pure Eliot, but there was also an echo of Arnold's *Culture and Anarchy* (1869). Eliot might still deplore the "thinness" of Arnold's conception of culture, but he had clearly joined him in pursuing game outside the literary preserve.

Eliot's apparent shift in interests already showed itself in the preface to *For Lancelot Andrewes* (1928), with its famous declaration that his point of view was "classicist in literature, royalist in politics, and anglo-catholic in religion." Each of these points to commitments which transcend literature, even Eliot's Classicism, which involved rejection of Romantic individualism and its social fruits. But though Eliot's views have long been on the record, they have aroused less understanding than controversy, perhaps because they were generally opposed to the dominant trends of the age. To the extent that his views are reflected in his poetry, the same pattern is observable, and not all of his critics distinguish between the role of a literary critic and that of a moralist, as Eliot himself did in *After Strange Gods* (1934). As the debates covered in this chapter will show, we are just beginning to understand Eliot's intellectual development, the meaning of his social criticism, and the social implications of his work.

The Development of a Social Critic

Eliot did not live to provide, as he had planned, a retrospective evaluation of his social criticism of the sort given his literary criticism in the title essay of *To Criticize the Critic* (1965). For hints of his view of his development, we must still turn to that essay. Eliot regrets the excessive quotability of the *For Lancelot Andrewes* preface without renouncing the views expressed, except that Classicism and Romanticism as "terms have no longer the importance to me that they once had" (p. 15). He attributes the emphasis on Classicism in his early criticism to the influence of Irving Babbitt—"with an infusion later of T. E. Hulme and of the more literary essays of Charles Maurras" (p. 17). Probably more important than such specific references is Eliot's general observation that too many of his critics have ignored his careful dating of his essays in collections and have assumed that views he uttered in one context and at one time are permanently held. It is certainly true that many accounts of Eliot's social criticism assume an identity of views between the Eliot of 1928 and the Eliot of 1948. The most useful studies of Eliot's social criticism have been produced by scholars who have taken the time to trace the development of Eliot's views.

For the early years, the most thorough study is John D. Margolis' *T. S. Eliot's Intellectual Development, 1922–1939* (1972). Although the main body of his study is concerned with the *Criterion* years, Margolis begins with a chapter on Eliot's development up to 1922, so that his coverage is a bit wider than suggested by his title. One of the strengths of his study, in fact, is his awareness of the importance of Irving Babbitt in shaping Eliot's early Classicism. Margolis provides extracts from Eliot's

1916 extension course syllabus on modern French literature which show Eliot scorning Romanticism and denouncing Rousseau, favorite targets of Babbitt. Babbitt is also credited with having led Eliot to other anti-Romantic thinkers like T. E. Hulme and Julien Benda. Margolis does not, however, devote much time to weighing the relative importance of various influences. His approach is essentially descriptive; his own opinions tend to disappear behind a mass of quotations, so that the reader must infer his judgments of relative significance from the selective attention he gives various Eliot statements.

In his account of the early years of the *Criterion*, for example, Margolis devotes particular attention to Eliot's debate with his friend John Middleton Murry (editor of *Adelphi*), a confrontation between Classicism and Romanticism. The effect is to reinforce Margolis' picture of Eliot's concerns in the early twenties as basically literary. Margolis has earlier noted the interest in religion in some of Eliot's early essays and reviews, but he seems almost too ready to find in the heavily literary pages of the early *Criterion* an adequate statement of its editor's intellectual interests. Margolis' concern to demonstrate the continuity of Eliot's intellectual development is appeased by suggestions that Eliot was searching for ordering principles which would help make poetry possible. Eliot's turn to open concern with politics and religion can then be treated as an outgrowth of his desire to create a healthy climate for literature.

Margolis' treatment of the period of Eliot's formal conversion (1926-28) thus gives special stress to the examples of Wyndham Lewis and Charles Maurras. Lewis is seen as having provided Eliot with the example of another artist who felt called upon by the times to speak out on larger issues in order that the social environment for art might be preserved. Margolis sees Maurras as primarily a negative example—that a literary man should stay out of partisan politics, that one could not effectively support a church in theory while staying out of it in practice. Eliot's conversion can thus be seen as a social duty. Margolis' tendency to play down the specifically religious element in Eliot's conversion is also seen in his treatment of the years immediately following the conversion. Here, Margolis stresses Eliot's various contributions, personal and editorial, to the debate over the New Humanism; the effect is rather to suggest that Eliot saw religious belief as an intellectual necessity to make his humanism complete. Margolis offers two reasons for Eliot's decision to become an Anglican rather than a Roman

Catholic: one is social, that the Roman Church was not a major spiritual force in England; the other is primarily intellectual, that Eliot saw Romanism as lacking in the spirit of humanism he continued to prize. Even if one concedes that an account of intellectual development need not be, at the same time, an account of spiritual development, Margolis' description of Eliot's conversion and its immediate effects seems bloodless, and one wonders whether this is not partly a result of basing this description almost entirely on Eliot's prose, with relatively little attention to the poetry.

In his treatment of the thirties, Margolis makes effective use of Eliot's correspondence with Paul Elmer More, another humanist who had drifted toward Anglicanism, though not, like Eliot, becoming a regular communicant. But Margolis does not seem very sympathetic to the direction in which Eliot was leading the *Criterion.* As it became less and less a purely literary review, and as Eliot's interests turned to drama, the quality of the journal declined. Concerned with abstract political theory, Eliot and the magazine were sometimes disturbingly blind to the import of political events. Moreover, Eliot was writing outside his area of expertise, and knew it. For Margolis, the end of the *Criterion* freed Eliot to follow his new interests in more appropriate formats; 1939 was the year of both *The Idea of a Christian Society* and the production of *The Family Reunion,* Eliot's first play for the commercial stage. Even *The Idea of a Christian Society* is marred, for Margolis, by the undefined character of Eliot's orthodoxy and his positive social ideals, and he suggests that its chief interest is the light it casts on Eliot's other work. Implicitly, this would seem to be the judgment Margolis passes on most of Eliot's extraliterary prose: its final value is in what it tells us about Eliot as a poet and dramatist.

If Margolis' book is at its best in dealing with Eliot as a humanist and Classicist, Roger Kojecký's study, *T. S. Eliot's Social Criticism* (1971), is at its best in dealing with Eliot as an Anglo-Catholic, and it does not really get rolling until Kojecký gets to the later years, when the characteristically Anglican concern with church and state came to dominate much of Eliot's prose. Kojecký opens with some observations on the degree to which Eliot's social criticism is in agreement with that of Arnold and Coleridge, especially the latter, who is given high praise in *The Sacred Wood.* This chapter makes some good points but is not really connected with the rest of the book. A biographical sketch of Eliot's early life is interesting in itself but is not handled so as to say much about its meaning for Eliot's later development. A chapter on Maurras and the Action Française is also primarily biographical; it makes the obvious points, but Kojecký does not state his conclusions about the importance of Maurras until near the end of the book, when he says that Eliot "does not appear to have studied the political writings of Maurras particularly closely" and "primarily valued his literary work, and in a general way the rationalistic elitism and royalism" (p. 223). Kojecký's treatment of Babbitt and the forces which led Eliot into his political and religious commitments is even more sketchy. A rather short list of works is treated in his brief chapter on Eliot as a poet and dramatist, and the *Coriolan* poems are seen as "ironically satirical" (p. 101). In *The Rock*, he notes that both fascism and communism are condemned, but (in a prose passage) the chief workman is allowed to express sympathy with the antimonetarism of Social Credit. Similar social views are noted in *Murder in the Cathedral*, and the resemblance of the guardians in *The Cocktail Party* to the Community of Christians, described in *The Idea of a Christian Society*, is insisted on. Since what Kojecký says about such matters is intelligent, one is tempted to wish that he had dealt with more works.

As matters stand, the chief value of the first half of Kojecký's book is in various incidental observations. Kojecký calls attention, for example, to Eliot's close connection with the Social Credit enthusiasts associated with the *New English Weekly*. This is evidence of Eliot's willingness to take proposals for radical economic reform seriously, though his enthusiasm for the program of the Social Credit school, if it had ever been warm, cooled by the end of the thirties. He also cites two previously unpublished Eliot comments on *After Strange Gods*, one of Eliot's more controversial performances. One, in a letter to More, refers to that book and *The Use of Poetry and the Use of Criticism* (1933) as "two bad jobs" that Eliot is glad to have behind him (1971, p. 103). The other is a reported remark to Helen Gardner that when he condemned D. H. Lawrence, "it was he rather than Lawrence, who was sick" (p. 94).

The later chapters of Kojecký's book benefit from his access to materials detailing Eliot's involvement with other Christians concerned with social issues. The ecumenical character of these contacts is especially interesting. They would seem to have grown out of Eliot's participation in the Oxford Conference on Church, Community, and State in 1937, which drew its delegates from more than forty countries and nearly as many denominations. Eliot addressed the Conference on the Oecumenical Nature of the Church and Its Responsibility toward the World and participated in a section concerned with economic issues. The next year, he was part of smaller, British meetings looking forward to setting up the World Council of Churches. These meetings created an interdenominational Council on the Christian Faith and the Common Life, which led to the founding of the *Christian News-Letter,* a periodical to which Eliot contributed and for which he served more than once as a guest editor.

If anything, the history of ecumenical enterprises is even duller than the history of institutional churches, but the reader who follows Kojecký's account of Eliot's involvement is soon rewarded. The same set of meetings gave rise to a small discussion group, called the Moot, which met several times a year between 1938 and 1947, and its discussions form the context of Eliot's later works of social criticism. Its members had a common concern for the propagation of religious values in British society, but they differed widely on means and even the details of ends. At the first meeting, for example, the minutes record Christopher Dawson as urging as a long-range goal "a totalitarian Christian Order" for society and Eliot as replying that "the best thing a totalitarian state could do would be to abdicate" (p. 164). This exchange accurately indicates the position Eliot soon took in *The Idea of a Christian Society*, though some readers have insisted on confusing his views with those of Dawson. Kojecký's account of the ideas discussed at the various conferences and within the small circle of the Moot contributes to our understanding of the dialogue to which that book was meant to contribute. The difficult notion of the church within a church of a Community of Christians, for example, is easier to understand when placed within the continuing discussion of the need for an ecumenical "order" or even "party" devoted to spiritual regeneration of the civil society. And the charge sometimes made, that the book expresses covert sympathies with fascism, is even harder to swallow when we see how much of what it had to say had its origin in assemblies called to consider ways of meeting the ideological threat posed by the totalitarian states then preparing to divide Poland between them.

Karl Mannheim was an early recruit to the discussions of the Moot, and our understanding of Eliot's treatment of Mannheim in *Notes towards the Definition of Culture* is clarified by Kojecký's tracing of the discussions within the Moot during the war. To some extent, the Moot would seem to have been a liberalizing influence on Eliot, encouraging him, for example, to accept the principle of social reconstruction. Although the framework was generally Christian, the political ideas held by members of the Moot were very diverse, and exposure to them both sharpened and moderated Eliot's. An appendix to Kojecký's volume reprints an Eliot paper for the Moot, "On the Place and Function of the Clerisy," which touches on the key questions of the functions of spiritual and intellectual elites. Since at least some of *Notes towards the Definition of Culture* is aimed at the general public, the Moot paper helps clarify ideas that sometimes are obscure in the book. Kojecký suggests that the book was written partly "to persuade" (p. 210), that is, as part of the general policy of propagating religious ideals.

Kojecký's analysis of Eliot's social criticism is less illuminating than his treatment of its background. His book ends with a series of rather indecisive evaluations, adding up to "in the long run any opinion of Eliot's social criticism, as such, will depend largely on individual attitudes towards Conservatism" (p. 224). Unwilling to assent to all of Eliot's views but determined to describe them from the inside, Kojecký leaves himself no standpoint from which to criticize those views. He cannot even say whether anyone would find it worth reading Eliot's social criticism if Eliot were not a major literary figure, though he appears to doubt it. Because he is weak on Eliot's early years and short on critical analysis, Kojecký's book is seriously incomplete as a study of Eliot's social criticism. Nevertheless, his use of the records of the Moot is extremely valuable and opens new avenues for research.

Few doubts about the value of Eliot's social criticism are expressed in Russell Kirk's *Eliot and His Age* (1971). Kirk writes as a partisan for Eliot, a "champion of the moral imagination" and a "critic of the civil social order" (p. 9). The book's framework is biographical, but Kirk did not become acquainted with Eliot until late in Eliot's life; so most of the information is taken from other published sources, though Kirk provides details on the American background of Eliot's "The Aims of Education" lectures (1950). Kirk's treatment of the poems and plays is sensible but a bit obvious. The valuable part of his book, then, is the way it relates Eliot's ideas to the man and his work. Kirk offers fewer academic trappings than Margolis or Kojecký, both of whom began work on their books as doctoral dissertations. But Kirk has mastered his material and, perhaps because he is a conservative himself, he has a surer grasp of the spirit of Eliot's thought.

Like Margolis, Kirk sees Irving Babbitt as an important influence. More given to argumentative generalizations than Margolis, Kirk even sees Eliot's later work as carrying out much of Babbitt's program—"in the apprehension of cultural continuity . . . in the reaction against romanticism; in the theories of education; in emphasis upon the essential and the succinct; in the rousing of the moral imagination" (1971, p. 30). Alive to the implicit cultural politics of Babbitt's Classicism, Kirk believes that the *Criterion* had political aims from the first, even though its first manifestos emphasized purely literary goals. He suggests that Eliot's interest in larger cultural issues was deemphasized at first out of deference to Lady Rothermore, its patron for the first three years, who wanted a fashionable journal of mainly artistic pretensions. This suggestion finds support in the changes the magazine underwent after Lady Rothermore withdrew her support, but more evidence on Eliot's original hopes would be desirable. The picture of Eliot which emerges is more self-consistent than that of Margolis—Kojecký conveys no real picture of the young Eliot. It follows, then, that Kirk gives even less weight than Margolis to the influences sometimes seen as affecting Eliot in the twenties; he argues that Eliot's conservatism in many ways remained an American federalism, that Babbitt taught Eliot most of what he found acceptable in Maurras, and that Hulme came only as a reinforcement. Eliot's movement from intellectual sympathy with the Established Church to personal assent to its doctrines is described as a primarily personal religious quest.

In general, Kirk puts the most favorable construction on Eliot's views, but he is not entirely uncritical, noting, for example, that the *Criterion* offered little practical guidance in the dark days of the thirties and that Eliot's interest in Social Credit theories of economics persisted rather longer than justified by their merit. Using quotations from the *Criterion* rather selectively, he provides persuasive defenses of Eliot against some standard charges. He notes an April 1929 "Commentary" in which Eliot views with alarm the apparent sympathy with fascism of writers like Shaw, Wells, and Wyndham Lewis. Using such evidence, Kirk can claim that Eliot was more prescient about the threat of fascism than other, more liberal writers. Kirk cites a September 1928 "Commentary" which argues that modern war is caused by economic and financial matters; this bolsters the argument that Eliot, a banker and successful businessman, was by no means naive about the importance of economics in modern politics. Passages which disparage economics are placed in the context of Eliot's view that economics must ultimately be ruled by ethics and ethics by theology. Eliot's professed monarchism is not seen as a commitment to authoritarianism but as an allegiance to legitimacy as the font of social order, as opposed to the dictatorships imposed by revolutions and ideologies as the price of order. Kirk notes that such views were enough in the air to find a sympathetic echo even in Shaw, whose *Apple Cart* came out in 1929.

The strength of Kirk's treatment of Eliot's social and political views lies in his sympathy with their assumptions. Kirk's conservatism is based on the need to balance potentially incompatible values like freedom and order; so he can take Eliot's similar efforts more seriously than critics who are reluctant to admit that values might be in conflict. He is surely right to say that *The Idea of a Christian Society* does not propose, or even imply, a theocratic state and that Eliot's defense of class structures in *Notes towards the Definition of Culture* is not meant to advocate an ossified class system. Kirk also offers useful insights into the immediate political occasions of some Eliot comments. He calls attention, for example, to a "dialogue" ("On the Eve," *Criterion*, Jan. 1925) in which Eliot, apparently revising work done by his first wife, has a character sharply criticize "those rich Liberals who play at pulling down the laws, the empire, and the religion of England" (cited 1971, p. 118). Kirk argues that the subject is the Liberal faction which entered the coalition of government headed by Labor's Ramsay MacDonald, a government which fell shortly before the story was published.

William Chace has a much less sympathetic view of Eliot's politics. Chace's account of Eliot's development (*The Political Identities of Ezra Pound and T. S. Eliot*, 1973) presents him as almost obsessed with politics, but committed to transcendence and independence in ways which make him a "suprapolitical" man. For Chace, Eliot's insistence on transcendent ideals is often a way of evading the duty to follow the logical consequences of his positions; his efforts to achieve balance seem merely inconsistencies. Although his tone is reasonable, his is essentially a destructive critique. Since he prefers to dwell on Eliot's internal inconsistencies, Chace's view is hard to pin down. He shares some of his subject's distaste for liberalism. In one unusually open passage, he speaks of Eliot as writing "in defense, sometimes muted, sometimes full-voiced, of the socio-economic structure he knows best. . . . That which Eliot defends might indeed be a regressive aspect of what is now meant by the class society of the West, but the regressive and progressive aspects of this society have more in common with each other than they do with the forces that threaten or would like to threaten it" (p. 190). But the nature of the "progressive" forces is left unspecified, so that some of the criteria by which Eliot is judged remain unclear.

Chace is at his best when exploring the ambiguities of Eliot's prose style. He argues that Eliot's early Classicism shifted easily from a cultural to a political stance as Eliot's interests shifted. Chace sees the 1924 *Criterion* essay on Hulme and the 1927 essay on Babbitt as showing Eliot busy redefining "classicism" as antidemocratic; one may wonder whether redefinition was really necessary, given the strongly anti-individualistic cast of Babbitt's humanism. Chace suggests that Eliot shifted from praising the "classicism" of Benda in 1926 to finding him infected with "romance" in 1928 because Benda had meanwhile (in *La Trahison des Clercs*, 1927) attacked right-wing ideologues like Sorel and Maurras. The validity of such examples depends in good part on whether one swallows Chace's assumption that Eliot's Classicism began as nonpolitical in its implications. Chace is perhaps more justified in complaining that the "orthodoxy" appealed to in *After Strange Gods* is covertly political and distressingly undefined.

For Chace, Eliot's impulses toward transcendence and independence go hand in hand. The 1930 essay on Baudelaire thus becomes "disguised autobiography" (p. 146). Eliot's Anglicanism, like Baudelaire's Satanism, was designed to lift him apart from the mob of the indifferent. Chace cites a remark that same year (in "Thoughts after Lambeth") that being a Christian could give one "an odd and rather exhilarating feeling of isolation." The fastidious need to be apart from the mob is seen as the factor that saved Eliot from excessive sympathy with the ridiculous English Fascists, or even with the simply unintelligent Conservative Party. Despairing of all available political alternatives, Chace's Eliot cultivates superiority at the cost of irrelevance. "Faith, for Eliot," says Chace, "was less a positive doctrine than a means by which he could retire from all conflict" (p. 207). Whatever one's personal religious views, one may feel that this is a rather reductive approach to the religious impulse. Exactitude in dogma is not a fair measure of religious feeling.

Clarity of doctrine is, however, a fair requirement of a social critic, and much of what Chace has to say about *The Idea of a Christian Society* is well taken. Chace argues that one cannot discuss political issues without taking seriously the issue of power and its use. He suggests that the rhetoric of dealing with an "idea" of Christian society functions in part to fend off troublesome questions about how such a state might be achieved. The issue of power must also be evaded because Eliot sees power as a corrupting force, which might well destroy his Christian state, even if it were successfully called into being. Unwilling to call upon force to change the direction of society, Eliot sees modern society as moving toward an apocalypse. Chace is perhaps too reluctant to concede the reasonableness of an apocalyptic view of modern history, particularly for someone writing, as Eliot was, on the eve of World War II.

Chace believes there is a similar lack of clarity in *Notes towards the Definition of Culture*, beginning with Eliot's failure to observe carefully his own distinctions among the various meanings of the word "culture": it appears as a way of life, now as an extramundane ideal, and is presented as consisting in part of "unconscious" ideas. Eliot would seem to reserve a more conscious culture for the upper levels of society, and Chace believes that this culture would be the controlling culture of the society. Chace appears to find the notion of varying cultures among classes at odds with the view of culture as a unifying force in society, although Eliot's sense of the possibilities of unity in diversity surely fits easily into what Kirk calls Eliot's American federalism.

In the end, Chace seems to be searching for something that isn't there, looking for a political philosophy in a writer for whom politics are incidental in a larger social philosophy. Chace's search is useful in a number of ways: he offers occasional insights into Eliot's literary work (like the importance of class stratification in the plays) and he puts his finger on some real problems in Eliot's social criticism. But for all the reasonableness of his approach, the picture he gives of Eliot is seriously misleading; even the yoking together of Pound and Eliot provides an inappropriate context. Some of his criticism rings true, but one learns less from Chace than from Margolis, Kojecký, or Kirk.

As an expression of Eliot's social criticism, the *Criterion* probably has to be judged a failure. That seems to have been Eliot's judgment, and it is the verdict offered by both John Peter ("Eliot and the *Criterion*," 1970) and Denis Donoghue ("Eliot and the *Criterion*," 1977). Both Peter and Donoghue feel the journal declined in its later years. Donoghue compares it unfavorably with Leavis's *Scrutiny* in consistency of purpose, and Peter points to its odd mixture of contributors in the thirties, very conservative clerical authors being found side by side with young Marxist authors like Auden and Spender. We might also think that *Criterion*'s openness to the latter says something about the relative place of art and ideology in Eliot's values.

Influences at Work

The sources of Eliot's social philosophy have been much less intensively sought than those of his poetry and criticism, no doubt because his social philosophy is considerably less important. Some of the sources are probably the same. Richard Wasson says that "many of Eliot's arguments against the humanists of his generation were adapted from arguments used by Bradley and other idealists against the humanistic pragmatism of William James, John Dewey, and their English ally F. C. S. Schiller" ("T. S. Eliot's Antihumanism and Antipragmatism," *Texas Studies in Literature and Language*, 1968, p. 445). Wasson demonstrates more similarity than adaptation, but his article suggests the congruence of Eliot's views on literature and society.

Whatever Eliot's difference with the New Humanists, he was obviously, and acknowledgedly, influenced by Irving Babbitt, and there is room for further study of this debt. George R. Elliott's "T. S. Eliot and Irving Babbitt" (1936) cites some cases but is mainly a defense of Babbitt against Eliot's later criticism of him. Kenneth Burke includes Eliot among "The Allies of Humanism Abroad" in Burke's contribution to a collective *Critique of Humanism* (1930), but he, too, is mainly concerned with the matters which separate Eliot from the American humanists. More study is needed, along the lines indicated in the books by Margolis and Kirk. The lack of such detailed studies is, in this case, probably due less to lack of interest in Eliot's intellectual origins than to the general neglect of Babbitt and the New Humanists.

There is, however, an important account of the influence of Hulme in Ronald Schuchard's "Eliot and Hulme in 1916: Toward a Revaluation of Eliot's Critical and Spiritual Development" (1973). Most accounts of Eliot's development assume that he was unacquainted with Hulme's prose until the appearance of the latter's posthumous *Speculations* in 1924. Schuchard believes that Hulme was an important figure as early as 1916 and that Eliot's "classicism even in 1916 was as much moral and 'religious' in its formulation and attitude as it was esthetic and literary" (p. 1084).

Schuchard thinks it possible that Eliot met Hulme between the spring of 1915, when Hulme was wounded and returned to England, and March 1916, when Hulme returned to the front. Hulme's essays were being published in *New Age*, along with essays by Pound which Eliot is known to have read there. Either Pound or A. R. Orage, the *New Age* editor, could have introduced the two, as could Bertrand Russell, Eliot's landlord at the time, who was then engaged in a lively controversy with Hulme over Bergson and other matters. Though Eliot has implied that he never met Hulme, Schuchard makes such a meeting seem almost probable.

Schuchard's case for Eliot's having read Hulme's essays by 1916 is even stronger. His clinching evidence is the nature of the syllabi for Eliot's Oxford extension courses, especially on contemporary French literature and thought. Schuchard describes this course as synthesizing ideas from Babbitt, Maurras, and Hulme. The evidence for Hulme's impact is threefold: Eliot's use of a Hulme translation of a Bergson text, his use of a Hulme translation (with an argumentative preface) of Sorel's *Reflections on Violence*, and the probable source in Hulme of Eliot's statement that "the classicist point of view has been defined as essentially a belief in Original Sin—the necessity for austere discipline," where the use of "Original Sin" strongly suggests Hulme. None of these is completely decisive. Eliot had presumably read Bergson and Sorel in French and may not have examined the translations, and a belief in original sin is still widespread. Moreover, some of the other doctrines for which Schuchard cites parallels in Hulme are also to be found in Babbitt, an earlier influence and one which Eliot freely acknowledged. But the probability that Eliot knew Hulme's work is established.

For the years between 1916 and 1924, Schuchard makes use of some Eliot references to Hulme's verse, a tiny body of work (five poems) even by Eliot's nonprolific standards; his knowledge of these poems (perhaps through Pound) may well imply a larger acquaintance with Hulme's work. Finally, there are many later references to Hulme and Hulme's theories, though these come after the publication of *Speculations* and Eliot's open conversion to principles much like Hulme's. Schuchard's summary, that "by 1916 Eliot knew Hulme's ideas well, and in them he found the keystone for his classicism" (1973, p. 1091), goes too far, even if we take the metaphor to make Hulme's thought the final stone in an arch formed by Babbitt's Classicism and Maurras' royalist Catholicism. Schuchard has shown that Eliot probably had some acquaintance with Hulme's work by 1916, but the evidence does not tell us how deep and enthusiastic his acquaintance was, and there are few signs of real influence. His tentative suggestion that Eliot may have concealed his debt to Hulme seems odd when we remember how openly he acknowledged his debts to Babbitt and Maurras, and Schuchard's view that Eliot concealed the moral and religious thrust of his Classicism seems unnecessary. Schuchard's more general point, that Eliot's Classicism was more moral and religious in tone than some of the remarks in *The Sacred Wood* encouraged readers to believe, is certainly valid, and critics (like Chace) who assume that his early interests were purely literary need to revise their ideas about Eliot's development. Whether Schuchard's claims for Hulme's role in that development hold up must await further biographical information, but he has shown that that role did not begin in 1924.

Schuchard has made it possible to explore Eliot's early development further by publishing Eliot's syllabi for his extension lecturing in a two-part article for the *Review of English Studies* ("T. S. Eliot as an Extension Lecturer, 1916–1919," 1974). The most thoroughly annotated syllabus is the first, for Eliot's 1916 course on modern French literature. The six lectures take up such provocative topics (for the Eliot scholar) as "The Origins: What Is Romanticism?" "The Reaction against Romanticism," "Royalism and Socialism," and "The Return to the Catholic Church." Eliot's annotations are often intriguing, as when he remarks of the royalists, Pierre Lassere and Maurras, that their views were fundamentally "sound, but marked by extreme violence and intolerance" (p. 166). The reading list is also of interest. About the same time, Eliot was also lecturing from another syllabus on modern English literature, the composition of which shows his thorough knowledge of Victorian literature. Other syllabi reprinted by Schuchard take us up to 1919 and cover Victorian literature, modern English literature (second year's work), and Elizabethan literature. As Schuchard points out, the course on the Elizabethans was especially important for Eliot's development as a poet and critic. Schuchard also reprints some passages from Eliot's official reports on his lecturing and provides useful background. All future accounts of Eliot's intellectual development will have to take account of these syllabi.

On Maurras' influence on Eliot, the best study to date is James Torrens' "Charles Maurras and Eliot's 'New Life' " (1974), though Torrens devotes most of his attention to Maurras' influence on Eliot's reading of Dante and to the influence of Dante on *Ash Wednesday*, an influence that does not seem especially relevant to the rest of his essay. Torrens covers Eliot's various tributes to Maurras as a writer and as an influence on himself. In Eliot's defense of Maurras in the *Criterion*, Torrens notes that Eliot speaks of having been reading Maurras for eighteen years, which would place Eliot's first reading of Maurras in his year in Paris as a philosophy student (1910–11). Torrens calls attention to the frequent description of the program of Maurras' Action Française as *classique*, *catholique*, and *monarchique*. And he suggests that Eliot's decision to translate and publish (in the *Criterion* in 1928) Maurras' thirty-year-old essay, "Prologue to an Essay on Criticism," may imply that the views expressed therein were especially close to Eliot's own. Torrens recognizes that Maurras was more extreme in his political views and cruder in his literary sensibility than Eliot, but he argues that the lesser man served Eliot as a kind of Virgil, guiding him toward a world of religious feeling that Maurras could not enter. We may hope that publication of Eliot's letters will shed further light on his response to Maurras. In any case, further work is needed on this relationship.

The religious thrust of Eliot's social criticism naturally raises the question of the influence of the Scholastic tradition, an issue raised but hardly settled in Hugh Bredin's "T. S. Eliot and Thomistic Scholasticism" (1972). Bredin begins with the assertion that "Eliot was proficient enough to write a number of book reviews on the subject in the *Times Literary Supplement* in the later nineteen-twenties" (p. 299); but how thorough a knowledge this presupposes depends on one's estimate of the usual competence of *TLS* reviewers in such areas.

Bredin's calling attention to these reviews is useful, but he is otherwise unconcerned with providing external evidence and content to demonstrate affinities between Eliot's views and Thomism. Bredin displays, in other words, the usual failings of the history-of-ideas approach.

Bredin suggests that Maritain was a mediating influence, perhaps because Maritain's *Three Reformers* was one of the books reviewed, but he does not note that Eliot had a long familiarity with Maritain's work. His study was probably written too early to take advantage of Kojecký's report that Maritain's *True Humanism* was the subject of a Moot discussion attended by Eliot in January 1939. Other references to Maritain are noted in Rebeccah Kinnamon's "Eliot's 'Ash Wednesday' and Maritain's Ideal for Poetry" (1973), though the connection between Maritain and *Ash Wednesday* that she suggests remains rather speculative.

Eliot's High Church Anglicanism was bound to find much to sympathize with in the writings of English Roman Catholic thinkers as well. David J. DeLaura has noted that Newman's analysis of society "played an influential role in T. S. Eliot's social writings in the 1930's and 1940's—a connection still ignored by readers of Eliot who know little of his extensive reading in the Victorian prose writers," though DeLaura, intent on other matters, does not pause to argue this case ("Arnold, Newman, and T. S. Eliot: A Note on the Disappearance of God," 1977). Despite substantial agreement on many matters, Eliot never was close to his contemporary, Chesterton. Russell Kirk explains why this is surprising ("Chesterton and T. S. Eliot," 1976). It would seem to be another case in which Eliot's literary values and allegiances proved more important than his religious and political sympathies.

The Social Critic as Reactionary

Given Eliot's conscious opposition to the dominant opinions of his age, many of those who have responded to his social criticism seem to take him as a simple reactionary, rather along the lines followed by Chace. Most of these critiques fail to understand the nuances of his position, and too many substitute counterassertions for rational argument. This is true even of one of the best statements of the essential liberal objections to Eliot's views, that given by Harold Laski in his *Faith, Reason and Civilization* (1944). Laski complains that Eliot's aristocratic Christianity diagnoses spiritual ills only to deny that the mass of men can ever be cured and saved, that Eliot's poetry and prose show his insistence on cutting himself off from his fellow men, that Eliot's ideal of the church neglects the corruption of that ideal, demonstrated by the historical record of Christendom. He puts this case very well, but it is based entirely on emotional assumptions—that there ought to be salvation for all, that poetry ought to be in contact with the people, that the church in power ought to be less corrupt than other human institutions. Less naive is Laski's objection that the kind of mild authoritarianism Eliot seems to recommend is not a real option, the true options of our time being democracy and totalitarianism. Even this objection would have more point if Eliot were as authoritarian as Laski thinks he is.

At their simplest, some critics take the position that Eliot must be wrong in criticizing liberalism, because everyone knows that liberalism is a "good thing," an argument one may agree with but not respect. Arthur T. Quiller-Couch, in *The Poet as Citizen* (1934), says that liberalism is the true source of the tradition Eliot praises, a response which comes to little more than playing with words. D. W. Harding says that the liberal spirit is that of the exploring child, while Eliot's Christianity is that of a fearful, defensive child, a metaphor scarcely worthy of *Scrutiny's* reputation for rationality ("Christian or Liberal?" 1939). Like Laski, Harding rejects Eliot's ideal Christian state on the grounds that Christian societies in the past have been repressive, committing the very error he condemns Eliot for, that of attributing to the dominant ideology of an age (Christianity for the Middle Ages, liberalism for today) all the sins and inadequacies of that age. Eliot is well aware that no society perfectly embodies its ideals. One might carry on an argument about the kinds of imperfections most likely to result in societies animated by different ideals, but few Eliot critics reach this level.

Sidney Hook ("The Dilemma of T. S. Eliot," 1945) also proposes to refute Eliot by simple reference to assumptions Eliot does not share. Discussing a preliminary magazine version of *Notes*, Hook writes that Elliot's supernatural faith "provides no principle of direction for the intelligent control of social change" (p. 69). Since distrust of all plans for rationalized social change is at the heart of Eliot's disagreements with Mannheim, one can hardly overturn Eliot's arguments by showing that they do not lead to a goal he rejects. The only alternative Hook can envisage is an authoritarian church watching over the culture and guiding the process of change—clearly not what Eliot had in mind.

John R. Harrison's *The Reactionaries* (1967) sets out to explain "a strange and disturbing phenomenon" (p. 1), the antidemocratic views of some of this century's greatest writers. His examples—Yeats, Wyndham Lewis, Pound, Eliot, and Lawrence—are a rather conventional set, although this grouping has the effect of placing Eliot with writers whose politics he did not share. Harrison's efforts to explain his subjects' views suffer from a radical failure in empathy, an inability to understand how anyone could have reservations about something as obviously good as democracy. One might well apply to him his own words on Eliot: "confused by seeing the situation but . . . unable to accept it" (p. 207). Eliot's admittedly elusive position seems particularly hard for Harrison to grasp; his chapter on Eliot is much the shortest and probably the least persuasive. Part of the problem is that Harrison does not seem to know Eliot's work very well. Most of his discussion is based on *Notes towards the Definition of Culture*, and although he quotes from two *Criterion* editorials, his summary of their general drift is less than accurate.

It is not true that Eliot "often expressed a preference for some kind of strict, authoritarian rule," and to say that he "did not openly sympathize with fascism to the extent that Lewis and Pound did" is to imply a covert sympathy that is not supported by the evidence (p. 148). Harrison suggests that imitating the literary techniques of the past led Eliot to adopt the outworn views expressed in those techniques; he would seem to be giving credit for a greater impact on ideas than literary forms are normally thought to possess. Baffled to the end, Harrison must concede that Eliot's views are legitimate in a sense: "if a man believes that great literature must continue to be written, whatever the cost to society, he will not feel that the position needs any other defense" (p. 160). This concession seems hardly necessary, since the position described is not Eliot's.

For Kathleen Nott, a strange and disturbing phenomenon is Eliot's rejection of what she takes to be the scientific world view. In *The Emperor's Clothes* (1954), she pictures Eliot as the leading representative of a dreadful tendency she calls "neo-scholasticism," a term she uses without any reference to genuine Scholasticism or to modern neo-Scholastic thought. Her "neo-scholastics" are, therefore, a rather motley crew. After Eliot, her chief examples are T. E. Hulme, Basil Willey, C. S. Lewis, and Dorothy Sayers (the latter as a lay theologian rather than as a detective-story writer). It is not surprising that Eliot seems to her the most important of these thinkers; and she returns to him again and again. She professes to be an admirer of Eliot's poetry and wholeheartedly agrees with his diagnosis of a seventeenth-century dissociation of sensibility. But for Nott, the "neo-scholastics" have sought to heal the split between thought and emotion by abandoning thought. Science, she believes, is man's only sure way of attaining knowledge, and is linked to liberal humanism by a common commitment to free inquiry.

Eliot, in fact, does not say much about science, so that Nott is, in effect, complaining about his sins of omission rather than sins of commission. His premises seem to her antiscientific, but since he rarely spells them out in detail, she is reduced to a form of shadow boxing. She justifies her discussion of lay theologians, like Lewis and Sayers, by adducing their willingness to spell out matters that Eliot is too prudent to discuss. One of the functions of "neo-scholastic" as a term is to allow Nott to blame careful thinkers like Eliot for the excesses of sloppy thinkers like Lewis and Sayers.

As one who is essentially a liberal humanist, it is natural for Nott to see all issues as ultimately to be decided by rational argument, but Eliot is intellectually consistent in seeing some issues as ultimately matters of faith. Eliot's reluctance to be more exact about the content of his faith is very "Anglican" of him, but here, at least, one may sympathize with Nott's frustration. She particularly objects to the doctrine of original sin; she seems to believe that science has disproved it, that it cuts us off from true morality, and even that it is finally opposed to the spirit of Christ. One may well disagree with her on all these points, may think that original sin is one of the more reasonable religious dogmas, and may feel that it is not fair for her to define this doctrine, for Eliot's benefit, in ways which suit *her* argument. Even so, it must be admitted that Eliot's failure to give a coherent account of what original sin means to him—other than very real and terrible—leaves him open to such criticism.

Nott dislikes what she can infer of Eliot's orthodoxy from his prose. She believes he advocates a rule-bound society, which could be established and maintained only by force. One feels that her dislike for his general stance has led her to misread his work. In her contributions to the Snow–Leavis "two cultures" controversy ("Whose Culture?" 1962) and to a recent Eliot symposium ("Ideology and Poetry," 1974), Nott repeats many of the same charges against Eliot, though with less emphasis on his rejection of science. The 1974 article, in particular, makes it clear that her defense of "science" against Eliot is really a way of attacking the assumed conservatism of Eliot's theology.

Nott's complaints against the antiscientific views of Eliot and the "neo-scholastics" echo complaints made much earlier by Max Eastman in *The Literary Mind* (1931). Writing in the midst of an ongoing controversy, Eastman knew the participants and their works better than Nott seems to, and he accordingly assigns Eliot a less important role than she does. Eliot appears as one leader among the "neo-classicists," who quarrel with the pure humanists only over the best way to oppose the march of science and the scientific attitude. He also appears as one who has led the retreat of literature into unintelligibility, a point which Eastman is prepared to argue at greater length than most who make this charge.

The inevitable "march of science," of course, is only one brand of historical inevitability, and with less general appeal in this century than the Marxist brand, which includes it. The contrast between Eliot the revolutionary poet and Eliot the reactionary critic has posed special problems for Marxist critics, many of whom have felt constrained to admire Eliot's early poetry. One common solution from the beginning has been to treat Eliot as a good man gone astray. The view is well put in an essay by Philip Rahv, written in the days before he became a pillar of the establishment left ("T. S. Eliot," 1932). In this essay, the Eliot of the first volume is a social rebel, exposing the "smug bourgeoisie of New England" (p. 18). But having made the positive step of rejecting the past, writes Rahv, Eliot relapsed into his ancestral reaction, as marked by the mysticism and obscurity of *The Waste Land*. His subsequent work cannot be good, since one cannot write good poetry based on reactionary assumptions in a revolutionary age. This is the same line of reasoning which makes it difficult for good Alabama Baptists to understand how Notre Dame can have such a good football team.

Even critics who are unwilling to dismiss *The Waste Land*

and later poems sometimes feel that the social implications of Eliot's espousal of tradition mean that his literary criticism must be dismissed along with his social criticism. In Alick West's *Crisis and Criticism* (1937), Eliot's appeal to literary tradition is presented as an attempt to shore up a crumbling bourgeois order. The objections D. S. Savage raises to Eliot's "orthodoxy" (*The Personal Principle*, 1944) are also based on an unduly authoritarian interpretation of what Eliot means by "tradition"—and, for that matter, what Eliot means by Christianity. Stanley Edgar Hyman's exploration of Eliot's use of "tradition" (in *The Armed Vision*, 1948) also produces an unduly static account, neglecting the role assigned the "individual talent."

Critics who are unwilling to abandon quite so much of Eliot's literary criticism are faced with the problem of explaining why Eliot can be both a perceptive literary critic and a reactionary social critic. S. J. Wyndham tries to answer this question in his "Outline for a Critical Approach to T. S. Eliot as Critic" (1948): Eliot is retrogressive in thought but retains some progressive features. His *mode* of thought is, in fact, progressive, although progressive elements survive in the *content* of his thought only as evasions and pretenses to fair-mindedness. Eliot is a medievalist at heart, but his methods are part of the revolution that began in the Renaissance with the origins of bourgeois society. Eliot's call for a literary criticism which deals with literature as literature, and not something else, is part of a larger process of specialization of intellectual labor. This is, in part, a source of strength, since it allows Eliot to apprehend literature better; it is also a weakness, for Eliot does not proceed from this understanding to reconnect literature with the rest of life. Although phrased as a complaint against Eliot, this sounds much like Eliot's suggestion that pure literary criticism needs to be completed by religious and moral criticism. Failing to make the necessary connections, says Wyndham, Eliot reduces evaluation to taste and thus to irrationalism. The resulting "open-mindedness" allows Eliot to express covert sympathy with reactionary political developments while pretending to remain above the battle.

The idea that Eliot's conservative but highly qualified statements are somehow meant to conceal even more shamefully reactionary views is widely shared among his critics to the left. In contrast to this are the comments of Brian Simon in his review of *Notes towards the Definition of Culture* ("The Defense of Culture," *Communist Review*, 1949). Concentrating on Eliot's views on education, Simon welcomes the book because it seems relatively open about the connections between a class-structured society and the defense of privilege in current educational practices. Eliot is then faulted for an Idealist notion of culture—that is, one which divorces culture from everyday life and its material base—which permits Eliot to see culture as the creation of a gifted few, ignoring the historical reasons (economic and social) why culture, in this sense, has been an elite preserve in the past. Eliot is seen as accepting Mannheim's analysis of the present disintegration of culture, differing only in the kinds of reactionary solutions advocated. This seems fair enough. Simon himself sees, instead, "the birth-pangs of the new society" and rejects Eliot's views as "the apotheosis of bourgeois individualism" (p. 768). Ignoring Simon's proclamation of the "greening" of Britain, one would think that bourgeois individualism would be better represented by the achievement elites of Mannheim. Simon seems too conscious of the points on which Mannheim and Eliot agree to give full value to their differences.

The conservative character of Eliot's social criticism made some find his great influence particularly disturbing. Rossell Hope Robbins responded by attacking "The T. S. Eliot Myth" in an article for *Science and Society* (1950); his fuller version of the same argument appeared the next year as a book (*The T. S. Eliot Myth*, 1951). Robbins describes Eliot's high critical standing as a result of a half-unconscious conspiracy to exalt a writer whose political views gave comfort to the Right. His early criticism aroused interest because few other critics were writing worthwhile criticism at the time, and his early verse won the allegiance of poets because of his technical innovations. Eliot's subsequent reputation has been protected by the general lack of acquaintance with his later poetry and prose, the most influential anthologies containing mostly early works. Robbins brings in the villainous influence of the Southern Agrarians on American New Criticism, arguing that their insistence on the autonomy of literature is a cover for a consistently conservative bias.

Robbins' attack takes much the same position as Rahv's, two decades earlier: Eliot is a good poet gone wrong. His conspiracy theory is a result of his need to explain why Eliot's inevitable advance into creative sterility has not been more widely recognized. Although Eliot saw *Four Quartets* as somewhat more accessible than *The Waste Land*, Robbins sees Eliot as becoming more and more obscure, partly as a result of writing for a coterie familiar with the increasingly arcane mystical sources he used and partly from a willful cult of mysticism and irrationality. The elitism and obscurity of Eliot's verse make him a natural ally for the forces of obscurantist reaction. Even the plays, the most public form Eliot has adopted, are intentionally obscure, with key points evaded by having characters proclaim that they are beyond understanding or (in *The Cocktail Party*) by having telephones and doorbells ring to interrupt much-needed explanations.

Although some of Robbins' animadversions on Eliot's dramaturgy are valid, his view of Eliot as intentionally obscure is certainly overdrawn. In the process, he provides a useful suggestion that Charles Williams' *Descent into Hell* is a source for *The Cocktail Party*, a suggestion he later published as a separate note ("A Possible Analogue for *The Cocktail Party*," 1953). His reading of Eliot's prose is distinguished by the same mixture of acute criticisms and rhetorical overkill. Charity is not the most conspicuous Christian virtue in Eliot's work, but accusing him of "an obvious hatred of people" (1951, p. 23) will not wash. Robbins also uses words like "fascism" too freely and too loosely; but he makes an intelligent case that Eliot does not meet his own tests for greatness as a poet. Since Eliot's admirers often suggest that his social criticism, whatever its faults as constructive thought, is useful as a negative critique of conventional liberalism, they should be grateful to Robbins for his negative critique of much of the conventional praise of Eliot.

Russell Ames goes even further than Robbins. His essay "Decadence in the Art of T. S. Eliot" (1952) takes as its thesis "that T. S. Eliot is even less a poet than his severest critics have said he is, that all of us who have *believed* in Mr. Eliot have been the victims of a general American decadence" (p. 193). The general decay referred to is that of capitalism; and Eliot is an example of it because he represents a concomitant decay in artistic forms and techniques. Ames does not maintain that "reactionary" artists are inevitably bad artists, but he regards all Modernism, whether that of Eliot or Schonberg or Picasso, as flawed by fragmentation of form and limitation of reality. Because Eliot's verse offers only atypical individuals like Prufrock, it is not even a good reflection of its decadent society. Much of Ames' article, in fact, is taken up with an attempt to establish that Marvell's "To His Coy Mistress" is a better poem than Eliot's "The Love Song of J. Alfred Prufrock," but the comparison establishes only that Ames likes the Marvell poem better and understands the Eliot poem less. The essay as a whole may well be accurate in its thesis about the social base of Modernism, but it is spoiled by Ames' inability to understand those whom he attacks or to articulate clearly his own rather bourgeois aesthetic prejudices.

Ames seems rather reasonable, however, when one compares him with a critic like Pauline Kogan. Her essay, "The Bourgeois Line on Culture and Anarchy in Matthew Arnold and T. S. Eliot" (1971), is of interest only because it is one of the few attempts to deal with Eliot from an avowedly Maoist position, although it might also amuse those who collect choice phrases of mindless Marxism. Kogan says that Eliot's "concern for the growth and for the survival of culture is in fact a concern for the growth and survival of an imperialist class" (pp. 9–10). It takes little perception to see that Eliot's defense of culture is the defense of a class society, for he says as much himself; unsupported epithets like "imperialist" do not add much. Kogan's assimilation of Arnold and Eliot to Hitler suggests a Manichean view of cultural history more than an intelligently Marxist one. Her apparent inability to distinguish between Arnold's and Eliot's views is mischievous even from a revolutionary standpoint. That Arnold and Eliot are not on the side of the triumphant march of Maoist thought is so obvious as to require no waste of proletarian paper. One's task surely should be to understand one's enemy, and one might well begin by noting the differences between Arnold's liberalism and Eliot's orthodoxy.

The Cultural Critic

The paradox of Eliot's conservatism is not that he is also a good poet but that he was a revolutionary poet, whose claims to speak for the poetic tradition were violently resisted by its self-appointed guardians. One would think that his role in modern poetry would give pause to those who read his social criticism as a call for a static society. Although one might expect that the most perceptive critiques of Eliot would come from those who share at least some of his conservative assumptions, a number of readers whose sympathies are much further left have more or less endorsed his critique of modern society.

A. L. Morton's "T. S. Eliot—A Personal View" (1966) recalls what "a liberating experience" (p. 286) *The Waste Land* was for young intellectuals of the first generation to encounter it. One of a number of young Marxists who published in the *Criterion,* Morton suggests that Eliot took Marxism seriously as an alternative analysis of society in a way he never took liberalism, and he gives Eliot credit for continuing social concern and poetic integrity as well as for standing "high among those men of our time who once helped me to a better understanding of the contemporary world" (p. 291). Even in Eliot's later prose, Morton finds some observations worthy of praise. Morton's Eliot sensed something terribly wrong with modern society but fell back on old solutions in an honorable but tragic defeat.

The outline of an intelligent Marxist response to Eliot and his social criticism appeared as early as V. F. Calverton's review of *After Strange Gods:* "T. S. Eliot: Inverted Marxism" (1934). For Calverton, Eliot's declaration of faith in the *Lancelot Andrewes* preface "sounded the death knell of the 19th century individualistic tradition" (p. 372). One cannot help remembering that Eliot opposed Romantic individualism long before he turned to Anglo-Catholicism, and that he traced its roots further back than Calverton's nineteenth century. Still, Calverton's basic point is worth considering: Eliot's espousal of tradition can be seen as a mirror image of the Marxist commitment to the future, with both rejecting liberal individualism and its social results. Both, as Calverton observes, "exalt orthodoxy" (p. 373). Logically, then, Calverton accepts Eliot's view that the decay of Protestantism is relevant to the current state of literature, for Calverton takes Protestantism to be the spiritual embodiment of a no longer viable individualism. For Eliot's conclusions and recommendations, Calverton has no use, but he can agree with him on the diagnosis.

Calverton's views are echoed in R. Hinton Thomas's "Culture and T. S. Eliot" (1951). Thomas explicitly reproves Robbins for underestimating Eliot's power as a poet, but he agrees that Eliot's politics are reactionary. Like Calverton, Thomas sees Eliot as one who saw through the extremes of bourgeois individualism but who chose a conservative, rather than a progressive, response. Eliot's "tradition" is timeless and thus ahistorical; the blending of past and present in *The Waste Land* and the search for timeless moments in the *Four Quartets* are part of the same attempt to escape from time. To escape from time, Thomas argues, is to escape from history and from the changes which destroy tradition. The ideas of the tradition are thus cut adrift from their material base; so Eliot must reject economics, along with all else that operates through time and history, such as science and secularism. Thomas sees the rejection of history as arising from Eliot's resistance to the new society which history is calling into being. In effect, Eliot enrolled in the counterrevolution.

The alternatives advocated in *Notes towards the Definition of Culture* seem to Thomas quite consistent with Eliot's earlier admiration for the Action Française. In each case, the society urged is a restricted democracy, with a hereditary class structure superimposed. Thomas argues that Eliot's ideal culture requires the maintenance of an exploited class, and that it bears the marks of having been conceived in a society dependent upon colonialism. His argument for the latter point is ingenious, though unconvincing. As a social critic, Eliot has spoken for his class, gaining acceptance for the notion that culture must be a minority product, and contributing to the process of mystification which helps prevent accurate social and political analysis. The assumption is that religious convictions can be explained by social forces and that writers are driven to speak for class interests—the common modern error being to apply to individual cases generalizations that are valid (at best) for large groups. Nevertheless, Thomas's willingness to put analysis ahead of rhetoric makes his essay one of the most stimulating Marxist appraisals of Eliot.

Thomas's general position is close to that of one of Britain's least orthodox socialists, George Orwell, whose comments on Eliot are scattered through the four volumes of *The Collected Essays, Journalism, and Letters of George Orwell* (1968). Wayne Warncke has surveyed Orwell's comments in a brief essay ("George Orwell on T. S. Eliot," 1972), and Brian Matthews has provided a fuller treatment (" 'Fearful Despair' and a 'Frigid, Snooty Muse': George Orwell's Involvement with T. S. Eliot, 1930–1950," 1977). Both find Orwell surprisingly sympathetic to Eliot, though obviously opposed to Eliot's political opinions. Orwell does not suggest that Eliot would have been a better poet had he held other opinions. He even suggests that Eliot might have been better off had he made fewer intellectual concessions to modern liberalism—better "feudalism," says Orwell, than "conservatism of the half-hearted modern kind" (1968, II, 242). This comment reminds one of Eliot's admission, in the preface to *Lancelot Andrewes*, that "royalism" might easily lend itself to "what is almost worse than clap-trap, I mean temperate conservatism." In a 1948 review of *Notes towards the Definition of Culture*, Orwell suggests that Eliot's defense of a class structure is undermined by his willingness to assume that there must simultaneously be elites which place the right men in the right jobs. Orwell also suggests that Eliot misses a strong argument against a meritocratic society: elites, being adoptive, can ossify by replacing themselves by men who resemble them and so are less dynamic than classes. Orwell believes, though, that Eliot is too pessimistic about the state of society; the condition of the common man, at least, is improving. As on so many topics, Orwell's uncommon common sense about Eliot is refreshing.

For many liberal and Marxist critics, Eliot's theological commitments vitiate his later poetry and render his social criticism irrelevant. But even those who share his faith have not always been entirely happy with his social criticsm. On the Protestant side, one can cite Reinhold Neibuhr, the prominent neo-orthodox theologian. Neibuhr gave *The Idea of a Christian Society* a respectful review ("Can Church Restrain State?" 1940). Like some Marxists, he agrees with Eliot's analysis of the problems of liberalism, and, going further, he agrees that its values are called into question by a growing secularism which divorces those values from the Christianity which is their only real ground. But he is uneasy with the constructive side of Eliot's book. Neibuhr concedes that Protestantism has been too critical in its relationship with the state, and even that "its lack of constructive power hastened the anarchy of modern life" (p. 27). But he fears that an established church may lead to pretension and corruption, losing contact with the valuable side of the critical spirit. This is well said, but it seems to ignore Eliot's willingness to retain the critical forces of humanism and liberalism in a Christian state. Eliot's ideal, in other words, is the elusive "middle way" that Anglicanism claims to follow between Protestantism and Catholicism.

D. L. Munby's *The Idea of a Secular Society* (1963) is a critique of Eliot from a perspective formed by the conservatism of Coleridge and, even more, the Anglicanism of F. D. Maurice. Munby believes that Christians must accept the pluralism of a secular society. On a practical level, he argues that modern society is by no means as badly off as critics like Eliot suggest;

on a theoretical level, he maintains that "such a society is framed more nearly in accordance with the Will of God as we can see it in Scripture, in the Incarnation, and in the way God actually treats men" (p. 34) than those societies which attempt to impose Christian norms on the mass of men. Munby is far more sanguine than Eliot about the effects and possibilities of the specialization inherent in a modern industrial order, insofar as that specialization is applied in economic, political, and intellectual matters. The specialized church, on the other hand, strikes Munby as a positive barrier to true Christianity. Much of what Munby says has only an incidental relation to Eliot; Eliot serves in this book as an occasion for Munby's expression of his own views. Munby thinks it "remarkable . . . how *much* agreement there is between the Christian view and the humanism of the West, in its modern secular form" (p. 64). We may remember that Eliot's essay "The Humanism of Irving Babbitt" describes secular humanism as a watered-down version of nineteenth-century liberal Christian thought; Munby's book shows that particular Christian tradition is still alive.

Somewhat more affirmative is Christopher Dawson's review of *Notes towards the Definition of Culture* ("Mr. T. S. Eliot on the Meaning of Culture," 1949). Dawson, an important Roman Catholic historian and apologist, was a fellow member of the Moot and therefore familiar with many of Eliot's arguments. In his review, he says Eliot is more in the tradition of Arnold than Eliot admits, and he applauds Eliot's effort to retrieve the word "culture" from the politicians and to call attention to those elements of culture—family, region, and religion—too often ignored by political ideologues. He scolds Eliot mildly for complaining that Mannheim's work envisaged an atomistic society. Dawson argues that Mannheim was simply descriptive, since we already have an atomistic society. Where he really parts company with Eliot is on the importance of transcendence. Dawson sees no salvation in class structures, and he thinks that Eliot fails to separate religion and culture clearly enough. Cultures, he says, we are born into; religion, to be sincere, requires an act of faith. One suspects that the problem, again, is Eliot's Anglicanism. The poems suggest that Eliot's personal religion is transcendent and mystical, but the prose suggests that his concept of the church is closely linked to particular cultures. Eliot's notion of regional diversity implies, as well, a universal church, embodied in differing national churches. Since both regret the secularist neglect of the religious dimension of culture, Dawson's review closes with praise for Eliot as a poet and social critic.

Although some of the best criticism of Eliot has been written by sympathetic figures like Dawson and Kirk, some of his other sympathizers have the effect of helping one understand Eliot's severest critics. Nott's denunciation of Eliot's alleged antiscientific views seems more reasonable when one reads Hyatt H. Waggoner's praise of Eliot for holding the same views, though what Nott calls "science" Waggoner calls "scientism" or "naturalism," loaded terms on the opposite side. Waggoner's praise is found in his chapter on Eliot in *The Heel of Elohim* (1950), which incorporates similar material in his earlier article, "T. S. Eliot and the Hollow Men" (1943). Waggoner sees Eliot's rejection of naturalism in ethics as the result of the influence of Babbitt, Bradley, Bergson, and Hulme. Evidently unacquainted with Eliot's dissertation, Waggoner discusses only the Bradley essay in *For Lancelot Andrewes*.

Waggoner tells us that Eliot condemns scientism for believing that mere facts can bring salvation, for robbing life of mystery, and for leading us away from faith into a shallow naturalism. The position is consistent with Eliot's beliefs, but it exists mainly as an intellectual construct of Waggoner's. At the same time, Waggoner praises Eliot for reflecting his age by using science in his poems, noting the presence of "such symbols as the nerves, the surgeon, astronomical conceptions of space, the rituals studied by anthropology, the earlier forms of life studied by historical geology and biology, details of physiology, dreams and hallucinations of a Freudian cast" (1950, p. 88)—a miscellaneous list, which does, perhaps, demonstrate that Eliot knows that science is around. Waggoner also insists that the doctrine of an "objective correlative" is somehow related "to the fact that ours is a scientific age" (p. 88). Waggoner's aim—a legitimate one—is to demonstrate that Eliot's Christianity is not antediluvian and has a place (perhaps a subordinate one) for science. One gets the feeling, though, that keeping science in its proper place is more important to Waggoner than to Eliot.

Another example is D. E. S. Maxwell's generally excellent introduction, *The Poetry of T. S. Eliot* (1952). Maxwell stresses Eliot's kinship with the Augustan Classicists, and he seems to relish the conservative cast of Eliot's thought. He responds to Eliot's critics by arguing that "extremist humanist philosophy looks forward to a new art which will speak with the voice of the state. Less extreme forms . . . prepare the way for this final prostitution" (p. 135). One cannot imagine Eliot, the student of Babbitt, using language so violent to condemn views in which he found much to admire.

G. H. Bantock is also a very sympathetic critic of Eliot's social criticism. Bantock's review of Kojecký's book, "T. S. Eliot's View of Society" (1973), faults Kojecký for failing to place Eliot's work in the context of the important political and social movements of the time—a fair criticism, which unfortunately applies also to Bantock's observations (in that review and elsewhere). Soon after the publication of *Notes towards the Definition of Culture*, Bantock responded in *Scrutiny* by stressing Eliot's educational philosophy ("Mr. Eliot and Education," 1949), dissenting mildly from some of Eliot's propositions. Twenty years later, Bantock produced a very short monograph, *T. S. Eliot and Education* (1969). His treatment of Eliot in this book is almost excessively respectful; for example, he twice quotes a rather fatuous remark to him by Eliot: "You can have equality; you can have culture; but you cannot have both"—commenting, with apparent approval, that such remarks are "unpalatable" to our age (1969, pp. 70, 87). Much of his monograph is taken up with extraneous matters. He begins, for example, with a brief account of Eliot's life and a somewhat longer account of Eliot as a poet. This padding is only partially justified by Bantock's effort to present Eliot as a poet with an unusually penetrating vision of society, making Eliot's poetry part of his credentials as a social critic.

Bantock (1969) also devotes as much attention to Eliot's social criticism in general as to his specific comments on education. His version of Eliot is perhaps less one sided than the Eliot perceived by critics from the Left, for Bantock's Eliot is not a simple reactionary but one who would shore up conservative forces in order to preserve a creative tension between the forces making for change in society and those which preserve continuity. If the value of conservative forces is stressed in Eliot's prose, it is because such values have too often been lost sight of by contemporary liberalism. Bantock performs a valuable service in calling attention to the balancing elements in Eliot's thought, though one cannot forget that the place assigned liberalism is subordinate and largely negative. Bantock sometimes accepts without criticism Eliot's efforts to balance what are really unequal alternatives, as when he praises Eliot for seeking a system which will avoid both "the petrification of a caste system" and "the deliquescence of excessive social mobility" (p. 29). To be fair,

Bantock's treatment of Eliot is not completely uncritical. Like many critics, he finds Eliot sliding from one definition of culture to another. Like a good product of *Scrutiny*, Bantock prefers what he takes to be Lawrence's more positive view of the possibilities of lower-class culture. And although he agrees with Eliot that the masses have no capacity for higher levels of consciousness, he finds Eliot unhelpful in saying what should be done with the lower orders.

Bantock's account of Eliot's educational philosophy is based almost entirely on *Notes towards the Definition of Culture* and the "Aims of Education" lectures in *To Criticize the Critic*. Although he begins and ends with references to Eliot's essay on Blake, he stresses only Eliot's apparent approval of Blake's self-education, neglecting his regret that Blake lacked a traditional framework within which to develop his ideas. Bantock also overlooks the occasional comments on Christian education in some of Eliot's periodical contributions of the forties. Although not definitive, Bantock's presentation of Eliot's ideas on education is accurate, and shows how Eliot's resistance to deemphasizing the classics, to democratizing educational opportunity, and to secularizing the educational process may be seen to be reasonable outgrowths of Eliot's overall position as a social critic. Bantock's strength is thus in showing the relationship between Eliot's general principles and particular prejudices; his weakness is that, rather complacently, he seems to accept both the principles and the prejudices.

Bantock takes no notice of Robert M. Hutchins' earlier essay, "T. S. Eliot on Education" (1950), though Eliot himself pays tribute to it in his 1950 lectures, "The Aims of Education," given at Hutchins' University of Chicago. Hutchins' essay contains inconsistencies of his own, inconsistencies almost inherent in Hutchins' democratic elitism, but it offers an account of the inconsistencies in Eliot's position which is far more acute than that of Bantock. He finds that in *Notes towards the Definition of Culture* Eliot fails to define what he means by "education" carefully enough, which Eliot concedes in his 1950 lectures. Eliot says Hutchins, knows there is a difference between education and schooling, but he shifts his meaning from one to the other as if he did not. Eliot complains that others wish to make education a social instrument, and yet his own educational views clearly derive from his desire for preserving a class structure. Eliot confuses meritocratic testing procedures (which Hutchins also dislikes) with equality of opportunity. Hutchins closes with a somewhat muddled comparison of Eliot with Burke, but his essay is valuable for the way it confronts Eliot's position with basic questions, questions Eliot was to try to answer in his lectures.

J. M. Cameron also seems to hold a high opinion of Eliot in "T. S. Eliot as a Political Writer" (1958), although the grounds on which he does so are unclear. Most of Cameron's essay is devoted to Eliot's writing about church and state, on which he seems to find Eliot consistently unclear. The essays of *For Lancelot Andrewes* are seen as naturally making readers think that the chief argument in favor of the Church of England is the aesthetic products of past adherence to it; *After Strange Gods* is flawed by the sinister influence of Maurras. The argument of *The Idea of a Christian Society* is hard to follow, perhaps "because some of the steps in the argument have been suppressed" (p. 147). In particular, Cameron complains that Eliot mixes theological and sociological categories, making it hard to see any relation between the universal church, which bears the ideals of the Christian society, and the national churches through which those ideals are to find expression. Having noted the elusiveness of Eliot's terms and dicta, Cameron justifies his admiration for Eliot by praising his freedom from that "logical rigour which springs from a mania for systematization. . . . The method employed by Mr. Eliot—the examination of particular questions in the light of general principles not too narrowly defined and not too inflexibly stated—is certainly the right one" (p. 150). Praise of this sort is rather astonishing, the more so because Eliot's political prose is notable for its failure to deal concretely with particular questions. Having evidently exhausted the possibilities of analysis, Cameron supports his praise of *Notes towards the Definition of Culture* by quoting two passages from it (on totalitarianism and modern atheism) and asking us to admire them, presumably for their lack of logical rigor.

The relation between church and state is also at the center of the issues explored in H. B. Acton's review of *Notes towards the Definition of Culture* ("Religion, Culture, and Class," 1950). For Acton, the key term is "incarnation," but even here it seems to him that Eliot is inconsistent, sometimes implying that only in primitive or future ideal societies can culture incarnate religion, and sometimes arguing that this is a condition of culture. The "incarnation," Acton assumes, must go beyond mere influence—must imply, in fact, that culture has a divine origin and a supernatural base. But Eliot is talking about essential form rather than origins, and Acton's speculations only complicate matters further. More to the point is his argument that Eliot is arguing for religion on a sociological basis, but this is fair only if we agree that the book is primarily Christian apologetics. Acton recognizes that Eliot's advocacy of classes is connected to his advocacy of regionalism, both based "upon his belief that a flourishing society must be neither too unified nor too differentiated" (p. 129), but he sees this tolerance of differences as in conflict with Eliot's Catholicism, which Acton thinks must inevitably be intolerant. The problem here is Acton's failure to recognize the characteristic Anglicanism of Eliot's views on church and state.

Acton's article is hard to classify with Eliot's critics of the left or right because he has no apparent axe to grind; William Barrett's review of *Notes towards the Definition of Culture* is hard to classify because it is hard to believe that its ideological stance is meant to be taken seriously ("Aristocracy and/or Christianity," 1949). This clever, shallow piece has received a wider audience than it deserves by being reprinted in a collection of *Kenyon Review* criticism. Barrett complains that the book exhibits a less vigorous prose style than that of Eliot's 1923 essay on Marie Lloyd; no real specifics are given, but Barrett argues that this alleged degeneration in style reflects a similar decay in quality of thought. Barrett would seem to prefer that Eliot be an out-and-out aristocrat on the lines of Ortega y Gasset or Nietzsche, and he accuses Eliot of evading the basic Nietzschean question: "What is to be done with the masses?" (p. 492).

Barrett's notion that Eliot might better have been a more thoroughgoing conservative reminds one of Orwell's comments, but Barrett seems to go further and to assume that Eliot longs for the landed aristocracy to rise and put down its inferiors by force. Accusing Eliot of religious snobbism, Barrett says that Eliot fails to recognize that there may be men who would like to believe, but cannot do so, because of real intellectual scruples; Eliot, of course, often indicated his sympathy for such "children at the gate." Barrett believes that Christianity is no longer a meaningful culture, that the urban lower classes have rejected it, and that it lives only among peasants. In hindsight, we may observe that the greatest growing force in Christianity since World War II has been neofundamentalist sects with a strong appeal to urban lower classes, although it is possible that this proves nothing about religion's ability to again become central to our culture. Barrett's view of the decline of the humanities is at least as bleak as Eliot's, but he notes that science has not shared in this decline and suggests that either the best brains are going into science or that science and technology are creating a new culture inimical to literature. Barrett concludes from this that we must choose (with Nietzsche, again) between primitivism and modern rationality, which is carrying a false dichotomy to extremes.

Barrett's distaste for the prose of *Notes towards the Definition of Culture* is not shared by Richard Rees ("T. S. Eliot on Culture and Progress," 1967). Rees has an unusual preference for the first portion of the book, with its destructive criticism of various progressive thinkers on education and culture; he admits that Eliot's presentation is one sided, but he praises the "verve and wit" (p. 105) of the prose and seems to feel that the victims deserve what they get. Although he recognizes that Eliot's use of theology sometimes verges on spiritual one-upmanship, Rees believes that Eliot's religious commitment makes the book more than " a mild conservative criticism of Mannheim's theory of elites" (p. 105).

Of all the various critiques of Eliot's social criticism, probably the most valuable is Raymond Williams' chapter on Eliot in his *Culture and Society* (1958), perhaps because Williams has thought more deeply about the issues which concern Eliot than have most of Eliot's critics. Unlike Rees, he dislikes the early chapters of *Notes towards the Definition of Culture*, saying that Eliot refuses to argue with his opponents, offering instead "the growling innuendoes of the correspondence columns" (p. 247). Even where Eliot offers definitions and generalizations, Williams finds the supporting illustrations and evidence insufficient. For example, Williams notes that although Eliot defines culture as "a whole way of life," the few specific references to cultural items are more limited in scope, implying either the high culture of cultural elites or the popular culture of the masses, but eliminating references to work or to technology. Williams accepts, however, Eliot's belief in levels of culture, for he sees this as a useful corrective to those simpler notions of democratic culture which assume that one can simply extend, unchanged, a single culture to all groups in society, a process generally envisaged in terms of extending the existing high culture to wider groups or the whole society. Williams also seconds Eliot's resistance to Mannheim's theories of elites, agreeing that a meritocratic society, based on formal education, would perpetuate narrow specialisms and disintegrate culture as an interactive whole. Williams' agreement here is based on different political assumptions from Eliot's; the theory of elites seems to Eliot a mere form of laissez faire thought. He has no sympathy with Eliot's defense of social classes, partly because Eliot's analysis separates social classes from their economic functions. He credits Eliot with a recognition that the "free economy," cherished by the "new" conservatives, is destructive of culture as a kind of wholeness, but he believes that Eliot implicitly recognizes the impracticality of his social ideals, which can at best find release in a holding action that shores up things as they are against the inevitable results of their internal contradictions.

Terry Eagleton's essay, "Eliot and a Common Culture" (1970), sees the difference between Eliot and Williams as arising from different views of consciousness. "Williams's common culture is at once more and less conscious than Eliot's: more conscious, because it engages the active participation of all its members; less conscious, because what will then be created according to this rule can neither be prescribed in advance nor fully known in the making" (p. 284). Eliot would presumably agree that the future of culture cannot be consciously planned. Eagleton is misled here by his tendency to see Eliot's orthodoxy as more static than it is, a tendency shared by most critics, except for relatively conservative ones like Bantock. But he is probably right to see Williams' as the best counterargument to Eliot's. The judgment which Eagleton and Williams reach on Eliot's social criticism is shared by most of Eliot's most perceptive critics: Eliot is useful in calling into question some complacent assumptions of modern liberalism, but weak in providing specific alternatives. Even sympathetic conservative critics are apt to agree, though less apt to see Eliot's conservatism as static and intolerant or to misperceive the Anglican character of Eliot's view of the church.

Eliot and Anti-Semitism

Most of the longer works in this chapter attempt to relate Eliot's social criticism to his poems. Among them, only Kirk devotes enough space to the task to do an adequate job, and much of Kirk's time is spent debunking the wilder excesses of

Eliot critics. The most extensively discussed issue in the social criticism of Eliot's poetry is probably his alleged anti-Semitism, a charge based on the presence of stereotyped figures like "Rachel nee Rabinovitch" (in "Sweeney among the Nightingales"), Bleistein (in "Burbank with a Baedeker: Bleistein with a Cigar"), and the "jew" who "squats on the window sill" (in "Gerontion"). To prove that anti-Semitic stereotypes of this sort are a natural consequence of Eliot's social philosophy, critics usually rely on a passage in *After Strange Gods* which praises the virtues of a relatively homogeneous population and indicates that his ideal commonwealth would not have large numbers of "free-thinking Jews." Critics usually say that Eliot should have known better than to say this at a time when Hitler had just come to power in Germany. His defenders reply that hindsight is demanding that Eliot should have been more perceptive than most of the world's political and religious leaders. Most of Eliot's critics from the left, discussed in the last section (like Harrison and Robbins), have at least touched on this issue, and a number of the sympathetic critics discussed earlier (like Kirk and Kojecký) have felt called upon to deal with it.

Discussions of the anti-Semitism of Eliot's work crop up at odd intervals, often set off by other matters. The only common denominator is that the charges are made by men whose sensitivities have been sharpened by the Holocaust. Wide circulation was given to the charge by Robert Hillyer, who wrote two articles for the *Saturday Review of Literature* attacking Eliot as the leader of those who gave the 1949 Bollingen Prize to Pound ("Treason's Strange Fruit," June 11, 1949a; "Poetry's New Priesthood," June 18, 1949b). Hillyer suggested that Eliot's critics showed "a decline in critical honesty" by refusing to deal openly with Eliot's anti-Semitism (1949b, p. 9), his example being Elizabeth Drew. Hillyer's level of understanding of Eliot is displayed in an odd reference to Eliot as "a disciple of Dr. Jung" (perhaps a result of misreading Drew) and in his assertion that Eliot is "neither scholarly nor deeply read" (1949a, p. 9; 1949b, p. 8). Hillyer's high ethical standards of rhetoric are exhibited in a passing reference to "the alien, or expatriate, T. S. Eliot" (1949a, p. 9). Nevertheless, he raised the issue of Eliot's anti-Semitism in a widely read middle-brow journal.

In 1957 Oscar Cargill gave the charge further currency in a note for another popular journal ("Mr. Eliot Regrets"). Cargill sees an admission of ethnic prejudices (against Jews, Irish, and other groups) in the "Little Gidding" passage about "motives late revealed." Since the passage is very general, dealing with things done in good faith that were nevertheless wrong, Cargill's argument is not terribly persuasive. Cargill also argues that the abandonment of *Sweeney Agonistes* was a result of Eliot's realization that prejudices did not fit in with his new Christian commitments; no special evidence is provided to prove this. Having found a particular apology in a general confession, Cargill goes on to find it insufficient, given the terrible nature of the offense. His self-righteousness is as strong as his evidence is weak.

George Steiner stirred another set of letters and articles on Eliot's anti-Semitism with some comments in his *Bluebeard's Castle: Some Notes towards the Redefinition of Culture* (1971). Although the book began as T. S. Eliot memorial lectures, Steiner begins by observing that *Notes towards the Definition of Culture* is "not an attractive book" (p. 3), and goes on to complain that it fails "to face the issue" of the Holocaust, or "to allude to it in anything but an oddly condescending footnote" (p. 33). The excessive respect in which Steiner is widely held make his linking of this sin of omission with the traces of anti-Semitism in Eliot's poetry important. One might note that Richard Clark argues that Steiner's criticism of Eliot is part of Steiner's general feeling that Christianity is a negative force in modern culture ("George Steiner on the 'Christian Barbarism' of Claudel and Eliot," 1973). Steiner's combination of high moral tone and sly innuendo is effective but annoying.

The issue has become important enough to be the subject of two long scholarly articles. The first of these, in 1972, J. A. Morris's "T. S. Eliot and Antisemitism," is unusual in adding to the canonical list of offending poems "A Cooking Egg," presumably (for Morris does not explain) on the basis of a line about "red-eyed scavengers." Like some other writers, Morris sees Eliot as linking Jews with images of repulsive animals. Observing that the vicious anti-Semitism of the Nazis also used bestial images for Jews, Morris seems to assert a virtual identity of the two viewpoints, the sort of logical fallacy often favored by those who wish to prove that their opponents are Fascists or Communists. Morris thinks it significant that the first English edition of *The Protocols of the Elders of Zion* appeared in 1920, "the very year that Eliot's antisemitic verses were first published" (p. 180)—not, of course, the year in which they were written. In a gesture at fairness, Morris admits that he does not know whether Eliot read the *Protocols*, or whether, if he did, he read a copy with a picture of the Jew-as-beast on its cover. With this equation of Eliot's view with the basest kind of ethnic slander, Morris couples Eliot's alleged medievalism with the medieval tradition of the Jew as anti-Christ and emissary of the devil. In *After Strange Gods*, he takes Eliot's occasional references to the powers of evil at work in the world as referring to a diabolic Jewish conspiracy. In the same volume he assumes that the reference to Virginia's having been "less invaded by foreign races" than England is aimed at Jews—although it seems more likely that this particular slander is aimed at the Irish and Italians. The famous phrase about the undesirability of "large numbers of free-thinking Jews" thus seems, to Morris, part of a sustained anti-Semitic argument. How seriously even Morris takes this nonsense is unclear, for he retreats into rhetorical questions when he makes his most outrageous assertions, but he seems to hold that Eliot was obsessed with a Jewish bogeyman about to destroy civilization.

Hyam Maccoby offers similar views in his essay "The Anti-Semitism of T. S. Eliot" (1973). He believes that anti-Semitism is an important and natural outgrowth of "the sacrificial view of life" Eliot acquired (via Henry Adams and Maurras) from the Christian tradition, and that Eliot continued to hold the same views long after he ceased to express them publicly (p. 68). Maccoby is capable of hyperbole—he describes the *After Strange Gods* passage as a proposal "to impose a quota on Jewish residents of the United States" (p. 68)—but he is generally fair in his discussion of the poems. Maccoby is certainly right to dismiss those critics who deny the presence of anti-Semitic stereotypes in the poems, and his arguments against various defenses are well taken. His discussion of the further mortification of Bleistein in the "Dirge," which was one of the rejected portions of the draft *Waste Land*, contributes to our understanding of the ways in which Eliot handles the theme of purgation. He is also more than generous to the poems in question, perhaps more generous than they deserve. "Burbank" is an artistic "triumph," says Maccoby, and "Gerontion" is a "superb poem" (p. 78). Maccoby is probably right in saying that Eliot was making poetic use of popular stereotypes which made the Jew the symbol of the interloper; it is less clear that he is accurate in saying that Eliot uses the Jew as a symbol of unregenerate humanity, and it seems purely speculative to say that Eliot (like Adams and Maurras) equates the Jew with the hated forces of social progress. Individuals who adhere to any of the great religious traditions may slip into expressing social prejudices which are opposed to the spirit of those traditions. The evidence Maccoby presents by no means proves that anti-Semitism was a deeply held attitude with Eliot, much less that it was connected with and long survived his increasing commitment to Christianity.

Morris Freedman's earlier discussion, "The Meaning of T. S. Eliot's Jew" (1956), was incongruously incorporated into a chapter in Freedman's *American Drama in Social Context* (1971). Freedman is not willing to apply the term anti-Semitic to *After Strange Gods*, and he sees the anti-Semitism of the early poems as symptomatic of Eliot's general failure to sympathize with humanity as a whole. Freedman distinguishes between Eliot's depiction of the lower classes, whose sexual life is (like Sweeney's) mechanical and listless, and of Jews, who seem to incarnate the animal side of man, lecherous and bestial. He sees Eliot's Jews as symbols of the Id and connects this with Conrad's use of Kurtz and, thus, with Eliot's "Mistah Kurtz—he dead," ending with the stunning question: "Is it significant that Kurtz's model in real life was named 'Klein'?" (p. 32). To which the answer is surely "No." Freedman's treatment is in many ways more sensible than that of Morris or Maccoby, but his desire to minimize the importance of anti-Semitic symbols in Eliot sometimes seems to derive from his understandable difficulty in joining Maccoby in admiring poems that contain such stereotypes.

Defenders of Eliot on this question have included conservatives like Kirk and socialists like Orwell: they have generally admitted the anti-Semitism in the early poems, but argued that it reflects no more than stupid or shallow prejudice, quite common in English society at the time. A few critics seem anxious to explain matters away entirely. Robert Fleissner exhibits some of this tendency in his damning review-article on Harrison's book, a good deal of which is devoted to defending Eliot on the issue of anti-Semitism ("Reacting to *The Reactionaries:* Libertarian Views," 1969). He objects, for example, to Harrison's statement that Eliot "is afraid the free-thinking of Jews strikes at the roots of Christian dogma, and destroys the premises on which religious orthodoxy is based" (Harrison [1967], p. 152). Fleissner argues that Eliot was too sensible to suppose that Jews were opposed to religious orthodoxy. To be fair to Harrison, the anti-Semitic stereotype involved here is not of the Orthodox Jew with a prayer shawl but of the free-thinking Jew as a type of cosmopolitan modernism, the great models being Marx and Freud. Fleissner later observes that Eliot refused to republish *After Strange Gods* and suggests that this refutes Harrison's use of that book. Even if one assumes that the decision was based on the book's one anti-Semitic passage, it is not unfair to take Eliot's words in that book as bearing some relation to his views at the time it was published. Eliot did not suppress the early poems which contain anti-Semitic passages, although in later editions of "Gerontion" the "jew" has been altered to "Jew." Fleissner says that Eliot simply "portrays the anti-Semitism that was evident in some circles at the time" (1969, p. 139). The word "portrays" suggests that Eliot was purely detached, but "expresses" would surely be a fairer word. There are no anti-Semites in these poems, but there are Jews, and Jews portrayed in a way which implies that the poems' persona accepts an anti-Semitic stereotype. For Fleissner, it seems important that Eliot said he was not an anti-Semite, that many Jews like Eliot's work, and that Eliot once gave a poetry reading at a Young Men's Hebrew Association (in 1961). All this suggests that Eliot was not a Nazi, that World War II made him more sensitive on such matters (as it did many others), and that such anti-Semitism as appears in a handful of early poems is incidental enough that it has been easily sloughed off by both the poet and his readers. That is not the same thing as saying it was never there.

When one turns to explications of the poems in question, one is sometimes surprised at the ease with which critics pass over the offending passages. Louis Locke's *Explicator* note on "Burbank with a Baedeker: Bleistein with a Cigar" (1945) deals solemnly with the various literary allusions in the poem, while identifying Bleistein simply as "the rich tourist from Chicago (Who has not known Bleistein?)." The sheer insensitivity of this paraphrase takes one's breath away, although the essay is chiefly of interest as an example of the dangers of the great Eliot-source-hunting game, which often threatens to substitute a poem's associations for the poem.

Besides Bleistein, "Burbank" confronts us with lines like "the Jew is underneath the lot" and the reference to "Sir Ferdinand/Klein," so that its portrait of social decay may depend so much on anti-Semitic stereotypes that readers unable to entertain them sympathetically cannot enter into the poem. The poem's attitude toward Burbank is, at least, ambiguous. There is a useful discussion of this point in Richard C. Turner's "Burbank and Grub-Street: A Note on T. S. Eliot and Swift" (1971). Taking issue with a critic, Elizabeth Drew, who has suggested that Burbank is a creative albeit impotent artist, Turner points out that two lines (beginning "who clipped the lion's wings") allude to Jonathan Swift's *A Tale of a Tub*, where they are part of the praise heaped by the supposed author on the hacks of his time. This allusion suggests that Burbank and his Baedeker are also intended as objects of satire, devices through which Eliot, like Swift, exposes the vulgarity of the "Moderns." Thus Burbank is simply Bleistein's philistine counterpart. With or without the Swift allusion, this seems a more reasonable reading of the poem, though it does not make it more attractive.

Eliot himself has been cited as saying that "Sweeney among the Nightingales" was an exercise in creating an atmosphere of foreboding. His critics, however, have often insisted on tying the poem down to specifics. The generally received opinion can be cited from Robert L. Lair's *Barron's Simplified Approach to T. S. Eliot* (1968), one of those handy guides designed to spare students (and teachers) the difficulty of thinking about poems for themselves. Lair instructs us that the poem is "a concise narrative of Sweeney's depraved existence and his death, set against the heroic legendary background of Agamemnon's murder in ancient Argos. In their two persons lies the contrast of a tarnished past splendor and the sordid vulgarity of the contemporary world" (p. 30).

Without dissenting from the social implications of this reading, James Davidson has offered an alternative reading in "The End of Sweeney" (1966). Davidson argues that Sweeney is such a low and comic character that he is not even worth killing; he is, "in fact, already dead," spiritually dead (p. 403). Davidson is just convincing enough to persuade one that the poem's ending is ambiguous and that we don't know what will be the end of Sweeney. Readers who want more details should seek them in the comic spirit of T. H. Thompson, who has ingeniously combined the various references to Sweeney in Eliot's poem to reveal the true secret in "The Bloody Wood" (1934): Sweeney murdered Mrs. Porter's daughter! Critics who lack a sense of humor should rest content with the poem as an exercise in atmosphere.

Too few of Eliot's critics seem gifted with either a sense of humor or a willingness to leave well enough alone. Neither quality is much in evidence in Everett A. Gillis's "Religion in a Sweeney World" (1964). Beneath its surface, Gillis sees the poem concerned with the "impotency of sacrificial death, which is developed through the middle portion of the poem by a thinly-disguised travesty of the Catholic Mass and generally throughout the piece by references to Agamemnon's tragic assassination" (p. 58). Although the disguise may seem thin to Gillis, the rest of us may have difficulty in seeing either Sweeney or Agamemnon as Christ-figures. Readers who recall Maccoby's insistence that Eliot's anti-Semitism is tied to a sacrificial view of religion will experience a mild shock of recognition when Gillis writes that "the presence of Rachel *née* Rabinovitch at the service—the source of the Communion wine—reminds us of the historical role of the Jews in Christ's passion and death which the Mass commemorates," although it is Gillis, rather than Eliot, who drags in the nonorthodox doctrine of the collective guilt of the Jews. For Gillis, Sweeney is the priest of this "Mass," which is meant to illustrate the depths to which religion has sunk in the modern world, in which Christ's death seems to have no more redemptive value than Agamemnon's.

Equally bland in its acceptance of the stereotype and unconvincing in its positive arguments is John Ower's essay "Pattern and Value in 'Sweeney among the Nightingales' " (1971). Here we are told that "the ancient religion of the Chosen People, at one time noble enough to be the progenitor of Christianity, has now in Eliot's opinion sunken into a crass materialism and a superficial internationalism which are well epitomized by the witch-like figure tearing at exotic fruits with her 'murderous paws' " (p. 152). Her "league" with the "person in the Spanish cape" is said to suggest "the degeneration of Romantic eroticism into the Decadent interest in sexual perversion" (p. 155), presumably because Ower somehow reads their "league" as lesbian in nature. Ower's general reading of the poem sees in it four spiritual planes in a complex relationship: "The civilization of ancient Greece is elaborately parodied in 'Sweeney among the Nightingales' by the third cultural plane of Nineteenth Century Romanticism. Although Romanticism is one step down the spiritual ladder from Classical Paganism, and two beneath Christianity, it is ironically brought much more into the foreground than either" (p. 154). Ower's poem is more allegorical and less interesting than Eliot's, to which it seems only distantly related.

The passages in "Gerontion" which are sometimes cited as anti-Semitic are more important to the poem than the minor role Rachel plays in "Sweeney among the Nightingales," but may be less of a problem for the reader than the passages in "Burbank." Still, it is surprising how few of the many interpretations of this difficult poem have much to say about the Jewish owner of the house, "spawned in some estaminet of Antwerp, / blistered in Brussels, patched and peeled in London." One of the few articles to tackle these lines is an *Explicator* note by Clark Griffith, "Eliot's 'Gerontion' " (1963). Griffith sees the poem as a religious meditation. The "jew" is Jewish because he is to be linked with those Pharisees who demanded a sign of Jesus. It is as a Pharisee that he is to be understood as the owner of the house of the speaker's mind, and the Pharisees are to be understood as having commenced "the skeptical and ultra-rationalistic tradition" which has brought us so much grief. At this point, Griffith seems to be replacing Eliot's libel on Jews with his own libel on the Pharisees, but he goes further. As a citizen of Antwerp, Brussels, and London, the "jew" is a representative man, so that "we are all Jews—Jews in the sense that, together with the Pharisees and the speaker, we all put naturalistic questions to a supernatural religion and, finding no answers, we all go on to make the same fatal rejection that they have made." It is this rationalistic cast of mind which condemns the Eucharist to be celebrated in whispers. The "jew" squats in the window, because the window opens symbolically on the possibility of escape into faith—as, Griffith would have it, does the window in "Sweeney among the Nightingales." The house is "rented" because the speaker once had faith but has lost it "in terror" and in excessive rationalism, so that the Pharisaical tradition (as Griffith defines it) is not natural to him. The "boy," indeed, represents Gerontion's younger self. Griffith might well have added to his argument the *After Strange Gods* reference to "free-thinking Jews," for that seems to be the stereotype he has in mind. If Eliot's Christianity matches this description, so much the worse for it.

One of the reasons why the "jew" of "Gerontion" seems less offensive than similar imagery in, say, "Burbank," is that "Gerontion" is a poem which seems to maintain a clear distance between the poet and his persona. E. San Juan, Jr., can thus speak of Gerontion as "preoccupied in reducing the Jew to the status of animal or fish," without assuming that Eliot is doing the same ("Form and Meaning in 'Gerontion,' " 1970, p. 117). For San Juan, as for some other critics, the Jewish owner may also suggest "the Lord, the power over secular and sacred realms" (p. 118). Gerontion is defeated "in his distrust of thought and language as the vehicle of transcendence, as a mode of self-knowledge," but Eliot triumphs "in his successful objectification of this persona in an aesthetically significant form" (p. 126). The only difficulty with this sharp separation is that Eliot himself may be said to have doubts about thought as a vehicle of self-transcendence. Still, San Juan's essay is one of the better explications of the poem, not least because it does not skip over passages which pose difficulties for his interpretation, a fairly common habit in dealing with this very difficult work.

The Poet as Social Critic

Efforts to discuss the social dimensions of Eliot's prose which do not get bogged down in the question of his anti-Semitism tend to dwell either on his bleak view of the modern world or on cloudier speculations about his view of history; relatively few discuss it with his essays of social criticism. A notable exception is Rajendra Verma's *Royalist in Politics* (1968), which begins as a discussion of Eliot's social philosophy but ends by devoting much of its space to his poetry. That is just as well, since Verma's treatment of Eliot's social criticism is mainly descriptive summary, with Verma serving as a cheering section, tossing in supporting quotations from Burke and the Dalai Lama. It does not help much to be told that some (not all) of Eliot's views resemble those of Oswald Spengler, when we are given no evidence of direct influence. Even in dealing with the poems, Verma sometimes strains one's sense of relevance, as when *The Waste Land*'s "Unreal City" sends him into a two-page account of Lewis Mumford's theories about the development of cities. His most interesting pages, in any case, have little to do with politics; instead, they discuss the ways in which the religious symbols of *The Waste Land* reappear with new meanings in *Ash Wednesday*. Given his task, this may not be entirely Verma's fault; the religious cast of Eliot's later poems makes it difficult to give them political readings.

Of Eliot's earlier poems, those like "Burbank" and "Sweeney among the Nightingales" are often read in terms of their depiction of a squalid present, while "Gerontion" is often treated as a meditation on history. *The Waste Land*, naturally, can be read as either or both.

While the general social philosophy at work in a poem like "Burbank" seems fairly obvious, there is nothing obvious about

"Gerontion." Various readings stress one or another of its multiple levels of reference—social, religious, personal—and the poem seems rich and confused enough to accommodate them all. Of those readings which stress its social criticism, one of the best is Ruth Bailey's *A Dialogue on Modern Poetry* (1939). For Bailey, the old man of the poem "is a dying civilization, *our* civilization, which is, in the poet's view, contemptible, pitiful, justly doomed" (p. 15). It has not fought a heroic struggle against barbarism, like the Greeks at the "hot gates" of Thermopylae; it has fought against itself, so that it is a civilization in decay. "Like its owner," says Bailey (rather blandly, for 1939), "this civilization is international and belongs nowhere; it has been knocked about from place to place; it is falling to pieces" (p. 21). The "depraved May" may have been the Renaissance, which helped usher in a secular, individualistic civilization, which has known the truth and rejected it. The end is coming, and the poet, who knows it, has not made this demonstration purposely. Admitting with refreshing honesty that she can only understand the general idea of the next passage—the seven lines beginning "I would meet you upon this honestly"—Bailey suggests that the speaker is replying to someone who objects to the anticipated doom, replying that the civilization has lost too much to be worth preserving. The poem ends with Gerontion still thinking, anticipating the destruction of all things. The religious dimension of the poem is not lost in Bailey's reading; it is subordinated to an apocalyptic vision of history.

Apocalyptic visions are much on the mind of Harvey Gross in his essay "*Gerontion* and the Meaning of History" (1958). Gross tells us that the poem is the "literary expression of Karl Mannheim's contention that historicism is the only possible *Weltanschauung* in an age dominated by historical force and obsessed with the idea of history" (p. 299). The expressed sense of history resembles that of Henry Adams in its despair—and even in its anti-Semitism. Gerontion is a more admirable figure to Gross than to Bailey. The poem's "backward devils" are the false prophets of Dante's fourth *bolgia*, but Gerontion is not among them. The difficult passage beginning "after such knowledge," is read as a closely reasoned argument for an attitude toward history. Gerontion's knowledge is his awareness of the irreversible decline of his civilization; he is prepared, even eager, for its violent end. Historical knowledge cannot save us, for our "vanities" enable us to distort it too easily. Trapped in a relentless historical process, in which our very heroism may father "unnatural vices," the individual seems helpless, though he is still held morally responsible. Gerontion can only die, but the historical process will go on—has "not reached conclusion"—and there may be cause for hope in the violent coming of "Christ the tiger," the transformation of Gerontion's set into "fractured atoms." Eliot does not, as some critics have charged, succumb to a merely mythic view of history, nor, says Gross, does he commit the Hegelian error of assuming that the historical process is morally right. He is, in fact, commenting "on an immediate historical crisis" (p. 304), the state of Europe after World War I, and he knows that we cannot be forgiven our knowledge.

Gross's apocalypse is far less Christian than Bailey's; as in Yeats' "The Second Coming," the coming of "Christ the tiger" seems to signal only a violent new start in a continuing historical process. Both Bailey and Gross seem too quick to assume that Gerontion's death, inevitable because of man's mortality, necessarily implies both spiritual death and the end of civilization as we know it. In an *Explicator* note, "Eliot's 'Gerontion,' 56–61" (1957), Robert M. Brown and Joseph B. Yokelson have noted the essential ambiguity of the poem on this point: "admitting despair, Gerontion is nevertheless 'waiting for rain.' " Brown and Yokelson see the poem as about the "deceptions of history," but for them the great loss has been man's separation from a vital relationship with God.

For John B. Vickery's "*Gerontion:* The Nature of Death and Immortality" (1958), the "personal or individual level of the poem serves as the focus" for its religious, historical, and natural levels (p. 101). To assert that the poem's persona serves as its unifying element may seem obvious, but most critics seem more interested in Gerontion's thoughts than in Gerontion himself. Vickery is also unusual in calling attention to the poem's "natural" level—the endless death and change of nature, linked to Gerontion's motality—and in seeing Gerontion as at least partially regaining "his divinity as a man . . . when he loses 'terror in inquisition' " (p. 101). Vickery is right in reasserting the importance of the literal level of the poem's opening picture of Gerontion's situation, and he can do so without denying that even in those lines suggestions of broader themes are to be found.

Vickery does not see Gerontion as regretting his failure to have fought for traditional values but as regretting his failure to have fought at all, not to have engaged himself with life.

Gerontion has recognized, but been unable to submit himself to, the power of Christianity, and the decay of his house is only the first step in the projection of Gerontion's sense of alienation and decay onto a larger screen. Although the darkness of his mind has kept him from apprehending the Word, he is at least linked to Christ by the "inverted communion" of "us he devours," a degree of insight which offers him more hope of salvation than the "perverted communion" of Mr. Silvero and the others (p. 108). He has been led to this insight by his meditation on the "contrived corridors" of history and his recognition of the inevitable mortality promised by "the wrath-bearing tree." But the act of accepting the devouring Christ enables Gerontion to accept his death and responsibility for his life, for, in Christ, death need not be the end, and life has meaning. He can now cease clinging to his senses and confront the irreversible processes of time. For Vickery, who may be stretching the evidence a bit at this point, the sea images of the next to last stanza suggest "the apparent threatened return of chaos," which is "in reality a prelude to Genesis and the divine creation upon which every man's existence is contingent" (p. 114). On the whole, Vickery is more persuasive in showing that the poem's scattered images can be consistently read in terms of Gerontion's meditations on the nature of death than he is in arguing that Gerontion achieves a real hope of immortality. Nevertheless, Vickery's essay accounts for far more of the poem's many difficulties than most critical accounts of it.

Like "Gerontion," *The Waste Land* can be read on many levels. Many of the critics interested in Eliot's social criticism (like Kirk, Harrison, Robbins) have found it possible to incorporate a discussion of *The Waste Land* in their analyses of Eliot's position. Kirk's review-essay on Valerie Eliot's edition of the poem's drafts ("The Waste Land Lies Unredeemed," 1972) takes account of the new evidence offered by the drafts; for Kirk, the poem relates the disordered state of the persona to that of his society. While Kirk repeats some of his earlier arguments, John T. Barry repeats Verma's suggestion that Oswald Spengler's *Decline of the West* may have been a source for Eliot ("*The Waste Land:* A Possible German Source," 1972). Barry is more specifically concerned with *The Waste Land* than Verma, and the case for reading that poem as about social decay would be strengthened if his new information were convincing. Unfortunately, only the first volume of Spengler's book was out when *The Waste Land* was written, and even that was not translated into English until 1926. The only external evidence Barry can cite of Eliot's familiarity with Spengler comes from after that year. Barry believes that the internal evidence of "similarities in theme, analogical method . . . and even wording, however accidental, are worth pointing out" (p. 431), but the similarities he points to suggest a vague affinity at most.

Of the interpretations of *The Waste Land* which focus on its social implications, the best is probably David Craig's "The Defeatism of *The Waste Land*" (1960). The original essay has been anthologized several times, but Craig's later book, *The Real Foundations* (1974), has a fuller version of the essay, expanded to reply to some critics of the original. Craig implicitly concedes that the poem is an artistic achievement of a high order; his quarrel is with the social viewpoint implicit in it and thus with critics who have praised the poem as a spiritual and cultural diagnosis as well as art. Even if the poem is a lyric product of "an almost despairing personal depression," it projects that depression "in the guise of an impersonal picture of society" (1974, p. 195). The reader, says Craig, is almost bound by the poem's form and content to react to that picture of society, whatever the author's original intent or later explanations. The poem's shifts from one scene and social class to another convey the image of a poet exploring a whole society, and the historical allusions suggest the degeneracy of the present by summoning up the image of an idealized past. Craig is not persuaded by arguments that, following the notes, lead to more realistic assessments of, say, Elizabeth and Leicester, for the poem conveys quite opposite impressions. Eliot's irony, as in "sweet ladies," strikes Craig as "just ordinary sarcasm" (pp. 198, 203).

The implicit comparisons work well in the poem, but they are fundamentally unfair, neglecting the sordid nature of much of the past and treating the present as if it could be summed up by a series of cheap seductions. The political affinities of the poem are clear in part V, in those portions glossed by Eliot as concerned with "the present decay of eastern Europe." The poem's references to "hooded hordes" especially offends Craig, who recalls that it was conceived at a time when ravages were committed by the armies of the Allied intervention.

The issue here is whether the vision of a society projected by the poem's protagonist is representative enough to amount to an accurate diagnosis of the state of postwar Europe; the issue is important even to those critics who give the poem a religious reading, for the persona's spiritual crisis is often taken as representative. One need not share Craig's political position to agree with him that the poem is inadequate as a general social diagnosis. That the poem's vision of things as they are is, nevertheless, widely shared may be gathered from the response of its readers over the years. Craig is not, however, justified in assuming that the poem necessarily evokes such responses. The merit of his essay is that it should discourage efforts to transform a fine lyric sequence into a Representative Poem of Our Time.

Just such a transformation is attempted by Harvey Gross in his chapter on Eliot in *The Contrived Corridor* (1971), which also contains a version of Gross's 1958 article on "Gerontion." To justify his historical interpretation of *The Waste Land*, Gross notes that Eliot's copy of Hegel's *Philosophy of History* is heavily underlined, while his copy of Weston's *From Ritual to Romance* contains some uncut pages. This may confirm one's doubts about interpretations built upon Weston, but it does not give strong support to interpretations built upon Hegel, whose works would be natural reading for a graduate student in philosophy, whether that student found Hegel deeply interesting or not. Gross argues, though, that "the substance of *The Waste Land* is not ahistorical or antihistorical myth but history as it might be philosophically understood" (p. 49). Its setting is a moment when historical process seems to have been stopped or suspended, leaving the reader to choose between alternative visions of history: the Christian framework and a cyclical Eastern framework. The "hooded hordes" and "maternal lamentation" may signal a new cycle or a new savior.

Gross's reading of *The Waste Land* is less persuasive than his general case for historical interpretation. Much of his time is devoted to its sexuality. When his historical thesis plays any part, one feels that the apocalyptic visions he invokes are more Gross's than Eliot's. Gross goes on to argue that the *Four Quartets* is concerned with a Christian interpretation of the historical process and with a direct consideration of the problem of historical knowledge. On the first of these concerns he is relatively convincing, and on the second, merely interesting. Although committed to the notion of the poet as prophet, Gross dislikes Eliot's Christianity for its Jansenism and so wants to strip Eliot's insights of their supernaturalism, leaving them "translated into secular hopes" (p. 62). It is unclear how we can do this without distorting the poem, and the effort certainly violates Eliot's cautions against pretending that literature can substitute for religion or philosophy.

Rather hard to classify is Richard Wasson's essay, " 'Like a Burnished Throne': T. S. Eliot and the Demonism of Technology" (1969), which purports to say something about the relationship between technology and art by an analysis of the first part of "A Game of Chess" in *The Waste Land*, but mostly talks about other matters. The passage is said to reveal the demonic side of technology, a point proved by reference to Siegfried Giedion's discussion of the demonism of mass-produced Victorian furniture. Eliot thus confronts technology through the "demonic mode," defined by reference to Northrop Frye and Paul Tillich. The essay ends with a modest hope that it has contributed to our understanding of the "relationship between technology and literary forms, between technology and the poles of human fear and hope" (p. 316). Certainly it does not add to our understanding of the relationship between technology and Eliot.

Another hard-to-classify sociological reading of *The Waste Land* is John Brooks Barry's "Eliot's 'Burial of the Dead': A Note on the Morphology of Culture" (1974), one of those essays in which a critic uses ideas he does not understand to explain a poem he seems unable to read. Eliot's view of history is attributed to Bradley and Hulme in ways which misinterpret Bradley's influence and overstate Hulme's. The nature of the influence attributed to Bradley is suggested by Barry's interpretation of a remark in Eliot's dissertation that "to realize that a point of view is a point of view is already to have transcended it." Says Bradley: "Eliot seems to mean that in the young culture a generally held concept of mortality was the basis of fear and escape from personality. But to the city dweller the fear of death, as an end to biography, has become as much an abstraction as the joy of life" (p. 67). Perhaps—the passage in Barry is confusing—this is meant to apply to "The Burial of the Dead" section, in which case it still makes little sense. Of the Madame Sosostris passage we are told: "Yet surely the point here is not ancient magic as a test of modern culture but the evaporation of a background, a mother-landscape to which all religion is form-bound and to which Eliot returns in 'East Coker,' the sixteenth century home of his English ancestors, and in those strangely terrifying reminiscences of the New England coast, 'The Dry Salvages' " (p. 69). The essay ends abruptly with the suggestion that somewhere—apparently in the last lines of "The Burial of the Dead"—one might see a connection with Charles I hiding at Little Gidding.

The crowds that cross London Bridge in "The Burial of the Dead" are largely absent in the later poetry, but they reappear in the *Coriolan* poems, "Triumphal March—1931" and "Difficulties of a Statesman." These poems have received little attention, perhaps because few have thought they would repay the struggle, with their obvious difficulties. Eliot's explanation, that the finished work was to be tied together through the character who appears as "young Cyril" in the first poem and a newly appointed telephone operator in the second, has not seemed terribly helpful.

One of the best separate treatments of these poems is found in Donald F. Theall, "Traditional Satire in Eliot's 'Coriolan' " (1951). Theall notes the previous appearances of the Coriolanus figure (in "A Cooking Egg" and *The Waste Land V*), and suggests that Eliot's interpretation of this Shakespearean hero may have been shaped by Wyndham Lewis's emphasis on Coriolanus' adolescent qualities. The choice of Coriolanus as a central figure is thus "tied up with a conception of the super-state as a phenomenon of emotional immaturity" (p. 195). The poems' almost Audenesque blending of the vulgar, the prosaic, and the mock-heroic is traced by Theall to the use of Joycean double plots. Dante references contrast the hollowness of the political triumph with the procession in "Earthly Paradise" at the end of the *Purgatorio*. In the second poem, a Virgil reference contrasts the pastoral tradition with life in the mechanized modern city.

A more recent, and slighter, effort has the virtue of linking these poems directly with Eliot's prose of social criticism. Balachandra Rajan's "A Note on the Coriolan Poems" (1978) takes off from William Empson's reflections on Eliot's remark (in *After Strange Gods*) that in poetry one must attend to reality, while in prose one could entertain ideals (Empson, "Eliot and Politics," 1975). For Rajan, *The Idea of a Christian Society*, strong on goals and weak on how to achieve them, illustrates the prose side of this remark. He sees greater strength in the Coriolan poems, both of which he reads as poems of failure, "a turning away from reality which constitutes the common ground of failure" (1978, p. 102). Rajan concludes that "in a decade in which political commitment was becoming necessary and honorable, the poems remind us that there is a poetic commitment to understanding by which the political incursion must be shaped" (p. 103). This is fair enough, though Eliot might have put the poetic commitment under some higher discipline.

Social satire of a less pretentious sort can also be found in some of the poems of *Old Possum's Book of Practical Cats*, as we learn from Molly Best Tinsley's "T. S. Eliot's *Book of Practical Cats*" (1975). Tinsley suggests that these poems provide a receptacle "for all the mischief and muddle that could find no place in the ordered universe of a classicist, royalist, and Anglo-Catholic" (p. 171). One of the attractive features of Tinsley's essay is that she never forgets that she is reading nonsense poems, so that she does not insist that the social implications she finds are somehow the true meaning of the poems.

When we turn to the *Four Quartets*, we find ourselves with poems which deliberately raise historical associations but do so in a context shaped by meditations on timeless moments. What this means in terms of Eliot's relation to his society is a matter of debate. Vincent Miller sees in these last poems final proof of "Eliot's Submission to Time" (1976). This submission consists in an acceptance of history and daily life as a necessary and purgative pain, to be endured on the road to salvation. On the other hand, Grania Jones ("Eliot and History," 1976) claims that Eliot is able to "redeem history only by denying its temporal aspects, despite the support of values which have often found it plausible that God should be at work in history" (p. 31). Only superficially modernistic in these poems, says Jones, Eliot accomplished "an audaciously anachronistic manoeuvre . . . by returning to the simplicity of exemplary history," thus showing the "courage to put history in its place" (pp. 46–47).

Although differences over the attitude taken toward history in the *Quartets* may appear to be differences in literary interpretation, they are based on differing value judgments about Eliot's social and religious framework. The attitude expressed in the *Quartets* is very close to that of the social criticism. One of the virtues of James Johnson Sweeney's "*East Coker:* A Reading" (1941) is its sensitivity to the social dimension of the poem; Sweeney is able to make good use of apposite quotations from Eliot's *Idea of a Christian Society*. Careful reading of Eliot's social criticism might save readers from some misinterpretations of his later poetry—Jones' assumption that Eliot denies all value to the temporal being a case in point. The balance between time and the timeless, sought in *Four Quartets*, is much like that in Eliot's essay, "Tradition and the Individual Talent," and like that essay, it is often overlooked. Balancing opposites is natural to Eliot's temperament, congenial to the Classicism he imbibed from Babbitt and others, and native to the Anglican tradition he embraced. Those who see no sense in the pursuit of the timeless moment may still reject the religious cast of Eliot's later poetry and of much of his social criticism. One can hardly understand Eliot and his work, however, without attention to his religious commitment. Our next chapter, then, turns to studies which concentrate on the religious dimension of his work.

References

Acton, H. B.
1950. "Religion, Culture, and Class," *Ethics* Jan., pp. 120–30.

Ames, Russell
1952. "Decadence in the Art of T. S. Eliot," *Science and Society* Mar., pp. 193–221.

Bailey, Ruth
1939. *A Dialogue on Modern Poetry*, pp. 9–31. London: Oxford Univ. Pr.

Bantock, G. H.
1949. "Mr. Eliot and Education," *Scrutiny* Mar., pp. 64–70.
1969. *T. S. Eliot and Education.* New York: Random House.
1973. "T. S. Eliot's View of Society," *Critical Quarterly* Spring, pp. 37–46.

Barrett, William
1949. "Aristocracy and/or Christianity," *Kenyon Review* Summer, pp. 489–96.

Barry, John Brooks
1974. "Eliot's 'Burial of the Dead': A Note on the Morphology of Culture," *Arizona Quarterly* Spring, pp. 63–73.

Barry, John T.
1972. "*The Waste Land:* A Possible German Source," *Comparative Literature Studies* Dec., pp. 429–42.

Bredin, Hugh
1972. "T. S. Eliot and Thomistic Scholasticism," *Journal of the History of Ideas* Apr.–June, pp. 299–306.

Brown, Robert M., and Joseph B. Yokelson
1957. "Eliot's 'Gerontion,' 56–61," *Explicator*, item 31.

Burke, Kenneth
1930. "The Allies of Humanism Abroad," in *The Critique of Humanism*, ed. C. Hartley Grattan, pp. 183–87. New York: Brewer and Warren.
Calverton, V. F.
1934. "T. S. Eliot: Inverted Marxism," *Modern Monthly* July, pp. 372–73.
Cameron, J. M.
1958. "T. S. Eliot as a Political Writer," in *T. S. Eliot: A Symposium*, ed. Neville Braybrooke, pp. 138–51. New York: Farrar, Straus and Cudahy.
Cargill, Oscar
1957. "Mr. Eliot Regrets," *Nation* Feb. 23, pp. 170–72.
Chace, William M.
1973. *The Political Identities of Ezra Pound and T. S. Eliot.* Stanford: Stanford Univ. Pr.
Clark, Richard C.
1973. "Review Article: George Steiner on the 'Christian Barbarism' of Claudel and Eliot," *Review of National Literatures*, pp. 119–25.
Craig, David
1960. "The Defeatism of *The Waste Land*," *Critical Quarterly* Autumn, pp. 241–52. Reprinted in *The Real Foundations*, pp. 195–212. New York: Oxford Univ. Pr., 1974.
Davidson, James
1966. "The End of Sweeney," *College English* Feb., pp. 400–403.
Dawson, Christopher
1949. "Mr. T. S. Eliot on the Meaning of Culture," *Month* Mar., pp. 151–57.
DeLaura, David J.
1977. "Arnold, Newman, and T. S. Eliot: A Note on the Disappearance of God," *Arnoldian* Winter, pp. 2–7.
Donoghue, Denis
1977. "Eliot and the *Criterion*," in *The Literary Criticism of T. S. Eliot*, ed. David Newton-DeMolina, pp. 20–41. London: Athlone.
Eagleton, Terry
1970. "Eliot and a Common Culture," in *Eliot in Perspective*, ed. Graham Martin, pp. 279–95. New York: Humanities Pr.
Eastman, Max
1931. *The Literary Mind.* New York: Scribner's.
Eliot, T. S.
1965. "To Criticize the Critic (1961)," in *To Criticize the Critic*, pp. 11–26. New York: Farrar, Straus and Giroux.
Elliott, George R.
1936. "T. S. Eliot and Irving Babbitt," *American Review* Sept., pp. 442–54.

Empson, William
1975. "Eliot and Politics," *T. S. Eliot Review*, pp. 3–4.
Fleissner, Robert F.
1969. "Reacting to *The Reactionaries:* Libertarian Views," *Journal of Human Relations*, pp. 138–45.
Freedman, Morris
1956. "The Meaning of T. S. Eliot's Jew," *South Atlantic Quarterly* Apr., pp. 198–206.
1971. "Mr. Eliot's Drama: His Jew and His Jazz Rhythms," in *American Drama in Social Context*, pp. 29–42. Carbondale: Southern Illinois Pr.
Gillis, Everett A.
1964. "Religion in a Sweeney World," *Arizona Quarterly* Spring, pp. 55–63.
Griffith, Clark
1963. "Eliot's 'Gerontion,'" *Explicator* Feb., item 46.
Gross, Harvey
1958. "*Gerontion* and the Meaning of History," *PMLA* June, pp. 299–304.
1971. "T. S. Eliot," in *The Contrived Corridor*, pp. 32–75. Ann Arbor: Univ. of Michigan Pr.
Harding, D. W.
1939. "Christian or Liberal?" *Scrutiny* Dec., pp. 309–11.
Harrison, John R.
1967. "T. S. Eliot," in *The Reactionaries*, pp. 145–60. New York: Schocken.
Hillyer, Robert
1949a. "Treason's Strange Fruit," *Saturday Review of Literature* June 11, pp. 9–11, 28.
1949b. "Poetry's New Priesthood," *Saturday Review of Literature* June 18, pp. 7–9, 38.
Hook, Sidney
1945. "The Dilemma of T. S. Eliot," *Nation* Jan. 20, pp. 69–71.
Hutchins, Robert Maynard
1950. "T. S. Eliot on Education," *Measure* Winter, pp. 1–8.
Hyman, Stanley Edgar
1948. *The Armed Vision*, pp. 73–105. New York: Knopf.
Jones, Grania
1976. "Eliot and History," *Critical Quarterly* Autumn, pp. 31–48.
Kinnamon, Rebeccah A.
1973. "Eliot's 'Ash Wednesday' and Maritain's Ideal for Poetry," *Georgia Review* Summer, pp. 156–65.
Kirk, Russell
1971. *Eliot and His Age*. New York: Random House.
1972. "The Waste Land Lies Unredeemed," *Sewanee Review* Summer, pp. 470–78.

1976. "Chesterton and Eliot," *Chesterton Review*, pp. 184–96.

Kogan, Pauline

1971. "The Bourgeois Line on Culture and Anarchy in Matthew Arnold and T. S. Eliot," *Literature and Ideology* (Montreal), pp. 1–14.

Kojecký, Roger

1971. *T. S. Eliot's Social Criticism*. London: Faber and Faber.

Lair, Robert L.

1968. *Barron's Simplified Approach to T. S. Eliot*. Woodbury, N.Y.: Barron's.

Laski, Harold J.

1944. *Faith, Reason and Civilization*, pp. 96–100, 180–82. New York: Viking Pr.

Locke, Louis G.

1945. "Eliot's Burbank with a Baedeker: Bleistein with a Cigar," *Explicator* May, item 53.

Maccoby, Hyam

1973. "The Anti-Semitism of T. S. Eliot," *Midstream* May, pp. 68–79.

Margolis, John D.

1972. *T. S. Eliot's Intellectual Development, 1922–1939*. Chicago: Univ. of Chicago Pr.

Matthews, Brian

1977. " 'Fearful Despair' and a 'Frigid, Snooty Muse,': George Orwell's Involvement with T. S. Eliot, 1930–1950" *Southern Review* (Australia) Nov., pp. 205–31.

Maxwell, D. E. S.

1952. *The Poetry of T. S. Eliot*. London: Routledge and Kegan Paul.

Miller, Vincent

1976. "Eliot's Submission to Time," *Sewanee Review* Spring, pp. 448–64.

Morris, J. A.

1972. "T. S. Eliot and Antisemitism," *Journal of European Studies*, pp. 173–82.

Morton, A. L.

1966. "T. S. Eliot—A Personal View," *Zeitschrift für Anglistik and Amerikanistic*, pp. 286–91.

Munby, D. L.

1963. *The Idea of a Secular Society*. London: Oxford Univ. Pr.

Neibuhr, Reinhold

1940. "Can Church Restrain State?" *Common Sense* Feb., pp. 26–27.

Nott, Kathleen

1954. *The Emperor's Clothes*. Bloomington: Indiana Univ. Pr.

1962. "Whose Culture?" *Listener* Apr. 12, pp. 631–32.

1974. "Ideology and Poetry," in *The Waste Land in Different Voices*, ed. A. D. Moody, pp. 203–20. London: Edward Arnold.

Orwell, George

1968. *The Collected Essays, Journalism and Letters*, ed. Sonia Orwell and Ian Argus. 4 vols. New York: Harcourt Brace Jovanovich.

Ower, John

1971. "Pattern and Value in 'Sweeney among the Nightingales,'" *Renascence*, pp. 151–58.

Peter, John

1970. "Eliot and the *Criterion*," in *Eliot in Perspecitve*, ed. Graham Martin, pp. 252–66. New York: Humanities Pr.

Quiller-Couch, Arthur T.

1934. *The Poet as Citizen*, pp. 44–66. Cambridge: Cambridge Univ. Pr.

Rahv, Philip

1932. "T. S. Eliot," *Fantasy* Winter, pp. 17–20.

Rajan, Balachandra

1978. "A Note on the Coriolan Poems," in *A Political Act: Essays in Honor of George Woodcock*, ed. William H. New, pp. 95–104. Vancouver: Univ. of British Columbia Pr.

Rees, Richard

1967. "T. S. Eliot on Culture and Progress," in *Literature and Politics in the Twentieth Century*, ed. Walter Laquer and George L. Mosse, pp. 99–108. New York: Harper and Row.

Robbins, Rossell Hope

1950. "The T. S. Eliot Myth," *Science and Society* Winter, pp. 1–28.

1951. *The T. S. Eliot Myth.* New York: Henry Schuman.

1953. "A Possible Analogue for *The Cocktail Party*," *English Studies* Aug., 165–67.

San Juan, E., Jr.

1970. "Form and Meaning in 'Gerontion,'" *Renascence* Spring, pp. 115–26.

Savage, D. S.

1944. *The Personal Principle*, pp. 91–112. London: Routledge.

Schuchard, Ronald

1973. "Eliot and Hulme in 1916: Toward a Revaluation of Eliot's Critical and Spiritual Development," *PMLA* Oct., pp. 1083–94.

1974. "T. S. Eliot as an Extension Lecturer, 1916–1919," *Review of English Studies* May, pp. 163–73; Aug., pp. 292–304.

Simon, Brian

1949. "The Defense of Culture," *Communist Review* Dec., pp. 763–68.

Steiner, George

1971. *In Bluebeard's Castle: Some Notes towards the Redefinition of Culture.* New Haven: Yale Univ. Pr.

Sweeney, James Johnson
1941. "*East Coker:* A Reading," *Southern Review* Spring, pp. 771–91.
Theall, Donald F.
1951. "Traditional Satire in Eliot's 'Coriolan,'" *Accent* Aug., pp. 194–206.
Thomas, R. Hinton
1951. "Culture and T. S. Eliot," *Modern Quarterly* Spring, pp. 147–62.
Thompson, T. H.
1934. "The Bloody Wood," *London Mercury* Jan., pp. 233–39.
Tinsley, Molly Best
1975. "T. S. Eliot's *Book of Practical Cats*," *Studies in American Humor* Jan., pp. 167–71.
Torrens, James
1974. "Charles Maurras and Eliot's 'New Life,'" *PMLA* Mar., pp. 312–22.
Turner, Richard C.
1971. "Burbank and Grub-Street: A Note on T. S. Eliot and Swift," *English Studies* Aug., pp. 347–48.
Verma, Rajendra
1968. *Royalist in Politics: T. S. Eliot and Political Philosophy.* New York: Asia Publishing House.
Vickery, John
1958. "*Gerontion:* The Nature of Death and Immortality," *Arizona Quarterly* Summer, pp. 101–15.
Waggoner, Hyatt H.
1943. "T. S. Eliot and the Hollow Men," *American Literature* May, pp. 101–26.
1950. *The Heel of Elohim: Science and Values in Modern American Poetry*, pp. 61–104. Norman: Univ. of Oklahoma Pr.
Warncke, Wayne
1972. "George Orwell on T. S. Eliot," *Western Humanities Review* Summer, pp. 265–70.
Wasson, Richard
1968. "T. S. Eliot's Antihumanism and Antipragmatism," *Texas Studies in Literature and Language* Fall, pp. 445–55.
1969. "'Like a Burnished Throne': T. S. Eliot and the Demonism of Technology," *Centennial Review*, pp. 302–16.
West, Alick
1937. *Crisis and Criticism*, pp. 35–49. London: Lawrence and Wishart.
Williams, Raymond
1958. *Culture and Society*. New York: Columbia Univ. Pr.
Wyndham, S. J.
1948. "Outline for a Critical Approach to T. S. Eliot as Critic," *Contemporary Issues* Winter, pp. 106–16.

Selected Additional Readings

Belgion, Montgomery
1948. "Irving Babbitt and the Continent," in *T. S. Eliot: A Symposium*, ed. Richard March and Tambimuttu, pp. 51–59. London: Editions Poetry.

Bush, Douglas
1949. "No Small Program," *Virginia Quarterly Review* Spring, pp. 287–90.

Cook, Eleanor
1979. "T. S. Eliot and the Carthaginian Peace," *ELH* Summer, pp. 241–55.

Czamanske, Palmer, and Karl Hertz
1952. "The Beginning of T. S. Eliot's Theory of Culture," *Cresset* July, pp. 9–21.

Fekete, John
1977. *The Critical Twilight: Explorations in the Ideology of Anglo-American Literary Theory from Eliot to McLuhan*, pp. 17–25. London: Routledge and Kegan Paul.

Greenberg, Clement
1953. "The Plight of Our Culture: Industrialism and Class Mobility," *Commentary* June, pp. 558–66.

Habedank, Klaus
1974. *Kultur- und Sozialkritik bei T. S. Eliot.* Hamburg: Hartmut Ludke.

Levy, William T.
1958. "The Idea of the Church in T. S. Eliot," *Christian Scholar* Dec., pp. 587–600.

Mordell, Albert
1951. *T. S. Eliot's Deficiencies as a Social Critic.* Girard, Kan.: Haldeman-Julius.

Murdoch, Iris
1958. "T. S. Eliot as a Moralist," in *T. S. Eliot: A Symposium*, ed. Neville Braybrooke, pp. 152–60. New York: Farrar, Straus and Cudahy.

Reckitt, Maurice B.
1939. "Views and Reviews: A Sub-Christian Society," *New English Weekly* Dec. 7, pp. 115–16.

Schwartz, Edward
1953. "Eliot's *Cocktail Party* and the New Humanism," *Philological Quarterly* Jan., pp. 53–58.

Strachey, John
1933. *The Coming Struggle for Power*, pp. 218–21. New York: Covici Friede.

CHAPTER 4

The Religious Poet

Few of its early readers regarded *The Waste Land* as religious poetry. It was read as expressing the disillusionment of a generation, and its poet was assumed to share the avant-garde disillusion with religion. Eliot's later public declaration of faith was a shock to many and seemed a betrayal to some. His most secular-minded critics still regard the religious character of his later poetry and drama as a serious defect. In his essay "Religion and Literature" (1935), Eliot acknowledged that many lovers of poetry assume that religious poetry is necessarily minor poetry. He concedes, moreover, that there is a considerable body of devotional poetry "which is the product of a special religious awareness, which may exist without the general awareness which we expect of the major poet." Critics who find Eliot lacking certain fundamental human sympathies needed for the greatest poetry are, in effect, denying him this general awareness, although they are scarcely justified in assuming, as some of those cited in the last chapter seem to, that such a deficiency is necessarily linked to his religious commitments. For good or for ill, the relevance of Eliot's faith to his later poetry and to his plays is generally recognized, and a number of critics have stressed the importance of the religious dimension in *The Waste Land* and other early poems.

Most discussions of the religious implications of Eliot's work have been written by critics sympathetic to his religious outlook. Some of this criticism, even when most lavish in its praise, has the effect of interpreting Eliot's poetry and drama in ways which deny him the general awareness Eliot himself thinks valuable. Pious interpretations of "The Hippopotamus," like those touched in our first chapter, read like those strange exegeses in which learned divines extract Christian typological morals from the more bloodthirsty passages of the Old Testament. Some of the interpretations of the *Four Quartets* dealt with in this chapter read rather like Sunday School primers and manage to make Eliot sound the same. Reductive explanations which transform poems and plays into exemplifications of mythic method, primers of mysticism, or demonstrations of doctrine do little to help us experience them as works of art. Even so, some attention to the religious dimensions of Eliot's work, particularly the later poems and the dramas, is necessary and useful. We may, perhaps, appreciate these works without sharing Eliot's particular variety of faith, but we can hardly hope to understand them without making some effort to come to terms with the way in which his religious concerns have affected the poems and plays.

The Early Christian

Eliot's passage from the apparent satire of "The Hippopotamus" and the desolation of *The Waste Land* into the folds of Anglicanism requires some explanation. The first attempts to explain this development assumed that the early poetry expressed a period of uncomfortable unbelief through which the poet passed on his way to a personally more satisfying belief. Critics of differing persuasions disagreed on whether the passage should be attributed to spiritual maturity or loss of nerve. This sort of explanation of Eliot's religious development oversimplifies the relation between belief and disbelief in a mind like Eliot's, but it has the virtue of corresponding to most readers' initial experience of Eliot's early poetry. Even today, it requires strenuous mental gymnastics to read in Christian terms most of the poems before "Gerontion" and *The Waste Land*, although some critics have demonstrated that it is possible to do so.

The view that Eliot's earliest verse had no particular spiritual overtones was shared by even the religiously inclined among his early critics, as one can see in Thomas McGreevy's *Thomas Stearns Eliot* (1931). McGreevy, an aggressively Roman Catholic Irish critic, indulges in many passing hits at Eliot's Anglicanism. For him, Eliot's earliest verse is "gentlemanly whimpering" or "disdainful wit," fortunately abandoned when the poet "was overtaken by a subject worthy of his powers," the great theme of "death and resurrection" (p. 34). In McGreevy's view, some of the early poetry is clever enough, and

"Prufrock" is a perfect poem of its adolescent kind. But cleverness is not enough for poems which touch on religious themes, and McGreevy sternly observes that in a poem like "Mr. Eliot's Sunday Morning Service," "the young versifier does not grasp the possible spiritual significance of the service. Or, if he does, he keeps it to himself" (p. 12). McGreevy is fully aware of the religious significance of *The Waste Land*, and prefers it to *Ash Wednesday*.

Some critics, of course, would claim that in early poems like the "Sunday Morning Service" Eliot is perfectly aware of the spiritual significance of his themes and is merely parodying the wicked modern world, which observes the rites and has lost the meaning. Everett A. Gillis finds many examples of this in his "Scurrilous Parody in T. S. Eliot's Early Religious Verse" (1972). Anglican services are parodied not only in the "Sunday Morning Service" but in the "Burial of the Dead" section of *The Waste Land*. The Mass is parodied in "Gerontion," "Sweeney among the Nightingales," and the beginning of section III of *The Waste Land*—though in this last case Gillis's explanation suggests that he is thinking instead of the boudoir scene, which opens section II. The purpose of such parodies, says Gillis, is "to demonstrate the decay of religious values generally, and of formal worship in particular, in the modern world," while serving as part of the "facade" by which Eliot "masks much of his early meaning" (pp. 43, 48). Although Eliot is a poet who sometimes dons masks, this comes close to looking like a "conspiracy theory" of poetic creation. Religious hypocrisy can be mocked and religious symbols utilized by believers and unbelievers alike, and speculating on the author's motives is sometimes less than helpful.

In "Mr. Eliot's Sunday Morning Service," for example, contrasts are drawn between "the unoffending feet" of Christ and the service being attended, and between the souls burning in purgatory and those who would buy forgiveness with "piaculative pence"; but such contrasts can be drawn by the devout and nondevout alike. Even on the surface, this is a difficult poem. An unabridged dictionary and references to scholarship will solve some of its difficulties—we can learn from Floyd C. Watkins, for example, in his "T. S. Eliot's Painter of the Umbrian School" (1964), that Piero della Francesca, whose *Baptism of Christ* hung in London's National Gallery, was most likely Eliot's reference. But such information does not help us resolve the poem's deeper ambiguities. Are we to take it as a satire, as its tone seems to suggest, or as a meditative lyric of experience, balanced somewhere between devotion and skepticism?

Something like a lyric reading of the poem is provided by Arvid Shulenberger in "Eliot's 'Mr. Eliot's Sunday Morning Service' " (1952). The poem is read as an internal monologue which begins with the entry of the priests, who are contrasted unfavorably with Origen, a great figure of the church, and more pointedly with an ascetic Umbrian mural of the baptism of Christ. But Anselm Atkins' "Mr. Eliot's Sunday Morning Parody" (1968) presents the poem as a parody of the verbose and abstruse speculation associated with Origen, who is to be identified, rather than contrasted, with the present "sapient sutlers of the Lord." Atkins also identifies Origen with the "masters of the subtle schools" at the end of the poem, while Shulenberger sees these as present-day learned men, unable to explain the decline of the church; Shulenberger points out that Origen was pre-Scholastic. Although Atkins' insistence that the entire poem is a parody of Origen seems unnecessarily esoteric, the overtones of "enervate Origen" suggest that Origen is not held up as a model to admire.

Ernest Schanzer's interpretation of "Mr. Eliot's Sunday Morning Service" (1955), anticipates Atkins in presenting the initial stanzas as a sustained contrast between the Word of God and the wordiness of the Fathers of the church. Schanzer does not, like Atkins, find this contrast dominating the remainder of the poem; in fact, he is unsure that the poem is unified at all. Schanzer takes the fifth and sixth stanzas to contrast the easy penitence of the pustular young with the true purgation of those in purgatory, but he admits that the contrast is not clear. Seeing no irony in "blest office of the epicene," Schanzer would have the bees of the seventh stanza contrasted favorably with the epicene priests (the "sable presbyters"), who are not fruitful and who presumably deserve the words of the epigraph, "two religious caterpillars." The introduction of Sweeney in the last stanza brings new contrasts—the stated one with the disputing Fathers and the implicit contrast between Sweeney's bath and Christ's "unoffending feet" or the souls burning in purgatory. Schanzer believes that the introduction of Sweeney "still further lessens the coherence of the poem" (p. 158). This is a fair point, but it derives much of its force from his implicit assumption that the reality of the Word is never in question, so that Sweeney's gross reality contrasts mainly with the speculative schools.

Schanzer had hoped to start a debate on the poem, but the principal reply was by David Holbrook, arguing that Schanzer had been too kind to the poem, which is emblematic of "Mr. Eliot's Chinese Wall" (1955). Admitting that there is a good Mr. Eliot who writes good poems, Holbrook waxes wroth against the bad Mr. Eliot, whose didactic mannerisms disguise "a recoil from human sexual potentialities" (p. 421). This recoil is the true unifying element in "Mr. Eliot's Sunday Morning Service," where it is only partly disguised by "the dishonest habit and manner" (p. 426). There is no doubt that the poem, as is not unusual with Eliot, expresses in some of its images a revulsion from the flesh, but to insist that the poem is somehow about such feelings is to carry healthy mindedness to extremes. The nondialogue between Schanzer and Holbrook offers us an apparent choice between taking anticlericalism as a sign of deep religious conviction or seeing it as a disguise for naturally procelibate sentiments.

Dealing with the poem as a satire does not necessarily make things simpler, certainly not in George Monteiro's "Christians and Jews in 'Mr. Eliot's Sunday Morning Service' " (1976). Monteiro sees himself as working along lines suggested by Hugh Kenner, who is not quite accurately cited as reading the poem as a satire on the decline of historical Christianity, from the ideal Christ of Origen to the Christ found in Sweeney. Monteiro wants to add to this the poem's alleged " 'semitic' element" (p. 20). Not only, we learn, is the epigraph taken from Marlowe's *The Jew of Malta*, but the poem's opening word (and line), "Polyphiloprogenitive," is very like "philoprogenitive," a word applied to Jews in two works Monteiro cites, without giving reason to believe that Eliot had read them. This might sound like we were dealing again with the "anti-Semitic Eliot" of some critics. Monteiro thinks that Eliot is prejudiced, but he argues that, in this poem, "to attack decadent Christians Eliot turns back upon them their own anti-semitism" (p. 21). How this is accomplished remains unclear. This is by no means the only case in Eliot criticism where importing an epigraph into the poem introduces more new confusion than clarity. More reasonable is Monteiro's final suggestion that the title shows Eliot satirizing his own superciliousness.

Monteiro sees Sweeney as another object of prejudice, turned against its holders, in "Mr. Eliot's Sunday Morning Service." Although that scarcely seems likely, one supposes that Sweeney can take care of himself. It does, however, seem a pity to find Grishkin, of the "friendly bust," reduced to a mere ideological cartoon in Sister M. Cleophas' interpretation of "Eliot's 'Whispers of Immortality'" (1949). In this reading, Grishkin "symbolizes materialism," and even "the Abstract Entities (modern philosophy) have succumbed to her." These interpretive abstractions are not irrelevant to the poem—as one feels about Monteiro's polyphiloprogenitive Jews in the other poem—but Cleophas manages to take a poem once praised by William Empson (*Seven Types of Ambiguity*, 1930) for its controlled use of ambiguity, and reduce it to a simplistic allegory of the modern condition. These are not major Eliot poems, but they deserve to be taken seriously. Still, to take such poems seriously one must first learn to take them lightly.

As a commentary and an antidote to ponderous attempts to read piety into the early Eliot, one should turn to Felix Clowder's "The Bestiary of T. S. Eliot" (1960), which applies this approach to Eliot's *Old Possum's Book of Practical Cats* (1939). The "Jellicle Cats," Clowder reveals, are evangelicals, whose enthusiasm ("like a jumping-jack") is mildly deplored by the Anglican Eliot. "Old Deuteronomy" is clearly the established church itself, secure in its many livings and dozing quietly. The three names of cats (in "The Naming of Cats") suggest the Trinity, with one of the names unknown to man, like the Hebrew name for God. Perhaps the entire book was "originally conceived *in posse* (or pussy) as *Old Parson's Book of Practical Catechumens*" (p. 37). Clowder's essay is presumably satiric, though no regular reader of Eliot criticism will be wholly sure. It makes a nice companion piece to Molly Best Tinsley's sociological reading of Eliot's cats (mentioned in an earlier chapter).

The tone of "Gerontion" is much more somber than that of the poems mentioned so far in this chapter, and here it seems fairly clear that we have a meditative lyric of experience, though most first readers of the poem may feel that they have had the experience and missed the meaning. Although the poem exists on many levels of meaning, many critics find the religious level dominant. Although Mervyn Williamson presents his 1957 essay on the poem as an attempt to challenge standard views of Eliot's development ("T. S. Eliot's 'Gerontion': A Study in Thematic Repetition and Development"), a Christian reading of "Gerontion" was already widespread. F. Dye, for example, calls it an exercise in "negative theology," exemplifying the wrong kind of relationship between God and man, so that Gerontion's lack of a "real relation with the supernatural" is responsible for his unsatisfactory relationship with the natural world of the senses ("Eliot's 'Gerontion,' " 1960). For Wolf Mankowitz, too, the sterility of Gerontion's setting is sexual only on the surface, and the real villain is the loss of Christian belief ("Notes on 'Gerontion,' " 1947). The mob has rejected Christ, and those who give him only lip service are little better off and feel a nameless terror. For Mankowitz, the "new year" which brings "Christ the tiger" is less a seasonal phenomenon than an apocalyptic one, and the terror is justified. Like his civilization, Gerontion faces death. Having lost his faith in ratiocination, he is even further from belief than the cosmopolitans. Intellectually, he knows that he must accept death, but he occupies his time with rationalization. He knows that he cannot be forgiven, but argues that he deserves forgiveness; he knows that his life is purposeless, but would not think it so. But nothing will avail him against death and his just devouring.

In his 1957 essay, Williamson shares this Christian reading of the poem. Like critics of a variety of persuasions, he reads "Gerontion" as closing on a note of despair which anticipates the opening passages of *The Waste Land.* What is unusual in his reading is an effort to show that "many of its allusions and symbols point toward Eliot's later poetry," especially *Ash Wednesday* and portions of *Four Quartets* (p. 111). The Andrewes passage in "Gerontion," for example, reappears in *Ash Wednesday V.* The wind of "a windy knob," not surprisingly, can be found in several later poems. Some of the resemblances suggested, like that between Gerontion's "Christ the tiger" and the leopards of *Ash Wednesday*, are not terribly close, but Williamson's efforts to suggest thematic continuity are at least suggestive.

Another relatively original Christian interpretation of this poem is Daniel R. Schwarz's "The Unity of Eliot's 'Gerontion': The Failure of Meditation" (1971), although the framework of his argument comes from Louis Martz. Schwarz sees the poem as modeled on Donne's *Second Anniversary*; in support of this, he notes Eliot's comparison of Lancelot Andrewes and Donne and some verbal echoes ("Thinke then"). The Donne poem serves as a model of successful meditation, by which we may explain the failure of Gerontion's efforts at meditation. The notion of "Gerontion" as a failed meditation does not require identification of a specific model; given the slim evidence, the Donne poem is probably best regarded as a model of a type rather than a specific source. Schwarz believes that seeing the poem as a failed meditation will help explain away "the apparently incoherent structure" of the poem, "the speaker's imprecision and incongruous combinations of sensual and spiritual images" (p. 55). The speaker can be seen to have recognized the spiritual insufficiency of preceding passages; unfortunately, this simply slaps a spiritual label on the general recognition that Gerontion's associative monologue is at least partly a debate with himself. Moreover, only a rigidly religious reading would see the poem's ambiguities as simple "imprecision" or find the yoking of sensual and spiritual images "incongruous." Such analyses insist on separating elements in the poem which the poet and his persona have fused together.

Roughly the same objections apply to readings of *The Waste Land* which ignore the personal elements in the poem's spiritual quest. Florence Jones, for example, in "T. S. Eliot among the Prophets" (1966), begins by positing a strawman interpretation of *The Waste Land*, as displaying "romantic nihilism" (p. 285), a view nowadays found only among naive readers (i.e., those who read the poem but not the critics). More to the point is her objection to readings which describe the relationship between time and the timeless as essentially different from that in *Four Quartets*. The Incarnation is in the poem, Jones argues, and by no means is diminished by the equation of Christ with fertility gods. The prophets, too, used imagery taken from fertility deities to praise Yahweh. This argument, though sound, means only that a Christian interpretation cannot be ruled out; but it does not require such an interpretation. The bulk of Jones' essay is devoted to an extended and unconvincing comparison of *The Waste Land* with the prophetic books, especially Jeremiah. Particular Old Testament echoes are certainly found in the poem, though Eliot's waste land resembles Ezekiel's visions more than Jeremiah's. Efforts to include the poem's sexual material in this framework by comparing, for example, Albert's bride in "A Game of Chess" with Israel as the unfaithful bride of the Lord carry no conviction. Nor are

Jones' arguments that a day of judgment is at hand at the end of the poem well supported with evidence.

A more sensible account of a biblical source is Peter Martin's " 'Son of Man' in the Book of Ezekiel and T. S. Eliot's *The Waste Land*" (1977). Eliot's note to line 20 refers us to the Book of Ezekiel, where God addresses Ezekiel as the "Son of man." Martin notes that the term also appears frequently in Daniel and that it has strong Christological connotations. But his essay concentrates on drawing parallels between the waste land of Ezekiel's vision and Eliot's, and he shows that these extend far beyond the passage referred to in Eliot's note. More tentatively, he suggests that Ezekiel, as the "Son of man," may have a better right to be thought of as the protagonist of the poem than does Tiresias. Martin finds the Book of Ezekiel a more consistent parallel to the action of the poem than either the Christ story or the Grail quest, but he disavows any effort to assert the "primacy of some single source" for a poem he sees as incorporating multiple references to images rich in "historical and archetypal associations" (p. 215).

The religious imagery in "Gerontion" and *The Waste Land* shows Eliot moving toward his later Christianity. Although the specifically Christian readings of earlier poems are not very convincing, hindsight allows us to see in some of them a concern with things of the spirit, fueled either by an instinctive faith not yet acceptable to reason, or by a need for an ordering principle in life. Zohreh Tawakuli Sullivan may have a point in arguing that Prufrock and the narrator of "Rhapsody on a Windy Night" share Gerontion's "frustrated search for illumination" ("Memory and Meditative Structure in T. S. Eliot's Early Poetry," 1977, p. 102). Sullivan probably overrates the influence of previous meditative poetry on these poems, and certainly reads them very much in the light of Eliot's later Christian work. Neither "Prufrock" nor "Rhapsody on a Windy Night" is primarily religious, and the absence of "illumination" from the poems does not imply a particular definition of "illumination" on the part of the poet. It is possible to see the early Eliot as a man in search of a faith, but there is more to the man and the poetry than that. Moreover, though Eliot was raised in an avowedly Christian culture, as a young man he was interested in a broader spectrum of faith than the Anglican Christianity he eventually adopted as his own.

The Seeker of Wisdom

Eliot took Indic studies as a graduate student at Harvard, wrote on comparative religion for his seminar with Royce, and maintained for much of his life a respectful attitude toward Indian religious and philosophical traditions. His studies left their imprint on both *The Waste Land* and the *Four Quartets.* Whether or not he at one time seriously considered becoming a Buddhist, he was obviously attracted to other faiths than Christianity at an early stage in his spiritual quest. Some critics have also credited him with an interest in the sort of esoteric and occult lore that often seems to go with Western interest in Eastern religion.

Eliot himself was inclined to deprecate his understanding of Hindu and Buddhist thought. In *After Strange Gods* (1934), he reports that his Indic studies left him in a state of "enlightened mystification," and he doubts that any Westerner can understand the Indian tradition without abandoning his own. Some critics have been loath to accept these judgments. B. N. Chaturvedi, for example, surveys "The Indian Background of Eliot's Poetry" (1965) and concludes that Eliot's remarks in *After Strange Gods* are at odds with his poetic practice. He cites the use of Buddha's Fire Sermon and the thunder of the *Brihadaranyaka Upanishad*, in *The Waste Land* as signs that Eliot was already attempting to integrate Indian traditions into his world view. The *Bhagavad Gita*, which Eliot called "the next greatest philosophical poem to the *Divine Comedy*" (in his 1929 Dante essay), is present in several of the *Four Quartets.* Chaturvedi sees all three Indic traditions as integrated in the *Four Quartets* and believes "it is doubtful whether Eliot would have been able to attain to the spiritual insight embodied in the latter if he had not made a study of the Indian scriptures" (p. 223). This assertion seems rather at odds with Chaturvedi's more defensible claim that the *Four Quartets* show "the basic unity of oriental and Christian mysticism" (p. 222).

Another general survey of Indic contributions to Eliot's work is William K. Bottorff's "Hindu and Buddhist Usages in the Poetry of T. S. Eliot" (1972). Bottorff also professes to go beyond identification to explication of such usages, but it is not clear what his reflections add to our understanding. Of the Fire Sermon of *The Waste Land*, he tells us that Eliot's note is misleading, since, whatever impression may be given by the Fire Sermon, the Sermon at Benares makes it clear that

"Buddha was no ascetic" (p. 113). This judgment adds little to our understanding of the use of the Fire Sermon in *The Waste Land.*

More importantly, Bottorff tells us that the words listed in the notes to line 308, as taken from Buddha's Fire Sermon, do not appear in the translation cited. A glance at the line in question makes one wonder whether Bottorff's point (or Eliot's note) changes much. If we accept Bottorff's point as significant, then we must doubt his other argument, that the Fire Sermon has influenced the particulars of the section to which it gives its name. The parallels cited are too general to be convincing, with the barely possible exception of Eliot's use of the term "indifference"—which Bottorff links with the word "indifferent," very differently used in the Fire Sermon (Warren translation).

Bottorff is more convincing in his treatment of "What the Thunder Said." He notes that Eliot reversed the order of the three commands of the thunder and, printing the original anecdote, Bottorff makes it clear that the reference to "control" means self-control, at least in its original context. His notion that Prajpati, the thunder deity, is implied, along with Christ, in "He who was living is now dead" seems less plausible. Finally, Bottorff deals briefly with the most obvious appearance of the *Bhagavad Gita* in the *Four Quartets*, the third section of "Dry Salvages"—"I sometimes wonder if that is what Krishna meant."

For a useful account, we may consult G. Nageswara Rao's essay " 'The Fire Sermon' in *The Waste Land*" (1972). Rao writes about the relevance of the Fire Sermon to the section named for it without forgetting that "Eliot was writing a poem and not a theological tract" (p. 101), mainly in terms of Buddha's call for self-discipline and an end to desire.

Other Buddhist references in Eliot's work have also been noted. Grover Smith's admirable source study, *T. S. Eliot's Poetry and Plays* (1956), suggests that an anecdote also found in Henry Clarke Warren's *Buddhism in Translation* may have contributed to the line "I do not know whether a man or a woman" in *Waste Land V.* G. Schmidt's "An Echo of Buddhism in T. S. Eliot's 'Little Gidding' " (1973) finds a close verbal parallel between material in Warren's chapter on fruitful and barren karma and Eliot's "There are three conditions which often look alike." In *The Cocktail Party*, Sir Henry's message, "Work out your salvation with diligence," echoes Buddha's last sermon, and R. Baird Shuman argues that Celia does so in the spirit of Buddhism ("Buddhistic Overtones in Eliot's *The Cocktail Party*," 1957). A more philosophical approach to analogies with Buddhist thought is taken in Harold E. McCarthy's "T. S. Eliot and Buddhism" (1952). Taken together, these articles do not demonstrate any lifelong interest in Buddhism on Eliot's part. They suggest that his early reading of Buddhist works left him with some lasting impressions.

In his note to line 402 of *The Waste Land*, Eliot indicates that the thunder's words come from the *Brihadaranyaka Upanishad* and he mentions a translation by Paul Deussen (1899). According to Mukhtar Ali Isani (1973), the presentation of the wisdom of the thunder in *The Waste Land* may owe something to the Deussen translation. Although the three commands of the thunder were originally addressed separately to gods, demons, and men, the translator suggested that this "was only a matter of form and did not indicate that each class was required to exercise only one of the three cardinal virtues" (p. 219). We are also told that in translating the key terms, Eliot may have relied on the *Sanscrit Reader* of Charles Lanman, under whom Eliot had studied at Harvard.

Lanman may also have influenced Eliot's interpretation of the thunder's sayings, a possibility exaggerated by M. E. Grenander and K. S. Narayana Rao in their discussion "*The Waste Land* and the Upanishads: What Does the Thunder Say?" (1971). Lanman discussed the legend in an essay included in *Anniversary Papers by Colleagues and Pupils of George Kittredge* (1913), and this makes it seem quite likely that he may have called attention to it in courses Eliot is known to have taken. Although aware that Eliot had read the Upanishads in the Sanscrit and in other translations, Grenander and Rao attribute great significance to the "changes" between Lanman's "be compassionate" and "control yourselves" and Eliot's "sympathize" and "control." A poet's natural preference for single-word imperatives would seem sufficient explanation.

Comparison of the Grenander-Rao and Isani essays suggests that this is one of those cases in which source study does not solve interpretive problems. In both essays, it is seen as significant that Eliot changed the original order of the thunder's commands. For Grenander and Rao, the distinctively human virtue of giving is placed first, and we then move up the hierarchy to the godlike virtue of "control." Grenander and Rao are aware that in the original legend each class is linked with the virtue it finds hardest to exercise–giving for men, self-control for gods. But they overturn this by assuming that Eliot's "control" is control of others, and thus a virtue to be practiced by those who have mastered the other two. Isani, on the other hand, argues that control is the final virtue because self-control requires preliminary channeling of the passions into giving. In more or less abandoning implicit references to gods and demons, in assuming that all three virtues are demanded of the protagonist, and in taking control to be self-control, Isani's interpretation is more convincing–but for reasons that have little to do with the source. If G. Nageswara Rao, in "The Upanishads and *The Waste Land*" (1973), is correct in arguing that there are other links, through Jessie Weston's references to Vedic hymns and Upanishadic passages in *From Ritual to Romance*, it seems likely that such sources will have little importance for our understanding of the poem.

Milton Miller's "What the Thunder Meant" (1969) deserves mention even so, because of the ingenuity with which it combines the *Upanishad* reference with other material. In the legend, the thunder says only "DA"; the gods, men, and demons must interpret it for themselves. The same need for interpretation, says Miller, is found in Kyd's *Spanish Tragedy*, and Eliot may have had in mind that Hieronymo means "Holy Name" or "bearing the Holy Name." The meaningful but mysterious speech and the need for the separate gift of interpretation are also like the biblical experience of glossolalia. What the thunder calls forth in the protagonist, the "fragments," are also a kind of Pentecostal glossolalia. The Pentecostal experience of the refining fire of the Holy Ghost thus answers the protagonist's quest, even though the waste land itself (the world) remains unredeemed. Miller himself writes in disorderly fragments, in need of interpretation, but his essay is suggestive so long as one does not feel called upon to take glossolalia as anything more than an analogy.

Eliot's praise of the *Bhagavad Gita* as a "philosophical poem" reminds us that the *Four Quartets* are also philosophical in this rather special sense. There is a direct reference to Krishna and the *Gita* in "Dry Salvages III", and some critics have found the *Gita*'s influence more pervasive. Russell T. Fowler argues that the *Gita* is important for both the form and theme of "Little Gidding" ("Krishna and the 'Still Point': A Study of the *Bhagavad Gita*'s Influence on Eliot's *Four Quartets*," 1971). Some of the points of similarity offered by Fowler are far too general to prove any specific influence; for example, images of spiritual progress as a journey or voyage. Narsingh Srivastava notes additional similarities, some of which are useful correctives to stereotyped Western views of Indic religions, as when Srivastava notes that "redemption through grace is as central to the teachings of Lord Krishna as it is to Christianity" ("The Ideas of the *Bhagavad Gita* in *Four Quartets*," 1977). The similarities pointed to by Fowler and Srivastava are sufficient to explain why Eliot could find it appropriate to introduce Krishna into a poem whose major religious symbols are Christian and to explain why Eliot admired the *Gita*. No profound influence of the *Gita* on Eliot has been proved.

K. S. Narayana Rao's "T. S. Eliot and the *Bhagavad Gita*" (1963) is far less general than its title might suggest. Rao is wholly concerned here with "To the Indians Who Died in Africa," a poem Eliot contributed to *Queen Mary's Book for India* (1943)—which reminds us that Eliot had little talent for occasional verse of this sort. Starting from the references to fruitful action in the last few lines, Rao maintains that the entire poem reflects the philosophy and situation of the *Bhagavad Gita*. In "*Addendum* on Eliot and the *Bhagavad Gita*" (1964), Rao comments on revisions Eliot made in the poem for *Collected Poems, 1909–1962*. Rao says the revisions weaken the philosophic content of the poem and make it less attractive for the Indian reader. Rao may be right about the revisions, but one doubts that the poem was ever weighty enough to bear the philosophy he would burden it with. Again, similarity of thought or situation is not enough to establish a real connection.

In his notes to *The Waste Land*, Eliot tells us that he is "not familiar with the exact constitution of the Tarot pack," but some readers have seen him as a master of its esoteric lore. David W. Evans, for example, tells us that Eliot "was somewhat better informed than his brief note would suggest" ("T. S. Eliot, Charles Williams, and the Sense of the Occult," 1954, p. 153), though Evans provides little evidence to prove the point. Two later critics have found evidence that Eliot's knowledge of the tarot deck was at least wider than that provided by Jessie Weston's book on the Grail motif. The key term is Eliot's use of "the man with three staves," for this card occurs only in a tarot deck designed by Arthur E. Waite, drawn by Pamela Colman Smith, and explained by Waite in *The Pictorial Key to the Tarot* (1910). This identification was first made by Gertrude Moakley in "The Waite-Smith 'Tarot': A Footnote to *The Waste Land*" (1954). Apparently unaware of Moakley's essay, Tom Gibbons published the same information in 1972 ("*The Waste Land* Tarot Identified"). Most tarot packs do not have pictures for the suit cards, but Waite's does, and his design for the Three of Wands shows a man looking out over the sea and leaning on one of three staves planted in the ground. The use of "staves" in Waite's description may indicate that Eliot had seen Waite's book. Both Moakley and Gibbons also point out that Waite's Hanged Man card and Waite's description of its meaning also fit Eliot's association of this figure with the Hanged God better than most traditional pictures for this card. Moakley also observes that the only conspicuous reference to blank cards in tarot packs occurs in an obscure item cited in Waite's bibliography. R. E. Scott has questioned Moakley's identification of the Waite pack, but it remains persuasive ("T. S. Eliot's *Waste Land*, 43–59 ['Eliot's Gypsy']," 1974).

Eliot's apparent acquaintance with Waite's deck could have resulted from nothing more than exposure to the conversation (and perhaps the cards) of a tarot enthusiast whose patter included some of Waite's lore. None of the three critics suggests deep involvement on Eliot's part. Evans argues that unfamiliarity with tarot may explain Eliot's association of "a very humble member of the suit cards, the Man with Three Staves, with the extremely important figure of the Fisher King" (p. 154), though Waite's picture for the card may be relevant here. Moakley sees Eliot's reference to "the traditional pack" of tarot cards as an indication that he did not know "what he was talking about" (p. 471), since the Waite deck, now widely available and hallowed by time, was then something of an innovation. Even so, Moakley goes on to find clues to "Belladonna, the Lady of the Rocks" and the Fisher King in Waite's designs for the Two of Swords and the King of Cups. Gibbons prefers to identify Belladonna with the Queen of Cups, and he finds over a dozen allusions to the tarot pack in *The Waste Land*. As a not unfair example of the evidence, we may cite Gibbons' remark that "kings occur in lines 66, 191, and 192" (1972, p. 564). If we can see a reference to the four kings of the tarot deck in the name King William Street, we can see almost anything we want to. Like other occult devices, tarot cards allow for an almost infinite series of correspondences. Readers who are familiar with the deck can find such correspondences, whether or not Eliot had more than a passing familiarity with tarot.

The question of Eliot's familiarity with tarot may seem more meaningful if we remember Yeats' extended dabbling with the occult. For the serious occultist, the correspondence allowed for or revealed by tarot may represent the underlying unity of the universe and point to the esoteric meaning behind all religion. It is as an adherent to the "perennial philosophy" of the occult tradition that Eliot is the last major figure considered in John Senior's *The Way Down and Out: The Occult in Symbolist Literature* (1959). Senior argues that the correspondences in Symbolist literature are not mere metaphors but seriously intended symbols of transcendent unity, meant not only to express that unity but to help the reader apprehend it for himself. As early as the "Preludes," Senior says, Eliot was searching out such epiphanies, moments in which we are suddenly suspended "on the brink of the eternity of Self-realization" (p. 173). Even "Prufrock" gets an "occult" reading, in this broad sense of the term.

Senior does not, however, maintain that Eliot was as fully immersed in the occult tradition as Yeats. *The Waste Land* is not "an occult work, in the sense that Blake's works are" (p. 178). Eliot, instead, is a spiritual searcher who has picked up material he is not yet prepared to understand, so that it "is not an entirely serious poem" (p. 179). Jessie Weston's book, Senior says, is based as much on occult sources like Waite as on any "scientific" anthropology. Senior's reading of *The Waste Land* is actually fairly conventional. Noting that Christ is present only by indirection in both it and *Ash Wednesday*, Senior suggests that Eliot is closer in spirit to those who see all religions as variations on one truth than Eliot will admit to in his prose. Despite the Christian imagery, *Four Quartets* also express this syncretic philosophy—"only the Holy Ghost is actually worshipped in Eliot's poetry" (p. 187).

The chief question about Senior's work is the relation between his "occult" tradition and the kind of mysticism Eliot's later work displays. Senior sees "occult" as the more inclusive term: "Mysticism is the form occultism took in Christendom as yoga is the form it took in India" (p. xviii). But the apparent similarity of the experiences achieved does not necessarily imply the kind of doctrinal agreement required for a "perennial philosophy." To the extent that Eliot's timeless moments are modeled on the Incarnation, they come to time from outside time, give meaning to the world without being of the world. Senior himself says: "But what is meaning? In *The Waste Land* there is none. In *Ash Wednesday* and *Four Quartets* . . . Eliot declares that whatever meaning events may have is not in the events themselves but is conferred" (p. 180). To an outsider, this seems rather different from the occult identification of the world with a universe of meaning or from the dismissal of the world as illusion found in some Eastern traditions. To say that *Four Quartets* "is based on occult doctrine" (p. 187) is too strong. Perhaps it would be fairer to say that this and other Eliot poems use images and convey experiences which can be interpreted in the light of occult doctrine—as what cannot?

The Mythic Poet

The picture of Eliot as a spiritual searcher delving in the occult tradition may gain some credence from *The Waste Land's* syncretic mix of Christian imagery, Indic wisdom, tarot cards, and vegetation myths. But we need not assume that these are identified with each other any more than is normally implied by the relation between tenor and vehicle in poetic metaphor. For some readers, all other mythic references are present as reflections of the central Christian mystery of death and rebirth. For others, all religious references reflect the sexual or social preoccupations of the protagonist. Readers of rather different persuasions, however, have been able to agree on seeing the Eliot of *The Waste Land* as a mythic poet who gives his work unity by manipulating familiar and unfamiliar myths, rather on the pattern of James Joyce in *Ulysses*. Madame Sosostris' brief appearance has given rise to a great variety of readings, several of them giving her mythic significance of one sort or another. Eliot's reference in the notes to Jessie Weston's *From Ritual to Romance* has encouraged lovers of fertility gods everywhere, and readings of the poem as a Grail quest are rather standard.

Madame Sosostris' name has proved remarkedly evocative. In 1950, Lysander Kemp suggested that she may be named after an Egyptian god-king Sesostris and (very tentatively, to be sure) that the misspelling might be a deliberate suggestion that she is only "so-so" ("Eliot's *The Waste Land*, I, 43–59") Later that year, Lyman A. Cotten agreed that Sesostris was a likely source but added that her name might also be meant to suggest the Greek roots *sos* ("alive and well," "certain") and *tris* ("thrice") —ironically, of course ("Eliot's *The Waste Land*, I, 43–46). The pseudo-Egyptian connotations of the tarot deck gave the Sesostris identification some plausibility, but Grover Smith may have ended this particular ancient parallel by finding a more immediate source, in his "The Fortune Teller in Eliot's *The Waste Land*" (1954), in Aldous Huxley's novel *Chrome Yellow* (1921). Huxley's Mr. Scogan disguises himself as "Madame Sesostris" to tell fortunes at a charity fair. In a communication to Smith, Eliot acknowledged this as a likely but wholly unconscious source. Smith, however, would like to make a connection between Scogan's disguise and the bisexuality of Tiresias.

The Huxley "solution," though, leaves us with a spelling change, from Sesostris to Sosostris. Noting this, Herbert Knust presented an alternative explanation in his "Tristan and Sosostris" (1966). The Sosostris passage, he observes, comes immediately after Eliot's allusion to Wagner's *Tristan and Isolde.* Since the allusion includes quotations from more than one scene, Knust believes that Eliot must have studied the drama closely. In it is a scene in which Tristan gives his name as "Tantris"; so we should "recognize Sosostris in Tantris, for the Latin prefix *tan* means *so* in English" (p. 237). Eliot's use of Latinisms and symbolic inversions elsewhere in the poem is seen as supporting this less-than-convincing identification.

Elsewhere, Knust has seen other echoes of Germanic myth and legend in *The Waste Land*, with Wagner as their likely source. In particular, the myth of one-eyed Wotan and Brunhild is seen as important to both the one-eyed merchant and Belladonna in *The Waste Land*'s fortune-telling scene and to the characters of Harcourt-Reilly and Celia in *The Cocktail Party* ("What's the Matter with One-eyed Riley?" 1965). Knust feels that his case is strengthened by reference to Sir James Frazer's *The Golden Bough*, the influence of which is acknowledged in the prefatory note to *The Waste Land.* Frazer includes Odin (Wotan) as an example of the hanged god, so that Eliot's reference to "the Hanged God of Frazer" in his note to line 46 may be specifically a reference to Wotan. Although one may not be convinced that Eliot had these northern myths in mind, Knust's essay is nevertheless stimulating, especially in dealing with *The Cocktail Party*. At the very least, this essay suggests that the archetypal patterns Eliot was dealing with have analogues in mythological traditions less familiar than the Greco-Roman.

Eliot's use of Frazer's *Golden Bough* receives a full chapter in John Vickery's study, *The Literary Impact of the Golden Bough* (1973). Like many writers of such studies, Vickery seems inclined to find his chosen influence lurking everywhere, so that the likely and the unlikely crowd together in his pages. Vickery believes, for example, that the copious examples, thematically connected, which characterized Frazer's method and that of the Cambridge anthropologists who followed him, may have contributed to Eliot's poetic technique, though this suggestion rests on nothing more than a fancied similarity. Most readers will also find it hard to picture the girl of "La Figlia che Piange" as a corn maiden or Gerontion as a "maimed priest-king" (p. 244).

More plausible, because it accounts for more of the poem, is Vickery's reading of "Sweeney among the Nightingales" as "an ironic and elegiac survey of the original form of religion, that is, the fertility cult" (p. 242). The departure of the moisture-giving moon leaves Sweeney alone to face death and the raven, which traditionally brings sterility. Orion and the Dog (signs of the cycle of fertility) are veiled, and the fruits the waiter brings are an ironic substitute for traditional rituals. The sacred heart of Dionysus is now imprisoned in a Christian institution, dedicated to chastity. Vickery's reading may be compared with an earlier Frazerian reading of the same poem by Elizabeth Rudisill Homann, who in "Eliot's 'Sweeney among the Nightingales,' 8" (1959) denies that the "horned gate" is equivalent to the classical "gate of horn" from which true dreams issued. Instead, in this reading, Sweeney is the animal-masked guardian of the sacred gate between life and death in the Dionysian rites. But the animals here are taboo animals, not fit for sacrifice and not associated with fertility. Sweeney is only a perverted bearer of his roles as priest and sacrifice, just as the lady in the cape is unaware of her function as a ritual prostitute and Rachel is a "debased Maenad." It is not clear whether the reader is supposed to be aware of all these associations.

Vickery sees the influence of *The Golden Bough* especially prominent in *The Waste Land*, where much of it is mediated through the Weston book. In addition to the usual Grail-quest symbols, Vickery finds the hyacinth girl offering the protagonist a sacred marriage, Stetson serving as a warrior-priest of Mars, Osiris as the corpse in the garden, and another sacred marriage being reenacted by a couple viewed by Tiresias. The dolphin of "A Game of Chess" recalls "both the hero, Anthony, and the sea-god described by Frazer as riding on a dolphin" (p. 258). The departed nymphs of summer were reenacting "the traditional sacrifice of their virginity to the river prior to their marriage" (p. 261). In later pages, Vickery finds echoes of older deities in poems like the Ariel poems and other later Eliot poems. One can at least feel that no likely Frazerian echoes are overlooked.

Eliot's prefatory note provides an even better warrant for looking in Jessie Weston's *From Ritual to Romance* for clues to the mythic structure of *The Waste Land.* The relevance of Weston's volume was well treated in early general assessments of Eliot by F. R. Leavis and F. O. Matthiessen. Somewhat more complete is an essay by Cleanth Brooks which appeared in the *Southern Review* in 1937 as "*The Waste Land:* An Analysis," and in Brooks' *Modern Poetry and the Tradition* (1939) as "*The Waste Land:* Critique of the Myth," and in many collections of Eliot criticism under one title or another. For those whose introduction to Eliot came through the American New Critics, Brooks' essay is probably the classic interpretation of *The Waste Land*, a standard view by which one can measure the orthodoxy of others. It is, in fact, so standard that it is sometimes less carefully read than it deserves. It repays rereading, however, by all who want to ponder the relevance of Weston's *From Ritual to Romance* to our reading of Eliot's poem. It is still one of the best interpretations offered by those who believe that "a knowledge of this symbolism is essential for an understanding of the poem" (1939, p. 137).

The points Brooks makes in connecting the poem with the Weston book are by now fairly familiar; indeed, some had already been made by earlier critics. The sterile waste land which confronts the protagonist is like that of the Grail stories, and the tarot cards which Madame Sosostris uses without full understanding relate the figures of the Grail quest to the fortunes of the protagonist. The loveless sexuality depicted in "A Game of Chess" reminds us of the rape which brought a curse on the land in the Grail story. The *Tempest* references, in this section and the next, are connected to the drowned god whose death was a prelude to resurrection and renewal of fertility. In the Fire Sermon, the protagonist is identified with the maimed Fisher King, both by the *Tempest* references and by the allusion to *Parsifal*, another Grail-quest story. Mr. Eugenides "is a rather battered representative of the fertility cults" (p. 153), whose apparent homosexuality marks the end of his "new cult" as "not life but, ironically, sterility" (p. 154). Phlebas, too, may be identified with those Syrian merchants who spread the fertility cults, as well as with the drowned god. The last section of the poem takes us to the Perilous Chapel, a place of initiation, to hear the voice of the thunder announcing the renewing rain.

One of the virtues of Brooks' reading, sometimes lost in his epigones, is his awareness of the intellectual questions raised by such interpretations. He admits that such structures of allusion may be only a "scaffolding," useful for some readers as a preparation for confronting the poem itself, raising the danger that "some readers will be tempted to lay more stress upon the scaffolding than they should" (p. 136). Brooks warns that his interpretation is not a substitute for the poem and "certainly is not to be considered as representing *the method by which the poem was composed*" (p. 171). Moreover, Brooks is well aware that the Weston book is only one element in the poem's organization. He gives special weight to the contrast between the death-in-life of the meaningless waste-land existence and the life-in-death promised by the sacrifice of Phlebas.

In some later critics, the Grail quest becomes "the method by which the poem was composed." Charles Moorman leans in this direction in his essay "Myth and Organic Unity in *The Waste Land*" (1958), later incorporated in his book *Arthurian Triptych* (1960). Moorman suggests that Eliot's "unified sensibility" resembles the primitive mythmaker's alleged inability to distinguish clearly between himself and the universe, this being one of those myths about primitive man invented by modern men, unable to distinguish between their imaginations and the evidence. Moorman calls this curious state of mind "sacramental," the model being the Mass. The unity of the poem is thus somehow "organic" rather than "mechanical." As he tells us twice, Eliot finds in Weston's version of the Fisher King and the waste land "a perfect objective correlative . . . to his own generalized emotion toward contemporary society" (1958, p. 198; cf. p. 201). The movement from allusion to structure, from unconscious myth to conscious ordering principle, is typical of the slippery uses of "myth" in much modern criticism.

Other critics, like Grover Smith in *T. S. Eliot's Poetry and Plays* (1956), routinely refer to the protagonist of *The Waste Land* as the "quester," implying a simple identification of the movement of the poem with the Grail quest. Recognition of other allusions does not necessarily help matters. William T. Moynihan's "The Goal of the *Waste Land* Quest" (1961) adds the role of Odysseus to the protagonist's burdens, leading to such striking identifications as that which links Mr. Eugenides with "the cannibalistic Polyphemus" (p. 177), presumably by way of the one-eyed merchant. The epic qualities Moynihan attributes to the poem are akin to the general tendency of critics who emphasize the Grail quest to exaggerate the narrative elements in the poem's structure. In such interpretations, the "scaffolding" becomes the poem.

If there is a troublesome aspect to the Cleanth Brooks version of *The Waste Land*, it is his insistence on the Christian use to which Eliot puts his Grail symbols. That the eclectic images deployed in *The Waste Land* ultimately refer back to Eliot's Christian tradition may very well be true, especially when we read the poem in the context furnished by Eliot's later development. But Brooks seems to downplay the more personal elements in the poem. Having connected the rape of Philomela with the rape of the maidens who serve the Grail shrine, Brooks writes: "Miss Weston conjectures that this may be a statement, in the form of a parable, of the violation of the older mysteries which were probably once celebrated openly, but were later forced underground. Whether or not Mr. Eliot noticed this passage or intends a reference, the violation of a woman makes a very good symbol of the process of secularization" (1939, p. 147). Even the tentative way in which Brooks expresses this does not prevent one from feeling that the critic's imaginative re-creation of the poem has got out of hand. Later it seems that the villain of the poem has been positively identified: "If secularization has destroyed, or is likely to destroy, modern civilization, the protagonist still has a private obligation to fulfill" (p. 164). Brooks' antipathies seem to be behind a suggestion that the dog of part I be identified with "humanitarianism and the related philosophies which, in their concern for man, extirpate the supernatural" (pp. 145–46). And though Brooks is too sophisticated to turn *The Waste Land* into a sermon, he tells us that "Eliot's theme is the rehabilitation of a system of beliefs, known but now discredited" (p. 171).

What is lost in a wholehearted stress on *The Waste Land* as a spiritual quest can be seen by comparing Brooks' interpretation with another well-known essay on the poem, one which also gives a prominent place to the use of Weston's book: George Williamson's "The Structure of *The Waste Land*" (1950), a reading later incorporated in his *Reader's Guide to T. S. Eliot* (1953). Like Brooks, Williamson sees "the anthropological framework" as "a means rather than an end," where "the end is concerned with both the development and the decline of religious feeling in modern man" (1950, p. 206). Many of the details of Williamson's reading follow the same line as Brooks'. But Williamson offers a different explanation of the attraction of *From Ritual to Romance* for the poet: "Miss Weston's treatment of the legend enables Eliot to see in the experience of sex the potentialities of the Fisher King and his Waste Land" (p. 191). For Brooks, the virtue of the fertility myths is that they hold the age-old promise of resurrection; for Williamson, the fertility myths are of use also because they connect the search for the divine with the mysteries of sexuality. Williamson's approach allows him to retain the personal level of significance in his reading of the poem.

On one other issue between them, Brooks is probably closer to most readers' experience of the poem than is Williamson. Williamson sees the protagonist as left, in the end, in the "knowing but helpless state of the Fisher King" (p. 206), while Brooks sees the protagonist as prepared for fruitful action. Most critics follow Brooks in finding a positive tone in the closing lines, though few go so far as to hear, as Richard D. Hathaway does, the "onomatopoetic character" of the last line as a sign of the "swish of falling rain" ("*The Waste Land*'s Benediction," 1963). Since Williamson recognizes that the poem has progression and movement, and since he and Brooks generally agree on what the protagonist has learned from the thunder, arguments over the protagonist's future spiritual state look suspiciously like debates over what becomes of Nora after the end of Ibsen's *Doll's House* or whether King Lear's successors will rule well. The more hopeful tone Brooks finds in the poem's closing obviously reflects the semi-Christian character of his "scaffolding," and those of us who share his reading may well, like Brooks, be reading *The Waste Land* by the light of Eliot's later poems.

Mythic echoes can be found in other Eliot poems as well, at least by critics and readers willing to define "myth" in the vague manner customary in literary discussions of it. Donald Stanford has revealed that "here we go round the prickly pear" in "The Hollow Men" is intended to "recall the ancient fertility rite of the ring dance and at the same time to comment ironically on the sterility of modern civilization which has lost much of its religion" ("Two Notes on T. S. Eliot," 1955). Audrey T. Rodgers opens her essay, "The Mythic Perspective of Eliot's 'The Dry Salvages' " (1974), with a particularly memorable sentence: "T. S. Eliot is seldom thought of as a mythic poet, yet all his poetry reflects the pattern of the quest—an essential ingredient of the mythic perspective" (p. 74). What is memorable about this sentence is that each of its three generalizations is false. With Joseph Campbell and others as guides, Rodgers is willing to take the "voyages" of "Dry Salvages" as a narrative journey, to take any journey as a symbolic quest, and to take any supernatural element as "myth."

Genesius Jones also employs a rather broad definition of the "mythic method" in *Approach to the Purpose* (1964), justified, in his case, by reference to Ernst Cassirer's philosophy of symbolic forms, ways in which the human mind attempts to order reality. Although his stress is on Eliot's religious vision and mythic method, Jones attempts to apply a variety of perspectives (also derived from Cassirer) to Eliot's work. His chapter on Eliot's relation to the French Symbolists, for example, is well worth reading. But Jones believes that "if there is a single key" to Eliot's thought, "it lies in the process of death, burial and resurrection" (p. 313). In "Burbank with a Baedeker: Bleistein with a Cigar," for example, "the epigraph is itself the background myth: a sort of modern version of the Vegetation Cults. Mr. Eliot elaborates its theme of organic renewal in considerable detail along the various perspectives by means of the mythic principle of concrescence and mythical space and time thinking" (p. 297). Such passages are neither readable nor illuminating. Nor is there much to be said for Jones' extremely affirmative reading of "The Hollow Men" as illustrating Eliot's movement from "death and burial" to "resurrection."

What is valuable in Jones' book is his emphasis on the continuity of Eliot's efforts to achieve transcendent order. Jones also casts some light on the continuity and development of Eliot's use of images like "street" or "stair." His final evaluation of Eliot's achievement draws on Father Guardini's distinction (*The End of the Modern World*, 1957) between the modern and the contemporary. The contemporary world appears as one in which nature is no longer infinite and benevolent but finite, complex, and relative—perhaps even unknowable. Culture no longer suggests a long vista of progress, and the power of man over nature and culture is less triumphant than frightening. Eliot's attempt to recover a lost tradition of wholeness is a response to this situation, and his great triumph is the mythic method: "*Four Quartets* tackles the task that was mooted in *The Faerie Queen* and brings it off triumphantly" (1964, p. 322).

Comparing the *Quartets* to *The Faerie Queen* may suggest to some that concentration on mythic method leads Eliot (or his critics) into a world of timeless moral allegory. But Richard Chase has complained that Eliot's grasp of tradition and fascination with primitive myth is at odds with "The Sense of the Present" (1945), which is basic to good poetry. This rather suggests Eliot's contrast between the special religious awareness and the general awareness we expect of major poets, and part of Chase's problem seems to be his evident antipathy to Eliot's religious views: "The world portrayed in 'The Waste Land' is no doubt sufficiently repulsive and discouraging, but not, I think, repulsive enough to justify the artist's exchanging it for the nameless utopia of mysticism" (p. 231). But Chase also seems to be a victim of Eliot's notes to *The Waste Land* and the critical excesses they have engendered. Of the Death by Water section, for example, Chase complains that "we are to think (as Eliot says in a note on this passage) of the asceticism of Augustine; we are to think of 'the drowned Phoenician sailor,' a card in the Tarot pack. Perhaps we are to think of the acqueous cosmogonies of certain Indian divines, perhaps of the part water plays in the fertility myths; perhaps we are to recall Miss Jessie Weston's *From Ritual to Romance*, which will furnish us with a hint about the effigy of Adonis which, cast upon the sea every year by the women of Egypt, floated on the current to Phoenicia; perhaps we are to recognize here an allegory of the cycles of time" (p. 229). The critical industry that has flourished since 1945 would allow this list to be extended a good bit. But Chase has misplaced one of Eliot's notes and misread their general intent; his real quarrel is with Eliot's critics.

If one turns from the notes and the critics back to the poem, *The Waste Land* does not seem terribly esoteric in its use of religious and mythic references. Of the Indic usages, the Fire Sermon is well known, and the legend of the thunder is sufficiently explained in the poem; only the closing line requires explanation for most readers. Eliot's use of the tarot deck is very free but not very puzzling. Most educated readers have some familiarity with the connection between fertility cults and the seasonal death and rebirth of gods. Additional knowledge of comparative anthropology or *From Ritual to Romance* is not required, though some may find that adds to their experience of the poem. In providing a key to these and other matters, essays like those by Brooks and Williamson can prove useful to many readers. But the web of associations which lies beneath the poem's surface should not alter one's sense of the real discontinuities of its surface; readings which insist unduly on its logical structure risk transforming a poem of experience into an argument. Arthur C. McGill's reading of *The Waste Land* (in his *The Celebration of Flesh*, 1964) is avowedly theological but spends less time on religious symbolism than many "literary" readings. McGill concentrates on the concrete experience of the poem, which can then be shown to have religious connotations and implications which can be understood in the light of Christian doctrine. In the long run, this may be a more objective approach than that which insists on finding doctrines in the poem, which are interpreted on the basis of aesthetic doctrines. The critical tendency to exaggerate the doctrinal content of Eliot's early poetry is even more prevalent in approaches to his later poetry.

The Anglican Poet

Eliot published little poetry between *The Waste Land* and his formal acceptance of Anglicanism in 1927. Although "The Hollow Men" may echo Dante and the "Sweeney Agonistes" fragments were to sport an epigraph from St. John of the Cross, the signs of his impending conversion were far from obtrusive. With "Journey of the Magi," the first of several Ariel poems published as Christmas poems by Faber, we enter into a period in which his poetry is not merely religious but Christian—not merely Christian, some would add, but Anglican, as seen in the liturgical framework of *Ash Wednesday*.

"The Hollow Men" is certainly concerned with spiritual states. The question of its place in Eliot's development as a religious poet is whether it is to be read as rehearsing the despair of earlier sections of *The Waste Land* or as looking forward to the tentative affirmations of the closing sections of *Ash Wednesday*. The most usual reading treats the hollow men of the poem as damned by their inability to choose. Friedrich W. Strothmann and Lawrence A. Ryan, on the other hand, in their "Hope for T. S. Eliot's 'Empty Men' " (1958) see the "multifoliate rose" in the closing lines of part IV as "the hope only / of empty men." Arguing that Eliot was already familiar with the work of St. John of the Cross, Strothmann and Ryan maintain that "empty" is not to be understood as the same as "hollow"—on the contrary, emptiness is "a condition of hope," part of the dark night of the soul, which may serve them as a preliminary of mystical ascent. In a later exchange of views with

Everett A. Gillis ("Hope for Eliot's Hollow Men?" 1960), Strothmann and Ryan reject the usual identification of the hollow men with Dante's trimmers, as advanced by Gillis, on the grounds that the hollow men are still alive. Gillis argues convincingly that Eliot simply wanted to avoid an unnecessary repetition of "hollow"—perhaps, one might add, to avoid a sense of closure at the end of his penultimate section. It is, in any case, hard to see why emptiness should be better than hollowness as a preparation for transcendence.

Gillis's views, in "The Spiritual Status of T. S. Eliot's Hollow Men" (1961), are avowedly traditional: "*The Hollow Men*, rather than embodying any affirmative note, however meager, is to be considered merely as an extension of Eliot's earlier poem—that it is, as it were, a *Waste Land* in little" (p. 475). References to Dante and the liturgy may point to the possibility of salvation, but they are distorted and without efficacy in the world of the hollow men. Harold F. Brooks, placing "The Hollow Men" somewhere between *The Waste Land* and the first Ariel poems (1966), agrees with Gillis that the hollow men are not saved (as Strothmann and Ryan believe), but argues that the possibility of a salvation they cannot summon the will to choose is genuinely part of the poem. But if Gillis is right in noting that there is no salvation in the poem, the signs which seem to point to it are ambiguous at best. For the reader who believes—or is overcome by his prior knowledge of Eliot's belief—the irony of the hollow men's failure to act upon their "hope only" may be an important part of his experience of the poem. But one cannot move from that to saying that the poem affirms belief. As J. G. Keogh says, "The Hollow Men" is "a poem about death which is not a Christian poem (at least it is not about Christians)" ("Eliot's *The Hollow Men* as Graveyard Poetry," 1969). Like "Gerontion" and *The Waste Land*, this poem may be in good part a product of Eliot's developing religious awareness—his Christianity, if one insists. But the doctrines which help one apprehend a spiritual state are not necessarily embodied in a depiction of such a state.

Eliot's Ariel poems were issued separately as Christmas poems. The first three—"Journey of the Magi" (1927), "A Song for Simeon" (1928), and "Animula" (1929)—form a natural bridge to *Ash Wednesday* (1930). Of these three, "Journey of the Magi" has received the most critical attention, probably because it treats one of the most familiar of all Christmas stories, and possibly because it is the best poem of the three. Most critics have noted that the opening lines are taken from one of Lancelot Andrewes' sermons on the Nativity. Many have also called attention to the way in which "six hands at an open door dicing," near the water mill, echoes Eliot's citation of "six ruffians seen through an open window playing cards at night at a small French railway junction where there was a water mill" as one of those recurring images which are somehow "charged with emotion" for those they haunt (in *The Use of Poetry and the Use of Criticism*, p. 148). The speaker of the poem is generally taken as a representative of the old dispensation, who has given intellectual assent to a new order he only partially understands. Grover Smith even compares the Magus to Gerontion (*T. S. Eliot's Poetry and Plays*, 1956).

If one sees the poem as about the change from the era of the Magi to that of Christ, then the landscape through which the Magi pass on their journey may be taken as emblematic of the religious past. For Robert B. Kaplan and Richard J. Wall, "the center" of Eliot's "Journey of the Magi" (1960) is the "white horse" which gallops away in line 25. Rejecting the Frazerian echoes found by some commentators, Kaplan and Wall suggest that the image probably comes from G. K. Chesterton's "Ballad of the White Horse," in which the departure of the white horse of the White Horse Vale signalizes the extinction of paganism. The line, they believe, divides the poem into two logical parts, one concerned with birth and death, the other with death and rebirth. Another ingenious interpretation of the horse is T. A. Smailes' "Eliot's 'Journey of the Magi' " (1970). Smailes suggests that a parallel exists with the change of loyalties demonstrated by innkeepers, who replaced their Stuart oak leaves with a Hanoverian white horse at the accession of George I. One finds it hard to imagine either association having much effect on one's reading of the poem.

In any case, the landscape the Magi traverse has Christian connotations as well. The most often noted are the "three trees on the low sky" and the men "dicing for pieces of silver." These look forward to the crucifixion and give a sinister cast to the poem's last line: "I should be glad of another death." In "T. S. Eliot's 'Journey of the Magi': An Explication" (1966), Arthur T. Broes finds many other New Testament references. The "running stream" is not simply the Jordan, where Christ was baptized; it is also Christ himself, as the water of life. Christ is like the mill as well, separating the wheat from the chaff and "beating the darkness." The white horse may be the white horse of Revelation, a symbol of death and disease, here vanquished by the coming of Christ. And the "empty wine-skins" recall the miracle at Cana. These references are much less clear than those to the crucifixion, and probably testify instead to the suggestive but nonspecific character of the imagery employed.

A more serious challenge to the normal reading of the poem is made in Rosemary Franklin's "The Satisfactory Journey of Eliot's Magus" (1968). Some critics have complained about the flat understatement of the Magus' comment on their arrival—"It was (you may say) satisfactory." Some have found it so inadequate as to cast doubt on the speaker's understanding of what he has witnessed. In "Eliot's 'Journey of the Magi' " (1954), John H. Wills even cites this line as evidence that the Magus is so preoccupied with the remembered suffering of his journey that he is blind to the later suffering of Christ. Franklin points out that the word "satisfactory" also carries a theological meaning of "atoning," stemming from a more general use as making amends or giving recompense. She supports this with Eliot's use of the theological meaning in *Murder in the Cathedral*, a reference to Christ's death as a "sacrifice, oblation and satisfaction for the sins of the whole world." A similar point has been made independently by R. D. Brown ("Revelation in T. S. Eliot's 'Journey of the Magi,' " 1972), who makes much of the appearance of similar phrases in a nativity sermon by Andrewes and in the Thirty-nine Articles, which define the Anglican faith. Although Franklin and Brown present this phraseology as arcane Christian lore, it was long a part of the Anglican *Book of Common Prayer* and recited by priests at every celebration of Holy Communion. Eliot would have heard this use of "satisfaction" many times; moreover, the place of the *Book of Common Prayer* in English literature is such that allusions implying familiarity with it are, in principle at least, perfectly fair. The Magus' parenthetical "you may say" preserves his ambivalence.

Even if the language used by the Magus points toward Christian dogma and liturgy, the Magus may be unaware of the full implications of his words. As Franklin says, the Magus asks whether this was birth or death, but the believing Christian sees a coming death which is the promise of rebirth. This seems more reasonable than Brown's insistence that the Magus affirms the revelation he has received. This is obviously one of those poems in which we must not make a simple identification of the speaker and the poet, whether to assume (as Smith seems to) that Eliot's religious commitment was still insecure or to argue (as Brown does) that Eliot's Christianity must be affirmed by the speaker. Like "The Hollow Men," "Journey of the Magi" has a reality of its own, which, like the larger world of experience, can be interpreted differently by believers and unbelievers.

Grover Smith (*T. S. Eliot's Poetry and Plays*, 1956) finds "A Song for Simeon" as despairing as "Gerontion," and other critics have shared his rather negative view of Simeon's prayer and prophecy. To be sure, the eighty-year-old Simeon, vouchsafed a sight of the infant Christ, prophecies trials and tribulations to come; to be sure, Simeon knows that he will never be a saint or martyr, and he is ready to die. But Simeon is no Gerontion, and neither the poem nor the gospels imply that salvation is reserved for those who have received the "ultimate vision." Of the various general treatments of Eliot's poetry which are widely circulated, only Hugh Kenner seems willing to recognize that Simeon is far better off spiritually than Gerontion. Nancy Gish gives a reasonably affirmative reading of the poem in "The Meaning of Incarnation in Two 'Ariel Poems' " (1973), but she seems somewhat unaware of previous critics and is only moderately helpful in her efforts at explicating the Magi and Simeon. John T. Hiers' essay on the same two poems offers similar interpretations and suffers from the same weaknesses ("Birth or Death: Eliot's 'Journey of the Magi' and 'A Song for Simeon,' " 1976).

The best reading of "A Song for Simeon" is in Audrey Cahill's *T. S. Eliot and the Human Predicament* (1967). Cahill confronts and rejects the Smith interpretation of the poem. Cahill does not overstate Simeon's spiritual achievements, but she notes that there is vicarious suffering as well as simple tiredness in a line like "I am dying in my own death and the deaths of those after me." Simeon has the humility "that is the prerequisite of grace" (p. 76), even if he has not yet received the peace he prays for. Even if one finds the poem ambiguous—we have the prayer and not the answer—its hopeful character deserves recognition.

In some ways, *Ash Wednesday* presents non-Christian readers with problems like those of "A Song for Simeon." The experience at the heart of the poem is clearly Christian in some sense, but the speaker does not seem to be enjoying it. If "A Song for Simeon" can be read as suggesting that the Incarnation may be a trial, *Ash Wednesday* can be read as making belief sound very much like despair. One can appreciate the poem without sharing its faith, but one probably needs some familiarity with the traditional Christian year, in which Ash Wednesday marks the beginning of Lent, a period of self-discipline and penance which, nevertheless, looks forward to Easter. Failure to note this has led some unwary readers to confuse the poem's humility with a simple failure to achieve faith. One might even say, with Paul Dolan, that "*Ash Wednesday* is completely a Lenten poem" ("*Ash Wednesday:* A Catechumenical Poem," 1967). The poem is a meditation in the Lenten spirit, and Eliot's incorporation of phrases from the liturgy of the Lenten season suggests that parts of the poem, at least, were inspired by the devotions prescribed for Lent. The Christian year itself, like the passage of the seasons, has a timeless, universalizing character, and if one generalizes Lent to the point of considering it a recurring spiritual experience of purgation, then Eliot's is certainly "completely a Lenten poem." The phrase has other connotations, however, for it suggests that *Ash Wednesday* is a narrowly Christian poem, inextricably tied to the liturgy which informs it. If that is so, and critics like Dolan sometimes seem to take it to be the case, then Eliot's religious poetry is, by his own definition, minor poetry, however excellent.

Dolan certainly carries the liturgical reading too far when he insists that *Ash Wednesday* is a "catechumenical poem," because many of its liturgical sources can be found in that portion of the Mass after which the unbaptized catechumens were once asked to leave. As Dolan admits, "Lord, I am not worthy" comes later in the Mass. His explanation that it comes "*before* Communion is received and is therefore one more reference to the state of the speaker as one anticipating the fulfillment of a spiritual experience" (p. 205) is well taken. But what it suggests is that the imagery drawn from the Mass is subordinate in the poem to the more general pattern of humble preparation suggested by the Lenten analogy.

Although Dolan does not mention them, two previous critics also attempted to tie *Ash Wednesday* to the pattern of the Mass: Carl Wooton, in "The Mass: *Ash Wednesday*'s Objective Correlative" (1961), and Gwenn R. Boardman, "*Ash Wednesday:* Eliot's Lenten Mass Sequence" (1962). Wooton finds the structure of the Mass "loosely imposed on the whole poem" (p. 31). The question, of course, is whether Eliot or Wooton is doing the imposing, and whether "loosely" is not simply an escape word to cover difficulties in the interpretation. Boardman is even more schematic, finding in the six sections of the poem parallels to the six Masses of the Lenten season, the six Acts of the Mass, and the six Remembrances in each Mass. Taken together, Wooton, Boardman, and Dolan provide a useful compendium of liturgical allusions in the poem, but their efforts to find the structure of the Mass in the poem are unconvincing. The pattern of the Mass (or the Anglican Holy Communion) embodies and channels a pattern of religious experience also found in the Lenten season. To the extent that it is successful, the poem is its own "objective correlative" for that experience, and the speaker's incorporation of references to Dante and the Mass are part of his effort to apprehend and convey his analogous experience.

The reductive tendencies of these critics may be further exemplified by their treatment of the "three white leopards" of *Ash Wednesday II*. These beasts have often brought out the worst in Eliot's critics, who seem unwilling to tolerate the suggestive and indefinite character of their symbolism, although Eliot always refused to explicate the passage as meaning anything other than what it said. The leopards recall the beasts Dante encounters early in the *Inferno*, and, as with Dante's beasts, one finds them variously identified. Thus Wooton is sure they symbolize the penitent's "trials and tribulations" (p. 36), while Boardman sees them as "representing the threefold nature of God, since the white leopard ('Once') is a traditional symbol of the Almighty" (p. 31). H. Z. Maccoby believes they represent "both the three stages of renunciation and the body of Christ" ("Two Notes on 'Ash Wednesday,' " 1966, p. 415). For F. Peter Dzwonkoski, Jr., "as it portrays the eating of human flesh and blood the feast of the leopards inverts the Christian practise of Holy Communion as a sacramental event" (" 'The Hollow Men' and *Ash Wednesday*: Two Dark Nights," 1974, p. 28). Efforts to reduce complex and ambiguous symbols to simple allegorical signs are obviously self-defeating. Efforts to reduce the poem to an allegory of the Mass or of some other doctrinal matter are harder to resist but equally wrongheaded.

Recognition that the poem is an effort to convey experience, rather than preach doctrine, is one of the merits of one of the earliest essays on *Ash Wednesday*, Allen Tate's "Irony and Humility," first printed in 1931 and reprinted in several collections of Tate's essays. Tate recognizes that Eliot makes use of certain conventional religious images, but he argues that Eliot transforms these images into immediate sensations, at once less specifically tied to particular referents (the Lady as Beatrice, or the Virgin, or a nun) and more specifically to the personal experience which the poem expresses. At the time, Tate was concerned to defend Eliot's poem from secular critics whose generalized reaction to all traces of religion blinded them to the merits of Eliot's poem. There is equal need to defend Eliot from devout critics whose equally generalized reaction to religious symbols threatens to obscure the personal use to which such symbols are put in *Ash Wednesday*.

As it happens, Tate's essay makes another point which, if it is accepted, undermines any strictly liturgical reading of the poem. Tate regards the opening stanza as an expression, ironic in tone, of an objective but temporary state. Some later critics have elaborated on this hint and taken it further, seeing in the opening section a spiritual state not merely temporary but misleading—Clifford Davidson, for example, in "Types of Despair in 'Ash Wednesday' " (1966). In the first section, the traditional despair of those alienated from God is combined with the modern despair of doubt; in later sections, the speaker finds his way to another traditional recognition, that his despair is the necessary first step toward regeneration. The liturgical echoes of the first section are thus ironic in effect, for their full import is not yet recognized by the speaker. Sister Margaret Patrice Slattery does not go quite this far in condemning the emotion expressed in the first section, but she sees its renunciation as incomplete, not bringing the kind of peace found in the last section. The contrast between the two is thus the key to her "Structural Unity in Eliot's 'Ash Wednesday' " (1968). Some such interpretation seems called for by the deliberate contrast between the opening lines of the first and last sections, as well as by our sense of the poem's movement. Liturgical echoes are not thereby ruled out, for such a progression can be thought of as part of the speaker's effort to meet the demands for penance of either Lent or the Mass; but the poem is about this effort, at first imperfect and incomplete, rather than about the conventional religious observances which may be its occasion.

Liturgical echoes are less commonly found in the poetry after *Ash Wednesday*, though they have been found in Eliot's plays. A rare attempt to find such echoes is James P. Sexton's essay "*Four Quartets* and the Christian Calendar," (1971), in which Sexton suggests that each of the *Quartets* is to be identified with a different holy day in the liturgical calendar. "Little Gidding's" fire associations naturally place it with Pentecost, and the lyric of "East Coker IV" makes explicit reference to Good Friday. The "Prayer of the One Annunciation" in "Dry Salvages II" and references to Mary elsewhere in that poem are said to establish the Annunciation as central to "Dry Salvages." The best evidence he can find for associating "Burnt Norton" with Ascension Day is a series of alleged puns and one use of the verb "ascend."

Also very strained and not very useful is Thomas Oden's attempt to show that " 'Burnt Norton' rehearses the celebration of the Holy Eucharist, which points to the Christ-event as an eschatological occurrence, recorded by a participant in this celebration, not as an objective description of the event celebrated, but as an existential response of agony, repentance, and faith in reference to the event" ("The Christology of T. S. Eliot: A Study of the *Kerygma* in 'Burnt Norton,' " 1960). Oden wants to link each section of the poem with a part of the last days of Christ—the Garden, the Crucifixion, the Descent into Hell, the Tomb and the Resurrection, the Creation of the Church—a sequence of identifications which does not become implausible until the last. Neither Sexton's nor Oden's efforts suggest that Eliot's later work is fruitfully explored through liturgy.

In the period of the Ariel poems, *Ash Wednesday*, and *Murder in the Cathedral*, the connection between Eliot the poet and Eliot the Christian believer is very close, but the result is not devotional poetry in a narrow sense but poetry which sometimes expresses the experience of devotion and sometimes makes use of the language of devotion. His work of this period, and earlier, incorporates material from Christian texts, in a way which secular-minded critics have sometimes found more daunting or less acceptable than his similar incorporation of allusions to the Western literary tradition. Bradley Gunter has suggested that "it is the Anglicanism that makes the later poetry, the plays, and the prose seem, to an audience largely alienated from the Church, so distinctively and disconcertingly modern" (1970, p. 45). Nevertheless, Eliot's allusions to the Christian tradition, well covered in Gunter's brief guide for students, do not always imply a different kind of relationship with the material alluded to than with more traditional literary sources. Eliot's personal estimation of Dante probably owes something to his sympathy with Dante's Christian outlook, but one could probably say the same about his personal estimation of Gautama Buddha. It may be only the complexities of living in a culture partly shaped by Christianity which makes Eliot's use of the associations of Christian authors and liturgical materials seem more of a stumbling block than his use of the Fire Sermon in *The Waste Land.*

Karen T. Romer's survey, "T. S. Eliot and the Language of Liturgy" (1972), suggests that we may think of Eliot's poetry in this period as displaying a special fascination with the traditional and evocative character of the liturgy. Beyond the incorporation of allusions, we can see the poetry as exploring the possible uses of a diction which draws on the liturgy for some of its character. As a man, Eliot was presumably drawn to liturgical language because it expressed his faith, but there is reason to believe he was earlier drawn to the technique of Laforgue partly because it could be used to express his existential situation at that point in his life. The poet, as a poet, discovers everywhere rhythms and other techniques which help him in his struggle to collect and convey his experience.

To insist that Eliot's relationship to the Christian tradition is often much the same as his relation to the literary tradition is not to deny the importance of Christianity for our understanding of certain Eliot poems. R. P. Blackmur's chapter, "T. S. Eliot: From *Ash Wednesday* to *Murder in the Cathedral*" in *The Double Agent* (1935), makes the obvious point that the work of this period "is penetrated and animated and its significance is determined by Christian feeling" (p. 190). It is, as Blackmur implicitly recognizes, a particular kind of Christian feeling, one which has much in common with other religious and philosophical traditions, and which differs much from other sensibilities one might also call "Christian." But Eliot found in the doctrines of the Anglican Church the faith which satisfied and helped to order his religious sensibility. Without some minimal attention to those doctrines—the meaning of Ash Wednesday, for example—it is difficult to understand some of his poems. Moreover, the coherence they give Eliot's outlook may be of utility to even the nonbelieving reader. We can understand Eliot, as we cannot understand Pound, writes Blackmur, because "the unity that is Mr. Eliot has an objective intellectual version in his Christianity. The unity of Mr. Pound—if there is one—is in a confusion of incoherent, if often too explicitly declared, beliefs" (p. 205). For Eliot the Christian, faith may serve as both the source and the explanation of religious experience. But for Eliot the poet, it is a "body of feelings, and not any intermediately necessary intellectualizations of them, which are his immediate concern; and ours, when we can bear on them"

(p. 202). Eliot is a religious poet because his view of life and his experience are colored by his commitment to Christianity, but Eliot the poet is seldom simply a mouthpiece for Eliot the Anglican. This point is clear enough in the early essays by Blackmur and Tate; it has too often been lost sight of by their successors.

The Dantesque Poet

The question of the relationship between poetry and belief is central to Eliot's 1929 essay on Dante, and passages with a religious import in Eliot's poetry are often graced with an allusion to Dante. "Little Gidding" includes a famous passage in imitation of Dante. In a broader sense, Dante appears to be Eliot's model for much of his religious poetry, offering an ideal of faith, poetic achievement, and breadth of vision. Critical approaches to Eliot's use of Dante are, in turn, very similar to critical approaches to his use of more general Christian references.

The best-known essay on "T. S. Eliot and Dante" is by Mario Praz (1937). Praz is inclined to stress the influence of Ezra Pound on Eliot's understanding of Dante, and he shows how remarks Pound makes in *The Spirit of Romance* (1910) are echoed by Eliot in *The Sacred Wood* (1920) and later writings on Dante. Like F. O. Matthiesen before him, Praz finds Eliot repeating ideas absorbed from the Harvard tradition of Dante studies, as exemplified in Charles Grandgent's *Dante* (1916) and Santayana's *Three Philosophical Poets* (1910). Praz is inclined to find in Eliot's study of Dante the origin of Eliot's most striking critical doctrines, the "objective correlative" and "impersonality," but this is to ignore the many other influences on those doctrines we have noted earlier.

Dante echoes can be found in Eliot's poetry in all periods, and Praz notes the major occurrences. His emphasis is on Eliot's effort to reproduce the lucid immediacy he found in his reading of Dante. Praz compares the imagery in "La Figlia che Piange" favorably with the more mannered Dantesque imagery of Dante Rossetti's "Blessed Damozel," a poem Eliot would also seem to have had in mind while writing his own poem. For Praz, *Ash Wednesday* is written in the spirit of the *Purgatorio*, perhaps especially canto XXX, and he notes that in *Dante* (1929) Eliot links that canto with Dante's *Vita Nuova,* reminiscences of which also appear in *Ash Wednesday.*

Most of what is valuable in Gabrielle Barfoot's survey, "Dante in Eliot's Criticism" (1972), has already been said by Praz. Barfoot's principal addition is to collect and exaggerate the significance of instances in which Eliot seems to use Dante as a touchstone for measuring the achievement of other poets. Barfoot also illustrates a major theme in critical efforts to assess Eliot's relationship to Dante as a great Christian poet: the suspicion that Eliot's praise of Dante rests too much on doctrinal grounds. Following the lead of F. R. Leavis, Barfoot objects to Eliot's use of Dante as a yardstick for measuring the "maturity" of the outlooks of other authors. In doing this, Barfoot is, of course, able to cite against Eliot his apparently conflicting statements on the relation between poetry and belief and his admissions that temperamental and ideological affinities may play some role in his appreciation of Dante. Barfoot points to additional inconsistencies in Eliot's later praise of Dante as a sign that the later poet's increasing commitment to religion blunted his critical perceptions. The critique is valuable, though one is tempted to remark that consistency was never Eliot's great virtue as a critic. Much of Barfoot's criticism, moreover, seems to derive from the same sort of ideological bias of which Eliot is being accused. Concentrating on Eliot's criticism should not prevent one from remembering that it was written by a poet, whose first attraction to Dante was to Dante as a poet, a point clearly made by Praz.

Most other commentaries on Eliot and Dante fall somewhere between Barfoot's insistence on doctrine and Praz's relative indifference to it. In "Dante through the Looking Glass: Rossetti, Pound, and Eliot" (1972), Ron D. K. Banerjee is closer to Praz, though he would prefer to reassert, against Praz, the importance of the Harvard tradition, as opposed to Pound, in shaping Eliot's understanding of Dante. Banerjee finds both Pound and Eliot influenced in their approach to Dante by Rossetti, whose "Blessed Damozel" serves as the point of departure for both Pound's "Donzella Beata" and Eliot's "La Figlia che Piange." Banerjee is even more apt than Praz to believe that Dante was a direct influence on "La Figlia che Piange," though he admits that "the complex interaction of allusions . . . rules out any attempts to relate it to Dante's poetry in any straightforward way" (p. 144). Although the Rossetti poem is certainly referred to, "La Figlia che Piange" is "an exorcism of Rossetti by way of Laforgue" (p. 147). How literally one takes the metaphor of "exorcism" presumably depends on how far along one believes Eliot was on the progress described in his 1929 Dante essay: "Rossetti's *Blessed Damozel*, first by my rapture and next by my revolt, held up my appreciation of Beatrice by many years." The ways in which Eliot's poem differs from Rossetti's may well owe something to the influence of Laforgue and even to Eliot's reading of Dante, as Banerjee suggests.

Graham Hough's essay, "Dante and Eliot" (1974), provides a useful summary of some previous efforts to assess the relationship. Hough's sympathies are with the Praz tradition, in which the emphasis is on the relationship of poet with poet rather than on religious affinities. Hough adds some nice examples of this poetic influence, pointing out that "I had not thought death had undone so many" gets part of its strength from a bold rescue of "undo" from the language of melodrama, an operation suggested by the literal translation of the verb in the Dante passage Eliot is appropriating. Hough suggests that Pound is the most important figure in the compound ghost of "Little Gidding," on the grounds that Pound, then in Italy, most resembles Brunetto (in hell). Hough's most original contribution is a stress on Dante as a major Continental figure who had not yet made a real impact on English poetry, earlier possibilities being cut short by the premature deaths of Shelley and Keats. As such, says Hough, Dante provided Eliot with an alternative to Shakespeare, always the great intimidating figure for English poets.

Eliot was certainly familiar with some previous efforts to introduce Dante's influence into English poetry. His general judgment on the poetry of Shelley was extremely negative, but in Eliot's 1950 address on Dante to the Italian Institute in London, he barely quoted Dante but cited thirty-three lines from Shelley, including thirty from *The Triumph of Time*. This last passage is praised as the most successful Dantesque passage in English poetry, superior to his own effort in "Little Gidding II." Glenn O'Malley ("Dante, Shelley, and T. S. Eliot," 1977) has called attention to this address, noting that this surprising tribute to Shelley is appropriate since Shelley and Eliot are "probably the two English poets who have outstripped all others in enhancing Dante's esteem" (p. 166). Moreover, Eliot had previously excepted the same passage from *Triumph of Time* from his usual criticism of Shelley; indeed, Eliot may have echoed the passage in "Sweeney Erect." In general, however, Eliot's critical understanding of Shelley remains, as we always thought, "very limited" (p. 174), with his references most often being to ghosts, like that of Rousseau, in the *Triumph of Time*. O'Malley also provides some analysis of Eliot's "Little Gidding" imitation of Dante and a surprisingly extended discussion of the brief prose translations of Dante in Eliot's 1929 essay. Geoffrey Carter, we may note, has found these translations based on the Temple Classics translation, with "such small alterations as someone with an elementary knowledge of Italian would be able to make" ("The Question of T. S. Eliot's Erudition," 1977, p. 452n). Carter also suggests that the Ugolino passage in *Waste Land V* rests on a mistranslation in the Temple Classics edition.

The Dante references in *The Waste Land* are identified in Eliot's notes. A number of critics have found Dantean imagery in "The Hollow Men." Some of these interpretations have been conveniently reviewed by Dagny Richter in "T. S. Eliot, Dante, and 'The Hollow Men' " (1971). What this demonstrates is that efforts to specify Dante references display an embarrassing lack of consensus, save on the "multifoliate rose" of section IV. Genesius Jones' book (1964, cited above) indicates that the "dream kingdom" is the *Inferno*; B. C. Southam (*A Guide to the Selected Poems of T. S. Eliot*, 1969) believes that it includes both the *Inferno* and the *Purgatorio*. The "other kingdom" thus becomes the *Purgatorio* in Jones and the *Paradiso* in Southam. The "twilight kingdom" can be seen as the seculiar world (Jones) or as a transition between the other kingdoms and, thus, like the earthly paradise (Southam). Considering such disputes, Richter reasonably concludes that the influence of Dante on "The Hollow Men" is important but diffuse; attempts to establish particular parallels between the different kingdoms and sections of the *Divine Comedy* are "an intellectual game . . . of minor importance" (p. 221). Among the studies of Dante and "The Hollow Men" *not* covered by Richter, the most important are a section of the Philip Headings book (discussed below) and Robert S. Kinsman's summary of *Inferno* and *Aeneid* references in "Eliot's 'The Hollow Men' " (1950).

The third of the Ariel poems, "Animula" paraphrases in its opening lines a passage from Dante's *Purgatorio* which Eliot quotes in his 1929 essay on Dante. The second stanza seems to repeat the message of the first, and in the last stanza we are asked to pray for various unknown figures. In a letter to a reader who asked about the invented names, Eliot suggested that Floret might recall "certain folklore memories" while Guiterriez and Boudin "represent different types of career, the successful person of the machine age and someone who was killed in the last war." Most critics of the poem cite this letter, which may be found in Ethel M. Stephenson's otherwise quite useless *T. S. Eliot and the Lay Reader* (1944, p. 49). The identifications have not altered the usual impression of the poem, which is that its purgatorial air makes it seem a rather grim poem, as Christmas verse goes.

T. A. Stroud ("Eliot's 'Animula,' " 1969) tried to strike a more positive note by suggesting that the active souls we are to pray for are to be sharply distinguished from the irresolute souls described in the first two stanzas. The latter he regards as so indecisive that they belong in the vestibule of Dante's hell. Speculating on the likely sins of the characters in the last stanza, Stroud invents an upward progression through the levels of hell. Dante, we might note, went in the opposite direction, though perhaps the way up and the way down are the same. Stroud does not succeed in making the poem sound more hopeful by dividing it into two unequal parts. And if we are to take Dante as our guide to the poem, the *Purgatorio*, from which the opening stanza is derived, would seem a more appropriate road map than the *Inferno*.

In his Twayne Series volume, *T. S. Eliot* (1964), Philip R. Headings *does* take Dante as his guide to the poem, and he gives the entire poem a far less gloomy reading than most critics. Headings sees in the poem "not only a restatement of Dante's theory of the soul . . . but also the clear statement of the psychology and philosophy basic to all of Eliot's major poetry" (p. 32), a heavy burden for a minor poem. The soul, innocent by nature, is easily misled and confused by the partial goods of the world. Trapped by the pattern of its choices, the soul "issues from the hand of time," unable to choose the good. The figures of the last stanza represent such lost souls. The speaker asks that "the reader or, more likely, the Virgin Mary" pray for them. That it is the Virgin Mary who is addressed is suggested by the last line, which is adapted from the "Hail Mary," with the substitution of "birth" for "death." The substitution has point, for the poem sees the strayed soul as "living first in the silence after the viaticum." The poem is not, then, a simple warning of the perils the soul faces in this world. It holds out the promise of a birth to follow death. As Statius explains to Dante (*Purgatorio*, XXV), the soul which has been freed from the flesh at last understands its true direction. And even after death, souls who have not sinned mortally may find purgation.

Headings's Dantean reading of "Animula" may obscure some of the differences between Dante and Eliot. The divine love which draws men to God in Dante is not a part of Eliot's poem, and the moral choices which the "simple soul" must learn to make are not presented in terms of the proper "ordering of love" (p. 36). If Eliot shares Dante's doctrine of the soul, he gives it a less positive statement. The almost complacent pessimism which some critics find in the poem is, in other words, a real feature of its tone. But Headings is a valuable reminder that a more positive and Christian interpretation of the poem is possible and even plausible. His entire monograph is worth reading and deserves to be more frequently consulted than it seems to be. As his reading of "Animula" suggests, Headings consistently reads Eliot in the light of Dante and the Christian tradition. Even Gerontion is seen as looking forward to life after death. Headings is particularly good on *Ash Wednesday*, the Eliot poem most densely strewn with Dante references. Headings may well provide the best account of the relationship between Eliot's work and the theology and poetry of Dante.

Excessive insistence on schematic parallels between Eliot and Dante is the weakness of Sister Mary Cleophas' "*Ash Wednesday:* The *Purgatorio* in a Modern Mode" (1959). Cleophas takes rather literally the not unfamiliar notion that *The Waste Land* is Eliot's *Inferno*, that *Ash Wednesday* is his *Purgatorio*, and that the *Four Quartets* are his *Paradiso.* Of these comparisons, linking *Ash Wednesday* with the *Purgatorio* is especially appropriate, for the poem has many intimate links with passages in the *Purgatorio*, as Headings and others have demonstrated. Eliot has a particular affinity for the *Purgatorio* throughout his work, which may say as much about his poetic temperament as about his theology. Cleophas would go further than most critics, holding that the *Purgatorio* is importantly connected to Eliot's structuring of the six lyrics which make up *Ash Wednesday*. She arrives at a conclusion less significant than she seems to believe: Eliot is "paralleling the *Purgatorio*" with a structure which is "analogous" to "the underlying spiritual structure" of Dante's poem (p. 349). That structure, as she describes it, is necessarily very general, a quest for purgation, hardly surprising in a poem which takes its title from Ash Wednesday. Cleophas shows, for those who doubt it, that the poem has movement, but her reading very much slights influences other than Dante on its composition.

The Mystic

If we accept, for the moment, the notion that Eliot's religious poetry is concerned more with religious experience than with religious doctrine, the question remains: What sort of religious experience does the poetry present us? In *Ash Wednesday* and, perhaps, *The Waste Land* we seem to be confronted with a process of purgation and self-discipline of the kind required of believers in most higher religions. The liturgical elements in *Ash Wednesday*, for example, suggest preparation for the reception of the Sacrament and for the miracle of Easter. Theologically, such moments of "grace" are usually regarded as open to all believers. At the same time, such purgative experiences can also be envisaged as preparatory steps in a process which leads to the mystical experience of union with the divine, a kind of experience attained, at its most intense, by far fewer than those who achieve the certainties of faith. Eliot's religious prose—and allusions in his poems—will demonstrate his familiarity with the writings of great Christian mystics. Do his works, then, particularly the *Four Quartets*, attempt to convey mystic experience? A number of critics have maintained just that.

It is in the *Four Quartets* that we are most likely to find such moments. The few suggestions of mystical experience earlier in the poetry are not convincing. Mother Mary Eleanor, for example, has argued that the passage of Eliot's Magi deliberately parallels the "way" described by mystics, like St. John of the Cross, from purgation, to illumination, to unity ("Eliot's Magi," 1957). Her reading has more plausibility than a hasty reading of the poem might suggest, but it is unlikely that even the Magus has achieved full illumination. Eliot's poetry through *Ash Wednesday* is probably more aptly described as taking its protagonists through purgation to the brink of illumination by faith.

In the *Four Quartets*, on the other hand, a variety of mystics are quoted or alluded to, and the sequence ends with a vision in which "the tongues of flame are in-folded / into the crowned knot of fire / and the fire and the rose are one." Mystical experience—or at any rate the experience of mystics—is obviously somehow involved with the poem. In an excruciatingly pious essay, Elizabeth Jennings writes that the poems reflect "Eliot's own conviction that poetry is not only a medium for the expression of mystical experience but itself an experience of a similar kind" (*Every Changing Shape*, 1961, p. 189). This point is not really argued in the essay, which is appreciative and homiletic in manner. Jennings also discusses Eliot's plays, saying that "unless we interpret the 'visions' of the chief characters in *all* Eliot's plays in a mystical sense, we cannot really understand them at all" (p. 167). Not many critics would agree with Jennings fully on either point, but quite a few are in partial agreement.

A less extreme form of this approach can be found in Sister Mary Cleophas' "Notes on Levels of Meaning in 'Four Quartets' " (1950). The "levels" here are those fourfold principles Dante discussed in his famous letter to Can Grande: literal, allegorical, moral, and anagogical. Her most connected argument links the *Four Quartets*, on the anagogical level, to the sequence of mystical life outlined by St. John; in this essay, the key terms are the Ascent of Mount Carmel, the Dark Night of the Soul, and the Living Flame of Love. The final vision of "tongues of flame" is thus akin to "Dante's sight of the Beatific Vision" (p. 116). This is a fairly cautious formulation, since what is seen is not necessarily grasped for oneself.

Much less cautious is Sister Bernadotte Counihan's "*Four Quartets:* An Ascent to Mount Carmel?" (1969). Counihan argues that Eliot follows "the exact teachings of ascetical and mystical theology concerning the mystical experience—to suggest, in fact, that by the 'still point' Eliot means exactly that mystical experience at its ultimate moment when time falls away and the soul is completely rapt in communication with God the Eternal" (p. 60). In addition to St. John of the Cross, Counihan cites the presence of St. Ignatius of Loyola, Dame Juliana of Norwich, and the anonymous author of *The Cloud of Unknowing*. The last two are quoted or paraphrased in parts of "Little Gidding," and the parallels between *Four Quartets* and the spiritual discipline advocated by St. Ignatius of Loyola have been discussed in detail by William T. Noon ("*Four Quartets: Contemplatio ad Amorem*," 1954). Eliot's acquaintance with these mystical guides and his poetic use of them is well established, but it is wise to remember that his use of other kinds of sources has sometimes been more creative than faithful.

Sister Mary Gerard, in fact, has found important differences in "Eliot of the Circle and John of the Cross" (1959). She does not find in *Four Quartets* the personal deity of St. John. If the "still point" represents mystical experience at all, it points to "the impersonal God of the philosophers, the God of the Neo-Platonic mystic, not the personal Incarnate God of the Christian mystic" (p. 126). The rose garden experience of "Burnt Norton" does not seem to be a "mystical union in St. John's sense, but only an experience of sudden insight into the pattern of reality with the resultant feeling of peace and wholeness" (p. 112). A concern for pattern, she argues, is more basic in *Four Quartets* than the search for union. Whether this represents a defect in Eliot's understanding of the Incarnation, as Gerard seems to believe, is debatable, but Gerard's essay raises legitimate questions about the nature of the experience being conveyed.

The curiously systematic accounts of the stages of spiritual life left us by the great mystics of all religious traditions can be used as tools for analysis without implying an ultimately theological judgment of the poems. A useful example of such analysis is the chapter on Eliot in Robert J. Andreach, *Studies in Structure: The Stages of the Spiritual Life in Four Modern Authors* (1964). Among its other virtues, Andreach's volume provides the most detailed comparison of Eliot's work with that of Gerard Manley Hopkins. Philip M. Martin's earlier *Mastery and Mercy* (1957) simply presents, side by side, rather conventional interpretations of *Ash Wednesday* and Hopkins' "Wreck of the *Deutschland*," while Peter Milward's essay, "Sacramental Symbolism in Hopkins and Eliot" (1968), is mainly interested in showing that the Christian ideal has produced in these men some good poetry. Andreach provides a good account of the similarities and differences of Hopkins and Eliot by following standard analyses of ascetic and mystical experience (by those authorities who link the two together).

Andreach does not find genuine mystical union in the poetry of either Hopkins or Eliot. He reads most of Eliot's poems as concerned with active purgation of the senses, with some of the protagonists of the plays having progressed to active purgation of the spirit. In Hopkins, this process of purgation is directed toward spiritual growth and leads to the next stage, illumination; in Eliot, purgation is necessary for "the rediscovery of the spiritual life" (p. 98). In Hopkins, the Incarnation is an accepted fact and a pledge of God's grace; in Eliot, the Incarnation must be recaptured so that grace will be possible. Eliot's emphasis on redemption of the past, on breaking out of time into the timeless, is part of the process of purgation, a step toward awakening, rather than a more advanced state, for memory itself is left behind in the achieved state of union. Trapped in secularized time, Eliot's poetic personae and dramatic protagonists must struggle simply to achieve an awakening to the reality of the spiritual world which exists beyond time.

Fayek M. Ishak's *The Mystical Philosophy of T. S. Eliot* (1970) quotes Eliot as saying, in a 1961 interview with the author, that his "solution is not final, but it is as far as" he can go (p. 148). The humility of the statement is apparent in *Four Quartets* as well. Ishak is willing to see in the *Quartets* "some touches of the illuminative vision of the mystic" (p. 145), but he agrees with Andreach in finding the poems essentially purgative and lacking in moments of mystic union. Their classification schemes are not entirely alike; the moments of illumination seen by Ishak are dismissed by Andreach as no more than spiritual awakening, while other critics would credit them as transcendent visions. Ishak's book is a grab-bag of Eastern and Western mysticism and derivative readings of Eliot's poetry, but it is worth attending to as a detailed study of Eliot's relationship to mystical thought.

Ishak's emphasis on Eliot's preference for the way of negation has recently been challenged by Nancy Gish ("The Significance of the Mystic in T. S. Eliot's Theme of Time," 1976). Gish's essay is sensible and persuasive, even when discussing Eliot's concept of time, the most boring of critical preoccupations in dealing with *Four Quartets*. She sees a variety of concepts of time at work in the *Quartets*, "in which the life of the mystic bears varying kinds of significance" (p. 174). Her key point, as for most of those who see progression rather than circling in the poems, is that "Little Gidding" affirms the possibilities of our life in time. Gish sees little of St. John of the Cross and the negative way in "Little Gidding"; she apparently sees Dame Juliana of Norwich as significantly more affirmative. In her reading, we still do not end "with the ecstasy of the mystic," but we end with "an affirmation that all shall ultimately be well though we do not achieve union here" (p. 176). This differs from Andreach and Ishak only in emphasis, but Gish's tone is a useful departure. The *Four Quartets* are certainly rich with references to the spiritual disciplines advocated by the mystics, but these disciplines can be followed and reflected upon by those with no expectation of achieving union for themselves. Too exclusive a concentration on the mystical sources of the poems can lead to judging the experience they present by standards they do not propose.

The Poet in the Rose Garden

Many problems of interpretation with which the *Four Quartets* confront the reader can be found in the first of the *Quartets*, "Burnt Norton." Written before the full sequence was conceived, "Burnt Norton" provided the pattern for the other *Quartets*, though the poem appears to have derived its pattern from *The Waste Land* and to incorporate discarded material from *Murder in the Cathedral*. Like the full sequence, "Burnt Norton" is often discussed as though it were composed of doctrine and philosophy rather than poetry.

How we interpret the opening poem in the sequence obviously has considerable bearing on what kind of progression, if any, we find in the *Quartets* as a whole. Perhaps for this reason, the most frequently discussed passage in the entire sequence is probably the rose garden passage in "Burnt Norton I." In an essay oddly titled "T. S. Eliot's Wasteland" (1967), John Carey argues that the rose garden passage is the key to the *Quartets* and that this moment, and much else in the sequence, presents us with a mystical union with God. The bird says "Go" because, in Scholastic philosophy, God is pure act. God is ultimate reality, as well, and communion with him is so intense an experience that "human kind / cannot bear very much" of it. Like the mystical interpretations already discussed, this one is unconvincing; it leaves out too much of what is happening in the text, and the lines it calls upon do not support its interpretation. The presences which fill the rose garden are unseen, or seen only as reflected in the pool. No union is implied by these images, only separation bridged by a moment's perception. We may add that a poem made up of moments of mystical union would seem to lack progression; and one wonders why the poet would have gone on to write the other *Quartets*.

The experience in the rose garden looks backward to Eliot's earlier poetry as well as forward to the other *Quartets*. The mention of "heart of light," for example, takes us back to the hyacinth garden of *The Waste Land*. Leonard Unger's famous essay, "T. S. Eliot's Rose Garden: A Persistent Theme" (1942), traces such earlier appearances of the garden theme in Eliot's poetry, including "La Figlia che Piange," the waiter's story in "Dans le Restaurant," "Portrait of a Lady," "Marina," and *Ash Wednesday*. Unger interprets Eliot's garden "experience" as like that Dante describes in the *Vita Nuova*, an early sexual awakening later identified with that love which leads us to God. The young girl, flowers, and water are recurring elements, as is a sense of inadequate response. In "Burnt Norton I," the recovery of the experience (which may never have occurred) is a product of will and deception and is only partially successful. Sexual elements are still present ("the lotos rose"); but later developments in "Burnt Norton" insist on the wider significance of the experience, and by the time we have reached "Little Gidding" the rose garden is identified with a redemption from history that is more than simply personal.

Robert D. Wagner's "The Meaning of Eliot's Rose-Garden" (1954) follows Unger in seeing a comparison with the *Vita Nuova* but neglects the sexual implications Unger finds in the comparisons. For Wagner, "the significant quality of the original experience (revived in the rose-garden) was its unselfconsciousness. We were then innocently at one with reality" (p. 26), but now must struggle to wrest from time and language a new reality, continuous with that we once experienced. Wagner's assumptions that the experience was innocent and that we were at one with reality are not backed up by any reference to the text. The assumption made by both Unger and Wagner, that we are dealing with a childhood experience, is hard to follow when the poem tells us that the passage to the rose garden leads "towards the door we never opened." The poem takes us, perhaps, "into our first world," but this is surely the garden of Burnt Norton, as well as the garden we never visited. Even the echoes which inhabit the garden are imperfectly apprehended.

It may be, of course, that Eliot was making use in this passage of a recurring image with personal emotional significance for him. Unger's survey of his various gardens of missed delight suggests that such may be the case. But what matters is not the image's origin but its use in a particular poem. Insofar as it suggests a childhood encounter with an adored woman, the *Vita Nuova* comparison does not help one understand the opening of "Burnt Norton." Where the two works touch is that the moment in the rose garden is interpreted, later in the poem, in terms which suggest spiritual awakening. The setting itself may recall the Garden of Earthly Paradise in Dante or the Garden of Eden, which was its model, though these are surely secondary associations at most. If we identify, as seems plausible, the children hiding in the leaves with "the children in the apple tree" of "Little Gidding V," then we are eventually (at the end of the *Quartets*) led to see the apple tree of Eden in the rose garden.

Eleanor Simmons Greenhill has hung upon these two passages a long essay, "The Child in the Tree: A Study of the Cosmological Tree in Christian Tradition" (1954), which sees the tree and children, found in some Grail myths, as more emblematic of the cross than of paradise. Although we are not really called upon to recall obscure Grail stories in reading "Burnt Norton," it is conceivable that the voices of the children, startling when first encountered, are eventually meant to remind us of Christ.

To speak of the way in which "Little Gidding's" closing passage may alter our perception of "Burnt Norton's rose garden is to notice that the experience of the rose garden is neither complete in itself nor fully understood when we first encounter it. In "Hints and Guesses in *Four Quartets*" (1954), Arnold P. Drew has found the basic method of the poem. Taking his cue from "Dry Salvages V," Drew insists that the poet pursues a deliberate vagueness because such "hints and guesses" are all that we can grasp, all that we can bear of ultimate reality, although "the hint half guessed, the gift half understood, is Incarnation." There is no doubt that this is the direction in which the *Four Quartets* move, but we cannot reduce the experiences which provide us with such hints and guesses to mere shadows of a greater reality. If they are not also natural experiences, occurring in time, they cannot point toward the Incarnation. And to read the results of the poet's meditations back into the experiences which are the objects of his thought is to violate the human reality and ambiguity of those experiences as we encounter them in the poem. Eliot criticism has its own Gnostic heresies.

A sense of the movement of the *Four Quartets* is one of the virtues of David Perkins' "Rose Garden to Midwinter Spring: Achieved Faith in the *Four Quartets*" (1962). The rose garden, he points out, is a secluded place, and its light is a transitory illusion. In "Little Gidding" the light reflected from the snow is real and all around the protagonist, while the experience itself takes place in the open, on the way to a place of devotion.

Moreover, the protagonist now understands more of the experience he undergoes. The differences between the opening and closing sections of the *Four Quartets* thus demonstrate the progress toward faith and community which have been made during the poems. Although Perkins' essay is weakened somewhat by insistence on the purely theological connotations of the passages and by an exaggerated stress on the childhood character of the rose garden experience, he clearly makes the important point that, in circling back to its initial moment of awakening, the poems are consolidating their gains, rather than completing a simple circle.

A temptation to see *Four Quartets* as coming full circle is encouraged by many lines in the poems which indicate their continuing concern with "the still point of the turning world" ("Burnt Norton II"). The image of the "still point" occurs in several Eliot works and is well enough known that Ethel F. Cornwall has used it as a key for exploring the work of a variety of writers (*The Still Point*, 1962). Her presentation of Eliot's conception of "the still point" is rather confused, but the obvious points emerge: The "still point" is to be equated with God, Christ the Word, the pattern-giving spiritual reality at the center of life. To this we may add the observation of H. Z. Maccoby, that the "still point" is not simply the Incarnation but also those moments in which our lives are illumined by awareness of the divine ("A Commentary on 'Burnt Norton,' II," 1970).

Because "Burnt Norton" rehearses so many themes of the *Quartets* as a whole, critical essays on the poem have often tended to concentrate on those passages most clearly relevant to the sequence as a whole. Even where the differences among the *Quartets* are acknowledged, concentrating on elements they have in common may slightly distort our view of them as individual poems. "Burnt Norton," written before the full sequence was conceived, especially deserves to be read on its own terms.

One of the longest separate essays on "Burnt Norton" is Paul D. Hahn's "A Reformation of New Criticism: 'Burnt Norton' Revisited" (1972). (The title may be a misprint: the running head in the journal is "A Reformulation of New Criticism," which better fits the author's efforts.) Unfortunately, the essay's length is not matched by depth of detail, for the author spends much time on pretentious and unnecessary critical preliminaries; the detailed reading is confined to the first two sections of the poem, so that the usual concentration on the rose garden and the "still point" is not much altered. Hahn's proposal to explicate the poem in terms of its experience rather than some "thesis" derived from it is sound enough, and points to the real weakness of much criticism of the *Quartets*. But his explication sometimes adds unnecessary difficulties, when there are quite enough already. To solve some problems he has created, Hahn tentatively proposes a "dual narrator" (p. 41), splitting the speaker of the poem into one who undergoes the experience and another who has already contemplated its meaning. The problems of point of view in *Four Quartets* are less serious than in much modern fiction, and the invention of special types of narrators does not seem called for.

Far more illuminating is "A Visit to Burnt Norton" (1974) by Barbara Everett, one of the few critics of the nineteen-seventies who regularly finds fresh things to say about Eliot that are also worth saying. Everett takes us back to the ruined house for which Eliot named the poem. "Almost all commentators quietly re-name it *The Rose Garden*," she observes, so that "it is often easier to find in critical discussions resumes of its statements than any very precise rendering of its feeling" (p. 201). She stresses that even the philosophical language of the poem, by virtue of becoming part of the poem, is presented as the feelings of a single speaker in a given place. Moreover, the poem yields more than mystical feelings, even if we think those are the ones Eliot emphasized in constructing later *Quartets* with it as model.

The opening passages may arouse as much uneasiness as joy. The speaker confronts a deserted house and its garden, alive with ghostly presences—"There they were, dignified, invisible"—which are not to be identified, as they sometimes are, with the children or the roses. If one remembers previous Eliot gardens, one may recall previous appearances of the children—not simply in "New Hampshire" (where they suggest mysticism) but in the suppressed "Ode" from *Ara Vos Prec* (where they have been violated). The line "Human kind cannot bear very much reality" occurs in *Murder in the Cathedral*, in a sense suggesting betrayal.

For Everett, then, the opening section of "Burnt Norton can be read as a kind of ghost story, recalling Eliot's early "Death of St. Narcissus" and, more closely, Henry James's *Turn of the Screw*. Besides the influence of James, Everett suggests the presence, behind a passage of "footfalls echo," of Charles Dickens in

A Tale of Two Cities. Again, the emphasis is social and psychological, stressing the narrative side of Eliot, his ability to create an atmosphere. On the other hand, emphasis on the house, rather than the garden, makes the poem "a study in consciousness, like 'Gerontion,' or 'Prufrock' or *The Waste Land* . . . a poem about 'living here,' not about 'how to live,' " (p. 219). The dogmatic side of the poem already seems dated, valid only as an expression of one sensibility at one time. The patterning of the *Quartets* as a whole, ingenious as it is, must be seen as an effort to give shape to "their sense of a vast wastage in human existence, the feel of anarchic air blowing through and through things" (p. 223).

Louis L. Martz's "The Wheel and the Point" (1947) is best known for its exploration of this imagery in Eliot's later work, but Martz provides additional sources which reinforce Everett's reading. He suggests that the poem has not only echoes of *Alice in Wonderland* (acknowledged in conversation by Eliot) but of two stories Eliot discusses in *After Strange Gods:* D. H. Lawrence's "The Shadow in the Rose Garden" and James Joyce's "The Dead." In the Lawrence story, a woman is confronted by a lover she had thought dead; in the Joyce story, a wife has a garden vision of a long-dead lover. None of these sources presents itself as an allusion to be recognized by the reader, and one may say the same for Everett's James and Dickens sources. What is significant at this point is that such echoes are plausible and *do* suggest themselves to sensitive readers like Everett and Martz. The ominous overtones they add to the rose garden passage are part of the ambiguity that confronts us if we approach the reading of "Burnt Norton" without insisting on reading its end into its beginning. In another context, Martz cites Eliot's 1931 essay "The *Pensées* of Pascal" (in *Selected Essays*), which praises Pascal as a type of the believer whose faith triumphs over rational skepticism by integrating that skepticism into a faith which transcends it.

Everett supports her reading of "Burnt Norton" by recalling that a skeptical tone has always been one of the strengths of Eliot's religious poetry. She insists that this tone persists in the *Quartets*—in the affectionate parody of Crashaw, which may modify our sense of "Little Gidding's" lyric on "the dove descending"; in the "strange bathos" (p. 210) of the "Dry Salvages" stanza, beginning "Pray for all those who are in ships," with its apparent echo of Corbière; and in the tone, recalling Clough, which gives a powerful passage in "East Coker" a momentary flash of wit with "the vacant into the vacant," counterpointing the solemnity of the passage with a tone of "insolence, of insubordination, and of calm farce" (p. 212). Essays like Everett's help us recognize the ways in which Eliot's religious poetry distinguishes itself from the sort of devotional verse it is sometimes mistaken for.

The Poet and Time

"Burnt Norton" begins with "time present and time past" and all the *Quartets* contain reflections on the passage of time and its intersection with the timeless. The "still point" gives meaning to the world of time, as the Incarnation gives a center and meaning to history. Reflections on time provide some of the poetic high points of the *Four Quartets.* The same cannot be said for critical reflections on Eliot's attitudes toward time, but there has been a fair amount of critical interest in the topic.

The world of time appears to us as a realm of constant flux and inevitable decay. Eliot's sense of time's change has been variously traced to Bergson (Staffan Bergsten, *Time and Eternity*, 1960) and Heraclitus (Merrel D. Clubb, Jr., "The Heraclitean Element in Eliot's *Four Quartets*," 1961). Such philosophical sources hardly seem required to explain what we find in the poem, but Clubb at least demonstrates that Heraclitus is relevant to the poem in ways which go beyond its epigraph.

Beyond this world of flux, and intersecting it, is the timeless. This is a widely shared notion, so it is not surprising that Morris Weitz can find traces of neo-Platonism in Eliot's philosophy of time ("T. S. Eliot: Time as a Mode of Salvation," 1952). Weitz does not really attempt to demonstrate any direct debt, and it seems likely that any neo-Platonic elements in Eliot come to him through modern Idealists and the Christian tradition. Bradley and St. Augustine are suggested by C. A. Patrides ("T. S. Eliot and the Pattern of Time," 1976). Even these influences, Patrides says, are "diffuse, not precise" (p. 165). Both the ceaseless flux and meaningless repetition of time horrify Eliot, but the Christian view of time allows him to see time as linear, moving purposefully under the shadow of eternity. Eliot's interest in the nature of time, says Patrides, can be seen in his translation and publication in the *Criterion* (1930) of an essay on Einstein by Charles Mauron.

Eliot's view of time has also been compared with that of Thomas Hardy, by Tom Paulin in his "Time and Sense Experience: Hardy and T. S. Eliot" (1976). The attempt does nothing to alter one's impression that Eliot and Hardy are poets with little in common. Both, we learn, tell us that time passes and makes all things pass. Hardy will not go beyond sense experience, while Eliot finds a religious answer to the ravages of time. Nevertheless, Eliot is a more negative poet than Hardy: "For if Hardy almost always points to death and despair lying just beyond the joyous affirmation of the dance, he can allow the dancers their moment of happiness" (p. 176).

A more affirmative view of Eliot's temperament is found in Bergsten's book, *Time and Eternity* (1960). Although his early references to Bergson are unconvincing, Bergsten's book is a useful survey of the various ideas about time which might have influenced Eliot. Bergsten's long consideration of the theories of time in various forms of mystical thought is particularly interesting, even when hard to relate specifically to Eliot. Bergsten is also sensitive to "history," concrete personal and social pasts, especially in the later *Quartets.*

Even so, the least persuasive portions of Bergsten's book are those in which he attempts to apply his key notions to the poems. His interpretation of the rose garden follows Unger with undue confidence: "It can hardly be doubted that the rose garden is meant to symbolize a vision of Reality or of the Divine and the prefiguration of this vision in the experiences of profane love" (p. 171). Nor does it add much to this interpretation to attach "eternity" as a label to the rose garden experience, so that "the First Section of 'Burnt Norton' is thus constructed round two themes, that of time in the first part and that of eternity in the second" (p. 172). Bergsten must then go on to explain Eliot's omission of words like "eternal" or "timeless" in this section as a deliberate decision to "hold back the explicit statement of the meaning of the experience in the garden until the conclusion of the poem" (ibid.). When his general argument does not get in his way, Bergsten's readings are often characterized by good sense.

Much of the *Four Quartets* may seem taken up with regret at the wastage of historic time and yearning for a timeless eternity, glimpsed only in moments, but "Little Gidding" affirms the value of both. The better readings of *Four Quartets* have always recognized the dual character of this affirmation, linking it often to the Christian doctrine of the Incarnation, but readings which concentrate on the poem's mystical sources sometimes lose sight of it, and unsympathetic critics have sometimes pictured the later Eliot as turning his back on society to work out a purely personal kind of salvation. Readings which stress the poet's acceptance of time are therefore useful.

This point is made in Nathan A. Scott Jr.'s discussion of Eliot in his *The Poetry of Civic Virtue* (1976). It is the early poetry, says Scott, which rejects society and despairs of history, participating in the characteristic modern withdrawal into an Orphic solitude of art-made worlds. It was Eliot's exploration of the implications of his new Christian position which persuaded him "that disabling though the burdens imposed by our human heritage may be, our most essential task remains that of seeking to 'fare forward.' Since there is no other dwelling place for us but historical time, he began to conclude that, despite all the taint and ambiguity in our history there can be no escaping the truth that 'Only through time time is conquered' " (p. 19). Eliot is certainly attracted to asceticism and the example set by ascetic saints, but his "negative way" is not, in the end, a rejection of the world so much as a descent into it. It is in the historicity of the world that we come in contact with eternity.

Many of the issues connected with Eliot's concept of time are brought together in Rajendra Verma's *Time and Poetry in Eliot's Four Quartets* (1979). We hear again of Heraclitus, St. Augustine, and a variety of Christian mystics. Special attention is given to Eliot's use of concepts from *Bhagavad Gita.* Dante and Yeats are summoned up as well, with much emphasis given to the contrast between Eliot's Christian concept of time and Yeats' attempt to redeem man from history through cyclic myths. Eliot, Verma concludes, "is not upholding conceptual tenets of Neo-Platonist approach to time which sets time against eternity" (p. 196). Although few of its major points are original, Verma's book has the merit of applying them in a section-by-section reading of the *Four Quartets.* Each *Quartet* and each section gets two readings, one purely expository and another more concerned with sources and comparisons. This structure maintains the flow of the poem in the explicatory chapters, but it leads to a certain amount of repetition. In an effort to keep pace with the poetic material under discussion, Verma's prose sometimes seems rather cloudy, for example, on "Burnt Norton II": "The opening does seem modulated on symmetrical phrases, but the clash and cohesion of a sharp visual imagery of the aromatic (garlic) sums up the essence of it all" (p. 36). His reading, however, demonstrates the relevance of time and the timeless to much of the *Four Quartets.*

The Doctrinal Poet

Discussions of time in the *Four Quartets* naturally focus on the poems' intellectual content, at the risk of divorcing thought from feeling. The temptation to read the sequence as doctrinal poetry is heightened by the discursive tone of many passages, especially those sections which discuss in prosy lines the making of verse. Even careful readers can take the poems in this fashion, for critical paraphrase turns many passages in these poems into apparently straightforward statements about the nature of life and art. Those who share Eliot's doctrinal commitments need not find it a problem to read the poems in this way, but some of the resulting readings seem to take too seriously his remark that "the poetry does not matter." Those unable to assent to Eliot's doctrines have often objected to those passages in the *Quartets* which seem to ask for such assent.

There is nothing inherently reductive about discussing a poem's thought, of course. William Blissett's early discussion of the *Quartets* as reflections on time and poetry gives a connected account ("The Argument of T. S. Eliot's *Four Quartets,*" 1946) without confusing poetry and philosophy. In another early essay on the poems' major themes, R. W. Flint stresses their prophetic and philosophic character but is prepared to admit that Eliot is a "philosopher who has less fear of the hobgoblin consistency than some of his colleagues and disciples" ("The *Four Quartets* Reconsidered," 1948, p. 70). Flint sees Eliot's religious position as poetically nonsectarian; despite the references to Christ, Eliot's doctrine of the Incarnation speaks more of the intrusion of the timeless into time than of traditional teachings about the nature of Christ. If one must stress the doctrinal character of the poems, Flint's approach has much to recommend it, though even Flint ends with some doubts as to whether the unspiritual multitude will be able to grasp the vision of the last lines of "Little Gidding."

Book-length studies of the *Quartets* abound, some of which, like Verma's, provide fairly detailed explications; but early efforts at line-by-line readings could be fairly brief. Raymond

Preston's *Four Quartets Rehearsed* (1946) and Constance de Masirevich's *On the* Four Quartets *of T. S. Eliot* (1953) are not much more than pamphlets. Most later explications run much longer, partly because they must take into account a greater volume of critical comment. Of the early efforts, Preston's is much the better, and its sixty-six pages cover most of what a reader needs to know. The overall interpretation follows lines laid down by Helen Gardner, and much of Preston's pamphlet is devoted to identifying sources or parallel passages and quoting them for the reader. Eliot read Preston's work in manuscript; so it benefits from some notes Eliot made. On the Heraclitan epigraphs, for example, Preston writes that "Mr. Eliot says that he was attracted by the *poetic suggestiveness* of the fragments" (p. viii). The comments from Eliot may do as much for the survival of Preston's study as its own good sense.

The fifties and sixties saw the publication of several longer explications of the *Quartets*, all of which overstress their doctrinal character: C. A. Bodelsen's *T. S. Eliot's Four Quartets* (1958), Peter Milward's *A Commentary on Eliot's "Four Quartets"* (1968), Daniel O'Connor's *T. S. Eliot's "Four Quartets"* (1969), and Harry Blamires' *Word Unheard* (1969). Bodelsen's work is somewhat less detailed than its successors, but provides a useful survey of interpretations from the fifties. Of the later books, O'Connor's is the least pretentious, a book intended for students and for reading the poems as exercises in Christian meditation.

Milward and Blamires illustrate the chief fault of doctrinal interpretations: they translate back into old familiar formulas the ideas Eliot labored to make new, so that his hard-won affirmations seem easy victories. Here, for example, is Milward on "East Coker IV" and its closing line ("Again, in spite of that, we call this Friday good"): "It is because we regard our bodies as substantial, that we shrink from suffering and death as evil. But our Christian faith teaches us the opposite truth: that suffering and death with Christ on the cross are the only means of eternal salvation. It is for this reason that '*we call this Friday good.*' Incidentally, it was for the Good Friday of 1940 that this lyric was originally composed" (p. 111). Whatever force Eliot has been able to give to the paradox of "Good" Friday is utterly dissipated in this explanation. Blamires, in turn, says that "East Coker IV" presents "the affirmative and joyful content of the doctrine of the Redemption and the Atonement" (p. 72). Although Blamires may be right about the doctrine, he misstates the tone of Eliot's lyric.

Pouring new wine into old bottles, such paraphrases threaten to deaden the reader's response to the experience of the poems, and one hopes that the students and general readers for whom such works are often intended will put off reading them until they are thoroughly familiar with the *Quartets*. If one already knows the poetry well, detailed paraphrases like those by Milward, Blamires, and others have the virtue of not skipping awkward passages and of allowing one to check one's response to the poems against that of another reader.

Essays devoted to individual *Quartets*, like studies of the work as a whole, often stress the doctrinal or mystical features. We have already noted several such studies of "Burnt Norton," and similar readings can be found for the other *Quartets*. In "A Reading of 'East Coker' " (1946), Francis J. Smith interprets the poem as concerned with "tradition," seeing that term in the harsh light cast by *After Strange Gods*. Smith's strength is his account of the poem's relationship to the purgative way of the mystics; his weakness is his reluctance to recognize any other aspects of the poem. This doctrinal approach leads him to reject as negative what the poem finds merely insufficient, as when Smith tells us that the dance "represents the meaningless, fitful expenditure of physical and emotional energy of the modern world" (p. 275). We might also wonder whether the archaic dangers are a very apt representative of anything in the modern world.

Jack Kligerman ("An Interpretation of T. S. Eliot's 'East Coker,' " 1962) acknowledges the sensuous harmony of the dance in "East Coker," along with the poet's final rejection of its merely natural ritual. Though often sensitive to the poem's shifts and progress in meaning, he wants to see at its end a mystical union, rather than simply achieved knowledge: "Eliot's communion seems to be both with himself and with God, and he has made this communion manifest in 'East Coker' " (p. 112). This turns poetry (or criticism) into a spiritual scorecard.

For those who find such doctrinal pronouncements hard to swallow, the discursive passages in the *Quartets* offer the most problems. They are particularly prosaic in "Dry Salvages," and their unpoetic tone is frequently referred to in the most famous essay on "Dry Salvages," Donald Davie's "T. S. Eliot: The End of an Era" (1956); and it may explain why there are not more essays on this *Quartet*. Davie's essay falls into two parts. The first makes a convincing argument that, taken by itself, "The

Dry Salvages" is simply not a very good poem. The second makes a less convincing argument that the badness is deliberate, that "The Dry Salvages" provides the *Four Quartets* as a whole the kind of false reconciliation Hugh Kenner has found operating within the individual poems of the sequence. "Dry Salvages" is necessary, in other words, to enable us to appreciate "Little Gidding." In trying to show that "Dry Salvages" is badly written, Davie proceeds by selective quotation, Eliot's critical method. It is hard to disagree with him about the opening passage of the poem, despite the praise it has received from other critics; surely, "worshippers of the machine" is not a cliché redeemed but a cliché pure and simple. And when one is forced to look at them, some of the rhymes in the "sestina" *do* look forced. As Davie notes, even those who praise the poem are uncomfortable with "I sometimes wonder if that is what Krishna meant– / Among other things–or one way of putting the same thing." Whether this adds up to a convincing indictment depends on one's ear as one reads the poem. But Davie's efforts to save the day by reading the poem as intentional parody, even if accepted, would justify only false positions and not bad poetry. One cannot be sure that Davie takes it seriously himself. For all his admiration for the *Quartets*, he sees them as a dead end. Eliot's, says Davie, is a post-Symbolist poetry in which the poetry literally "does not matter," so that even the drabness of "Dry Salvages" is acceptable if drabness is what we wish to express. Davie would just as soon return to beauty.

Some similar problems are raised by the best-known essay on "Little Gidding," D. W. Harding's review of the poem for *Scrutiny:* "We Have Not Reached Conclusion" (1943). Harding's review is mainly a brief explication of the poem. It is still worth reading as such, though Harding drastically underrates the sympathy with which the poem treats the ghost encountered in section II. But at the end of his review, after a brief summary of "Little Gidding V," Harding comments: "In most of Mr. Eliot's poems the intellectual materials which abound are used emotionally. In much of this poem they are used intellectually, in literal statement which is to be understood literally (for instance, the opening of section III). How such statements become poetry is a question outside the range of this review. To my mind they do, triumphantly, and for me it ranks among the major good fortunes of our time that so superb a poet is writing" (p. 219). In the next issue of *Scrutiny* (Summer 1943) was R. N. Higinbotham's "Objections to a Review of 'Little Gidding.' " Higinbotham complained that Eliot had failed to assimilate his intellectual materials and that Harding had evaded the issue, a position to which F. R. Leavis took vigorous exception in the same issue ("Reflections on the Above.")

The issue in this dispute over "Little Gidding" is like that raised by Davie's article on "The Dry Salvages," since many of the passages singled out by Davie as bad poetry are discursive passages embodying the kind of intellectual materials Harding is speaking of. How far one can admit the discursive, prosy tone to a poem without rending the poetic fabric is a technical question of craft. But such passages exhibit, with particular clarity, the doctrinal predispositions behind the poet's meditation on his experience. They seem to exhibit and evoke a separation between thought and feeling of the very sort Eliot helped persuade us to distrust. From this we may be led to see much of the entire sequence as composed of statements which invite, even coerce, our assent.

Such a progress seems evident in the considerable reservations Leavis has since expressed about the *Four Quartets* in *The Living Principle* (1975). Leavis continues to hold that Eliot is a major poet and even that the *Four Quartets* are an important work. But he is convinced that one's response to the poems requires an initial negative judgment. In part, what Leavis objects to seems itself a product of such a judgment—his Eliot is characterized by "fear of life and contempt (which includes self-contempt) for humanity" (p. 205), by an insistence "on humanity's utter abjectness and nullity" (p. 255), and "on the unreality, the unlivingness, of life in time" (p. 179). Although Leavis is hardly alone in holding this picture of Eliot, it is an unfair characterization of Eliot's temperament and an inaccurate characterization of what is said in the *Four Quartets.* Such problems are perhaps inevitable when a critic like Leavis, given to forceful exaggeration impatiently confronts a poet and critic like Eliot, given to self-doubt and equivocation. Leavis also seems to attribute Eliot's reflections on the limitations of language to his Americanism (p. 222) and his religious stance. Leavis manages to exaggerate Eliot's position while taking exception to it.

There are really two problems, then, with Leavis's "judgment and analysis" of lines like "Go, go, go, said the bird: human kind / Cannot bear very much reality." Leavis says they "imply both a conception of 'reality' that I must repudiate for myself, and a perverse judgment of 'human kind' " (p. 177). The first problem is that Leavis may have misjudged the implications of the lines. The second problem is that Leavis assumes that a lyric moment in the poems demands of him fundamental assent or dissent—the other side of the same moral view of literature that allows him to praise Eliot for having exposed the philistinism of our time. This side of Leavis's argument seems dispensable, along with his tortured discussions of "sincerity," his stereotyped views of Americans, and his parochial assumption that "the truly important thinkers" of the century are "Alexander, Whitehead, and Collingwood" (p. 235).

At the same time, Leavis raises important questions about whether the poems' moments of affirmation are earned or simply willed. If we take the poems as an argument, their affirmations are obviously not justified conclusions, based on reasoned discourse. Even Leavis does not quite treat the poems as an argument, but he maintains that they implicitly treat Eliot's spiritual condition as somehow representative, and for this Leavis has some warrant in the text. If we take representativeness as essential to the strategy of the poems, then any failure to command the reader's assent to their ultimate vision means that the poems have fallen short on their own terms. It is possible, however, to regard passages in which Eliot speaks of "most of us" as more concerned to deny the speaker's uniqueness (which would constitute spiritual pride) than to assert his representativeness. We would still face, though, the question of whether the poems convince us that they have earned for themselves their affirmations. This, to use Lionel Trilling's dichotomy, is less a matter of "sincerity" than "authenticity."

Graham Hough's reservations in "Vision and Doctrine in *Four Quartets*" (1973) are primarily of this sort. In key passages of the sequence, including a number of the lyrics, he writes, "I think I see will doing the work of the imagination" (p. 126). One may disagree with his description of the poems as characterized by "sectarian dogmatism" (p. 110), but it is hard to see how one would go about refuting the simple assertion that certain passages have a willed quality to them. Nevertheless, when leveled by careful readers like Leavis and Hough, such opinions deserve respect. Also of interest is Hough's explanation for the alleged unevenness of the *Quartets*. Eliot's natural genius, he suggests, was for fragmentary verse that is itself a way of discovering what it means: "The predetermined doctrine, expressed appropriately enough in a predetermined form, that we find in the *Quartets* is not in harmony with

Eliot's natural and intrinsic poetic methods" (p. 125). Since our view of Eliot's "natural" methods depends partly on our judgment of those in what we think are his best poems, this argument is potentially circular.

Of such recent attacks on the doctrinal overtones of the *Four Quartets*, Leavis's has probably received the most attention, both because of his eminence as a critic and because, as R. P. Bilan observes, his recent views are "rather unsettling in light of his original acclaim of the poem" ("F. R. Leavis's Revaluation of T. S. Eliot," 1978). Bilan traces the change to changes in Leavis's ideology as a critic; he finds Leavis's latest essay at its best when least determined by ideological bias. P. H. Butter's "*Four Quartets:* Some Yes-buts to Dr. Leavis" (1976) also contains a passing reply to Hough. In response to Leavis, Butter shows how Leavis's account of Eliot "either over-states the negative attitude or under-states the positive" (p. 31). In response to Hough's observation that the finest moments in the *Quartets* are natural (rather than Christian) epiphanies, Butter argues that Eliot is simply holding true to a religious sensibility which can experience only such "hints and guesses" and must interpret them as best it can. Butter is convincing on both points.

Although not conceived as a reply to Hough, William V. Spanos' essay "Hermeneutics and Memory: Destroying T. S. Eliot's *Four Quartets*" (1978) is relevant to Hough's complaint about the predetermined character of the *Quartets*. Identifying Modernism with spatial organization, Spanos says that the *Four Quartets* move beyond the modernism of their initial conceptions. Using a Kierkegaardian distinction between recollection and repetition, Spanos says that the poems are not locked in the closed circle of recollection (like "Prufrock") but move forward with repetitions that are always new. The poet, we are told, does not find fulfillment but a need for new voyages; more dubiously, we hear that he does not find a presence but an *absence* at the "still center." The *Quartets* are poems of words, and the words will not stand still. Despite the occasional spurts of jargon which mark efforts to introduce new critical perspectives, and despite a tendency to assume that clinching quotations from Heidegger help, Spanos has a nice sense of the way in which the meditations move (rather than circle). "East Coker," in particular, responds well to his approach, with his terms providing a nice summary of the progress between the opening, "In my beginning is my end" (recollection), and the closing, "In my end is my beginning" (repetition). Although Hough may be right in seeing a predetermined form as a problem in the later *Quartets,* Spanos makes a good case that the sequence was not dominated by predetermined doctrine and remained a poetry of exploration.

While Spanos turns the *Four Quartets* into a postmodern poem, Roger Sharrock has offered a different reading in his "*Four Quartets* as a Post-Christian Poem" (1977). This is less exciting than it might sound, for Sharrock means that Eliot was writing a Christian poem for a post-Christian age. That may sound rather like Hough's complaint, but Sharrock has well in mind Eliot's distinction between religious poetry which is purely devotional and that which retains the general awareness we ask of all poetry. Sharrock is thus inclined to minimize the specifically Christian references in the poem. He points out, for example, that there is a more explicit reference to what Krishna said in the *Bhagavad Gita* than to the various Christian mystics alluded to in the poem. The poem attempts to present itself in common terms, with the various Christian references functioning as "a kind of liturgical ground-bass for personal meditations and reflections on certain moments and stages of an individual conversion" (p. 148). Sharrock may go a bit too far in minimizing the Christian aura of the poem, but he is right in suggesting that it has been exaggerated.

Sharrock's observations about the difficulties of a Christian poet in a secular age were anticipated in R. P. Blackmur's "Unappeasable and Peregrine: Behavior and the *Four Quartets*" (1951). Although written in Blackmur's usual dense style and organized in random fashion—he refers to it as "these notes" (p. 71)—this may still be the best essay on the *Four Quartets,* packed with suggestive generalizations and comments on individual lines that somehow act on one's sense of the poem as a whole. Blackmur argues that Eliot's sense of his age has forced him "to make present in his poetry not only Christian dogma and Christian emotion, but also the underlying permanent conditions, stresses, forces with which that dogma and emotion are meant to cope"—in other words, "to give the actual experience of [religion] *in its conditions*" (p. 57). This special burden is part of the poetry's power and a source of its weakness. The ingenuity of the poem's order, which we find it easier to recognize and admire, is, in fact, a response to the pressures of the experience the poem must contain. In the end, the poem is about its own process of creation—about Eliot's efforts to find and convey a sense of meaning and order in experience which few of his readers will share.

Whether Eliot succeeds, and at what points he succeeds, in shaping that experience into poetry that will last is a matter for future generations of readers to determine. If the poem is the static doctrinal poem that some of its admirers and detractors take it to be, it is hard to imagine posterity's taking much interest in it. But we have learned to see the order that lies beneath the surface disorder of *The Waste Land;* perhaps we can learn to see the disorderly pressure of experience that lies beneath the formal surface of the *Four Quartets.*

The Religious Dramatist

There is a close relationship between the *Four Quartets* and Eliot's plays, particularly *Murder in the Cathedral* (1935) and *The Family Reunion* (1939), both in language and theme. It is not surprising, then, that critical treatments of his dramas have often stressed their religious dimensions. This is particularly true, of course, of *Murder in the Cathedral,* with its liturgical language and saintly hero. But critics have found religious themes lurking not far below the surface of all of Eliot's plays.

Carol H. Smith's study, *T. S. Eliot's Dramatic Theory and Practice* (1963), argues that Eliot's plays are "intended to lead the audience to a sense of religious awareness by demonstrating the presence of the supernatural order in the natural world. . . . In each of his plays he has portrayed the plight of the individual who perceives the order of God but, forced to exist in the natural world, must somehow come to terms with both realms" (p. 31). The fragmentary *Sweeney Agonistes* (1932) thus becomes a "spiritual pilgrimage" (p. 75), with Sweeney as a Lazarus figure. The tormented Harry of *Family Reunion* "has been born of the marriage of human will and divine spirit; he is, like all men, a child of earth and heaven. (Agatha's love affair with his father is intended to convey *her* love for the divine)" (p. 143). Eliot's last play, *The Elder Statesman* (1958), is a tale of "divine resolution and reconciliation to God's will through human love" (p. 214).

Smith's Eliot is also a regular practitioner of the mythic method. Harry is to be identified "with the spirit of the new year struggling for rebirth" (p. 137). The struggle for Colby's allegiance in *The Confidential Clerk* (1953) reenacts "the ritual battle between the old and the new" (p. 211). Alex, in *The Cocktail Party* (1949), "carries out the function of the ritual cook who is instrumental in the purification of the impure old god" (p. 180). These mythic readings may acquire some plausibility from Eliot's acknowledged use of Greek drama as a basis of his plots and from his established interest in the work of Gilbert Murray and others in the Cambridge school of anthropology. They do not, in general, add much to our understanding of the plays, and one feels they reflect more faithfully the critical fashions of the years in which Smith wrote her book than they do the plays she is dealing with.

Emphasizing spiritual values and mythic order, Smith sees all the plays as fables, not open to criticism in naturalistic terms. Her study, accordingly, gives little attention to the merely human side of characters and their author; and one feels this as a weakness in her treatment of *Family Reunion* and *The Elder Statesman.* Her approach is most illuminating in dealing with *The Cocktail Party*, where constant libations rather encourage thoughts of ritual and myth, and Eliot's efforts to secure our acquiescence in Celia's martyrdom require explanation as a religious fable. Smith's treatment of *Murder in the Cathedral* is conventional in its interpretation of the play's theology and unconvincing in its references to ritual drama; but, given her emphasis on the religious and nonrealistic elements in Eliot, it is not surprising that she finds this play "Eliot's most successful integration of his dramatic theories" (p. 110).

Smith's approach is shared by a number of essays which attempt general estimates of Eliot's plays. Wanda Rulewicz agrees with Smith in her "Myth and Ritual in the Drama of T. S. Eliot" (1975) and develops similar points at less length. Hugh Dickinson's discussion of Eliot in *Myth on the Modern Stage* (1969) recognizes that the myths Eliot uses are so deeply buried that few audiences will recognize them unprompted; but Dickinson regards this burial as regrettable, an unnecessary concession to naturalism. Other critics stress the spiritual elements in Eliot's plays. Richard Kennedy, for example, describes the "mystic way" as the dominant theme in both *Family Reunion* and *The Cocktail Party* and suggests that its difficulties as dramatic material may explain their failure to match the achievement of *Murder in the Cathedral* ("Working Out Salvation with Diligence: The Plays of T. S. Eliot," 1964). Peter Kline, on the other hand, is inclined to credit Eliot with having found an original and highly individual way of giving dramatic life to the subject of spiritual awakening ("The Spiritual Center in Eliot's Plays," 1959). And Charles I. Glicksberg tells us that

Eliot's plays hold "up a shining vision of the journey that must be taken if one is to emerge at the end spiritually saved" ("The Journey that Must Be Taken: Spiritual Quest in T. S. Eliot's Plays," 1955).

Eliot's plays are static enough without being reduced to ritual reenactments or spiritual message boards, and such treatments take us even further from the surface of his work than similar approaches to his poetry—though with the possible excuse that the surface of his drama is less rewarding than that of his poetry. The single-minded application of mythic or spiritual categories to Eliot's later drawing room comedies is particularly annoying. Thomas E. Porter, for example, devotes a chapter of his *Myth and the Modern American Drama* (1969) to a relentlessly mythic interpretation of *The Cocktail Party*, and then complains that "the realistic surface gives way before the ritual underpattern" (p. 75), a criticism more clearly deserved by his essay than by Eliot's play.

There is, of course, a genuine religious level of meaning even in Eliot's later plays. Critics of the plays, like critics of his later poetry, differ in the extent to which they see this religious dimension as expressed primarily in renunciation. *The Cocktail Party* is a case in point. The play's psychiatrist and resident *deus ex machina*, Sir Harcourt-Reilly, offers Celia the choice of two ways, which correspond in some sense to the affirmative and negative ways one hears so much about in criticism of the *Four Quartets*. Celia chooses the second way, finding saintly martyrdom; Edward and Lavinia, we understand, take the first, reconciling to each other and their everyday world. Although Reilly says that neither way is better, his description of the first way, as bringing together (sometimes) "two people who know they do not understand each other, / breeding children whom they do not understand," has struck many critics as scarcely equal to the heroism of Celia's choice. "Although both ways of life may be equal," says Leo Hamalian, it looks like "Celia's way is a little more equal" ("Mr. Eliot's Saturday Evening Service," 1950).

Some critics simply ignore Reilly's assertion that neither way is better and make Celia the center of the play, the latest in a series of questing protagonists who transform the lives of more ordinary people. Most of the general essays on Eliot's plays (cited earlier) take this approach, as does C. J. Vincent's essay on *The Cocktail Party*, "A Modern Pilgrim's Progress" (1950). Hamalian notes the problem but still regards Celia as the central character. Inclined toward a ritual reading of the play, he supplies a number of mythic parallels from Jessie Weston's *From Ritual to Romance.* Although this way of reading the play makes it fit well with *Family Reunion* and *Murder in the Cathedral*, pushing Edward and Lavinia into the background seems at odds with the strategy of the play, whose last act has them onstage and Celia dying offstage.

Eliot himself later thought the last act anticlimactic, since the essential choice has been made, but surely its portrait of the consequences of Edward's choice is as important as its report of the consequences of Celia's. Among critical accounts of this, Thomas Hanzo's suggestion that Edward and Lavinia demonstrate healthy Kierkegaardian despair has the merit of recognizing that some sort of progress is made by them, but the disadvantage of describing it in terms alien to the play's religious climate ("Eliot and Kierkegaard: 'The Meaning of Happening' in *The Cocktail Party*," 1959). Hanzo winds up describing the plays as failures for failing to convey the message he attributes to them. This may not be unfair, but it is rather circular.

Edward and Lavinia are led to acceptance, rather than despair, and the real difficulty is that making the best of what one has does not seem like very much, compared to Celia's martyrdom. Another approach to this problem is to argue that all parties have chosen correctly "*according to the spiritual capacity of the individual,*" an approach taken in John J. McLaughlin's Thomistic reading, "A Daring Metaphysic: *The Cocktail Party*" (1950). A similar notion of appropriate levels seems to be at work in Robert A. Colby's "The Three Worlds of *The Cocktail Party:* The Wit of T. S. Eliot" (1954). Taking his categories from Eliot's *Idea of a Christian Society*, Colby places Celia among the Community of Christians, Reilly and his fellow "Guardians" in the Christian State, and Edward and Lavinia in the Christian Community. In both of these formulations, one senses a certain spiritual elitism; the two ways may be equal, but those who take them are not—Celia's way thus appealing as a kind of religious executive elevator.

If one holds, though, that the play intends to show both paths to salvation as valid, one may be driven to conclude that it fails. The situation is rather like that in the *Four Quartets*, which ends by affirming both time and the timeless, but with what many readers find unequal conviction. This seems to be the conclusion of Newby Toms in his essay "Eliot's *The*

Cocktail Party: Salvation and the Common Routine" (1964). Toms makes a good case for Eliot's effort to work out a salvation for ordinary people like Edward and Lavinia; this, says Toms, is the really original part of the play, saintly characters like Celia being less unusual. For Toms, it is the extremity of Celia's crucifixion that breaks the precarious balance between the two ways, so that we end the play with the two kinds of choices, seen as opposed rather than complementary.

John Edward Hardy also insists that Harcourt-Reilly's restoration of the marriage of Edward and Lavinia is central to the play ("An Antic Disposition," 1957)—and is inclined to credit Harcourt-Reilly with divine attributes in the process. More affirmative than Toms about the play's ending, he sees "no splitting of the worlds" (p. 59) and no preference for the infinite at the expense of the finite.

To the extent that Eliot's plays point toward the infinite, similar questions can be raised about most of them. Ronald Gaskell's essay " 'The Family Reunion' " (1962) is one of those which argues that Eliot was mistaken to adopt more naturalistic conventions for his plays after *Murder in the Cathedral.* He argues that "a play that presents natural and supernatural as intersecting planes will have dramatic force only if the writer is convinced of the reality of both—as the author of *Everyman* is; as Eliot is in *Murder in the Cathedral,* Claudel in *Partage de Midi*" (p. 301). It might be better to say that it must convince the audience of the reality of both, as *The Family Reunion* obviously does not convince Gaskell. A critical response to Gaskell by C. A. Scrimgeour argues that Gaskell devotes too much attention to the role of Harry, to which Gaskell responds that the dramatic center is "the consciousness of Harry" (1963). This exchange has a rather bookish air; it is difficult to get a character's "consciousness" on stage, and easier to make natural worlds convincing than to embody supernatural planes. Whether or not one finds the presentation convincing, Eliot is surely interested in this—and perhaps in all of his plays—in moments in which the natural world is transformed by contact with the timeless. In a jargon-ridden but stimulating essay, William V. Spanos has dubbed this the "strategy of sacramental transfiguration" ("T. S. Eliot's *The Family Reunion:* The Strategy of Sacramental Transfiguration," 1965). The connections between the dramatist and the poet of the *Quartets* run deep.

The Poet in the Cathedral

Among Eliot's plays, *Murder in the Cathedral* is a special case. Although portions of the play are in prose, the play's poetry displays a full-throated lyricism that contrasts sharply with the deliberately "transparent" poetry of most later plays. While later plays take their plots from Greek drama and their surface form from contemporary commercial drama, this play takes its plot from ecclesiastical history and its form from liturgy. In "Poetry and Drama" (1951; in *On Poetry and Poets*, 1957), Eliot remarks that he felt more at ease in writing recognizable verse both because it was a historical subject and because "it was a religious play, and people who go deliberately to a religious play at a religious festival expect to be patiently bored and to satisfy themselves with the feeling that they have done something meritorious." The play has since been produced for secular audiences, however, and may well prove the most durable of Eliot's dramas.

Specifically religious sources for the structure of this play have naturally been sought. One of the most obvious possibilities is to see Becket as reenacting the redemptive sacrifice of Christ—in the play, Becket says that "just as we rejoice and mourn at once, in the Birth and in the Passion of Our Lord; so also, in a smaller figure, we both rejoice and mourn in the death of martyrs." Carol Smith (1963) makes this connection and would like to see more specific parallels as well—like one between Thomas's tempters and the temptations of Christ in the wilderness. The only convincing parallels, however, are the general ones inherent in the nature of Christian martyrdom. Robert N. Shorter presented the case for Becket in "Becket as Job: T. S. Eliot's *Murder in the Cathedral*" (1968), though he admits that the analogy applies only to the first half of the play. Shorter argues that Becket and his temptations are more Job-like than Christlike, but his essay is more persuasive in refuting interpretations of Becket as a Christ figure than in establishing his likeness to Job.

Since the Christian Mass also reenacts Christ's sacrifice, those who see Becket reenacting the pattern of Christ may find the play's structure determined by the pattern of the Mass. Anne LeCroy has suggested the particular influence of the memorial Mass once celebrated for Thomas (and still found in the Anglican missal) in "*Murder in the Cathedral:* A Question of Structure" (1969). The resemblances, again, are rather general—the liturgical nature of much of the play's diction and the central place occupied by the sermon, which serves as an interlude between the two acts. The connections of the play with any specific liturgy are no stronger than those evinced by medieval morality plays. Jerry V. Pickering's essay "Form as Agent: Eliot's *Murder in the Cathedral*" (1968), though mostly summary, makes the useful point that both the morality plays and liturgy are models which lead to the audience's involvement in the play's action.

Martin L. Kornbluth's "A Twentieth-Century *Everyman*" (1959) explores the similarities between *Murder in the Cathedral* and the best known of all morality plays, overstating them considerably in the process. It is easy to agree that the tempters are projections of Becket's mind, but harder to agree that the chorus and priests are "present only as they are a part of Becket's conscience" (p. 26). Kornbluth's analogies between Thomas and Everyman rest on the same bases as the analogies between Thomas and Christ or Job; all three are tempted and resist.

Eliot acknowledged having had in mind the verse patterns of *Everyman*, and it is likely that various other religious legends were on his mind as he worked on the play; but the most obvious sources for his play were historical. Reviewing these, J. T. Boulton has concluded that Eliot "adhered faithfully to the outline, and often to the detail, of the events described by contemporary witnesses" ("The Use of Original Sources for the Development of a Theme: Eliot in *Murder in the Cathedral*," 1956). Boulton's essay would be more convincing if it were not based on translations unavailable to Eliot, but he shows that a number of details in the play can be traced back to the sources. Grover Smith (*T. S. Eliot's Poetry and Plays*, 1974) has traced the probable source of the translated narratives Eliot used. Even so, Smith speaks of the "peculiarly unhistorical treatment of the protagonist's character," by which he means that Eliot does not agree with "the common judgment of Becket as overweeningly arrogant" (p. 183). This suggests a rather naive notion of historicality. It is also a bit unfair in that Eliot deliberately chose to deal with Becket at a point just before he accepts martyrdom, and Eliot shows us pride and arrogance as traits Becket struggled to overcome.

Smith concedes that Eliot's Thomas makes a more convincing saint than the more balanced picture in Tennyson's drama on Becket. Tennyson's play is also used for comparison in John

Peter's "*Murder in the Cathedral*" (1953). In Peter's essay, the difference in the treatment of sources reflects Tennyson's uncertainty in treating his materials. Peter also praises the play at the expense of Eliot's later dramas, the psychological and religious elements of which he thinks ill integrated. Peter grants that *Murder in the Cathedral* is more limited, less ambitious than the later dramas, but he argues that it is also more successful.

Louise Rouse Rehak also finds *Murder in the Cathedral* superior to Tennyson's *Becket* and Eliot's later plays, but she does so with reluctance ("On the Use of Martyrs: Tennyson and Eliot on Thomas Becket," 1963). Rehak finds a number of saving virtues in Tennyson's play, particularly its more human qualities, which she contrasts favorably with what she takes to be Eliot's theological escapism. Eliot's alleged disdain for the merely human invalidates his dramas for Rehak, though she will admit that *Murder in the Cathedral* is effective theater. As theater, it commands the power of ritual, and "ritual," says Rehak, "posits a central mystery—to be attained by a sacrifice of humanity" (p. 58). One need not embrace the views of those who see ritual figures behind every great drama to believe that Rehak's view of ritual's relation to life and drama is unduly limiting.

One can, in fact, hold that it is the ritual and sacramental structure of the play which allows it to present the intrusion of the timeless into time. Something of this sort is the gist of William V. Spanos' "figural" interpretation of the play ("*Murder in the Cathedral:* The *Figura* as Mimetic "Principle," 1963), though Spanos differs from many Eliot critics in finding the same "figural aesthetic" at work in later Eliot dramas as well. Michael Beehler combines hints from Spanos and Derrida in "*Murder in the Cathedral:* The Countersacramental Play of Signs" (1977), producing sentences like this: "But it is precisely this central absence which allows the historical sign to appear, for, as we have seen, the sign dies (disappears) in the presence of the silent presence" (p. 377).

It is hard to avoid feeling that both Eliot's admirers and his detractors overstress the ritual and theological elements in this drama—and his other plays as well. *Murder in the Cathedral* has liturgical overtones, which may have real effects on believers in the audience; and it has theological implications as well, which may affect, one way or the other, both believers and nonbelievers. It is, however, first and foremost a drama. Even discussions of it as a drama often reflect religious presuppositions. There is, for example, considerable discussion of whether *Murder in the Cathedral* can properly be called a "tragedy." The discussion is usually based on generic presuppositions which would exclude most Greek tragedy and much of Shakespeare. To these are sometimes added questions as to whether a "Christian" or a "modern" tragedy is possible, questions which conflate literary and ideological categories. One turns back with relief to one of the earliest and best essays on *Murder in the Cathedral*, that by Francis Fergusson in *The Idea of a Theater* (1949). Fergusson does indeed find ritual patterns in the play, and he speaks of it as "theological"—in this case a mild hyperbole, meant to indicate that its purpose is to demonstrate particular theological notions. But Fergusson recognizes that the play itself produces a true imitation of human action, even though the real world may be scarcely appealed to. In Fergusson's Aristotelian terminology, the play's "final cause" may be theological but its "formal cause" is the imitation of a human action.

This distinction is one that should be kept in mind in considering all of Eliot's religious drama and poetry. It is likely that in *Murder in the Cathedral* Eliot hoped to send the audience home aware of its complicity in the secularism of the knights who murder Thomas. It is likely that, in his other plays, he hoped to touch a spiritual nerve or two. It is even possible to see some didactic intent in sections of *Four Quartets*. But Eliot is not a didactic poet or a didactic dramatist, in the sense that his poetry and drama are decisively shaped by such hopes and intentions.

In his religious poetry, religious experience is the object of imitation and not the desired end. One can say much the same of his drama, to the extent that it is religious at all. Discussions of the religious dimension of Eliot's work can be valuable in helping us understand the experience the work conveys. When such discussions translate the poetry into dogma and the drama into doctrine, they stand between us and the work.

References

Andreach, Robert J.
1964. *Studies in Structure: The Stages of the Spiritual Life in Four Modern Authors*, pp. 72–101. New York: Fordham Univ. Pr.

Atkins, Anselm

1968. "Mr. Eliot's Sunday Morning Parody," *Renascence*, pp. 41–43, 54.

Banerjee, Ron D. K.

1972. "Dante through the Looking Glass: Rossetti, Pound, and Eliot," *Comparative Literature* Spring, pp. 136–49.

Barfoot, Gabrielle

1972. "Dante in Eliot's Criticism," *English Miscelany*, pp. 231–46.

Beehler, Michael

1977. "*Murder in the Cathedral:* The Countersacramental Play of Signs," *Genre* Fall, pp. 329–38.

Bergsten, Staffan

1960. *Time and Eternity: A Study in the Structure and Symbolism of T. S. Eliot's Four Quartets.* Stockholm: Bonniers.

Bilan, R. P.

1978. "F. R. Leavis's Revaluation of T. S. Eliot," *University of Toronto Quarterly* Winter, pp. 151–62.

Blackmur, R. P.

1935. *The Double Agent*, pp. 184–218. New York: Arrow.

1951. "Unappeasable and Peregrine: Behavior and the *Four Quartets*," *Thought* Spring, pp. 50–76.

Blamires, Harry

1969. *Word Unheard: A Guide through Eliot's Four Quartets.* London: Methuen.

Blissett, William

1946. "The Argument of T. S. Eliot's *Four Quartets*," *University of Toronto Quarterly* Jan., pp. 115–26.

Boardman, Gwenn R.

1962. "*Ash Wednesday:* Eliot's Lenten Mass Sequence," *Renascence* Fall, pp. 28–36.

Bodelsen, C. A.

1958. *T. S. Eliot's Four Quartets: A Commentary.* Copenhagen: Rosenkilde & Bagger.

Bottorff, William K.

1972. "Hindu and Buddhist Usages in the Poetry of T. S. Eliot," in *From Irving to Steinbeck*, ed. Motley Deakin and Peter Liska, pp. 109–24. Gainesville: Univ. of Florida Pr.

Boulton, J. T.

1956. "The Use of Original Sources for the Development of a Theme: Eliot in *Murder in the Cathedral*," *English* Spring, pp. 2–8.

Broes, Arthur T.

1966. "T. S. Eliot's 'Journey of the Magi': An Explication," *Xavier University Studies*, pp. 129–31.

Brooks, Cleanth

1937. "*The Waste Land:* An Analysis," *Southern Review* Summer, pp. 106–36.

1939. *Modern Poetry and the Tradition*, pp. 136–72. Chapel Hill: Univ. of North Carolina Pr.

1963. *The Hidden God*, pp. 68–97. New Haven: Yale Univ. Pr.

Brooks, Harold F.

1966. "Between *The Waste Land* and the First Ariel Poems: 'The Hollow Men,'" *English* Autumn, pp. 89–93.

Brown, R. D.

1972. "Revelation in T. S. Eliot's 'Journey of the Magi,'" *Renascence* Spring, pp. 136–40.

Butter, P. H.

1976. "*Four Quartets:* Some Yes-buts to Dr. Leavis," *Critical Quarterly* Spring, pp. 31–40.

Cahill, Audrey F.

1967. *T. S. Eliot and the Human Predicament.* Pietermaritzburg, South Africa: Univ. of Natal Pr.

Carey, John

1967. "T. S. Eliot's Wasteland," *Cithara*, pp. 3–38.

Carter, Geoffrey

1977. "The Question of T. S. Eliot's Erudition," *Notes and Queries* Oct., pp. 451–52.

Chase, Richard

1945. "The Sense of the Present," *Kenyon Review* Spring, pp. 218–31.

Chaturvedi, B. N.

1965. "The Indian Background of Eliot's Poetry," *English* Autumn, pp. 220–23.

Cleophas, Sister Mary

1949. "Eliot's 'Whispers of Immortality,'" *Explicator* Dec., item 22.

1950. "Notes on Levels of Meaning in 'Four Quartets,'" *Renascence* Spring, pp. 102–16.

1959. "*Ash Wednesday:* The *Purgatorio* in a Modern Mode," *Comparative Literature* Fall, pp. 329–39.

Clowder, Felix

1960. "The Bestiary of T. S. Eliot," *Prairie Schooner* Spring, pp. 30–37.

Clubb, Merrel D.

1961. "The Heraclitean Element in Eliot's *Four Quartets*," *Philological Quarterly* Jan., pp. 19–33.

Colby, Robert A.

1954. "The Three Worlds of *The Cocktail Party:* The Wit of T. S. Eliot," *University of Toronto Quarterly* Oct., pp. 56–59.

Cornwall, Ethel F.

1962. *The Still Point*, pp. 17–63. New Brunswick, N.J.: Rutgers Univ. Pr.

Cotten, Lyman A.

1950. "Eliot's *The Waste Land*, I, 43–46," *Explicator* Oct., item 7.

Counihan, Sister Bernadotte
1969. "*Four Quartets:* An Ascent to Mount Carmel?" *Wisconsin Studies in Literature*, pp. 58–71.
Davidson, Clifford
1966. "Types of Despair in 'Ash Wednesday,'" *Renascence* Summer, pp. 216–18.
Davie, Donald
1956. "T. S. Eliot: The End of an Era," *Twentieth Century* Apr., pp. 350–62.
De Masirevich, Constance
1953. *On the* Four Quartets *of T. S. Eliot.* New York: Barnes and Noble.
Dickinson, Hugh
1969. *Myth on the Modern Stage*, pp. 207–18. Urbana: Univ. of Illinois Pr.
Dolan, Paul J.
1967. "*Ash Wednesday:* A Catechumenical Poem," *Renascence* Summer, pp. 198–207.
Drew, Arnold
1954. "Hints and Guesses in *Four Quartets*," *University of Kansas City Review* Spring, pp. 171–75.
Dye, F.
1960. "Eliot's 'Gerontion,'" *Explicator* Apr., item 39.
Dzwonkoski, F. Peter, Jr.
1974. "'The Hollow Men' and *Ash Wednesday:* Two Dark Nights," *Arizona Quarterly* Spring, pp. 16–42.
Eliot, T. S.
1957. "Poetry and Drama" (1951), in *On Poetry and Poets*, pp. 75–95. New York: Farrar, Straus.
Empson, William
1930. *Seven Types of Ambiguity*, pp. 98–101. London: Chatto and Windus.
Evans, David W.
1954. "T. S. Eliot, Charles Williams, and the Sense of the Occult," *Accent* Spring, pp. 148–55.
Everett, Barbara
1974. "A Visit to Burnt Norton," *Critical Quarterly* Autumn, pp. 199–224.
Fergusson, Francis
1949. *The Idea of a Theater*, pp. 210–22. Princeton: Princeton Univ. Pr.
Flint, R. W.
1948. "The *Four Quartets* Reconsidered," *Sewanee Review* Winter, pp. 69–81.
Fowler, Russell T.
1971. "Krishna and the 'Still Point': A Study of the *Bhagavad*

Gita's Influence on Eliot's *Four Quartets*," *Sewanee Review* Summer, pp. 406–23.

Franklin, Rosemary
1968. "The Satisfactory Journey of Eliot's Magus," *English Studies* Dec., pp. 559–61.

Gaskell, Ronald
1962. "*The Family Reunion*," *Essays in Criticism* July, pp. 292–301.

Gerard, Sister Mary
1959. "Eliot of the Circle and John of the Cross," *Thought* Spring, pp. 107–27.

Gibbons, Tom
1972. "*The Waste Land* Tarot Identified," *Journal of Modern Literature* Nov., pp. 560–65.

Gillis, Everett A.
1961. "The Spiritual Status of T. S. Eliot's Hollow Men," *Texas Studies in Language and Literature* Winter, pp. 464–75.
1972. "The Scurrilous Parody in T. S. Eliot's Early Religious Verse," *Descant* Spring, pp. 43–48.

Gillis, Everett A., Lawrence A. Ryan, and Friedrich W. Strothmann.
1960. "Hope for Eliot's Hollow Men?" *PMLA* Dec., pp. 635–38.

Gish, Nancy K.
1973. "The Meaning of Incarnation in Two 'Ariel Poems,'" *Michigan Academician* Summer, pp. 59–69.
1976. "The Significance of the Mystic in T. S. Eliot's Theme of Time," *Studies in Medieval Culture*, pp. 169–76.

Glicksberg, Charles I.
1955. "The Journey that Must Be Taken: Spiritual Quest in T. S. Eliot's Plays," *Southwest Review* Summer, pp. 203–10.

Greenhill, Eleanor Simmons
1954. "The Child in the Tree: A Study of the Cosmological Tree in Christian Tradition," *Traditio*, pp. 323–71.

Grenander, M. E., and K. S. Narayana Rao
1971. "*The Waste Land* and the Upanishads: What Does the Thunder Say?" *Indian Literature* Mar., pp. 85–98.

Gunter, Bradley
1970. *Guide to T. S. Eliot.* Columbus: Merrill.

Hahn, Paul D.
1972. "A Reformation of New Criticism: 'Burnt Norton' Revisited," *Emporia State Research Studies* Summer, pp. 5–64.

Hamalian, Leo
1950. "Mr. Eliot's Saturday Evening Service," *Accent* Autumn, pp. 195–212.

Hanzo, Thomas
1959. "Eliot and Kierkegaard: 'The Meaning of Happening' in *The Cocktail Party*," *Modern Drama* May, pp. 52–59.

Harding, D. W.
1943. "We Have Not Reached Conclusion," *Scrutiny* Spring, pp. 216–19.
Hardy, John Edward
1957. "An Antic Disposition," *Sewanee Review* Winter, pp. 50–60.
Hathaway, Richard D.
1963. "*The Waste Land*'s Benediction," *American Notes and Queries* Dec., pp. 53–54.
Headings, Philip R.
1964. *T. S. Eliot.* New York: Twayne.
Hiers, John T.
1976. "Birth or Death: Eliot's 'Journey of the Magi' and 'A Song for Simeon,'" *South Carolina Review* Apr., pp. 41–46.
Higinbotham, R. N.
1943. "Objections to a Review of 'Little Gidding,'" *Scrutiny* Summer, pp. 259–61.
Holbrook, David
1955. "Mr. Eliot's Chinese Wall," *Essays in Criticism* Oct., pp. 418–26.
Homann, Elizabeth Rudisill
1959. "Eliot's 'Sweeney among the Nightingales,' 8," *Explicator* Feb., item 34.
Hough, Graham
1973. "Vision and Doctrine in *Four Quartets*," *Critical Quarterly* Summer, pp. 108–27.
1974. "Dante and Eliot," *Critical Quarterly* Winter, pp. 293–305.
Isani, Mukhtar Ali
1973. "The Wisdom of the Thunder in Eliot's *The Waste Land*," *English Language Notes* Mar., pp. 217–20.
Ishak, Fayek M.
1970. *The Mystical Philosophy of T. S. Eliot.* New Haven: College and Univ. Pr.
Jennings, Elizabeth
1961. "Articulate Music: A Study of the Mystical Content in the Plays and *Four Quartets* of T. S. Eliot," in *Every Changing Shape*, pp. 163–89. London: Andre Deutsch.
Jones, Florence
1966. "T. S. Eliot among the Prophets," *American Literature* Nov., pp. 285–302.
Jones, Genesius
1964. *Approach to the Purpose.* London: Hodder and Stoughton.
Kaplan, Robert B., and Richard J. Wall
1960. "Eliot's 'Journey of the Magi,'" *Explicator* Nov., item 8.
Kemp, Lysander
1950. "Eliot's *The Waste Land*, I, 43–59," *Explicator* Feb., item 27.

Kennedy, Richard S.
1964. "Working Out Salvation with Diligence: The Plays of T. S. Eliot," *Wichita University Studies*, pp. 1–11.
Keogh, J. G.
1969. "Eliot's *The Hollow Men* as Graveyard Poetry," *Renascence* Spring, pp. 115–18.
Kinsman, Robert S.
1950. "Eliot's *The Hollow Men*," *Explicator* Apr., item 48.
Kligerman, Jack
1962. "An Interpretation of T. S. Eliot's 'East Coker,'" *Arizona Quarterly* Summer, pp. 101–12.
Kline, Peter
1959. "The Spiritual Center in Eliot's Plays," *Kenyon Review* Summer, pp. 457–72.
Knust, Herbert
1965. "What's the Matter with One-eyed Riley?" *Comparative Literature* Fall, pp. 289–98.
1966. "Tristan and Sosostris," *Revue de Litterature Comparee* Apr.–June, pp. 235–45.
Kornbluth, Martin L.
1959. "A Twentieth-Century *Everyman*," *College English*, pp. 26–29.
Leavis, F. R.
1943. "Reflections on the Above," *Scrutiny* Summer, pp. 261–67.
1975. *The Living Principle*, pp. 155–264. New York: Oxford Univ. Pr.
LeCroy, Anne
1969. "*Murder in the Cathedral:* A Question of Structure," in *Essays in Memory of Christine Burleson*, ed. Thomas G. Burton. Johnson City, Tenn.: Research Advisory Council, East Tennessee State Univ.
Maccoby, H. Z.
1966. "Two Notes on 'Ash Wednesday,'" *Notes and Queries* Nov., pp. 413–15.
1970. "A Commentary on 'Burnt Norton,' II," *Notes and Queries* Feb., pp. 53–59.
Mankowitz, Wolf
1947. "Notes on 'Gerontion,'" in *T. S. Eliot: A Study of His Writing by Several Hands*, ed. B. Rajan, pp. 129–38. London: Dennis Dobson.
Martin, Peter A.
1977. "'Son of Man' in the Book of Ezekiel and T. S. Eliot's *The Waste Land*," *Arizona Quarterly* Autumn, pp. 197–215.
Martin, Philip M.
1957. *Mastery and Mercy*, pp. 84–148. London: Oxford Univ. Pr.

Martz, Louis L.
1947. "The Wheel and the Point: Aspects of Imagery and Theme in Eliot's Later Poetry," *Sewanee Review* Jan.–Mar., pp. 126–47.

Mary Eleanor, Mother
1957. "Eliot's Magi," *Renascence* Autumn, pp. 26–31.

McCarthy, Harold E.
1952. "T. S. Eliot and Buddhism," *Philosophy East and West* Apr., pp. 31–35.

McGill, Arthur C.
1964. *The Celebration of Flesh: Poetry in Christian Life*, pp. 38–91. New York: Association Pr.

McGreevy, Thomas
1931. *Thomas Stearns Eliot.* London: Chatto and Windus.

McLaughlin, John J.
1950. "A Daring Metaphysic: *The Cocktail Party*," *Renascence* Autumn, pp. 15–28.

Miller, Milton
1969. "What the Thunder Meant," *ELH* June, pp. 440–54.

Milward, Peter
1968. *A Commentary on T. S. Eliot's* Four Quartets. Tokyo: Hokuseido Pr.
1968. "Sacramental Symbolism in Hopkins and Eliot," *Renascence* Winter, pp. 104–11.

Moakley, Gertrude
1954. "The Waite-Smith 'Tarot': A Footnote to *The Waste Land*," *Bulletin of the New York Public Library* Oct., pp. 471–75.

Monteiro, George
1976. "Christians and Jews in 'Mr. Eliot's Sunday Morning Service,'" *T. S. Eliot Review*, pp. 20–22.

Moorman, Charles
1958. "Myth and Organic Unity in *The Waste Land*," *South Atlantic Quarterly* Spring, pp. 194–203.
1960. *Arthurian Triptych*, pp. 127–48. Berkeley: Univ. of California Pr.

Moynihan, William T.
1961. "The Goal of the *Waste Land* Quest," *Renascence* Summer, pp. 171–79.

Noon, William T.
1954. "*Four Quartets: Contemplatio ad Amorem*," *Renascence* Autumn, pp. 3–10, 19.

O'Connor, Daniel
1969. *T. S. Eliot's Four Quartets: A Commentary*. New Delhi: Aarti Book Centre.

Oden, Thomas C.
1960. "The Christology of T. S. Eliot: A Study of the *Kerygma* in 'Burnt Norton,'" *Encounter* (Indianapolis), pp. 93–101.

O'Malley, Glenn
1977. "Dante, Shelley, and T. S. Eliot," in *Romantic and Modern: Revaluations of Literary Tradition*, ed. George Bornstein, pp. 165–76. Pittsburgh: Univ. of Pittsburgh Pr.

Patrides, C. A.
1976. "T. S. Eliot and the Pattern of Time," in *Aspects of Time*, ed. Patrides, pp. 159–71. Toronto: Univ. of Toronto Pr.

Paulin, Tom
1976. "Time and Sense Experience: Hardy and T. S. Eliot," in *Budmouth Essays on Thomas Hardy*, ed. F. B. Pinion, p. 192–204. Dorchester: Thomas Hardy Society.

Perkins, David
1962. "Rose Garden to Midwinter Spring: Achieved Faith in the *Four Quartets*," *Modern Language Quarterly* Mar., pp. 41–45.

Peter, John
1953. "*Murder in the Cathedral*," *Sewanee Review* Summer, pp. 362–83.

Pickering, Jerry V.
1968. "Form as Agent: Eliot's *Murder in the Cathedral*," *Educational Theatre Journal* May, pp. 198–207.

Porter, Thomas E.
1969. *Myth and the Modern American Drama*, pp. 53–76. Detroit: Wayne State Univ. Pr.

Praz, Mario
1937. "T. S. Eliot and Dante," *Southern Review* Winter, pp. 525–48.

Preston, Raymond
1946. "*Four Quartets*" *Rehearsed.* New York: Sheed and Ward.

Rao, G. Nageswara
1970. "The Unfinished Poems of T. S. Eliot," *The Literary Criterion*, pp. 27–35.
1972. " 'The Fire Sermon' in *The Waste Land*," *Visvabharati Quarterly*, pp. 97–107.
1973. "The Upanishads and *The Waste Land*," in *Literary Studies*, ed. K. P. K. Menon, pp. 195–200. Travandrum, India: D. A. Sivaramasubramonia, Aiyer Memorial Committee.

Rao, K. S. Narayana
1963. "T. S. Eliot and the *Bhagavad Gita*," *American Quarterly* Winter, pp. 572–78.
1964. "*Addendum* on Eliot and the *Bhagavad Gita*," *American Quarterly* Spring, pp. 102–3.

Rehak, Louise Rouse
1963. "On the Use of Martyrs: Tennyson and Eliot on Thomas Becket," *University of Toronto Quarterly* Oct., pp. 43–60.

Richter, Dagny
1971. "T. S. Eliot, Dante, and 'The Hollow Men,' " *Moderna Sprak*, pp. 205–23.

Rodgers, Audrey T.
1974. "The Mythic Perspective of Eliot's 'The Dry Salvages,'" *Arizona Quarterly* Spring, pp. 74–94.

Romer, Karen T.
1972. "T. S. Eliot and the Language of Liturgy," *Renascence* Spring, pp. 119–35.

Rulewicz, Wanda
1975. "Myth and Ritual in the Drama of T. S. Eliot," *Studia Anglica Posnaniensia*, pp. 138–47.

Schanzer, Ernest
1955. "Mr. Eliot's Sunday Morning Service," *Essays in Criticism* Apr., pp. 153–58.

Schmidt, G.
1973. "An Echo of Buddhism in T. S. Eliot's 'Little Gidding,'" *Notes and Queries* Sept., p. 330.

Schwarz, Daniel R.
1971. "The Unity of Eliot's 'Gerontion': The Failure of Meditation," *Bucknell Review* Spring, pp. 55–76.

Scott, Nathan A., Jr.
1976. *The Poetry of Civic Virtue*, pp. 1–39. Philadelphia: Fortress Pr.

Scott, R. E.
1974. "T. S. Eliot's *Waste Land*, 43–59 ('Eliot's Gypsy')," *American Notes and Queries* Dec., pp. 57–58.

Scrimgeour, C. A., and Ronald Gaskell
1963. "*The Family Reunion*," *Essays in Criticism* Jan., pp. 104–6.

Senior, John
1959. *The Way Down and Out: The Occult in Symbolist Literature*, pp. 170–98. Ithaca: Cornell Univ. Pr.

Sexton, James P.
1971. "*Four Quartets* and the Christian Calendar," *American Literature* May, pp. 279–81.

Sharrock, Roger
1977. "*Four Quartets* as a Post-Christian Poem," *Aligarh Journal of English Studies*, pp. 144–66.

Shorter, Robert N.
1968. "Becket as Job: T. S. Eliot's *Murder in the Cathedral*," *South Atlantic Quarterly* Autumn, pp. 627–35.

Shulenberger, Arvid
1952. "Eliot's 'Mr. Eliot's Sunday Morning Service,'" *Explicator* Feb., item 29.

Shuman, R. Baird
1957. "Buddhistic Overtones in Eliot's *The Cocktail Party*," *Modern Language Notes* June, pp. 426–27.

Slattery, Sister Margaret Patrice
1968. "Structural Unity in Eliot's 'Ash Wednesday,'" *Renascence* Spring, pp. 147–52.

Smailes, T. A.
1970. "Eliot's 'Journey of the Magi,'" *Explicator* Oct., item 18.
Smith, Carol H.
1963. *T. S. Eliot's Dramatic Theory and Practice.* Princeton: Princeton Univ. Pr.
Smith, Francis J.
1946. "A Reading of 'East Coker,'" *Thought* June, pp. 272–86.
Smith, Grover
1954. "The Fortune Teller in Eliot's *The Waste Land*," *American Literature* Jan., pp. 490–92.
1956. *T. S. Eliot's Poetry and Plays.* Rev. 1974. Chicago: Univ. of Chicago Pr.
Southam, B. C.
1969. *A Guide to the Selected Poems of T. S. Eliot.* New York: Harcourt Brace Jovanovich.
Spanos, William
1963. "*Murder in the Cathedral:* The *Figura* as Mimetic Principle," *Drama Survey* Oct., pp. 206–23.
1965. "T. S. Eliot's *The Family Reunion:* The Strategy of Sacramental Transfiguration," *Drama Survey* Spring, pp. 3–27.
1978. "Hermeneutics and Memory: Destroying T. S. Eliot's *Four Quartets*," *Genre* Winter, pp. 523–73.
Srivastava, Narsingh
1977. "The Ideas of the *Bhagavad Gita* in *Four Quartets*," *Comparative Literature* Spring, pp. 97–108.
Stanford, Donald L.
1955. "Two Notes on T. S. Eliot," *Twentieth Century Literature* Oct., pp. 133–35.
Stephenson, Ethel M.
1944. *T. S. Eliot and the Lay Reader.* London: Fortune Pr.
Strothmann, Friedrich W., and Lawrence A. Ryan
1958. "Hope for T. S. Eliot's 'Empty Men,'" *PMLA* Sept., pp. 426–32.
Stroud, T. A.
1969. "Eliot's 'Animula,'" *Explicator* Oct., item 14.
Sullivan, Zohreh Tawakuli
1977. "Memory and Meditative Structure in T. S. Eliot's Early Poetry," *Renascence* Winter, pp. 97–105.
Tate, Allen
1931. "Irony and Humility," *Hound and Horn* Jan.–Mar., pp. 290–97.
Toms, Newby
1964. "Eliot's *The Cocktail Party:* Salvation and the Common Routine," *Christian Scholar* Summer, pp. 125–38.
Unger, Leonard
1942. "T. S. Eliot's Rose Garden: A Persistent Theme," *Southern Review* Spring, pp. 667–89.

Verma, Rajendra
1979. *Time and Poetry in Eliot's Four Quartets.* Atlantic Highlands, N.J.: Humanities Pr.

Vickery, John B.
1973. *The Literary Impact of the Golden Bough*, pp. 223–79. Princeton: Princeton Univ. Pr.

Vincent, C. J.
1950. "A Modern Pilgrim's Progress," *Queen's Quarterly* Autumn, pp. 346–52.

Wagner, Robert D.
1954. "The Meaning of Eliot's Rose-Garden," *PMLA* Mar., pp. 22–33.

Watkins, Floyd C.
1964. "T. S. Eliot's Painter of the Umbrian School," *American Literature* Mar., pp. 72–75.

Weitz, Morris
1952. "T. S. Eliot: Time as a Mode of Salvation," *Sewanee Review* Jan.–Mar., pp. 48–64.

Williamson, George
1950. "The Structure of *The Waste Land*," *Modern Philology* Feb., pp. 191–206.
1953. *A Reader's Guide to T. S. Eliot.* New York: Noonday Pr.

Williamson, Mervyn W.
1957. "T. S. Eliot's 'Gerontion': A Study in Thematic Repetition and Development," *Texas University Studies in English*, pp. 110–26.

Wills, John H.
1954. "Eliot's 'Journey of the Magi,' " *Explicator* Mar., item 32.

Wooton, Carl
1961. "The Mass: *Ash Wednesday*'s Objective Correlative," *Arizona Quarterly* Spring, pp. 31–42.

Selected Additional Readings

Ayers, Robert W.
1978. "*Murder in the Cathedral:* A Liturgy Less Divine," *Texas Studies in Literature and Language* Winter, pp. 579–98.

Bowers, John L.
1965. *T. S. Eliot's "Murder in the Cathedral": A Public Lecture.* Cape Town: Univ. of Capetown, Dept. of English.

Fry, Francis White
1978. "The Centrality of the Sermon in T. S. Eliot's *Murder in the Cathedral*," *Christianity and Literature*, pp. 7–14.

Gish, Nancy K.
1978. "Thought, Feeling and Form: The Dual Meaning of 'Gerontion,' " *English Studies* June, pp. 237–47.

Kantra, Robert A.
1968. "Satiric Theme and Structure in *Murder in the Cathedral*," *Modern Drama* Feb., pp. 387–93.

Naik, M. K.
1969. "The Characters in Eliot's Plays," in *Indian Essays in American Literature*, ed. Sujit Mukherjee and D. V. K. Raghavacharyulu, pp. 61–70. Bombay: Popular Prakashan.
1972. "Some Ambiguities in Eliot's Plays," *Panjab University Research Bulletin (Arts)*, pp. 25–30.

Orsini, Gian N. G.
1954. "T. S. Eliot and the Doctrine of Dramatic Conventions," *Transactions, Wisconsin Academy of Sciences, Arts and Letters*, pp. 189–200.

Pankow, Edith
1973. "The 'Eternal Design' of *Murder in the Cathedral*," *Papers in Language and Literature* Winter, pp. 35–47.

Schmidt, Gerd
1978. *Die Struktur des Dramas bei T. S. Eliot.* Salzburg: Institut fur Englische Sprache und Literatur, Univ. Salzburg.

Sharoni, Edna G.
1972. " 'Peace' and 'Unbar the Door': T. S. Eliot's *Murder in the Cathedral* and Some Stoic Forebears," *Comparative Drama*, pp. 135–53.

Simpson, Louis
1975. *Three on the Tower.* New York: Morrow.

Vance, Thomas
1976. "New Verse, Ancient Rhyme: T. S. Eliot and Dante," *Parnassus* Fall/Winter, pp. 135–53.

Webb, Eugene
1975. *The Dark Dove*, pp. 194–236. Seattle: Univ. of Washington Pr.

Williams, Raymond
1963. "Tragic Resignation and Sacrifice," *Critical Quarterly* Spring, pp. 5–19.

CHAPTER 5

The Traditional Poet

Despite the influence of Eliot, the dominant critical assumptions of our time are still, in many ways, Romantic. We honor writers, even Eliot, for their originality and individuality, and we speak of poets who have found their own voice. If we turn back to "Tradition and the Individual Talent," there is still something surprising about Eliot's praise of the role of tradition in forming a poet's sensibility; there is something almost shocking about his assertion that "the most individual parts of his work may be those in which the dead poets, his ancestors, assert their immortality most vigorously." Eliot did, however, succeed in rehabilitating "tradition" as a term, as one can see in the titles of such modern critical landmarks as Cleanth Brooks' *Modern Poetry and the Tradition* (1939) or F. R. Leavis's *The Great Tradition* (1948). Associated phrases like "the historical sense," also entered into the vocabulary of praise used in modern criticism. Critics have labored to show that the most revolutionary modern works were in living continuity with the significant traditions of English and European letters. For Eliot and some of those who followed him, terms like "tradition" and "historical sense" helped bridge the gap between their avant-garde literary tastes and their conservative religious and social attitudes. For all of them, Eliot's rhetoric provided an original strategy for pursuing the perennial battle between literary generations, allowing the advocates of contemporary literature to lay claim as well to the best of the past.

Eliot's poems have been taken as exemplars of the hard-won "historical sense" he praised. Bristling with epigraphs from obscure works and dense with quotations and allusions, his early poetry almost forced readers to read it in relation to literary tradition. Readers who tracked Eliot's allusions back to their original sources did not always improve their understanding of Eliot's poetry, but they improved their acquaintance with the tradition; the famous "Notes" to *The Waste Land* are a very good reading list, whatever their value for interpreting the poem. Many critics have found Eliot's allusions essential to understanding his poems, but not all of those who agree on this are happy with this "poetry of allusion."

Although Eliot praises the value of tradition for the poet, "Tradition and the Individual Talent" also argues that the existing "ideal order" of works "is modified by the introduction of the new (the really new) work of art among them." Eliot's early criticism, as well as his poetry, helped to modify that "ideal order" in the minds of many readers. The "ideal order" that Eliot set before his readers begins, conventionally enough, with the Greco-Roman classics, but Eliot's picture of the English poetic tradition was less usual. *Hamlet,* it seems, is an artistic failure, and Milton is a bad influence. The Romantics and Victorians are not part of the true tradition at all. The later Elizabethans and the Metaphysical poets, on the other hand, are given new prominence. From nineteenth-century English poetry, attention is redirected toward nineteenth-century French poetry. The relationship between such revaluations and the qualities of Eliot's work is fairly obvious, and Eliot himself has since noted that his early criticism was "a by-product of my private poetry-workshop; or a prolongation of the thinking that went into the formation of my own verse" ("The Frontiers of Criticism," 1957). We must attribute its influence to the truth of his observation that a "really new" work affects our understanding of past literature.

Partly because he helped reshape our understanding of that tradition, it is now easy to see Eliot as part of the English literary tradition. We can, moreover, see him as part of that tradition in ways which go beyond those suggested by his early criticism, for critics have shown that his work maintains a great deal of continuity with the Romantics and Victorians he spoke of so harshly. Finally, Eliot's efforts to revive poetic drama as a popular medium, albeit only partially successful, can be seen as part of a long series of such efforts by English poets working in the long shadow of Shakespeare.

The Prophet of Tradition

Although "Tradition and the Individual Talent" is especially important, references to "tradition" occur in many of Eliot's essays. In *T. S. Eliot and the Idea of Tradition* (1960), Sean

Lucy demonstrates that Eliot's praise of tradition is connected with his Classicism, his social criticism, his rejection of the idiosyncratic diction of Milton and the idiosyncratic theology of Yeats, his Anglicanism, and his insistence on the value of minor poets. Lucy is less useful in dealing with Eliot's poetry and drama: he makes some of the obvious points about Eliot's use of traditional forms and borrowing from earlier writers, but his use of the term "realist" for Eliot and others who react against Georgian writers and late nineteenth-century Romanticism does not seem especially apt. Even in dealing with Eliot's criticism, Lucy's strength is description rather than analysis. Abstracting from Eliot's criticism those passages relevant to the idea of tradition may also have the effect of making that criticism seem more theoretical than it really is. Lucy, indeed, believes that Eliot "almost always uses judgments of literary detail to discover, extend, or clarify a literary principle" (p. vii); the opposite would be more nearly true, and the theoretical consistency Lucy finds in Eliot does not demonstrate a theoretical purpose.

Lucy himself seems to hold to a more Romantic critical position than Eliot, assigning far more weight to the individual talent. Responding to "What Is a Classic?"—for example—Lucy objects that "it is true that each good poet does something for a literature that can never be done again, but the reason that it can never be done again is that no one else could write the poetry which he has written" (p. 12). Eliot's poetry is seen as "a very bad direct model" for younger poets because it is a "very *personal* poetry" whose completeness "is a result of a sense of unique and inviolable personality which is to be found in all his work" (p. 160). Lucy would like to distinguish this from the more obtrusive personality of Shelley in his poems, but the criticism, perhaps well taken, again suggests some distance between Eliot's principles and Lucy's.

Lucy recognizes that Eliot's idea of tradition is by no means new, crediting Eliot instead with applying it more thoroughly and consistently than most previous critics. Eliot's sources are given only brief attention, with Arnold singled out for special attention. Among the sources mentioned only in passing by Lucy, F. H. Bradley deserves more consideration, for such Eliotic notions as the "ideal order," formed by existing works of art, are more explicable in a Bradleyan framework. One of the first to call attention to Bradley's importance in this regard was E. P. Bollier, in "Mr. Eliot's 'Tradition and the Individual Talent' Reconsidered" (1957). Bollier also cites earlier poets who advocated somewhat similar ideas (Wordsworth, Coleridge, and even Shelley), noting that Eliot's criticism has thus "been both traditional and original in the sense in which he has used those terms" (p. 117).

P. G. Ellis's account, "The Development of T. S. Eliot's Historical Sense" (1972), finds that Eliot's idea of tradition "has more in common with the critical theories of Pater than with those of Arnold" (p. 301). The evidence that Eliot was familiar with Pater's criticism is convincing, and Ellis quotes some intriguing passages from a Paul Elmer More essay on Arnold, Pater, and Wilde which Eliot is known to have read. Of Eliot's likeness to Pater, Wilde, and Yeats, Ellis writes: "All use the terminology of the biological sciences, of organic growth and development, to describe the process by which tradition is formed, and a language deriving from Platonism to describe the relationship between the present and the past, between the individual and tradition" (p. 291). These similarities do not, perhaps, indicate that Pater was an important influence, but they may help us place Eliot's ideas within an intellectual tradition.

A somewhat more interesting, because more surprising, source has been proposed by David Ward, who argues that Eliot's idea of tradition "owes a very great deal to Eliot's early interest in anthropology" ("Eliot, Murray, Homer, and the Idea of Tradition: 'So I Assumed a Double Part,' " 1968, p. 50). Ward calls attention to the linking of tradition and impersonality in some lectures (later published) at Harvard by Gilbert Murray while Eliot was a student. It is conceivable that Murray and other English anthropologists of the time had some part in shaping Eliot's thinking about tradition, although "a very great deal" seems overenthusiastic.

Less convincing as a source is James Russell Lowell, brought forward as "a strong possibility" by Brian Murray in "Tradition and the Eliot Critical Talent" (1976, p. 15). Murray shows a number of similarities, both in their views on tradition and in other matters: both liked Donne, and made similar comments on Coleridge. Murray has no evidence that Eliot ever read Lowell, though he is convinced "there were many reasons why Eliot should have" (p. 15). Murray also seems convinced that Eliot deliberately concealed his debt to Lowell, perhaps as part of a campaign to play down his own American origins. Murray believes that Lowell is an important link in Eliot's intellectual origins even if one is forced to assume that the influence was indirect. This suggests a certain lack of familiarity with the English critical tradition and with Eliot criticism as well. Readers who recall the interminable search for the origins of the "objective correlative," discussed in an earlier chapter, will be surprised to hear that critics have devoted insufficient attention to the sources of Eliot's criticism.

Given that Eliot's critical generalizations can be shown as parallel to a number of previous critics, one might wonder why he keeps returning to the theme of the poet's possible relation to his cultural tradition. Alan Weinblatt suggests that working out this relationship was a matter of personal urgency for Eliot ("T. S. Eliot and the Historical Sense," 1978). Unlike Eliot, Weinblatt sees no special advantage in poets' possessing the "historical sense"—a burdensome sense of past accomplishments which seem to leave little for a modern poet to do. Judging himself by the standards of the past, Weinblatt's Eliot devotes much of his criticism to an effort to deal with his "fear of being doomed to failure by history" (p. 285). One strategy is to whittle away at the reputations of one's distinguished predecessors, as in Eliot's handling of Shakespeare and Milton. Eliot's immediate predecessors, of course, are treated with "massive antipathy": "From Wordsworth to Arnold to Swinburne to Lawrence, Eliot's best-known comments display vitriol at worst" (p. 286). A similar defensive strategy is seen behind Eliot's compensating praise of non-English classics and minor authors, with whom the strain of competition is less enervating. The very unpopularity of his poetry, its failure to achieve (except among the elite) the acclaim won by Virgil, Dante, and Shakespeare, only reinforced, in Weinblatt's view, Eliot's fears that he lived in a twilight age for poetry. Weinblatt's tone is a bit too melodramatic—only by the bland standards of academic criticism does Eliot's criticism qualify as "vitriol" or "vituperative" (p. 295), and perhaps not even by those. But Weinblatt's appeal to what Harold Bloom has called the "anxiety of influence" may explain why a poet, writing out of his poet's workshop, should repeatedly return to the idea of tradition.

Weinblatt (following W. J. Bate) sees the burden of the past as a central problem for all modern poets; and that may explain some of the influence of Eliot's idea of tradition, for a number of those who followed him were likewise poet-critics. Eliot's reputation as a poet naturally increased his influence as a critic; he was the logical leader for what Roger Sharrock, among others, has termed "The Critical Revolution of T. S. Eliot"

(1971). Sharrock notes the ways in which Eliot's critical writings served to pave the way for his poetry, both in his revaluation of past figures and in his praise of tradition, which made Eliot's historical self-consciousness seem a boon to be desired by all poets. He also observes that, despite Eliot's praise of impersonality, the criticism succeeds in capturing something of the special flavor of the poets Eliot discusses. Sharrock's stated concern is "with establishing the tone of Eliot's criticism" (p. 26). Such characteristics as its "emphatic precision" and "habitual insinuation" (pp. 27, 30) certainly contributed to its rhetorical effectiveness.

One of the best attempts to capture the tone of Eliot's early criticism is John Douglas Boyd's "T. S. Eliot as Critic and Rhetorician: The Essay on Jonson" (1969). Boyd suggests, in passing, that Eliot's praise of the "historical sense" in "Tradition and the Individual Talent" is phrased in terms which are "peculiarly *anti*-historical" (p. 175), for its insistence that one see the whole of the past as existing simultaneously tends to obscure the significant differences between historical periods. Eliot is, of course, aware of such differences, but there is some justice in Boyd's description of the relevant passage as exemplifying "a common Eliot ruse: the formulation of a striking, often paradoxical 'insight,' through a covert and perhaps unconscious manipulation of the meaning of certain key words" (p. 176). Boyd's analysis of Eliot's essay on Jonson admittedly concentrates on Eliot's more questionable rhetorical moves. It shows how Eliot's air of authority and precision, his ambiguous diction, and his circular organization may lure the reader into accepting some dubious generalizations with the genuine insights. Speaking on behalf of tradition, Eliot sometimes seems to speak *for* it as well, uttering *ex cathedra* judgments based on an apparently limitless erudition. In the end, he did more than rehabilitate the word "tradition"; he altered our sense of the literary past it stood for.

The Allusive Poet

Although few of his later poems are as dense with quotation and allusion as *The Waste Land,* Eliot was an unusually allusive poet throughout his career; the "historical sense" he praises in his criticism is ostentatiously embodied in his poems. The poems may express a personal vision of a mind at the end of its tether, but they do so through fragments of the "mind of Europe." Critics have spent over a half century ferreting out real and fancied sources and arguing over their relevance to our understanding of his work. For Eliot's creative work, Grover Smith's *T. S. Eliot's Poetry and Plays: A Study in Sources and Meaning* (1956; 2d ed., 1974) is the standard study of sources. Smith has been an indefatigable searcher for sources, and he incorporates the most significant results of other searchers. It would be a rash critic, indeed, who would publish a new Eliot source without checking to see if Smith has anticipated him. No equivalent work exists for Eliot's criticism. Chaviva Hosek and Viiu Menning's *Index to References in T. S. Eliot's Selected Essays* (1967), based on the 1951 edition, is a useful tool for investigating the sources of Eliot's criticism.

As practiced by Eliot, Pound, and others, this is sometimes called the "poetry of allusion." Readers with little taste for Eliot have sometimes called it pedantry, or even plagiarism. Eliot's cheerful dictum that "immature poets imitate; mature poets steal" ("Philip Massinger," 1920) has not pleased all his critics. "Literary kleptomania," for example, is one of the principal charges made against Eliot in Arthur Davidson's privately printed pamphlet, *The Eliot Enigma* (1956), a diatribe by an admirer of Longfellow, to whom the pamphlet is dedicated. Most critics, however, have assumed that Eliot's quotations and allusions are meant to be noted by the reader, and that they are meant to contribute to the sense of the poem.

A particularly interesting discussion of the problems posed by Eliot's use of quotations appeared in *Essays in Criticism*, beginning in 1969. The journal's editor, F. W. Bateson, may be said to have fired the first gun in his essay for another journal in 1968, "T. S. Eliot: The Poetry of Pseudo-Learning." Bateson begins by attacking the scholarship displayed in Eliot's criticism. Bateson finds fewer errors and less excitement in Eliot's later criticism, suggesting to him that "dogmatism and recklessness of assertion, underlying and feeding on the master illusionism of fact, were the indispensable prerequisites" of the effect of Eliot's early criticism (p. 17). Though dismissing as "plagiarism" the quotations in "Gerontion," Bateson finds them functional in *The Waste Land* and some other early poems, only to become "functionless" in *Four Quartets* (pp. 20, 25). Bateson explains Eliot's parade of learning (and Pound's) as "an aspect of his Americanism" (p. 24). Eliot is seen as an intellectual tourist, out to conquer Europe with his guidebooks in hand, putting them aside when he successfully became part of the English establishment. This (very English) explanation may have some truth in it, but it also reminds us that critics and editors (like poets) may feel some animus toward potentially overwhelming influences. On a more positive note, Bateson sees the use of allusion as part of Eliot's and Pound's strategy to break the impasse of pure poetry. Poetry having been revived, allusiveness has proved, he believes, no longer useful.

The debate in *Essays in Criticism* began with an April 1969 essay by William H. Pritchard, "Reading *The Waste Land* Today." Echoing some of Eliot's later doubts about the extent to which the famous notes have turned readers away from the poem and sent them in pursuit of stray allusions, Pritchard states the extreme case for ignoring all such matters. Eliot's poetry, he says, is a poetry of the surface, like that Eliot praises in his essay on Jonson. It is a kind of creative satire which does not yield complex characters or a clear progression of meaning. In the end, the poem exists for us as a series of passages of varying quality, comprising a whole which we admire despite its imperfections. The merit of such a reading is that it redirects our attention to the text and reasserts the fragmentary character of its surface; the disadvantage is that it seems to despair unnecessarily of making any sense of the text or the links between its fragments.

In the same issue of *Essays in Criticism*, John Lucas and William Myers responded to Pritchard with a very different view, in "*The Waste Land* Today." The allusions, they note, are not just in the notes, they are part of the poem; and the question is what they are there for. Lucas and Myers find no satisfactory answer to this question, probably because they pursue the will-o'-the-wisp of Tiresias. They find no unifying personality in the poem, and certainly not the poet. Juliet McLaughlin replied to this with a defense: "Allusion in *The Waste Land*" (1969). The poet does not need to be present in the poem, she argues, since he can control it through allusions. In the years since these essays were published, we have come to see *The Waste Land* as a very personal poem, and all of this persona hunting and control-through-allusion seems unnecessary—even in terms of Eliot's "impersonal" theory, which did not deny that poems are written by poets.

William Myers, in "Allusion in *The Waste Land*" (1970), agrees that the use of allusions is a central issue, although Myers digresses several times to remark how mad certain lines of verse in the poem seem to him to be. Myers says that the very use of allusions, to give a sense of timelessness, prevents one from knowing whether the guiding consciousness is (like Dante) a reliable guide to an external waste land or (like Baudelaire) part of the evil described: "Distinctions between self and society and between health and sickness, which must be made if the poem is to have value, are carefully obscured" (p. 122). Such distinctions do not have to be made, of course, and critics who are unable to tolerate ambiguity must be very careful in choosing works of literature for discussion. This point was made in replies to Myers by Francis Berry and by Bernard Bergonzi, both under the same title: "Allusion in *The Waste Land*" (1970).

In April 1970, A. L. French's contribution to this discussion appeared as "Death by Allusion?" Fresh from an article in the same issue of *Essays in Criticism*, disposing of Marlowe's *Dr. Faustus*, French raised questions rather like those of Myers: "Doesn't the insistent presentation of barrenness and emptiness in *The Waste Land* claim, by its very frequency, that modern life *is like this?* Wouldn't we regard with some surprise a critic who said that *King Lear* was just about one old man and his children and had no wider bearing or significance? Doesn't all literature implicitly claim to talk not merely about 'this thing' but about 'such classes of things'?" (p. 270).

These questions would have more force if French seemed willing to distinguish between levels of meaning or between the work and its interpretation. Works of literature, including *The Waste Land*, rarely "claim" the kind of significance critics are accustomed to find in them; *The Waste Land* is a poem, not an argument. More to the point, perhaps, is French's argument that the effect of the allusions is to expose the thinness of the sensibility which creates the contemporary characters and scene of the poem, although French's comparison between the vividness of Shakespeare's Cleopatra and the shadowy character of the lady in "The Game of Chess" rather slights the difference in characters and genres involved. In any case, it is possible to see the comparative thinness of sensibility as one of the poem's themes. Like the Eliot he finds in *The Waste Land*, French seems one of those sensibilities who are most fulfilled in expressing distaste.

Lucas and Myers, this time individually, delivered some of the final blows in this controversy. John Lucas' reconsideration, "*The Waste Land* Today" (1970), is mainly devoted to replying to Bernard Bergonzi, especially Bergonzi's assertion that the pub scene in "A Game of Chess" was meant as something of a music-hall turn. Lucas disagrees with this, though he really does not argue the point. He takes the disagreement as another sign of the poem's ultimate evasiveness and incoherence, though other explanations certainly occur to one—the inadequacies of contemporary criticism, for one. Insisting that a poem yield a single clear interpretation is, in any case, a hard requirement to make of a poet who doubts the possibility of interpretation.

William Myers' "Aesthetic and Ethical Judgments" (1971) devotes most of his response to Berry and this relationship. In terms that Eliot presumably would not object to, Myers argues that these forms of judgment cannot be wholly divorced, that the poem relies on certain moral traditions and raises certain moral perceptions, which it fails to satisfy. One cannot escape the feeling, however, that it is simplistic moral and ethical judgments that Myers wants to find, though he may be right in condemning the moral vision of the typist sequence.

One might expect that prolonged discussion of important questions in a high-quality journal would produce less disappointing results than the contributions just discussed. The problems, insofar as they can be identified, would seem to be common to much Eliot criticism (and contemporary criticism generally): unarticulated assumptions and impressionism posing as objectivity. Critical exchanges are likely to be useless unless those who participate make clear their assumptions about the nature of literature and of criticism. It is characteristic that Myers' theoretical generalizations come at the end of the discussion rather than at the beginning; even then, Myers does not clearly relate his general position to his specific criticisms. Although most participants seem to assume that objective interpretation is possible, in practice they take their own subjective experience as normative. One has little sense that they are listening to each other in hope of correcting the merely accidental and personal elements in their response. This is criticism as a game with ill-defined rules, not as a common enterprise.

Of the participants, A. L. French produced a much more useful treatment of the issue some years earlier in "Criticism and *The Waste Land*," published in the *Southern Review* (Australia) in 1964. French argued that critics had paid excessive attention to the notes, with resulting neglect of the personal elements in the poem. With F. R. Leavis's *New Bearings in English Poetry* as his polemical target, French gives a less distorted account of the poem.

Staffan Bergsten's "Illusive Allusions, Some Reflections on the Critical Approach to the Poetry of T. S. Eliot" (1959) may still be the most perceptive essay on this topic. Bergsten is concerned with the development of critical principles that would provide criteria for distinguishing between a true source and a critic's fancy, between "the source of a literary allusion and its function within the poem," and "between an allusion proper and a mere reminiscence" (pp. 10, 11). He shows how some of these distinctions might be made, for example, in discussions of "Burbank with a Baedeker: Bleistein with a Cigar." He also makes useful distinctions about the role and nature of allusions in Eliot's earlier and later poetry. Bergsten, naturally, has little difficulty in finding horrid examples of overfanciful or irrelevant source studies. Bergsten concludes that those who interpret a poem in relation to its sources should rule out "irrelevant, private associations by making general consensus among qualified readers a criterion, and by choosing among several in themselves acceptable alternatives of interpretation, the one that accounts for the greatest number of details" (p. 18). The only difficulty with this is that most of the critics whom Bergsten attacks are presumably "qualified readers."

There are certainly deliberate allusions in Eliot's poetry, as well as cases in which Eliot unconsciously echoed an earlier writer's work. Both are clearly related to Eliot's belief that the poet should submit himself to the tradition. Readers who share something of Eliot's immersion in the Western literary tradition may find that recognizing allusions and sources adds to their experience of the poetry. (Disagreements over the importance of these recognitions for interpretation are hard to resolve by rational argument.) Readers sympathetic to Eliot's Classicism and Catholicism are likely to prefer the kind of consensual orthodoxy Bergsten would like to see prevail; those whose critical faith is Romantic and Antinomian may choose to heed their inner voice instead. One would hope, however, that assertions about Eliot's intentions and methods of composition would be governed by respect for normal standards of probability and argument. By such standards, allusions and sources play a much larger role in Eliot criticism than in Eliot's poetry.

The Classical Poet

Western Christendom has generally thought of itself as in continuity with Greco-Roman civilization, and the "tradition" to which Eliot appeals is an ideal in which "the whole of the literature of Europe has a simultaneous existence and composes a simultaneous order" ("Tradition and the Individual Talent"). For those who see Eliot as practicing the poetry of allusion, his place within that order may be with the Alexandrians, also self-conscious and erudite cosmopolitans with a sense of living at the end of an age. Paul MacKendrick makes the most of such comparisons in an essay primarily devoted to urging a more favorable estimate of the Alexandrians ("T. S. Eliot and the Alexandrians," 1953). If one looks at the actual uses Eliot makes of classical literature, his references to ancient literature and mythology do not go beyond those quite common in the English poetic tradition.

It is Virgil, rather than the Alexandrians, whom Eliot offers us as a model classic—in terms that may suggest that Virgil has served as well as a model for Eliot. It was before the Virgil Society that Eliot gave his 1944 address "What Is a Classic?" and it may therefore seem unsurprising that Virgil is the norm arrived at therein. But Eliot's interest in Virgil has been fairly steady. Reviewing the book in which the 1944 volume was reprinted (*On Poetry and Poets*, 1957), Frank Kermode could write (with some exaggeration) that "the historical issue that dominates this book is the status of Virgil" ("T. S. Eliot on Poetry," 1958, p. 133). Kermode sees a connection with Eliot's interest in Dante, who took Virgil as his mentor: Virgil and Dante together stand for the continuity and temporal wholeness that Eliot values. D. S. Carne-Ross's essay on Eliot and the classics notes that one effect of this linkage is that Eliot seems to value the classics mainly for their role in ushering in Christianity ("T. S. Eliot: Tropheia," 1965). Although paying due tribute to Eliot for his advocacy of the classics, Carne-Ross sees Homer as closer to our own age, precisely because he is less tied to the "collapse of the great intellectual structures" we have experienced (p. 20).

Those intellectual structures are, of course, the tradition to which Eliot appeals, and Carne-Ross is correct to see Eliot's choice of Virgil as in part an ideological one—the early Eliot wrote about Seneca instead. James P. Condon's "Notes on T. S. Eliot's 'What Is a Classic?': The Classical Norm and Social Existence" (1977–78) offers a few comments on the social qualities Eliot values in Virgil. One is reminded of Eliot's remark in another essay ("Virgil and the Christian World," 1951) in *On Poetry and Poets* that he "preferred the *world* of Virgil to the *world* of Homer—because it was a more civilized world of dignity, reason and order." But the order of Virgil's world, as ours, was precarious, and it is this which helps create the spiritual and literary kinship (rather than influence) which Andrew V. Ettin finds connecting the *Four Quartets* with Virgil's *Georgics* ("Milton, T. S. Eliot, and the Virgilian Vision: Some Versions of Georgic," 1977). The "world" of *The Waste Land* seems much less Virgilian, and the parallels Bernard F. Dick finds with the descents to hell in the *Odyssey* and the *Aeneid* seem overingenious ("*The Waste Land* and the *Descensus ad Infernos*," 1975).

Petronius would seem a more likely presence in *The Waste Land*, which sports an epigraph from his *Satyricon*, but it seems that the epigraph itself (not an important passage in Petronius) is all that is relevant. Helen H. Bacon's "The Sibyl in the Bottle" (1958) is mainly an introduction to the *Satyricon*, a work brief enough and racy enough that readers who are interested in tracking down Eliot's sources might as well read it for themselves. Such parallels as she finds with Eliot's work are not at all convincing, a stricture which applies as well to Francis Noel Lees' "Mr. Eliot's Sunday Morning *Satura:* Petronius and *The Waste Land*" (1966). The most convincing parallels are matters of tone more than substance, and the best discussion of these is in M. K. Naik's "Thalia in the Desert: Varieties of Comic Experience in *The Waste Land*" (1976). Naik is primarily concerned with exploring the often neglected comic strain in *The Waste Land.* Grover Smith has shown that the epigraph is a sentence which Rossetti had "turned into English doggerel verse" (1974, p. 304), which suggests the possibility of secondhand quotation and casts further doubt on claims for the epigraph's contribution to our understanding of the poem. One is tempted to doubt, as well, the importance of the Ovid and Sappho references in Eliot's notes, although critics enamored of Tiresias as a persona have found the Ovid passage relevant.

References to classical literature, as opposed to classical myth, are much less common in Eliot than in Pound. Greek poets make relatively few appearances in Eliot's poetry. The *Waste Land* passage where Eliot notes a Sappho reference echoes Robert Louis Stevenson more clearly. Charles Child Walcutt has noted a passing Homeric reference in "Eliot's 'Sweeney Erect' " (1976). The passage on Phlebas in *Waste Land IV* recalls the *Greek Anthology* epitaphs in tone, though Herbert Musurillo's singling out of the *Garland* of Meleager would add nothing to our understanding of *The Waste Land* even if it rested on more solid evidence ("A Note on *The Waste Land* [Part IV]," 1956).

Roman poets are also fairly rare. Smith notes the Catullus fragment, quoted in "Ode." F. J. Lelievre's "Parody in Juvenal and T. S. Eliot" claims no more than "a measure of common ground" between the two writers (1958, p. 25). Similarly, Ronald W. Janoff finds no direct influence of Horace on Eliot, even though Janoff finds Eliot closer in spirit "to Horace than to any other poet in antiquity" (1965, p. 31). The manifest differences between Juvenal and Horace may suggest the limitations of such purely comparative studies; any point of resemblance with one is a point of difference with the other.

Once one strips away fanciful references and etymologies, most of Eliot's references in his poetry to classical literature—and, for that matter, to classical history, legend, myth, and philosophy—do not take us far beyond the range of reference one might expect of a reasonably well educated man. Knowledge of specific literary contexts is rarely required of the reader. The Catullus reference in "Ode" may be an exception, but "Ode" is hardly an important work. Another possible exception is the Senecan epigraph (from *Hercules Furens*) to "Marina." If one takes the epigraph as part of the poem (always an uncertain point in discussing Eliot), it is possible to agree with Grover Smith (1956) that the epigraph may affect our sense of the poem by way of contrast. Paul J. Dolan's observation that the same line may have been used by Milton in *Paradise Lost* ("Milton and Eliot: A Common Source," 1966), however, is of purely historical interest.

When one turns to Eliot's drama, the situation is somewhat different, though perhaps less so than it has seemed to some critics. Greek drama is clearly in Eliot's mind in most of his efforts to revive poetic drama. An epigraph from Aeschylus was attached to *Sweeney Agonistes* (1932) after the first magazine publication of its "Prologue," and since this and "Agon" were published together they have carried the subtitle "Fragments of an Aristophanic Melodrama." The epigraph suggests the myth of Orestes, as the eventual title suggests the story of Samson and Milton's *Samson Agonistes*. The immediate relevance of either to the action of the fragments preserved seems very slight, and Charles L. Holt's suggestion that Samson and Orestes "function as oversouls to the action of the play" ("On Structure and *Sweeney Agonistes*," 1967, p. 44) is a bit mystical. Orestes may be relevant as an emblem of guilt, but that does not make Aeschylus' play relevant to Eliot's fragments.

Aeschylus presumably is relevant to Eliot's original and unrealized intention, which Sears Jayne describes as "an ambitious attempt to combine in one work a music hall melodrama, a Greek tragedy, and a theological poem" ("Mr. Eliot's Agon," 1955, p. 397). The reference to Aristophanes in the eventual subtitle points toward (and dignifies) the music-hall elements in the poetry; no direct reference to any Aristophanic play appears likely, so what we have is another signpost pointing to Eliot's intentions. A theater audience, like the reader of a poem, presumably attends to what is before it, rather than to the author's hopes for reviving poetic drama; but a director may well be guided by such clues to an author's intentions. If we read Eliot's play, we are presumably serving as directors for a mental performance. The unfinished character of *Sweeney Agonistes* is another problem, for it is tempting to use what one knows about Eliot's original plans (covered in Jayne and in Grover Smith's book) as a way of linking the surviving fragments. The practical and theoretical difficulties of such use are considerable, and Jayne's solution is probably the best. Jayne argues that, whatever Eliot's original intention, *Sweeney Agonistes,* as we have it, should be read as a poem rather than as a play. "Seen from this point of view," says Jayne, "*Sweeney Agonistes* is at least as 'finished' as most of Eliot's poems, and it has a special interest for the critic in that it is the only poem in which Eliot takes as his central theme the irony of his own situation as a poet in the modern world" (p. 395). Jayne's explication of this play-turned-poem is worth reading.

Sweeney Agonistes is certainly a special case. But it seems, despite various critical attempts to show otherwise, that Eliot's use of Greek drama in his plays is more relevant to his formal intentions than to any attempt at interpretation. This is certainly the case with his handling of the choruses for *The Rock* and in *Murder in the Cathedral*, and it seems increasingly true for the later plays, more and more loosely related to their Greek models. Although *The Confidential Clerk* is avowedly based on *Ion* by Euripides, and *The Elder Statesman* can be seen as akin to *Oedipus at Colonus* by Sophocles, knowledge of the Greek plays does little to affect our interpretation of Eliot's. Critics who have explored the relationship between Eliot and his models have devoted more attention to his first two "commercial" dramas, *The Family Reunion* and *The Cocktail Party*.

For these plays we have the advantage of being able to read Eliot's acute criticisms in his 1951 essay "Poetry and Drama."

For Eliot, "the deepest flaw" in *The Family Reunion* "was in a failure of adjustment between the Greek story and the modern situation. I should either have stuck closer to Aeschylus or else taken a great deal more liberty with his myth" (*On Poetry and Poets*, 1957, p. 90). Like many other critics, Eliot sees his modern Furies as embarrassing on stage; he says that no means of presenting them has proved satisfactory and advises eliminating them in the future. "More serious," in Eliot's view, is our inability to determine "whether to consider the play the tragedy of the mother or the salvation of the son" (p. 90), another sign of an ill-adjusted relationship with his Greek model. Having drawn these lessons, Eliot tells us that in *The Cocktail Party* he was determined to eliminate all ghosts and choruses and to use his Greek model "merely as a point of departure" (p. 91), concealing it, in fact, as best he could. He observes that he succeeded so well in this last aim that he had difficulty convincing acquaintances that it was, indeed, based on the *Alcestis* of Euripides. He adds that "those who were at first disturbed by the eccentric behaviour of my unknown guest . . . have found some consolation in having their attention called to the behaviour of Heracles in Euripides' play" (p. 91).

Eliot would be one of the last to claim special authority for an author's criticism of his own work, but his comments on *The Family Reunion* are essentially just. Perhaps for reasons that reflect his inner life, parts of Aeschylus' *Oresteia* have "lingered in Eliot's memory with singular persistence," as noted in Warren Ramsey's survey, "The *Oresteia* since Hofmannsthal" (1964, p. 371). The trilogy supplied "Sweeney among the Nightingales" with Agamemnon and the nightingales, as well as the epigraph to *Sweeney Agonistes*. Of *The Family Reunion*, Ramsey observes that "the play seems to have grown away from the legend" in the course of Eliot's work on it (p. 370). Parallels remain, of course. They have been explored at length in Maud Bodkin's pamphlet *The Quest for Salvation in an Ancient and a Modern Play* (1941) and more briefly (but sufficiently) by Ramsey, and by Rudolf Stamm ("The Orestes Theme in Three Plays by Eugene O'Neill, T. S. Eliot, and Jean Paul Sartre," 1949). But Harry's guilt is not the same as Orestes' and his salvation is not the same. There is no doubt that the *Oresteia* affected Eliot's handling of his theme, but our knowledge of the source has no clear bearing on our interpretation of Eliot's play.

The most obvious borrowing from Aeschylus is Eliot's use

of the Furies. Generally regarded as a misjudgment on Eliot's part, the Eumenides of *The Family Reunion* have been defended by Leo Hamalian on the grounds that they are central to Harry's liberation from guilt. Hamalian makes this argument in "Wishwood Revisited" (1960). The Eumenides are certainly to be associated with Harry's guilt and salvation, but they remain emblematic rather than functional.

Vinod Sena has provided a useful analysis of the problems raised by the Eumenides in "Eliot's *The Family Reunion:* A Study in Disintegration" (1967). In particular, he notes that Eliot describes them in terms that closely recall the Aeschylean Furies (before they become the Eumenides), while assigning them a different kind of spiritual function. Sena's analysis implicitly supports Eliot's comments on the play's failure to maintain a stable relationship with its Greek model. A secondary argument in Sena's essay, that the play fails by following too closely its predecessor, *Murder in the Cathedral*, is more original but less persuasive.

Eliot concealed the relationship of *The Cocktail Party* to *Alcestis* well enough that it took his own revelation to set critics off exploring parallels. The first critical suggestion of a classical source seems to have been the quite different and unconvincing parallel suggested in John M. Yoklavich's "Eliot's 'Cocktail Party' and Plato's 'Symposium' " (1951). Since then, critics have taken up the relationship with an enthusiasm that neglects Eliot's indication that Euripides served only as "a point of departure."

Of the early efforts, Ulrich Weisstein's "*The Cocktail Party:* An Attempt at Interpretation on Mythological Grounds" (1952) begins with the Alcestis myth but quickly becomes a mishmash, in which Weisstein applies his great learning to the play with little regard for common sense. Weisstein misreads the play badly, but his suggestion that it moves from mythology in the first part to religion in the last has some merit. William Arrowsmith's "Transfiguration in Eliot and Euripides" (1955) is well written and much referred to, but too general to be terribly useful. A distinguished Classicist, Arrowsmith argues that Euripides is a greater dramatist than Eliot, and one can hardly disagree. But his argument that this is because Eliot's version of Christianity makes everyday experience too drab to be redeemed by poetry is no more convincing than most such ideological arguments.

Robert Heilman offers a much more detailed comparison in

"*Alcestis* and *The Cocktail Party*" (1953). Heilman begins by noting that the only specific parallel endorsed by Eliot, between Heracles' and Harcourt-Reilly's conduct at parties, "is of no help whatsoever in assessing the serious role of Sir Henry Harcourt-Reilly" (p. 105), but he goes on to find a number of other parallels, incidentally betraying a rather limited understanding of Euripides' play. The question is whether these parallels are of any help in interpreting Eliot's play. If Heilman is correct in asserting that Eliot "has boldly split Alcestis into Lavinia and Celia," we have learned something interesting about Eliot's way of making use of models; the resulting deviation from the model, however, means that we cannot use the model as a guide to interpretation.

Points where Heilman's analysis finds Eliot closest to his model are often weak points. When the guest raises, within the play, the parallel between Lavinia's desertion and death, Edward objects that the figure of speech seems a bit "dramatic." Heilman writes that "by 'dramatic' Edward doubtless means theatrical, improbable—a judgment that might almost seem to have point if we did not see that the metaphor is drawn from the literal story in Euripides" (p. 108). Two objections can be raised to this sort of argument. The first is that we do *not* see the parallel with Euripides unless we have been warned to look for it; and our not seeing it is hardly a sign of lack of our perception, when Eliot has taken pains to conceal the connection. A second objection is that our perception of the analogy with *Alcestis* does not free Eliot of the obligation to make his play theatrically probable in terms of its own situation; this objection applies, as well, to Eliot's example of the boisterous behavior of Heracles and the "unidentified guest." Heilman's defense of the thematic relevance of the death-desertion metaphor is somewhat persuasive, but to the extent that the guest's remark is a mere echo of Euripides, it seems like a private joke of the playwright's.

John E. Rexine's exploration, "Classical and Christian Foundations of T. S. Eliot's *Cocktail Party*" (1965), returns to the free-association mode of Weisstein's article. Rexine draws parallels with other Greek myths and *The Waste Land*, as well as with Euripides' play. He argues that "to understand the parallels is to understand the full complexity of Eliot's artistry" and that "*The Cocktail Party* is worthy of the classical standard set by Euripides" (p. 21); but most of his suggestions are too far fetched to contribute much to our understanding or to the play's stature. Fond of finding symbolism in names (a trivial, though harmless, critical pastime), Rexine believes, for example, that Harcourt-Reilly's name, an Anglo-Irish compound, suggests the mixture of divine and mortal ancestry in Heracles. Inspired by a Minotaur reference in one of Reilly's speeches, Rexine finds that legend echoed "in the story of Delia Verinder and her brother who was kept rather quiet—the brother locked away can easily be the Minotaur, the castle in the North the labyrinth at Cnossus, and the island Crete" (p. 24), though one might think they could "easily be" any number of other things with equal facility.

Kenneth J. Reckford, somehow convinced that Eliot must have implied that he took more from Euripides than plot parallels, argues that Eliot was inspired as well by Euripides' tragic-comic treatment of his themes ("Heracles and Mr. Eliot," 1964). While "Eliot's Christian beliefs give specific point and reference to the Euripidean story, *Alcestis* in turn informs Eliot's ideas with vigor, warmth, humanity" (p. 17). If *The Cocktail Party* possesses vigor, warmth, and humanity—and lack of those qualities is a frequent charge against it—it is hard to see how one would demonstrate that they come from the *Alcestis*. To both the specific and general parallels adduced by Reckford, it is tempting to respond with his dismissal of the obscene origins of Harcourt-Reilly's song: "What matters is not what the song was once, but what it says now" (p. 6).

Most subsequent comments on the relation between Euripides and Eliot repeat parallels found in essays already mentioned. In *The Meddling Gods* (1974), Hazel E. Barnes argues that the relationship is an "essential ingredient" (p. 57) of our understanding of *The Cocktail Party*, but the most interesting passages deal with the play as a kind of antiexistentialist drama that still takes much from what it opposes. In particular, Barnes believes the restored life of Edward and Lavinia is intentionally unattractive—not so much a reply to Sartre as a demonstration of the insufficiency of life on a purely human (or humanistic) plane. Lavinia thus becomes the true analogue to Euripides' Alcestis, while Celia stands in heroic contrast as an Alcestis who does not return (one wonders whether an Alcestis who does not return is still an Alcestis in any meaningful sense). In any case, it is unlikely that Eliot meant Edward's and Lavinia's new life to be quite as unattractive as Barnes finds it. Although Euripides may have provided Eliot with his "point of departure," their ways diverged; literary sources, like personal sources, may have little to do with the meaning of the work they evoke.

The Symbolist Poet

Eliot's ideal "tradition" may have included all European literature since Homer, but much of that tradition does not appear to have affected his work. His 1955 lecture "Goethe as a Sage" applauded Goethe as one of the "Great Europeans," but most of his previous remarks on Goethe had been negative. The best evidence for northern literature influencing Eliot is the possible influence of Ibsen on his plays, as traced by Kristian Smidt (*The Importance of Recognition*, 1973) and others. Ilse E. Hochwald's contention that there is an important relationship between "Eliot's *Cocktail Party* and Goethe's *Wahlverwandtschaften*" (1954) rests on general similarities in dramatic situations and unconvincing parallels in names. Similarly unconvincing are efforts to relate Eliot's work to Russian literature, like Gabriel Motola's argument in "The Mountains of *The Waste Land*" (1969) that the mountains come from Turgenev or Temira Pachmuss's essay, "Dostoevsky and Eliot: A Point of View" (1976). Outside of Eliot's frequent use of Dante (discussed in the last chapter), Continental literature enters his work mainly through his long interest in nineteenth-century French poetry.

Eliot discovered the poetry of Laforgue through reading Arthur Symons' *The Symbolist Movement in Literature* while an undergraduate at Harvard, and efforts to reproduce the characteristic Laforguean tone and technique soon appeared in his own poetry. He went on to read and learn from a number of French Symbolists. The main lines of criticism in assessing Eliot's debt to these poets were set early by the chapters on Eliot in Rene Taupin's *L'Influence du Symbolisme français sur la poésie américaine* (1929) and Edmund Wilson's *Axel's Castle* (1931).

Another study, still of some interest, is M.-J.-J. Laboulle's "T. S. Eliot and Some French Poets" in the *Revue de Littérature Comparée* (1936). All three studies see the most important relationship as that with Laforgue, as a source for themes and situations in Eliot's early poetry, as well as of techniques and borrowed lines. It was also generally agreed that Laforgue and the others were less important in Eliot's later poetry. Wilson and Laboulle very sensibly note the ways in which Eliot differs from his models even when he seems to be following them closely.

One minor difference of opinion is over Apollinaire, included as both a Symbolist and an influence on Eliot by Taupin. Laboulle disagrees on both points and says that Eliot told him he had never read anything by Apollinaire. This has not kept Grover Smith (1956) from suggesting Apollinaire's *Les mamelles de Tirésias* as a source for *The Waste Land* or Georgio Melchiori from suggesting the same play as a source for *Sweeney Agonistes* ("Eliot and Apollinaire," 1964). Neither of these suggestions carries much conviction.

Later general treatments of Eliot's debt to French literature can be found in E. J. H. Greene's *T. S. Eliot et la France* (1951), Enid Starkie's *From Gautier to Eliot: The Influence of France in English Literature* (1954), and Francis Scarfe's "Eliot and Nineteenth-Century French Poetry" (1970). Greene's is the most useful and thorough for readers interested in exploring the matter in detail. His book covers Eliot's critical debt to French critics like Remy de Gourmont, as well as his use of various poets. Of particular interest is Greene's discussion of Eliot's four poems in French, in which Corbiere is the most obvious influence. Except for "Dans le Restaurant," which received attention from critics hoping to cast light on the portion of it used in *The Waste Land IV*, these poems have received little critical notice. Readers primarily interested in poetic influences may find Scarfe's essay sufficient. Scarfe notes the principal borrowings, rejects some unconvincing suggestions, and explains some of Eliot's points of difference with his models. His conclusion is more negatively phrased than those of the earliest critics who discussed this question, but seems to be in line with the conclusions reached by Wilson and Laboulle: "Eliot's 'debt' to French poetry was mainly to what he had read at an early, impressionable age, and . . . his subjection to this was by no means total" (1970, p. 60).

A rather reserved assessment of Eliot's debt to Laforgue is also found in Ronald Schuchard's " 'Our Mad Poetics to Confute': The Personal Voice in T. S. Eliot's Early Poetry and Criticism" (1976), although his argument is in some way a simple extension of Wilson's. Schuchard's argument is that "Eliot *was* intrigued by the Laforguean method of subtly mocking or ironically undercutting the explicit, implicit, or expected sentimentalism of a dramatic situation, but he turned the ironic technique of deflating the emotional sentimentalism in the poem against Laforgue by further mocking the philosophical sentimentalism underlying Laforgue's lunar symbolism" (p. 214). Schuchard supports this by analysis of the lunar symbols in Eliot's first Laforguean poems and by external biographical evidence. Schuchard's essay falls into two loosely related parts.

The first, theoretical portion argues that Eliot criticism has given too little attention to the author's personal voice, assimilating it to the general voice of a modern sensibility that Eliot rejected. Schuchard's accentuation of the difference between Eliot and Laforgue helps set Eliot off from other forms of modern irony.

Although Laforgue's influence is usually seen as confined to the early poetry, Leonard Unger has given good reasons for seeing an echo of Laforgue's prose "Hamlet" in Eliot's "Animula" and, possibly, in the second chorus of *Murder in the Cathedral* ("Laforgue, Conrad, and Eliot," in *The Man in the Name*, 1956). In his introduction to a 1966 collection of his Eliot essays (*T. S. Eliot*), Unger cites Eliot as having recommended the translation in the Symons book of the passage Unger had cited, in preference to the translation Unger himself had used. This may suggest that the Symons book was the source; in any case, it suggests the extent to which it had impressed itself on Eliot's memory.

In many ways, the influence of Baudelaire would seem to have been more intellectual than poetic, although, as Greene notes, Eliot seems to have read Baudelaire even before encountering the Symons work. Eliot's most direct statement on the topic occurs in his 1950 "A Talk on Dante" (1952), rather than in his better-known essays on Baudelaire. In his 1950 lecture, he says that he learned from Baudelaire certain possibilities for poetry—use of the sordid modern city, the mingling of reality and fantasy. At the same time, Eliot says that he may be "indebted to Baudelaire chiefly for half a dozen lines out of the whole of *Fleurs du Mal*." These remarks are not contradictory, for a young poet may perceive in a handful of lines by another new poet possibilities for his own work. Moreover, Eliot's remarks do not generally conflict with the view that Baudelaire, as a *source* for Eliot's poetry, is mainly confined to *The Waste Land*, particularly the first section thereof. Eliot's exploration of the possibilities revealed by Baudelaire may still have been guided primarily by Laforgue, the later Elizabethans, and other models.

A number of attempts have been made to suggest a larger role for Baudelaire in Eliot's development. Kerry Weinberg's monograph, *T. S. Eliot and Charles Baudelaire* (1969), is at any rate the longest such attempt, though it is weakened by Weinberg's imperfect acquaintance with Eliot criticism and lack of sympathy with precisely those aspects of Eliot which set him apart from Baudelaire. As in too many comparative studies, Weinberg does not distinguish carefully between parallels resulting from temperamental affinity, parallels resulting from intellectual influence, parallels showing use of a source, and parallels meant as allusions. Weinberg argues that Baudelaire also influenced Eliot indirectly by influencing Laforgue, but without showing that the ways in which Baudelaire influenced Laforgue were the aspects of Laforgue which influenced Eliot. Weinberg's comparison of the two poets' views on aesthetics and religion adds relatively little to previous accounts; more original is an attempt to find a Baudelairian coloring to the opening passage of *Waste Land II.* Although some of the parallels listed are less convincing than those with the better-known Shakespearean models, it is possible that Baudelaire was one of many influences on Eliot's handling of the passage. A comparison of Eliot and Baudelaire on cats, however, is not very persuasive. Weinberg concludes with a chapter noting (and exaggerating) the differences in the comments on Baudelaire in Eliot's "Baudelaire in Our Time" (1927) and "Baudelaire" (1930).

Two essays on Baudelaire and *The Waste Land* deal primarily with thematic resemblances which might demonstrate some indirect influence: Judith A. Berry, "The Relevance of Baudelaire to T. S. Eliot's *The Waste Land*" (1966), and Sister M. Cecilia Carey, "Baudelaire's Influence on *The Waste Land*" (1962). Of the two, Carey's is the better, clearer in analysis and more cautious in conclusions. Wallace Fowlie's essay in the Tate collection (1967), "Baudelaire and Eliot: Interpreters of Their Age," is appreciative and comparative in tone and method, and of interest chiefly to those who enjoy such exercises for their own sake.

Eliot's use of these writers is most obvious in his early poetry. In the same period, he also drew on French criticism, notably that of Remy de Gourmont, whose influence on the essays of *The Sacred Wood* is acknowledged in the preface to the 1928 edition. Glenn S. Burne's essay, "T. S. Eliot and Remy de Gourmont" (1959), provides a balanced account of this influence and its limits, which has also been discussed by Taupin, Greene, and some critics discussed in earlier chapters. Eliot's interest in Gourmont and in the Symbolist tradition may reflect his own Romanticism, and it served to justify the fragmentary and opaque surfaces of his early poetry—all very different from the models and principles represented by his classical sources and Dante. As a critic, Eliot was never entirely comfortable with the philosophical implications of the Symbolist tradition. As James Torrens has shown, his praise of its most distinguished twentieth-century representative, Paul Valery, never included whole-hearted endorsement of the notion of a pure or autonomous poetry ("T. S. Eliot and the Austere Poetics of Valéry," 1971a). E. P. Bollier has suggested that a good deal of Eliot's criticism can be seen as responding to Valery's position, which was both attractive and unacceptable to Eliot ("La Poésie Pure: The Ghostly Dialogue between T. S. Eliot and Paul Valéry," 1970).

To the extent to which Eliot increasingly rejected the poetic assumptions of the Symbolist tradition, he was also questioning his own poetic method, which had been partly formed on Symbolist models. As a critic, Eliot might prefer classical order and Dantesque faith, but his age was Romantic and secular, and neither order nor affirmations of faith come easily in Eliot's poetry. The *Four Quartets* are Eliot's major effort to remake his own poetry.

Barbara Everett has provided a brilliant exploration of the relationship in "Eliot's 'Four Quartets' and French Symbolism" (1980), setting the *Quartets* in the context of Eliot's long lover's quarrel with Symbolism, pointing to Symbolist analogues for passages in the *Quartets,* and tracing the way they both translate Symbolism into English poetry and transcend its limitations. "The first movements of the *Quartets,*" says Everett, "are genuinely symbolist poetry, sensuous, hypnotic, self-blazoning emblems of a created timelessness" (p. 33). Through the other voices of the *Quartets,* Eliot tries to achieve a philosophical style which can give order and public meaning to his work. Much more than a source study, Everett's essay is a model exploration of the complex relationship between a poet and his models.

The Elizabethan Poet

Eliot's early poetry also reflects deliberate efforts to learn from Elizabethan and Jacobean dramatists, and his relationship with the English literary tradition is most obvious in his essays on the Elizabethans and poetic allusions to them. Eliot has little to say about earlier periods of English literature and makes few allusions to them; the principal exception is the opening passage of *The Waste Land,* where it is hard to escape the allusion to the opening of Chaucer's *Canterbury Tales.* One of the few critical efforts to go further is Rodney Delasanta's effort to draw a parallel between *The Waste Land* bartender, who says "HURRY UP PLEASE IT'S TIME," and the host of the *Tales*, who urges the pilgrims not to lose time ("The Bartenders in Eliot and Chaucer," 1971). Serious discussion of Eliot's relationship to the English poetic tradition must still begin with his relationship to the Elizabethans.

Of Eliot and the Elizabethans, we may say that in his criticism he is surprisingly reserved about Shakespeare and surprisingly enthusiastic about some other figures. As a poet, Eliot acknowledged learning a great deal from some of the later Elizabethans. The mass of Shakespeare allusions in his work indicates that he had studied Shakespeare's works closely, and minor works as well as the major plays.

Along with many incidental references, Eliot wrote two full essays on Shakespeare, "Hamlet and His Problems" (1919) and "Shakespeare and the Stoicism of Seneca" (1927). Although both appeared in his 1934 collection, *Elizabethan Essays*, he eliminated them from his 1956 collection, *Essays on Elizabethan Drama*, along with a third essay, "Four Elizabethan Dramatists." On rereading his essays, Eliot reports, he was surprised to find that he thought his essays on other dramatists remarkably good; the three rejected essays "embarrassed me by their callowness, and by a facility of unqualified assertion which verges, here and there, on impudence" (1956, p. vii). He offers as explanation the theory that "an immature youngish man," like Eliot when he wrote them, can appreciate the minor figures fully, while "for the understanding of Shakespeare, a lifetime is not too long" (p. viii).

Philip L. Marcus has traced the development of Eliot's views on Shakespeare through Eliot's lifetime in a workmanlike essay for *Criticism* ("T. S. Eliot and Shakespeare," 1967). Through the twenties, says Marcus, Eliot was repelled by the form and philosophy of much of Shakespeare's work, a dissatisfaction "considerably aggravated by his turning during the 1920's to Catholicism and its greatest poet, Dante" (p. 68). This personal response accounts not only for the famous essay on *Hamlet* but for the grudging character of Eliot's praise of Shakespeare in the early criticism. Only such a personal response can explain the acute critic in Eliot, responding so favorably to J. M. Robertson's efforts to explain away much of the Shakespearean canon as non-Shakespearean. The turning point is marked by Eliot's introduction to G. Wilson Knight's *The*

Wheel of Fire (1930). Knight seems to have turned Eliot's interest to the patterning of symbols in Shakespeare and enabled him to accept much of what he earlier thought irrelevant material. A reference in Knight may have led Eliot to another book he mentions in his introduction to Knight's book, Colin Still's *Shakespeare's Mystery Play* (1921). He might have read Still earlier—even have found in him hints for the connection of *The Tempest* with mystery cults and other elements of *The Waste Land*—but it would seem to be Knight who led him to accept the sort of argument Still advanced. His references to Shakespeare increasingly stressed the positive, even to the point of contradicting his earlier views; an example of this is his praise, in "Poetry and Drama," of a speech by Horatio (in *Hamlet*) which he had earlier singled out for condemnation.

However callow the later Eliot may have thought them, it was his early essays on Shakespeare which have had the greatest influence. C. B. Watson's discussion, "T. S. Eliot and the Interpretation of Shakespearian Tragedy in Our Time" (1964), also stresses the ideological roots of Eliot's early strictures on Shakespeare. Eliot's insistence that Shakespeare had no philosophy, or an inferior philosophy, and Eliot's alleged aversion to the self-glorification of Shakespearean heroes are traced by Watson to Eliot's ignorance of and bias against Renaissance humanism. Since Marcus and Watson seem to have reached agreement on this point independently, one hesitates to disagree, but it seems odd that Eliot's references to Shakespeare should have grown more favorable even as his commitment to Anglicanism (and Dante) deepened. If Marcus can find Eliot's receptiveness to Robertson's arguments surprising, his openness to the wildly subjective prose of G. Wilson Knight seems even more so. Eliot's suggestion that one appreciates Shakespeare more as one matures seems less problematic.

Watson, as it happens, devotes little time to Eliot's changes of opinions. Though he recognizes that Eliot was not guilty of all the sins of those who were influenced by him, Watson wants to hold Eliot responsible nevertheless. He notes that Eliot's endorsement of Knight's book was duly guarded, but then writes as though Eliot had single-handedly encouraged the further development of subjectivist interpretation. Often enough, Watson quotes some critical outrage, quotes Eliot in support of his own position, and then condemns Eliot for having given rise to such thinking. Anyone who has undertaken to survey recent interpretations of a given author (Eliot, for example) can sympathize with Watson's dismay, but Eliot surely does not deserve all the blame for what one finds.

James Torrens has written two essays on this topic: "T. S. Eliot and Shakespeare: 'This Music Crept By' " (1971b) and "Eliot's Poetry and the Incubus of Shakespeare" (1977). Although the two essays are genuinely independent, they share a common stress on the personal, as opposed to the ideological, sources of Eliot's early resistance to Shakespeare. In the 1971 essay, for example, Torrens notes that Eliot found less of that sense of decadence which made the later Elizabethans fit his purpose and that he remained somewhat "overawed" (p. 81) by him—wary of a potentially overwhelming influence, uncertain that he could do him critical justice. In the 1977 essay, Torrens says that Shakespeare "intimidated Eliot, though he enticed him too, by his greatness" (p. 407). Although recognizing the thoroughness of Marcus' survey, Torrens says that he hopes his own 1971 essay will show "the richness and complexity even of Eliot's earlier feeling toward Shakespeare" (1971b, p. 83n), and it does so.

The genuineness of Eliot's attraction to Shakespeare is attested by his repeated use of Shakespeare in his work, especially during the very period when his published views of Shakespeare were most critical. Both of Torrens' essays touch on this. The 1971 essay has some particularly interesting remarks on Eliot's "fascination with the late romances" (p. 94), with their music and their achieved serenity. The 1977 essay is mainly devoted to the poetry. Torrens suggests that, though Eliot may have seen Hamlet partly through the eyes of Laforgue, "in reminding his character Prufrock that he is not Prince Hamlet, Eliot reminds himself, with a smile, that he is not quite Shakespeare" (1977, p. 410). Most attracted to those plays of Shakespeare which seemed relevant to his own inner turmoil, Eliot may well have been tempted to identify himself with Hamlet's apparent ambivalence toward women, Torrens suggests; so Eliot's comments on Shakespeare's failure to objectify his feelings might be almost autobiographical. Much of Torrens' essay reviews the Shakespearean echoes in *The Waste Land*, particularly the references to *The Tempest*, a story of "mock drowning" which becomes " a ceremony of renewal" and reconciliation (p. 412). Torrens' 1977 essay provides a useful and sometimes original survey of the many Shakespearean echoes and allusions one may find in Eliot's poetry.

The *Hamlet* reference in "The Love Song of J. Alfred Prufrock" is quite possibly the most-discussed Shakespearean passage in Eliot. One major question is what sort of figure Prufrock has in mind for himself. The most usual conclusion is found in Grover Smith's volume: "he confesses that he is only a pompous fool, a Polonius instead of a Hamlet (and recognizing this fact, partly a wise Fool too)" (1974, p. 17). Among those who disagree, we may cite Robert Fleissner's argument, in "Prufrock Not the Polonius Type" (1975), that Prufrock more closely resembles the foolish Osric than Polonius. Fleissner argues that Polonius is neither "obtuse" nor a "fool," but it is quite conceivable that Prufrock thinks of Polonius in just such terms.

Similarly, Ian S. Dunn argues that Prufrock is "not a Fool, but a fool" (1963), a failed "proof-rock" who cannot function in Touchstone's role as a social critic. Dunn's view seems less subtle than Prufrock's description of himself as "almost, at times, the Fool." Although readers of Eliot's poem who are also familiar with Shakespeare are bound to find such associations coming to mind, one wonders whether any attempt to pin down exact analogues for Prufrock (even Polonius) adds much to what the passage itself tells us about his self-image.

Touchstone reappears in John M. Major's attempt to find a connection in "Eliot's 'Gerontion' and *As You Like It*" (1959), where Gerontion's "dry brain" is traced to Jacques's description of Touchstone's "brain" as "dry as the remainder biscuit / after a voyage." This would seem to be one of those possible sources which do not function as allusions; Major himself claims no more than that "the dry-brained Touchstone and the melancholy Jacques" and the play they appear in were part of many Elizabethan plays in Eliot's mind when he wrote "Gerontion" (p. 30). Although the epigraph, taken from *Measure for Measure*, is relevant to the poem, its context does not seem to be, and the same can be said for the other Shakespearean echoes which have been found in this poem.

The *Tempest* references in *The Waste Land*, acknowledged in the notes, certainly function as allusions for those familiar with the Shakespeare play. Moreover, they help connect the first three parts of the poem with part IV, "Death by Water"— "Those are pearls that were his eyes." Those critics who follow Eliot's notes naturally tend to blend the figure of Ferdinand with that of the quester-hero; if it is correct to assume that Eliot had in mind Still's association of *The Tempest* with old mysteries, this blending acquires a further justification. Because these echoes recur throughout the poem, it may be only reasonable to allow our sense of *The Tempest* as a whole to affect our reading of *The Waste Land*—Smith, for example, writes that the speaker of the poem "can expect, if not the joy of Ferdinand, then at any rate the liberation of Prospero" (1974, p. 98). On the other hand, the efforts of Torrens (1977) to find additional specific references to *The Tempest* in part V of *The Waste Land* (e.g., Ferdinand's "controlling hands") seem unnecessary; Torrens himself does not press them very far.

The other Shakespearean plays whose echoes may be found in *The Waste Land* do not seem to have the same kind of range of reference. The opening passage of "A Game of Chess" is obviously modeled on the passage of *Antony and Cleopatra* cited in Eliot's notes. The passage is a familiar one and presumably functions as an allusion for many readers. The presence of Philomel and other resemblances have encouraged a number of critics to find an echo of *Cymbeline* (act II, scenes 2 and 4). Although the *Cymbeline* passages may well have been in Eliot's mind, their utility as allusions is less certain, and the alleged contrast with the chaste Imogene makes an uneasy blend with the contrast with the sensuous Cleopatra. Even less convincing is Harry M. Schwalb's attempt to find in the scenes from *Antony and Cleopatra* a conscious model for the whole of Eliot's "A Game of Chess" (1953), when all that Schwalb can show is some very loose analogies.

A number of critics have traced the title of Eliot's "The Hollow Men" to *Julius Caesar* (IV, ii), where the phrase occurs in a speech by Brutus, even though this involves rejecting Eliot's account of its sources. The identification goes back at least to George Williamson's *A Reader's Guide to T. S. Eliot* (1953). A part of section V, directly based on a line of Valery, also recalls an earlier speech by Brutus (*Julius Caesar*, II, i): "Between the acting of a dreadful thing / And the first motion, all the interim is / Like a phantasm"—lines Eliot quoted in an introduction to a book of Valery's. The Shakespearean part of this connection was noted as early as 1950 by Paul Fussell, Jr. ("A Note on 'The Hollow Men' "). The most complete argument for the relevance of these resemblances is Sydney J. Krause's "Hollow Men and False Horses" (1960). Krause contends that Eliot's poem is "fairly riddled with . . . ironies which, hanging just below the surface, are easily nudged into realization if one has in mind the stress Brutus places on pretentiousness and self-deceit" (p. 371). That Brutus stresses "self-deceit" is not at all clear, however, particularly in the passages which are said to serve as sources for "The Hollow Men." Krause's subsequent interpretation of Eliot's poem is defensible, but it owes little to the alleged allusions to *Julius Caesar.*

At least twice, Eliot used Shakespearean situations as points of departure: in the Coriolan poems (already discussed) and in "Marina." In the latter, Eliot takes from Shakespeare's *Pericles* the scene in which the shipwrecked Pericles finds that he is reunited with his daughter, Marina. As Elspeth Cameron has noted, Eliot's view and use of the Shakespeare play owes a great deal to the Shakespeare criticism of G. Wilson Knight, "both in its emphasis on the transcendental quality and in its special concern with the recognition scenes" ("T. S. Eliot's 'Marina': An Exploration," 1970, p. 181). A very different kind of recognition scene is suggested by the Senecan epigraph, but no critical effort to make use of the epigraph in interpreting the poem has yet justified itself. The relevance of *Pericles* seems more certain; it explains the poem's title and shipwreck imagery. That is, however, a very limited kind of relevance, since the identity of Marina with the daughter addressed is probably clear enough without the Shakespearean association, and the sea imagery is self-justifying.

Paul J. Dolan's "Eliot's 'Marina': A Reading" (1969) describes the spiritual movement of the poem without reference to *Pericles*, and Harold Cook's sensitive reading concludes that the debt to Shakespeare does not go beyond the "initial mood, certain parallel images, and the search for an ideal Marina which suggests the search of Pericles for his daughter Marina" ("A Search for the Ideal: An Interpretation of T. S. Eliot's 'Marina,' " 1954).

There are several reasons why it seems better to view *Pericles* as simply a point of departure for Eliot than as a sustained allusion, though the latter course is adopted by Elspeth Cameron (1970), Grover Smith (1974), and W. J. Barnes ("T. S. Eliot's 'Marina': Image and Symbol," 1963). The first is that thinking of the speaker of the poem as Pericles involves the reader in referring to an imagined situation which is not part of the poem itself. The second is that the *Pericles* which serves as a point of departure is G. Wilson Knight's and thus at least one degree removed from Shakespeare's. A third is that critics who persist in carrying the Periclean connection through the poem seem led to find further allusions in unconvincing analogies. And a final, rather debatable argument is that allusions to *Pericles*, a work not really part of normal tradition, lack the justification that attaches to allusions to a *Hamlet* or a *Divine Comedy*. Other things being equal, one ought to prefer interpretations which do not rely on such allusions.

Rather similar conclusions may apply to Eliot's use of less important Elizabethans. There is no doubt of Eliot's interest in these writers, recorded in many of his early essays. Nor is there any doubt that he learned from them. The verse of "Gerontion," in particular, shows how he worked to master the rhythms of their dramatic verse. "Gerontion" is, moreover, a tissue of quotations and paraphrase of Elizabethan verse, and many similar debts are owed in *The Waste Land*. Eliot's poetry has done almost as much as his criticism to send later critics searching through the dramas of obscure Elizabethans. Our knowledge of his sources has gone far beyond that provided by the notes to *The Waste Land*. Few of the newly found sources, however, are essential to our understanding of Eliot's poetry, and most do not even function as the sort of incidental allusion which heightens the pleasure of the reader who recognizes it. The critical tendency to overrate such discoveries threatens to reduce Eliot's poetry to its sources.

As an example, we may take I. B. Cauthen's discovery in "Another Webster Allusion in *The Waste Land*" (1958). The repeated "nothings" in "A Game of Chess" recall Lear and Ophelia to Smith, but Cauthen believes that he has found "a close verbal echo" (p. 498) in *The White Devil* (V, vi), where a character, asked what he is thinking responds:

> Nothing; of nothing: leave thy idle questions,
> I am ith way to study a long silence,
> To prate were idle, I remember nothing.
> Thers nothing of so infinite vexation
> As mans own thoughts.

Although the echo is not very close, it is closer than Lear or Ophelia, and it is from a scene that Eliot himself cites in one of his (less relevant) notes.

Cauthen later reported that Eliot himself had "no doubt that the page from Webster's play was at the back of my mind" ("An Unpublished Letter by T. S. Eliot [1962]," 1978, p. 22). But if we agree that this was a source—perhaps one of many—are we also to take it as an allusion, a case in which the poem's "texture is enriched by the connotations which the allusion brings" (1958, p. 499)? It is hard to see why. The similarities suggested are very general—both men "have come to this inarticulate state through their association with women" (p. 499)—and so are the contrasts. Although *The White Devil* is not an obscure play, this passage is neither well known nor particularly striking. Cauthen may have found his reading of Eliot's poem enriched by the train of associations set off by recollection of the Webster passage, but he does not make a convincing case that this is, or should be, the case for other readers.

Critics have found Eliot borrowing from a surprising number of Elizabethan authors, but few such borrowings function as allusions which the reader must grasp to understand the poem, as one must, perhaps, with the *Hamlet* reference in "The Love Song of J. Alfred Prufrock" or even the *Tempest* references in *The Waste Land*. The greater weight given the Shakespearean references reflects his more central place in the English poetic tradition, which Eliot never denied, however grudging some of his acknowledgments may have been. It is true, of course, that in his criticism Eliot did much to reshape our understanding of that tradition. As part of that reshaping he brought new attention to dramatists whose merits had been overshadowed by Shakespeare; in other periods of English literature, Eliot's reshaping of the tradition took a more revolutionary turn.

The Reshaper of Tradition

In recent years there has been something of a reaction against the conventional view of Eliot as the reshaper of this century's sense of the English poetic tradition. His praise of the Metaphysicals, we are told, was not original and reflected his misunderstanding of them and their time. His denigration of Milton was less severe than sometimes believed and reflected his immediate concerns with technique. In reacting against the Romantics and Victorians, Eliot simply reflected his age, which was itself simply sharing in the usual reaction of any generation of vigorous poets against the manner and methods of their immediate predecessors. As we shall see, there is a good deal of truth in all this. As the leading poet-critic of his age, Eliot has often been singled out as a representative figure and his views given more weight than they, perhaps, deserve. Separating the influence of his contributions from the influence of others is often very difficult; a good deal is apt to depend on the relative weight one in general assigns "great men," as opposed to the

Zeitgeist. But Eliot *was* the leading poet-critic of his age; opinions he shared and even took from others acquired special authority for many when he expressed them. Leaving aside, for the moment, the complicated question of his relation to the Romantics and Victorians, Eliot must still be held to have had considerable impact on poetic fashions in his time.

For the Metaphysical poets in particular, it seems clear that a number of critics were led to these poets by Eliot and read them in the light of his work. When a critic like Cleanth Brooks sets out to demonstrate the relationship of modern poetry to the tradition, he has in mind a tradition, shaped by Eliot's criticism, in which the Metaphysicals play an important part. That Eliot's opinions were derived from Grierson hardly matters in such a case. One American scholar-critic, especially interested in the Donne tradition, George Williamson, has also written extensively (and perhaps better) on Eliot. The first and better part of Williamson's 1927 *Sewanee Review* essay, "The Talent of T. S. Eliot" (printed separately in 1929), is devoted to a comparison of Eliot and Donne, considerably exaggerating their points of resemblance in use of erudition, diction, kinds of conceits, meter, and, of course, unified sensibility. The difficulty is that Donne comes out looking very much like a seventeenth-century Eliot, an error which may be said to have originated with Eliot.

This tradition in Donne and Eliot criticism lasted some time, though never without its scholarly opponents. It can be seen, for example, in David Morris's *The Poetry of Gerard Manley Hopkins and T. S. Eliot in the Light of the Donne Tradition* (1953). Morris treats Hopkins and Eliot separately, and so contributes to the comparative study of those two authors, but he contributes little that is new. He is no more able than most to disentangle the Donne corpus from the Metaphysicals in general as a source for Eliot, and, as he recognizes, he treats as similarities many technical devices which Eliot, like the Metaphysicals, took from other sources, notably the late Elizabethans. In one of the last gasps of this vein of criticism, Sunil Kanti Sen sees a deep kinship in his *Metaphysical Tradition and T. S. Eliot* (1965). This is not surprising, since he sees the Metaphysicals very much through Eliot's eyes. Eliot resembles Donne, in particular, because of his erudition, his condensed style, and his ability to combine thought, feeling, and wit. Sen recognizes that Eliot's style is more "elliptical" (p. 116) than Donne's and finds him less personal as well, probably a sign that he reads Eliot, too, through the lens of Eliot's criticism.

It would, of course, be absurd to assume that the Metaphysicals had remained unread and unloved between the time that Samuel Johnson ruled them out of the English poetic tradition and the time that T. S. Eliot ruled them central to it. Mary Thale, for example, has found remarkable agreement in "T. S. Eliot and Mrs. Browning on the Metaphysical Poets" (1968). Thale calls attention to a series of essays in which Mrs. Browning anticipated Eliot in holding "that English poetry progressed until the late seventeenth century, when it deviated from its true path" (p. 255). The Metaphysicals figure in her scheme as the last flowering of Elizabethan greatness. Although the very idea has a certain perverse appeal, it does not seem, as Thale suggests, "possible that Eliot adopted" his views from those of Elizabeth Barrett Browning, but her study says something about the lack of originality of Eliot's formulation and about the affinity of his sensibility with some Victorians. Thale may have reason to wonder whether "just as Mrs. Browning extended the Elizabethan era fifty years beyond that queen, a later generation will extend the Victorian era by so much—or more" (p. 258).

By the turn of the century, interest in Donne and the Metaphysicals was growing. Herbert Grierson's critical edition of Donne in 1912 and his Metaphysical anthology, which occasioned Eliot's famous 1921 essay, were themselves products of a gradual alteration in opinion through the nineteenth century. Reviewing over fifty items in which Eliot comments on Donne, E. P. Bollier has concluded that "Eliot has said little about Donne specifically, and most of what he has said is commonplace" ("T. S. Eliot and John Donne: A Problem in Criticism," 1959, p. 104). Bollier does not deny that Eliot helped promote the Donne revival, but he suggests that Eliot also made use of it, needing a major English nondramatic poet to serve as a counterexample in his attack on other established reputations. Eliot's cooler tone toward Donne later thus reflects his decreased need to use Donne as a critical weapon, along with his own genuine distaste for aspects of Donne's work.

Bollier's essay is complemented by Elsie Leach's exploration of Eliot's changing attitudes toward the other Metaphysicals ("T. S. Eliot and the School of Donne," 1972). Not surprisingly, Leach concludes that "the changing emphases of Eliot's criticism parallel developments in his own verse" (p. 163). Leach gives special attention to the steady rise of George Herbert's verse in Eliot's estimation, which is traced "to the fact that his later poetry has certain affinities with Herbert's (whereas it was never much like Donne's)" (p. 175). Leach also shows that Eliot's changing views reflected in part the various scholars he relied on at different periods—when Eliot was most influenced by Mario Praz's work, Crashaw received high praise.

To be fair to Eliot, it must be observed that surveys like Bollier's and Leach's reveal little beyond what Eliot himself has said about his changing critical opinions, Eliot having spent much of his last twenty years as a critic qualifying the confident generalizations he made in his first few years. In "To Criticize the Critic" (1961) and in the book of the same title (1965), Eliot acknowledges some of those whose advocacy of Donne preceded his own, says whatever influence his own advocacy may have had was due to the age's taste for his poetry (and thus those poets it may have resembled), and notes that he now reads Herbert more than Donne. Such changes, Eliot says, "[do] not necessarily involve a judgment of relative greatness; it is merely that what has best responded to my need in middle and later age is different from the nourishment I needed in youth" (1965, p. 23).

In "To Criticize the Critic," Eliot says that even his critical generalizations "had their origin in my sensibility," for example, " 'dissociation of sensibility' may represent my devotion to Donne and the metaphysical poets, and my reaction against Milton" (1965, p. 20). Eliot's dictum that some unfortunate bifurcation of thought and feeling took place after the Metaphysicals has had a lively critical life of its own, perhaps aided by the very looseness of Eliot's usage, which has allowed "dissociation of sensibility" to be applied to a variety of phenomena. F. M. Kuna's "T. S. Eliot's Dissociation of Sensibility and the Critics of Metaphysical Poetry" (1963), however, is primarily an all-out attack on the doctrines found in Eliot's 1921 essay on the Metaphysicals, all of which, says Kuna, "can be applied adequately only to modern poetry" (p. 248). Kuna does not cite Frank Kermode's *Romantic Image* (1957), but his position is not unlike Kermode's. Kermode sees Eliot as very much within the Romantic and Symbolist tradition. "Dissociation of sensibility" and the rest of Eliot's comments on Donne are thus part of the modern poet's search for a golden age in which the conditions that affect him did not exist.

Studies like this are probably correct in seeing "dissociation of sensibility" as an unhistorical doctrine that says more about Eliot's time than about Donne's. To the extent that they encourage us to see Eliot as simply projecting his own ideals upon Donne and the Metaphysicals, however, they are as misleading as those studies which read Donne only through Eliot's eyes. Much of what Eliot says about the Metaphysicals, after all, was based on scholars like Grierson, who also praised the Metaphysicals' combination of argument and emotion and their passionate thought. If the tradition of Donne criticism on which Eliot relied overemphasized such features and the striking conceits which seemed to exemplify them, it was partly because the Donne revival felt the need to defend those features of the Metaphysicals which Johnson had denounced. What we have in this case, is another conflict in temperament between those who delight in perceiving similarities and those who delight in making distinctions. Eliot uses the rhetoric of fine distinctions, but his critical imagination is most stirred by similarities to his own poetic concerns, as in the Metaphysicals. When Eliot speaks of the tradition as having one simultaneous existence, he naturally invites correction from those who stress the "pastness" of the past. But to enlist wholeheartedly on one side or another of such debates is to sacrifice part of the truth about our relation to history, and it would be a pity if the critical pendulum now swung in that direction.

The most significant of Eliot's borrowings from the Metaphysicals are covered in Grover Smith's volume. Most are simply sources. A few, like the Marvell reference in *Waste Land III*, are incidental allusions; in that case, the ironic contrasts implied are in the rhythm of the lines, but certainly more vivid for the reader who recalls "To His Coy Mistress." Three critics have labored to establish a relationship between Marvell's "The Garden" and Eliot's "Gerontion": Edgar F. Daniels ("Eliot's 'Gerontion,' " 1959), Elsie Leach (" 'Gerontion' and Marvell's 'The Garden,' " 1975), and John J. Pollock (" 'Gerontion' and 'The Garden': Another Perspective," 1977). They do not agree on the interpretive significance of this source, and their arguments that it is a source are weak.

In Eliot's 1921 review-essay on the Metaphysicals, Milton appears as one of those to blame for "dissociation of sensibility," and Eliot's later conversion to Anglicanism did little to increase his taste for Milton's Puritanism. By 1947, however, Eliot explains his earlier condemnations of Milton as necessitated by his generation's efforts to develop a more colloquial diction for poetry. Milton's influence would have been baneful then, but other virtues might make his poetry useful now. As E. P. Bollier notes, the strictures against imitating Milton's verse remain in effect ("T. S. Eliot and John Milton: A Problem in Criticism," 1958). Bollier sees Eliot's eventual recognition as consistent with his long-held principles. Less charitably, William York Tindall ("The Recantation of T. S. Eliot," 1947) describes it as "less confession than rationalization" (p. 436).

Tindall goes on to suggest that Eliot's 1947 position is meant to give the reader a clue to the Miltonic qualities of *Four Quartets,* where Eliot freely indulges in the poetry of statement, with little regard for the old requirement that thought and feeling be fused. B. Rajan's "Milton and Eliot: A Twentieth-Century Acknowledgment" (1978) also stresses the resemblances between Milton and the later Eliot, bolstering them by finding Miltonic echoes in *Four Quartets.* Eliot's notes to *The Waste Land* cite an incidental allusion to *Paradise Lost;* and Robert J. Andreach, encouraged by Eliot's "recantation," has argued for much larger correspondences in his "*Paradise Lost* and the Christian Configuration of *The Waste Land*" (1969). Taking a suggestion of Genesius Jones, Andreach identifies "the young man carbuncular" of *Waste Land III* with Milton's Satan in *Paradise Lost.* The hyacinth garden naturally is seen as echoing the lost Eden, and this and the typist scene are pictured as the pivotal scenes of Eliot's poem. Andreach's approach is less arbitrary than this summary may suggest, but his argument is much less convincing than Rajan's more modest efforts to show Miltonic echoes in *Four Quartets.* Even in the latter case, Milton's presence does not seem very significant, but perhaps is enough to demonstrate again that Eliot's changing critical positions reflect his poet's workshop.

Milton's relation to Eliot is only one of a number of topics dealt with in Helen Gardner's 1965 pamphlet, *T. S. Eliot and the English Poetic Tradition.* Gardner speaks of Eliot's kinship with Milton and Pope, "great literary poets, poets whose minds are stored with poetry, who deliberately borrow, reflect or imitate, and also unconsciously find words finely used before them the right words for their purpose" (p. 9). He is like Pope, too, in composing in snatches; thought of as a Classical and intellectual poet, Eliot almost always begins with fragments of intensely realized moments. Finally, Eliot resembles Pope in coming "at the close of a long period of brilliant and irregular genius" (p. 12). Since Gardner's lecture, the publication of *The Waste Land* manuscript, with its long-cancelled passage in heroic couplets, suggests that Eliot admired and worked to master some of Pope's technical effects. The possible echoes of Pope which have been found in his finished poems, however, are not very important. As examples of such sources (without much interpretative bearing) we may cite Jeffrey Hart's attribution of "patched and peeled" in Eliot's "Gerontion" to Pope's "peel'd, patch'd" in *The Dunciad* (III, 115) ("T. S. Eliot: His Use of Wycherley and Pope," 1957) and Jae Ho Lee's parallel between "East Coker IV" and some lines from Pope's "Essay on Man" ("Alexander Pope in Eliot's 'East Coker,' " 1963).

Of the other eighteenth-century writers, it appears that Eliot himself has confirmed the presence of "The Ghost of Swift in *Four Quartets*" (Maurice Johnson, 1949), making the ghost of "Little Gidding" more "compound" than ever. George T. Wright's "Eliot Written in a Country Churchyard: The Elegy and *Four Quartets*" (1976) argues that Gray's poem is "a possible base from which Eliot evolved *Four Quartets*" (p. 228). Wright's parallels show that *Four Quartets* can be seen as part of a tradition which includes Gray's poem and that Eliot shares certain qualities with Gray. To assume that Gray's poem was Eliot's model, however, would be to ignore most of what we know about the process of the composition of the *Four Quartets*.

Looking at the criticism, then, we are left with an Eliot who was Elizabethan and Metaphysical in his youth, Miltonic and "eighteenth century" in his later years—changes in his poetry reflected to some extent in his critical prose. That his writings on the English literary tradition generally reflected his current poetic concerns does not diminish their interest or validity, despite some *ad hominem* criticism they have received. That he has been found to reflect so many periods of English literature, at one time or another, may suggest that his poetry was more important than his prose in reshaping our sense of that tradition, to the point where we find shadows of Eliot in much of the past.

Reluctant Romantic, Last Victorian

Eliot is now part of our tradition. For those of us who do not share his vision of the tradition existing in some simultaneous present, Eliot figures in our past as the successor of those Romantics and Victorians he so often seemed to condemn. Eliot had been raised on their verses but thought to put them by on reaching maturity. But their imprint can still be found on his criticism and his poetry. Our increased sense of the personal element in Eliot's work makes it easier to relate him to his nineteenth-century predecessors, but the simple passage of time probably plays at least as important a role. Posterity almost always tends to "smooth out" the past, to group together men who thought themselves opposed and to speak of continuities where contemporaries saw sharp breaks. There is a danger in this of losing sight of the qualities that made Eliot's verse seem shocking and that still are vital to our experience of it—but this is a danger of all attempts to relate Eliot to poetic tradition. If we are to see him as a "traditional" poet at all, it is important to see him in relation to the Romantics and Victorians.

While Helen Gardner's pamphlet *T. S. Eliot and the English Poetic Tradition* (1965) speaks of Eliot's kinship with Milton and Pope, Gardner also stresses his relation to nineteenth-century poetry. Eliot's overt rejection of this poetry, she suggests, results partly from his efforts to come to terms with an inheritance which affected him deeply. The nineteenth century was a period of great "thumpers," and poets like Swinburne and Kipling had an uneasy fascination for Eliot; he sought a counter-music in the French Symbolists. Nevertheless, Eliot's poems ring with occasional strong lines or passages with an insistent triple pulse, as in "we have lingered in the chambers of the sea." When Eliot uses four strong stresses, he breaks them with a marked caesura—"Being read to by a boy, waiting for rain." The power of strong stresses is more easily admitted into his later poetry. Gardner finds Eliot's diction like Browning's in its ability to use the full range of the language, from colloquial to pedantic words, though she does not suggest Browning as an influence. Eliot is also characterized as being, particularly in *Four Quartets*, "a master of the distinctly English poetry of mood as expressed through images of place" (p. 24), a vein of poetry especially common in the great Victorians. In the hands of Gardner, such comparisons do not diminish the individuality of the poets involved; they help us see Eliot's poetic manner as partly a development of his predecessors'.

Eliot plays two roles in George Bornstein's study, *Transformations of Romanticism in Yeats, Eliot, and Stevens* (1976). As a critic, Eliot's role is largely negative: "In creating a literary theory to justify modern poetry, Eliot read his objections to the late, decadent romanticism that surrounded him back into the early, strong variety," achieving a victory "won at the cost of warping literary history" (p. 15). But the poet's quarrel with Romanticism is seen as more complex, part of an internal war. The creative imagination exalted by the Romantics is associated by Eliot with sexual drives and other internal forces that threaten to disrupt the personality and must be controlled with external constraints–irony, distance, dogma. Eliot was thus Romantic in spite of himself, illustrating his comment (on Baudelaire) that poets in a Romantic age could be anti-Romantic only in tendency. Bornstein sees "The Love Song of J. Alfred Prufrock" as a deliberate anti-image of Eliot's previous neo-Romantic efforts. In other useful remarks, Bornstein shows how the Romantic "imagination" is present, devalued and regretted, in "La Figlia che Piange"; how close "Gerontion" comes to the Romantic lyric; how Shelley influenced "Sweeney Erect"; and how the *Four Quartets* are designed to wait "for imagination to erupt" and to catch such upheavals in "a context of restraint" (p. 153). The advantage of Bornstein's approach is that it identifies some of the Romantic elements in Eliot without losing sight of his ambivalence toward them.

Although Gardner and Bornstein have good reason to stress the personal reasons for Eliot's apparent rejection of Romanticism, it should be recalled that Romanticism poses real theoretical difficulties, some of which are at the heart of the issues Frank Kermode discusses in *The Romantic Image* (1957). These difficulties were bound to emerge as its implications were worked out, and could hardly escape the attention of a pupil of Irving Babbitt, whose anti-Romanticism is currently unfashionable but hardly disproved. If Eliot was Romantic because he could not help but be, it is at least possible that he was anti-Romantic because he thought he should be.

Narrower in focus than Gardner or Bornstein but similar in conclusions is A. Walton Litz's " 'That Strange Abstraction, "Nature" ': T. S. Eliot's Victorian Inheritance" (1977). Litz suggests that Eliot can be seen as "an heir of the nineteenth century, one of the 'last Victorians' " (p. 471). Eliot's apprentice work was pseudo-Victorian, and rejecting it entailed rejecting them. The early Eliot thus appears as a special construct, anti-Victorian out of personal and poetic needs. The later Eliot, adopting the role of a Victorian sage and moving toward landscape poetry, was more generous to the Victorians in his criticism and more like them in his poetry. Of special interest is

Litz's careful tracing of revisions through the years in Eliot's essay, on Tennyson's *In Memoriam* as a sign of his increasing sympathy with Tennyson and his age. Litz's stress on Eliot's likeness to the Victorians is valuable, so long as we do not think of the Victorians in terms of the stereotypes Eliot helped promote.

When we look at Eliot's relationships with particular writers, he certainly seems closer to the Victorians than to the earlier Romantics. Despite the respect Eliot sometimes shows for Coleridge's criticsm, for example, efforts to show direct influence have not been convincing. Attempts to find Coleridge echoes in Eliot's creative work are even less so—for example, Mary Ellen Rickey's " 'Christabel' and 'Murder in the Cathedral' " (1963). Florence Marsh's "The Ocean Desert: *The Ancient Mariner* and *The Waste Land*" (1959) is a purely comparative study. Marsh finds both poems concerned with the need for rebirth, but she thinks Coleridge "wiser" in seeing the need for rebirth as something rare, where Eliot sees it as universal. Without suggesting that Eliot was a secret Pentacostalist, one may observe that his is a perfectly orthodox Christian position and that the experience of being "born again" is much more common than Marsh thinks.

Wordsworth, too, has enough points of resemblance with Eliot to allow critics to write comparative essays. Marion Montgomery's *T. S. Eliot: An Essay on the American Magus* (1969) suggests the influence of Wordsworth, along with Browning and even E. A. Robinson, so that Eliot is both "our greatest intellectual poet" and, "perhaps, our greatest romantic poet" (p. 1). Montgomery's graceful prose makes his many publications on Eliot pleasant reading, but his argument here is not persuasive. Although the likenesses he points to do not support a claim of influence, they do suggest Eliot's kinship with the Romantic tradition. In another survey, "The Romantic Tradition: Wordsworth and T. S. Eliot" (1959), James Benziger notes that both poets began as poetic revolutionists, reforming poetic diction. The *Prelude and Four Quartets* are also said to comment "upon each other" (p. 277)—no doubt another sign of Wordsworth's prescience. Admitting that differences exist, Benziger concentrates on resemblances between the religious sensibilities reflected in their poetry. Both Montgomery and Benziger seem to regard as relatively minor differences which Eliot took much more seriously. This is not necessarily unfair, and may be said to illustrate the tendency of posterity to accent continuities; but without any historical framework, such comparative studies do not get us very far.

Some of the connecting links between Wordsworth and Eliot are given in Christoper Clausen's "Tintern Abbey to Little Gidding: The Past Recaptured" (1976), which opens with the memorable suggestion that "much of the most important Victorian and twentieth-century English poetry is a search for Wordsworth's childhood" (p. 406). Clausen examines lost churches, lost faiths, and lost childhoods as they appear in various verses from "Tintern Abbey" to "Little Gidding." Clausen seems to think that the latter poem has brought the quest to an end by solving the original problem; if such quests are done with, it is more likely to be a sign that the long Age of Romanticism is over, and that is by no means as certain as some critics believe. But Clausen does not press his argument too far; his essay is refreshingly free of the oppressive solemnity which afflicts criticism of both Wordsworth and Eliot.

Alice Levine's comparative essay, "T. S. Eliot and Byron" (1978), is at its best in pointing to the ambivalent character of Byron's Romanticism and Eliot's Classicism, and her extended comparison of *The Waste Land* with *Childe Harold's Pilgrimage* as quest poems is of some interest. She says that "Byron's guards against direct expression—his ironic stance, the abundantly allusive and satiric content of *Childe Harold* and *Don Juan* (poems principally of self-revelation) and his method of dramatic poses and self-contradicting voices—betray the incipience of a problem, as well as its poetic solution, that in the twentieth century would even more intensely affect us, affecting our relation to words themselves" (p. 538). Levine's study thus goes beyond a simple comparison of two writers and casts light on their relation to a common tradition.

Robert Langbaum's *The Poetry of Experience* (1957) identifies the problem as our old friend, "dissociation of sensibility," which he blames on Newton and Locke rather than on Milton and Dryden. Whatever the merits of this diagnosis, Langbaum is probably on sound ground in seeing in dramatic lyrics (like those of Byron) the precursors of the dramatic monologues with which his book deals. Eliot plays a fairly important role in Langbaum's book, being identified as the most innovative twentieth-century exponent of this tradition. Langbaum is well aware of the differences between Eliot and poets like Browning, and he spends little time on questions of influence. It is possible, after all, that Eliot's most important model was the Elizabethan drama's soliloquy, itself an important model for the Victorians. Langbaum's book, nevertheless, indicates one important respect in which Eliot's poetry can be seen as a natural development from that of the great Victorians. A. N. Kincaid's "The Dramatic Monologue: Eliot's Debt to Browning" (1972) makes some of the same points, without citing Langbaum. It does not carry out its implicit promise to demonstrate Eliot's "debt" to Browning, nor does it give adequate recognition to other nineteenth-century dramatic monologues.

Although Eliot may seem to us to have a number of points in common with Robert Browning, who was also a "difficult" poet in his time, the only certain use of Browning in Eliot's work is the quotation from "A Toccata of Galuppi's," which forms part of the mélange of Venetian references serving as an epigraph to Eliot's "Burbank with a Baedeker: Bleistein with a Cigar." Stephen Brown's attempt to connect the same Browning poem with "The Love Song of J. Alfred Prufrock" rests on no more than a series of superficial parallels between the two dramatic monologues ("A Reader's Note on Similarities between Browning's 'A Toccata of Galuppi's' and Eliot's 'The Love Song of J. Alfred Prufrock,' " 1977). Much the same can be said of Martin Puhvel's attempt vis-à-vis Childe Roland, "Reminiscent Bells in *The Waste Land*" (1965). Even less justification exists for James F. Loucks' attribution in "A Second Browning Allusion in Eliot's 'Burbank' Poem" (1976a), which engages in excesses of interpretation on the basis of the similarity between Eliot's "but this or such was Burbank's way" and Browning's "and this, or something like it, was his way" ("How It Strikes a Contemporary"). The similarities noted by Harold F. Brooks in " 'The Family Reunion' and 'Colombe's Birthday' " (1952) would not suggest a significant influence of Browning's play on Eliot's, even if they were more certain. Christopher D. Murray's suggestion in "A Source for 'Prufrock'?" (1978) of a letter of Elizabeth Barrett Browning rests on closer verbal parallels than most of the Robert Browning sources suggested, although even this has no interpretative significance.

Tennyson echoes in Eliot's poetry are better attested. The most convincing can be found in Grover Smith's book, but few of them seem significant allusions. Even "O swallow swallow," in *Waste Land V*, does not gain much from tracing it back to Tennyson's *The Princess*, though its context in Eliot's poem makes us suspect a deliberate allusion. Eliot's third "Five-Finger Exercise" opens with another borrowing from *The Princess*—

"The long light shakes across the lake," which may remind us of other lines in which Eliot cultivates such Tennysonian effects. Critics have also seen analogies between *The Waste Land* and Tennyson's *In Memoriam* and *The Holy Grail.* Some efforts to pursue the first of these analogies were mentioned in our first chapter; on the latter, we may cite Linda Ray Pratt's "The Holy Grail: Subversion and Revival of a Tradition in Tennyson and T. S. Eliot" (1973). Pratt's main point seems to be that although Eliot's form is more modern, his approach to the Grail quest is more traditional, Tennyson's more secular approach treating the Grail quest itself as one source of Camelot's downfall.

What is striking about Eliot's use of Victorian literature is less his debt to any one writer than the sheer range of debts that have been more or less convincingly shown by critics. Such sources rarely function as allusions—to that extent, Eliot is consistent with his ruling most of these writers out of the major tradition. But they testify to the lifelong effect of Eliot juvenile enthusiasms. Swinburne, for example, is pictured as a baneful influence on poets in most of Eliot's criticism, but it seems likely that "I Tiresias" is an echo of Swinburne's "Tiresias"—an identification made by Smith and further supported in A. V. C. Schmidt's "Eliot, Swinburne and Dante: A Note on 'The Waste Land,' Lines 215–48" (1976a). With somewhat less certainty, Phlebas' Phoenician heritage has been traced to a William Morris poem Eliot had mentioned in a review (Margaret Gent, "The Drowned Phoenician Sailor: T. S. Eliot and William Morris," 1970). Smith's book lists several borrowings from Dante Gabriel Rossetti, and Loucks gives us some reason to believe that a rhyme was lifted from Thomas Hood ("T. S. Eliot's 'A Cooking Egg': An Echo from Thomas Hood," 1976b). Hans Borchers has even found in the famous opening image of "Prufrock" an echo of some lines by W. E. Henley ("The Patient Etherised upon a Table: A New Source," 1978). This list of poets includes several who embodied all that Eliot rejected in Victorianism.

Edward Fitzgerald is a rather special case. The *Rubaiyat* was an adolescent enthusiasm of Eliot's, but the clearest Fitzgerald reference in Eliot's poetry is not to Fitzgerald's poetry but to a biography of Fitzgerald published in 1905 by A. C. Benson. Two passages from Benson's book are paraphrased in the opening stanza of "Gerontion." The first of these was identified early in Eliot criticism by F. O. Matthiesson. In 1949, John Abbot Clark discovered both uses for himself ("On First Looking into Benson's *Fitzgerald*," 1949). Unfortunately, Clark goes on to claim a great many other parallels that are less acceptable. Gerontion, he says, is Fitzgerald; Prufrock is Fitzgerald; and *The Waste Land* is a sort of "twentieth century *Omar*" (p. 267). It is hard to be sure how serious Clark is about some of these claims, which are without sufficient support for us to take them seriously. A. F. Beringhouse, who does not cite Clark, appears to be perfectly serious about his even more extreme claim that "*The Waste Land* is a revamping of dramatic monologues by Edward Fitzgerald and James Thomson" ("Journey through *The Waste Land*," 1957, p. 79). The "themes, symbols, and a general plan of development" came from the *Rubaiyat*, while "character, setting, and form" came from Thomson's *The City of Dreadful Night*. Beringhouse argues with the loose criteria for evidence common in such source studies. More modest, though trivial even if true, is Jon Bracker's effort to trace Eliot's "some talk of you and me" to the *Rubaiyat*'s "some little talk awhile of me and thee / there was and then no more of thee and me" ("Eliot's 'The Love Song of J. Alfred Prufrock,' 89," 1966).

A fairly impressive list of Victorian prose fiction sources for Eliot could also be compiled from various critics, if one were credulous enough. Grace B. Briggs' link in "Stevenson's 'The Ebb-Tide' and Eliot's 'The Hollow Men' " (1977) ultimately depends on their using the same nursery rhyme, though Briggs gives some other parallels. Martha Fodaski finds "Oscar Wilde's Swallow in *The Waste Land*" (1976), where most critics would see Tennyson. Wilde's *The Happy Prince* has some thematic parallels to offer but lacks the "O" shared by Eliot and Tennyson. A. V. C. Schmidt's yoking together, "Crumpets in 'Coriolan,' Muffins in 'Pickwick' " (1976b), is possible if one assumes that Eliot and Dickens could not have arrived separately at the joke of having a sanctus bell mistaken for a muffin seller's. George Levine's study, "*The Cocktail Party* and *Clara Hopgood*" (1958), is a purely comparative study, which suggests no influence of Mark Rutherford's novel on Eliot's play and little reason for the essay's existence.

The case for Eliot's borrowing from two of his immediate predecessors, Rudyard Kipling and Joseph Conrad, is clearer. Some of the many Kipling echoes listed in Grover Smith's book are less than striking, but Eliot has confirmed at least two: the ghostly children from Kipling's story "They" in "Burnt Norton I" (first noted by Helen Gardner), and the title "The Hollow Men" as a combination of William Morris's "The Hollow Land" and Kipling's "The Broken Men." Eliot himself is the source of this last identification, which Smith finds "so ingenious and improbable that the explanation might be a joke" (1974, p. 101). Eliot's thorough acquaintance with Kipling's work and his almost puzzled admiration for it is, in any case, on record in Eliot's 1941 edition of Kipling's verse and his introduction to that volume.

Eliot's interest in Conrad is also beyond question. Even before the publication of *The Waste Land* manuscripts, it was known that Eliot had one time thought of using a quotation from Conrad's *Heart of Darkness* as an epigraph for *The Waste Land*, and another quotation from *Heart of Darkness* serves as an epigraph to "The Hollow Men." The best discussion of the relevance of *Heart of Darkness* to these and later Eliot poems is the 1956 Leonard Unger article. Unger appends notes on a number of other possible Conrad sources, and other critics have added to this list some trivial or unconvincing cases.

In their discussion of these sources and the sources suggested by Unger, later critics have often failed to exhibit the caution of Unger's awareness of the way in which multiple sources may lurk behind particular lines. In Conrad's *Youth*, for example, Marlowe refers to the lost joy of youth as "the heat of life in the handful of dust"; in "The Return," there is a reference to "fear" turning "one's heart into a handful of dust." Both of these inevitably remind us of "fear in a handful of dust" in *Waste Land I.* Unger notes the two Conrad passages, notes another use of "handful of dust" in some Donne sermons, and notes the Ecclesiastian ring of the phrase itself. Unger speculates on the meaning and origin of this common use but does not insist on a single explanation.

In contrast, Rosemary Franklin's essay, "Death or the Heat of Life in the Handful of Dust?" (1969) identifies the passage from *Youth* as *the* source and constructs large hypotheses to "explain" Eliot's alteration of "heat of life" to "fear" as deliberately ironic. To the extent that there is merit in her argument that Eliot's "dust" can thus be associated with both life and death, the meanings she finds are so much a part of the biblical and liturgical associations of dust that no Conrad reference seems necessary, especially since she has seized upon the less convincing of two Conrad sources. Similarly, Daniel J. McConnell's essay, " 'The Heart of Darkness' in T. S. Eliot's *The Hollow Men*" (1962), is much more schematic and heavy handed than Unger's, which it does not cite. What is disturbing in such cases is not the tendency of Eliot criticism to repeat itself—its unmanageable bibliography may make that almost inevitable—but that Eliot criticism sometimes seems to become less, rather than more, sophisticated in the process.

Eliot's use of nineteenth-century literature includes a number of borrowings from less "literary" authors. The best attested of these are from Sir Arthur Conan Doyle, portions of whose work Eliot is known to have been able to recite from memory. The most blatant of the Doyle allusions is the "Baskerville hound," which rears its head in one of the "Five-Finger Exercises" ("Lines to Ralph Hodgson Esqre."). Several other Doyle sources have been published more than once—another example of Eliot criticism repeating itself. James Johnson Sweeney seems to have been the first to note that the use of "grimpen" in "East Coker II" may come from the Grimpen Mire in Doyle's *Hound of the Baskervilles* ("*East Coker:* A Reading," 1941). Grover Smith called attention to a colloquy in *Murder in the Cathedral* which is based on a passage in Doyle's "The Musgrave Ritual" ("T. S. Eliot and Sherlock Holmes," 1948). Nathan L. Bengis later reported a letter from Eliot confirming the conscious use of the Doyle story in the play ("Conan Doyle and Mr. T. S. Eliot," 1951), which did not prevent Constance Nicholas from publishing it as a new discovery ("The Murders of Doyle and Eliot," 1955). That Macavity, the "mystery cat," was Professor Moriarity, Sherlock Holmes' nemesis, was first revealed by H. T. Webster and H. W. Starr ("Macavity: An Attempt to Unravel His Mystery," 1954), an identification rediscovered by Katharine Loesch ("A Dangerous Criminal Still at Large," 1959) and Priscilla Preston ("A Note on T. S. Eliot and Sherlock Holmes," 1959). Preston adds to the Macavity identification two lines from "Gus, the Theatre Cat," which refer to "The Final Problem." The same lines had been noted earlier by Don Hardenbrook (" 'T. S. Eliot and the Great Grimpen Mire' by Gaston Huret III," 1956), though Hardenbrook does not cite the specific Doyle source.

The use of Doyle, even in a work like *Murder in the Cathedral,* is not really surprising. A poet's sources will generally be works which have somehow embedded themselves in his mind, either because he has read them recently or because he was profoundly affected by them when he read them in the past. Eliot seems to have kept reading Doyle's Sherlock Holmes stories all his life. Although he may not have returned as often to the great Romantic and Victorian poets, they had been his first introduction to poetry, and he did not forget them. Only a handful of his nineteenth-century sources are important allusions, but in reminding us of Eliot's early immersion in that literature they remind us that he shared many qualities with his predecessors. Eliot certainly struggled to be Classical and anti-Romantic in tendency, but he was the product of a Romantic age. As we place him in the context of tradition, we may see him as a reluctant Romantic and one of the last Victorians.

The Poet in the Theater

Eliot's fascination with poetic drama is one of his most obvious links with the English poetic tradition. Reviving poetic drama in English was a prospect that had fascinated many of the Romantics and Victorians, though Eliot was probably influenced chiefly by his analysis of their failures. In one sense, Eliot succeeded where they failed. His dramas are not "closet dramas." *Murder in the Cathedral* has genuine theatrical power; though it is not well suited to the commercial stage, it has continued to receive productions in other venues. *The Cocktail Party* was thoroughly successful in commercial terms, and Eliot's other contemporary plays have received more or less successful professional productions. If the object of poetic drama is to bring poetry to the theater in a fashion which will appeal to ordinary theatergoers, then Eliot's solution must be considered a success. Even friendly critics, however, have questioned whether his plays can be considered distinguished as either poetry or drama. Some have argued that Eliot's later dramatic verse sacrifices too much to the worn-out theatrical conventions within which he chose to work.

Subhas Sarkar's *T. S. Eliot the Dramatist* (1972) is one of the best of the many books on Eliot to come from the Indian subcontinent. A repeated theme of Sarkar's study is that all of Eliot's poetry is the product of "a dramatic imagination" (p. 27). The poetry is seen as beginning with character portraits and moving on to create more objective situations. Eliot's turn to poetic drama is thus both an effort to reach a wider audience and a natural outgrowth of his gifts. Sarkar reviews Eliot's theories about poetic drama and gives sensitive and sympathetic (but not very original) interpretations of the individual plays. Two difficulties, however, suggest themselves in connection with this account of Eliot's development. The first is that one may well see Eliot's later poetry as making much less use of personae and other masks. The second is that Tennyson and Browning were equally masters of the dramatic lyric, while their plays suggest that such mastery may not be connected with gifts for the drama.

A more theoretical account is Hans Osterwalder's *T. S. Eliot: Between Metaphor and Metonymy* (1978), in which Osterwalder takes his approach from Roman Jakobson. The key distinction here is between two master tropes, the metaphoric revelation of similarities and the metonymic exploitation of contiguity. These tropes are linked with such other dyads as romantic/realistic and static/dynamic. As a heuristic device, this allows Osterwalder to explore common characteristics at many levels of the plays—structure, theme, characterization, syntax, semantics, and morphophonemics. Eliot's critical writings on poetry and drama are seen as initially holding a balance between metaphoric and metonymic poles, perhaps even tending toward the latter. Eliot's middle period sees him veering toward a largely static, metaphoric theory of drama, and his later writings find him pleading again for balance. Eliot's critical terminology is translated into these terms. In the 1928 "Dialogue on Dramatic Poetry," for example, one speaker insists that Ibsen had greater dramatic ability (metonymic) than Tourneur, but will not last as long because he lacks poetic excellence (metaphoric). The plays are read as initially consistent with the theory—*Sweeney Agonistes* balancing metonymic and metaphoric elements, *Murder in the Cathedral* being almost exclusively metaphoric. In the later plays, however, "metonymic realism has been emphasized at the level of poetry" (p. 111), despite the later theory's stress on balance.

If Osterwalder's dualistic framework takes most of Eliot's reflections on poetry and drama into account, it may be a sign of a weakness in Eliot's thinking, namely, a persistent tendency to set the two terms in opposition with each other. Although one of the speakers in the 1928 "Dialogue" says that "all poetry tends toward drama, and all drama toward poetry," and though Eliot defends Elizabethan rhetoric in his 1919 essay " 'Rhetoric' and Poetic Drama," Eliot's later criticism appears to accept as given the stage conventions of twentieth-century realistic drama. His 1950 lecture "Poetry and Drama (1957)," which contains some of his most acute self-criticism, criticizes *The Family Reunion* for "the introduction of passages which called too much attention to themselves as poetry." Determined to master the art of dramatic construction, Eliot acknowledges that his avoidance of obtrusive poetry in *The Cocktail Party* may make it "an open question whether there is any poetry in the play at all." He expresses the hope that after putting one's poetry "on a very thin diet to adapt it to the needs of the stage," one might eventually feel free to "make more liberal uses of poetry and take greater liberties with ordinary colloquial speech," but it is hard to see any such development in the later plays. One might also object that the language of drama is never an exact rendering of "ordinary colloquial speech" and that the language of Eliot's later plays simply reflects a set of conventional theatrical ways of having people speak on stage.

Archibald MacLeish's essay, "The Poet as Playwright" (1955), is directed against Eliot's conclusion that poetry can openly appear on the modern stage only when prose is inadequate. MacLeish believes that this assumes too much about the inevitability of the modern audience's preference for prose. If Shakespeare's plays succeed on the modern stage, it is because they create their own expectations, their own conventions. The problem is adapting modern verse to the demands of dramatic action, but this need not lead to giving up on poetry, except at rare points in the action. The weaknesses of MacLeish's poetic dramas do not affect the validity of his arguments, while his success—and that of Christopher Fry—may suggest that modern audiences are, in fact, willing to accept poetry less unobtrustive than Eliot's.

Eliot's doubts about the effect on audiences of the heightened language of poetry may have been reinforced by his contacts with the world of the theater, but they may equally have been a product of his inner inhibitions, which helped shape his poetic and public personae in other ways. The theater figure he worked with most closely through the years was E. Martin Browne, a director who more than shared Eliot's commitment to religious drama and poetic drama. Browne has written frequently about their collaboration, most extensively in *The Making of T. S. Eliot's Plays* (1969). Although expressing the belief that Eliot's later plays will continue to be produced, Browne is evidently one of those who prefer the earlier dramas: "By adopting this pattern of ironic social comedy, Eliot placed upon his genius a regrettable limitation. He tied himself to social, and still more to theatrical, conventions which were already outworn when the plays were written" (p. 342). Although Browne's account, copiously illustrated with passages from early drafts, shows that Eliot sought and needed advice on theatrical construction, the evidence presented indicates that the prosaic tone of Eliot's later verse was a result of Eliot's intentions rather than revisions mandated by his director. Browne's book is a basic source for any study of Eliot's plays. As director of *The Rock,* he persuaded Eliot to write the choruses for it, and Eliot sought him out as producer of *Murder in the Cathedral.* Browne was actively involved with all of Eliot's subsequent plays.

One of the sources of the flat tone of the verse in the later plays is the use of long lines with relatively few strong stresses. The regularity of these stresses, perhaps only dimly perceived by the audience, is what allows us to speak of this as "poetic" drama. Browne provides an interesting analysis of the way the verse pattern reinforces the sense and some discussion of how it should be handled by actors in performance, although he concedes that "the verse pattern is firmer" in *Family Reunion* than in the later plays (p. 298). In "Poetry and Drama," Eliot describes this pattern as "a line of varying length and varying number of syllables, with a caesura and three stresses."

Not all critics find this pattern, however. Marjorie Lightfoot, for example, is guided by another passage in "Poetry and Drama," in which Eliot praises Yeats' *Purgatory* ("*Purgatory* and *The Family Reunion:* In Pursuit of Prosodic Description," 1965). Analyzing *Purgatory* as consisting of fairly regular four-stress accentual lines, Lightfoot finds similar lines in *Family Reunion* and attributes them to the influence of Yeats. *The Cocktail Party*, by her analysis, is even more regular (90 percent) in its reliance on a four-stress norm. What is clearest here is how much accentual verse depends on the vagaries of the individual ear, especially when it is taken far from a syllabic norm and is interspersed with irregular lines and other variants. If the shadow of rhythmic regularity is the principal poetic contribution to Eliot's later plays, one wonders if audiences can be affected by rhythms critics cannot agree on.

Alternatively, one might decide that Eliot's formal description of his practice is simply wrong, and that critics who accept it have been misled by accepting his authority. In an article on

The Cocktail Party, Lightfoot reports on her prosodic analysis of a cast recording edited by the director and approved by Eliot, again finding a four-stress pattern ("The Uncommon Cocktail Party," 1969). Lightfoot reports that Eliot responded to her findings by saying that "he wrote by ear and did not concern himself with rules of scansion" (p. 383). Lightfoot's analysis may well be correct. Perhaps the cast recording could be subjected to objective analysis by one of the machines linguists have taken to employing in matters of phonology.

Whether Eliot's lines prove to have three or four or more stresses, critics who dislike the later plays often base their unfavorable evaluations partly on what Spencer Brown calls its "loose, or limp, blank verse" ("T. S. Eliot's Latest Poetic Drama," 1954). Though Eliot has adopted various personae, he suggests, the voice in his poetry has always been distinctively his own, and no new voices emerge in his plays. Brown also accuses Eliot of failing to create living characters and of failing to extract what humor is left in the dramatic situations he adopts. He concludes by regretting that "the most important poet now writing in English" should "feel so strong a vocation to be a second-rate playwright" (p. 372). Brown's only explanation is that Eliot has somehow fallen victim to the "tradition . . . that poets must try to write plays" (p. 372).

The fully rounded characters which Brown and others find lacking in Eliot's plays are, perhaps, not to be expected in the kind of comedy Eliot was writing in *The Cocktail Party* and its successors. P. G. Mudford, for example, tries to establish a relationship in "T. S. Eliot's Plays and the Tradition of 'High Comedy' " (1974). The "tradition" Mudford appeals to, however, is less a living dramatic tradition than a critical construct which sounds rather like Northrop Frye's "high norm" satire: "High comedy is that kind of comedy in which the humorous revelation of individual folly, through behavior and situation, raises social and moral issues which are themselves often seen in the perspective of some further metaphysical belief" (p. 127) Mudford's examples include *Midsummer Night's Dream*, *Tartuffe*, and *Don Giovanni*—not a terribly coherent group. Mudford suggests that the kind of articulateness Eliot's high comedy requires limits the social range to an unrepresentative set of characters, though a look at Mudford's examples of "high comedy" will show that other dramatists have not been so limited. If there is a dramatic tradition within which Eliot is working and which limits his characters, it is obviously the tradition of drawing room comedy. Noel Coward seems a more obvious comparison than Moliere.

Critics who prefer Eliot's earlier work have offered additional reasons for the relative failure of the later plays. Eliot is often seen, for example, as naturally more sympathetic to the driven Harry of *Family Reunion* than to the blander characters of the later dramas. It is possible, of course, that in such cases it is the critic who prefers the more driven Eliot of the earlier plays *and* poems to the blander Eliot of the later plays *and* the *Four Quartets*. Other critics simply deny that Eliot ever mastered the stagecraft he labored at. Mary Rahme maintains that Eliot lacked awareness of the "histrionic sensibility," of the poetry which emerges through action rather than language (1968). Although she employs it rather more heavy handedly, Rahme echoes some criticisms of Francis Fergusson–for example, "T. S. Eliot's *Poetry and Drama*" (1957). That Eliot did in fact, recognize that powerful effects could be achieved through action and dramatic form should be clear, and Rahme, at least, is unfair to Eliot as a critic.

Whether Eliot as a playwright possesses the histrionic sensibility is another question. Drawing room comedy is a talky form at best, and even the complicated plot of *The Confidential Clerk* does not produce dramatic onstage situations. From this, critics like Bernard Knieger have concluded that "all five plays are essentially static" (1961, p. 388). Knieger believes that Eliot would have done more for poetic drama had he "persisted in the direction of *Murder in the Cathedral*" (p. 392), where the full resources of poetry are employed. Others see *The Family Reunion,* where the poetry is present though somewhat subdued, as the lost model, while still others regret the abandonment of *Sweeney Agonistes* and its fresh, modern rhythms.

There are, of course, critics with a less negative view of the later plays–critics for whom *Murder in the Cathedral* was a magnificent dead end that Eliot was wise to turn away from. These critics stress Eliot's lifelong determination not to repeat himself, to master new forms. Although he admits that Edward and Lavinia's reconciliation at the beginning of act III is a bit tedious, John Lawlor gives the play high praise in "The Formal Achievement of 'The Cocktail Party' " (1954). Bonamy Dobree's essay, "*The Confidential Clerk*" (1954), credits Eliot with creating "a new kind of play, new in the form used as a vehicle for an idea, new in the way the impact on the audience is effected" (p. 131), praising particularly the verse form adopted though finding the characters unlovable (and unloved by Eliot). Rudd Fleming goes even further in his praise of *The Elder Statesman:* "More clearly, or at least more neatly, than any other work *The Elder Statesman* expresses Eliot's continued faith in the 'European mind' and in its art-works as the 'objective correlative' of that 'mind' eternally shaping itself into an *ecclesia poetarum* within which to find one's own right place is the way of salvation and life" (1961). Fleming arrives at this conclusion by exaggerating the play's connection with *Oedipus at Colonus*, and he seems to equate such statements of faith with dramatic effectiveness.

As such essays may suggest, it is possible to see Eliot's development as a dramatist very much in Eliot's terms. That is more or less the case in David E. Jones' *The Plays of T. S. Eliot* (1960), which may still be the best book-length treatment of its subject. Jones is not uncritical in his approach to Eliot's plays, though he sometimes seems less critical than Eliot himself, as when he suggests that *Murder in the Cathedral* "may even be the greatest religious play ever written" (p. 215). Jones nevertheless sees *Murder in the Cathedral* as "very much a special case" (p. 81) which did not solve the general problem of creating a new form for poetic drama. *Sweeney Agonistes* is also seen as a dead end, with few inherent possibilities of development, and the choruses from *The Rock* get short shrift. Jones is less hard on *The Family Reunion* than Eliot, and approves its lyric interludes, but he agrees with Eliot that the poetic runes are too obtrusive and that the Eumenides are unsuccessful. Although Jones betrays occasional qualms about the thinness of the poetry and the flatness of some characters in the later plays, he generally treats them as advances. Even more convinced than Eliot that a religious sense of wholeness is required for the creation and appreciation of poetic drama, Jones approves the indirection with which Eliot presents religious matters to secular audiences, while seeing this necessary indirection as a possible source of weakness in the works.

Jones is simply following Eliot's lead in stressing the problems of creating a poetic drama and in making much of the religious themes of Eliot's plays. The effect of such criticism, however, is to keep the plays in what Katharine Worth has termed "the not very jolly corner labelled 'verse and religious drama' " (1970, p. 148). Seeing Eliot in less moribund terms is the virtue of Worth's 1970 essay, "Eliot and the Living Theatre," and her chapter on Eliot in *Revolutions in Modern English Drama* (1973). Worth praises the theatrical inventiveness and dramatic possibilities of *Sweeney Agonistes.* Its fragments may be the only dramatic verse of Eliot's as highly charged as his best poetry, and Worth's recognition of its value is welcome. *The Family Reunion* is seen as more fully human than its successors, and Worth gives a persuasive description of a performance in which the Eumenides were more effective than in those performances Eliot describes. Of particular interest is her suggestion of the Pinteresque qualities of Eliot's later plays: Reilly sipping gin and water is "a Coward character poised for a leap into a Pinter scene" (1973, p. 63) and *The Cocktail Party* has "a claim to be considered the first black comedy in the postwar English theatre" (p. 55).

Such analogies point to real features in Eliot's later plays, including the way they alter and undermine the conventions they work within. In his poetic dramas, Eliot is certainly the traditional poet discussed in this chapter—a poet rich in references to the classics and anxious to restore the English tradition of poetic drama. But he is also the subversive poet and iconoclastic critic who helped reshape our sense of tradition—in other words, the modern poet we must discuss in our next and final chapter.

References

Andreach, Robert J.
1969. "*Paradise Lost* and the Christian Configuration of *The Waste Land*," *Papers on Language and Literature* Summer, pp. 296–309.

Arrowsmith, William
1955. "Transfiguration in Eliot and Euripides," *Sewanee Review* Summer, pp. 148–72.

Bacon, Helen H.
1958. "The Sybil in the Bottle," *Virginia Quarterly Review* Spring, pp. 262–76.

Barnes, Hazel E.
1974. *The Meddling Gods*, pp. 55–93. Lincoln: Univ. of Nebraska Pr.

Barnes, W. J.
1963. "T. S. Eliot's 'Marina': Image and Symbol," *University of Kansas City Review* Summer, pp. 297–305.

Bateson, F. W.
1968. "T. S. Eliot: The Poetry of Pseudo-Learning," *Journal of General Education* Apr., pp. 1–15.

Bengis, Nathan L.
1951. "Conan Doyle and Mr. T. S. Eliot" (letter), *Times Literary Supplement* Sept. 28, p. 613.

Benziger, James
1959. "The Romantic Tradition: Wordsworth and T. S. Eliot," *Bucknell Review* Dec., pp. 277–86.

Bergonzi, Bernard
1970. "Allusion in *The Waste Land*," *Essays in Criticism* July, pp. 382–85.

Bergsten, Staffan
1959. "Illusive Allusions: Some Reflections on the Critical Approach to the Poetry of T. S. Eliot," *Orbis Litterarum*, pp. 9–18.

Beringhouse, A. F.
1957. "Journey through *The Waste Land*," *South Atlantic Quarterly* Jan., pp. 79–90.

Berry, Francis
1970. "Allusion in *The Waste Land*," *Essays in Criticism* July, pp. 380–82.

Berry, Judith Andrew
1966. "The Relevance of Baudelaire to T. S. Eliot's *The Waste Land*," *Susquehana University Studies* June, pp. 283–302.

Bodkin, Maud
1941. *The Quest for Salvation in an Ancient and a Modern Play.* London: Oxford Univ. Pr.

Bollier, E. P.
1957. "Mr. Eliot's 'Tradition and the Individual Talent' Reconsidered," *University of Colorado Studies in Language and Literature* Jan., pp. 103–18.
1958. "T. S. Eliot and John Milton: A Problem in Criticism," *Tulane Studies in English*, pp. 165–92.
1959. "T. S. Eliot and John Donne: A Problem in Criticism," *Tulane Studies in English*, pp. 103–18.
1970. "La Poésie Pure: The Ghostly Dialogue between T. S. Eliot and Paul Valéry," *Forum* (Ball State Univ.), pp. 54–59.

Borchers, Hans
1978. "The Patient Etherised upon a Table: A New Source," *Yeats-Eliot Review*, pp. 9–13.

Bornstein, George
1976. *Transformations of Romanticism in Yeats, Eliot, and Stevens*, pp. 1–26, 94–106. Chicago: Univ. of Chicago Pr.

Boyd, John Douglas
1969. "T. S. Eliot as Critic and Rhetorician: The Essay on Jonson," *Criticism* Spring, pp. 167–82.

Bracker, Jon

1966. "Eliot's 'The Love Song of J. Alfred Prufrock,' 89," *Explicator*, item 21.

Briggs, Grace B.

1977. "Stevenson's 'The Ebb-Tide' and Eliot's 'The Hollow Men,' " *Notes and Queries* Oct., pp. 448–49.

Brooks, Harold

1952. " 'The Family Reunion' and 'Colombe's Birthday,' " *Times Literary Supplement* Dec. 12, p. 819.

Brown, Spencer

1954. "T. S. Eliot's Latest Poetic Drama: Where Are the Eagles and Trumpets?" *Commentary* Apr., pp. 367–72.

Brown, Stephen

1977. "A Reader's Note on Similarities between Browning's 'A Toccata of Galuppi's' and Eliot's 'The Love Song of J. Alfred Prufrock,' " *Browning Society Notes* Mar., pp. 33–34.

Browne, E. Martin

1969. *The Making of T. S. Eliot's Plays.* London: Cambridge Univ. Pr.

Burne, Glenn S.

1959. "T. S. Eliot and Rémy de Gourmont," *Bucknell Review* Feb., pp. 113–26.

Cameron, Elspeth

1970. "T. S. Eliot's 'Marina': An Exploration," *Queen's Quarterly*, pp. 180–89.

Carey, Sister M. Cecilia

1962. "Baudelaire's Influence on *The Waste Land*," *Renascence*, pp. 185–92, 198.

Carne-Ross, D. S.

1965. "T. S. Eliot: Tropheia," *Arion* Spring, pp. 5–20.

Cauthen, I. B., Jr.

1958. "Another Webster Allusion in *The Waste Land*," *Modern Language Notes* Nov., pp. 498–99.

1978. "An Unpublished Letter by T. S. Eliot (1962)," *Yeats-Eliot Review*, pp. 22–23.

Clark, John Abbot

1949. "On First Looking into Benson's *Fitzgerald*," *South Atlantic Quarterly* Apr., pp. 268–69.

Clausen, Christopher

1976. "Tintern Abbey to Little Gidding: The Past Recaptured," *Sewanee Review* Summer, pp. 406–24.

Condon, James P.

1977–78. "Notes on T. S. Eliot's 'What Is a Classic?': The Classical Norm and Social Existence," *Clasical Journal* Dec.–Jan., pp. 176–78.

Cook, Harold E.
1954. "A Search for the Ideal: An Interpretation of T. S. Eliot's 'Marina,'" *Bucknell Review* Dec., pp. 33–41.
Daniels, Edgar F.
1959. "Eliot's 'Gerontion,'" *Explicator* May, item 58.
Davidson, Arthur
1956. *The Eliot Enigma: A Critical Examination of* The Waste Land. London: Arthur Davidson.
Delasanta, Rodney
1971. "The Bartenders in Eliot and Chaucer," *Neuphilologische Mitteilungen*, pp. 60–61.
Dick, Bernard F.
1975. "*The Waste Land* and the *Descensus ad Infernos*," *Canadian Review of Comparative Literature*, pp. 35–48.
Dobree, Bonamy
1954. "*The Confidential Clerk*," *Sewanee Review* Jan., pp. 117–31.
Dolan, Paul J.
1966. "Milton and Eliot: A Common Source," *Notes and Queries* Oct., pp. 379–80.
1969. "Eliot's 'Marina': A Reading," *Renascence* Summer, pp. 203–6, 222.
Dunn, Ian S.
1963. "Eliot's 'The Love Song of J. Alfred Prufrock,'" *Explicator* Sept., item 1.
Eliot, T. S.
1952. "A Talk on Dante," *Kenyon Review* Spring, pp. 178–88.
1957. "Poetry and Drama," in *On Poetry and Poets*, pp. 75–95. New York: Farrar, Straus.
Ellis, P. G.
1972. "The Development of T. S. Eliot's Historical Sense," *Review of English Studies* Aug., pp. 291–301.
Ettin, Andrew V.
1977. "Milton, T. S. Eliot, and the Virgilian Vision: Some Versions of Georgic," *Genre* Summer, pp. 233–58.
Everett, Barbara
1980. "Eliot's 'Four Quartets' and French Symbolism," *English* Spring, pp. 1–37.
Fergusson, Francis
1957. *The Human Image in Dramatic Literature*. New York: Doubleday.
Fleissner, Robert F.
1975. "Prufrock Not the Polonius Type," *Research Studies* Dec., pp. 254–55.
Fleming, Rudd
1961. "*The Elder Statesman* and Eliot's 'Programme for the Metier of Poetry,'" *Wisconsin Studies in Contemporary Literature*, pp. 54–64.

Fodaski, Martha
1976. "Oscar Wilde's Swallow in *The Waste Land*," *American Notes and Queries* June, pp. 146–48.
Fowlie, Wallace
1967. "Baudelaire and Eliot: Interpreters of Their Age," in *T. S. Eliot*, ed. Allen Tate, pp. 299–315. New York: Delacorte Pr.
Franklin, Rosemary F.
1969. "Death or the Heat of Life in the Handful of Dust?" *American Literature* May, pp. 277–79.
French, A. L.
1964. "Criticism and *The Waste Land*," *Southern Review* (Australia), pp. 69–81.
1970. "Death by Allusion?" *Essays in Criticism* Apr., pp. 269–71.
Fussell, Paul, Jr.
1950. "A Note on 'The Hollow Men,'" *Modern Language Notes* Apr., pp. 254–55.
Gardner, Helen
1965. *T. S. Eliot and the English Poetic Tradition* (Byron Foundation Lecture). Nottingham: Univ. of Nottingham.
Gent, Margaret
1970. "The Drowned Phoenician Sailor: T. S. Eliot and William Morris," *Notes and Queries* Feb., pp. 50–51.
Greene, E. J. H.
1951. *T. S. Eliot et la France*. Paris: Boivin.
Hamalian, Leo
1960. "Wishwood Revisited," *Renascence* Summer, pp. 167–73.
Hardenbrook, Don
1956. "'T. S. Eliot and the Great Grimpen Mire' by Gaston Huret III," *Baker Street Journal*, pp. 88–93.
Hart, Jeffrey
1957. "T. S. Eliot: His Use of Wycherley and Pope," *Notes and Queries* Sept., pp. 389–90.
Heilman, Robert B.
1953. "*Alcestis* and *The Cocktail Party*," *Comparative Literature* Spring, pp. 105–16.
Hochwald, Ilse E.
1954. "Eliot's *Cocktail Party* and Goethe's *Wahlverwandtschaften*," *Germanic Review*, pp. 254–59.
Holt, Charles L.
1967. "On Structure and *Sweeney Agonistes*," *Modern Drama* May, pp. 43–47.
Hosek, Chaviva, and Viiu Menning
1967. *An Index to References in T. S. Eliot's Selected Essays*. Montreal: For the authors.
Janoff, Ronald W.
1965. "Eliot and Horace—Aspects of the Intrinsic Classicist," *Cithara* Nov., pp. 31–44.

Jayne, Sears
1955. "Mr. Eliot's Agon," *Philological Quarterly* Oct., pp. 395–414.
Johnson, Maurice
1949. "The Ghost of Swift in *Four Quartets*," *Modern Language Notes* Apr., p. 273.
Jones, David E.
1960. *The Plays of T. S. Eliot.* Toronto: Univ. of Toronto Pr.
Kermode, Frank
1957. *The Romantic Image.* London: Routledge and Kegan Paul.
1958. "T. S. Eliot on Poetry," *International Literary Annual*, pp. 131–34.
Kincaid, A. N.
1972. "The Dramatic Monologue: Eliot's Debt to Browning," *Browning Society Notes* July, pp. 4–11.
Knieger, Bernard
1961. "The Dramatic Achievement of T. S. Eliot," *Modern Drama* Feb., pp. 387–92.
Krause, Sydney
1960. "Hollow Men and False Horses," *Texas Studies in Language and Literature* Autumn, pp. 368–77.
Kuna, F. M.
1963. "T. S. Eliot's Dissociation of Sensibility and the Critics of Metaphysical Poetry," *Essays in Criticism* July, pp. 241–52.
Laboulle, M.-J.-J.
1936. "T. S. Eliot and Some French Poets," *Revue de Littérature Comparée* Apr.–June, pp. 389–99.
Langbaum, Robert
1957. *The Poetry of Experience.* New York: Random House.
Lawlor, John
1954. "The Formal Achievement of 'The Cocktail Party.' " *Virginia Quarterly Review* Spring, pp. 431–52.
Leach, Elsie
1972. "T. S. Eliot and the School of Donne," *Costerus*, 31: 163–80.
1975. " 'Gerontion' and Marvell's 'The Garden,' " *English Language Notes* Sept., pp. 45–48.
Lee, Jae Ho
1963. "Alexander Pope in Eliot's 'East Coker,' " *Notes and Queries* Oct., p. 381.
Lees, Francis Noel
1966. "Mr. Eliot's Sunday Morning *Satura:* Petronius and *The Waste Land*," in *T. S. Eliot*, ed. Tate, pp. 345–54. New York: Delacorte Pr.
Lelievre, F. J.
1958. "Parody in Juvenal and T. S. Eliot," *Classical Philology* Jan., pp. 22–26.
Levine, Alice
1978. "T. S. Eliot and Byron," *ELH* Fall, pp. 522–41.

Levine, George
1958. "*The Cocktail Party* and *Clara Hopgood*," *Graduate Student of English* (Minneapolis) Winter, pp. 4–11.

Lightfoot, Marjorie J.
1965. "*Purgatory* and *The Family Reunion:* In Pursuit of Prosodic Description," *Modern Drama* Feb., pp. 256–66.
1969. "The Uncommon Cocktail Party," *Modern Drama* Feb., pp. 382–95.

Litz, A. Walton
1977. " 'That Strange Abstraction, "Nature" ': T. S. Eliot's Victorian Inheritance," in *Nature and the Victorian Imagination*, ed. U. C. Knoepflmacher and G. B. Tennyson, pp. 470–88. Berkeley: Univ. of California Pr.

Loesch, Katharine
1959. "A Dangerous Criminal Still at Large," *Notes and Queries* Jan., pp. 8–9.

Loucks, James F.
1976a. "A Second Browning Allusion in Eliot's 'Burbank' Poem," *Notes and Queries* Jan., pp. 18–19.
1976b. "T. S. Eliot's 'A Cooking Egg': An Echo from Thomas Hood," *Notes and Queries* July, pp. 299–300.

Lucas, John
1970. "*The Waste Land* Today," *Essays in Criticism* Oct., pp. 497–500.

Lucas, John, and William Myers
1969. "*The Waste Land* Today," *Essays in Criticism* Apr., pp. 193–209.

Lucy, Sean
1960. *T. S. Eliot and the Idea of Tradition.* London: Cohen and West.

MacKendrick, Paul
1953. "T. S. Eliot and the Alexandrians," *Classical Journal*, pp. 7–13.

MacLeish, Archibald
1955. "The Poet as Playwright," *Atlantic Monthly* Feb., pp. 49–52.

Major, John M.
1959. "Eliot's 'Gerontion' and *As You Like It*," *Modern Language Notes* Jan., pp. 28–31.

Marcus, Philip L.
1967. "T. S. Eliot and Shakespeare," *Criticism* Winter, pp. 63–79.

Marsh, Florence
1959. "The Ocean Desert: *The Ancient Mariner* and *The Waste Land*," *Essays in Criticism* Apr., pp. 126–33.

McConnell, Daniel J.
1962. " 'The Heart of Darkness' in T. S. Eliot's *The Hollow Men*," *Texas Studies in Literature and Language* Spring, pp. 141–53.

McLaughlin, Juliet
1969. "Allusion in *The Waste Land*," *Essays in Criticism* Oct., pp. 454–60.
Melchiori, Georgio
1964. "Eliot and Apollinaire," *Notes and Queries* Oct., pp. 385–86.
Montgomery, Marion
1969. *T. S. Eliot: An Essay on the American Magus*. Athens: Univ. of Georgia Pr.
Morris, David
1953. *The Poetry of Gerard Manley Hopkins and T. S. Eliot in the Light of the Donne Tradition: A Comparative Study*. Bern: Francke.
Motola, Gabriel
1969. "The Mountains of *The Waste Land*," *Essays in Criticism* Jan., pp. 67–69.
Mudford, P. G.
1974. "T. S. Eliot's Plays and the Tradition of 'High Comedy,'" *Critical Quarterly* Summer, pp. 127–40.
Murray, Brian
1976. "Tradition and the Eliot Critical Talent," *Connecticut Review* May, pp. 2–15.
Murray, Christopher
1978. "A Source for 'Prufrock'?" *Yeats-Eliot Review*, p. 24.
Musurillo, Herbert
1956. "A Note on *The Waste Land* (Part IV)," *Classical Philology* July, pp. 174–75.
Myers, William
1970. "Allusion in *The Waste Land*: A Reply," *Essays in Criticism* Jan., pp. 120–22.
1971. "Aesthetic and Ethical Judgments," *Essays in Criticism* Apr., pp. 107–8.
Naik, M. K.
1976. "Thalia in the Desert: Varieties of Comic Experience in *The Waste Land*," in *Studies in American Literature: Essays in Honour of William Mulder*, ed. Jagdish Chander and Narindar S. Pradhan, pp. 212–19. Delhi: Oxford Univ. Pr.
Nicholas, Constance
1955. "The Murders of Doyle and Eliot," *Modern Language Notes* Apr., pp. 269–71.
Osterwalder, Hans
1978. *T. S. Eliot: Between Metaphor and Metonymy*. Bern: Francke.
Pachmuss, Temira
1976. "Dostoevsky and Eliot: A Point of View, *Forum for Modern Language Studies* Jan., pp. 82–89.
Pollock, John J.
1977. "'Gerontion' and 'The Garden': Another Perspective," *American Notes and Queries* Oct., pp. 22–24.

Pratt, Linda Ray
1973. "The Holy Grail: Subversion and Revival of a Tradition in Tennyson and T. S. Eliot," *Victorian Poetry* Winter, pp. 307–21.
Preston, Priscilla
1959. "A Note on T. S. Eliot and Sherlock Holmes," *Modern Language Review* July, pp. 397–99.
Pritchard, William H.
1969. "Reading *The Waste Land* Today," *Essays in Criticism* Apr., pp. 176–92.
Puhvel, Martin
1965. "Reminiscent Bells in *The Waste Land*," *English Language Notes* June, pp. 286–87.
Rahme, Mary
1968. "T. S. Eliot and the 'Histrionic Sensibility,'" *Criticism* Spring, pp. 126–37.
Rajan, Balachandra
1978. "Milton and Eliot: A Twentieth-Century Acknowledgment," *Milton Studies*, pp. 115–29.
Ramsey, Warren
1964. "The *Oresteia* since Hofmannsthal: Images and Emphases," *Revue de Littérature Comparée* July–Sept., pp. 359–74.
Reckford, Kenneth J.
1964. "Heracles and Mr. Eliot," *Comparative Literature* Winter, pp. 1–18.
Rexine, John E.
1965. "Classical and Christian Foundations of T. S. Eliot's *Cocktail Party*," *Books Abroad* Winter, pp. 21–26.
Rickey, Mary Ellen
1963. "'Christabel' and 'Murder in the Cathedral,'" *Notes and Queries* Apr., p. 151.
Sarkar, Subhas
1972. *T. S. Eliot the Dramatist*. Calcutta: Minerva.
Scarfe, Francis
1970. "Eliot and Nineteenth-Century French Poetry," in *Eliot in Perspective*, ed. Graham Martin, pp. 45–61. New York: Humanities Pr.
Schmidt, A. V. C.
1976a. "Eliot, Swinburne and Dante: A Note on 'The Waste Land,' Lines 215–248," *Notes and Queries* Jan., pp. 17–18.
1976b. "Crumpets in 'Coriolan,' Muffins in 'Pickwick,'" *Notes and Queries* July, pp. 298–99.
Schuchard, Ronald
1976. "'Our Mad Poetics to Confute': The Personal Voice in T. S. Eliot's Early Poetry and Criticism," *Orbis Litterarum*, pp. 208–23.
Schwalb, Harry M.
1953. "Eliot's 'A Game of Chess,'" *Explicator* Apr., item 46.

Sen, Sunil Kanti

1965. *Metaphysical Tradition and T. S. Eliot*, pp. 80–119. Calcutta: K. L. Mukhopadhay.

Sena, Vinod

1967. "Eliot's *The Family Reunion:* A Study in Disintegration," *Southern Review* Autumn, pp. 895–921.

Sharrock, Roger

1971. "The Critical Revolution of T. S. Eliot," *Ariel* Jan., pp. 26–42.

Smidt, Kristian

1973. *The Importance of Recognition: Six Chapters on T. S. Eliot.* Tromsϕ: Peder Norbye.

Smith, Grover

1948. "T. S. Eliot and Sherlock Holmes," *Notes and Queries* Oct. 2, pp. 431–32.

1956. *T. S. Eliot's Poetry and Plays: A Study in Sources and Meaning*. Chicago: Univ. of Chicago Pr. 2d ed., 1974.

Stamm, Rudolf

1949. "The Orestes Theme in Three Plays by Eugene O'Neill, T. S. Eliot, and Jean Paul Sartre," *English Studies* Oct., pp. 244–55.

Starkie, Enid

1954. *From Gautier to Eliot: The Influence of France in English Literature, 1851–1939*. London: Hutchinson Univ. Library.

Sweeney, James Johnson

1941. "*East Coker:* A Reading," *Southern Review* Spring, pp. 771–91.

Taupin, Rene

1929. *L'influence du Symbolisme français sur la poésie américaine.* Paris: Honoré Champion.

Thale, Mary

1968. "T. S. Eliot and Mrs. Browning on the Metaphysical Poets," *College Language Association Journal*, pp. 225–58.

Tindall, William York

1947. "The Recantation of T. S. Eliot," *American Scholar* Autumn, pp. 431–37.

Torrens, James

1971a. "T. S. Eliot and the Austere Poetics of Valéry," *Comparative Literature* Winter, pp. 1–17.

1971b. "T. S. Eliot and Shakespeare: 'This Music Crept By,'" *Bucknell Review* Spring, pp. 77–96.

1977. "Eliot's Poetry and the Incubus of Shakespeare," *Thought*, pp. 407–21.

Unger, Leonard

1956. "Laforgue, Conrad, and Eliot," in *The Man in the Name*, pp. 190–242. Minneapolis: Univ. of Minnesota Pr.

1966. *T. S. Eliot: Moments and Patterns*. Minneapolis: Univ. of Minnesota Pr.

Walcutt, Charles Child
1976. "Eliot's 'Sweeney Erect,'" *Explicator* Winter, pp. 31–32.

Ward, David
1968. "Eliot, Murray, Homer, and the Idea of Tradition: 'So I Assumed a Double Part . . .'" *Essays in Criticism*, pp. 47–59.

Watson, C. B.
1964. "T. S. Eliot and the Interpretation of Shakespearian Tragedy in Our Time," *Etudes Anglaises* Oct.–Dec., pp. 502–21.

Webster, H. T., and H. W. Starr
1954. "Macavity: An Attempt to Unravel His Mystery," *Baker Street Journal* Oct., pp. 205–10.

Weinberg, Kerry
1969. *T. S. Eliot and Charles Baudelaire*. The Hague: Mouton.

Weinblatt, Alan
1978. "T. S. Eliot and the Historical Sense," *South Atlantic Quarterly*, pp. 282–95.

Weisstein, Ulrich
1952. "*The Cocktail Party:* An Attempt at Interpretation on Mythological Grounds," *Western Review* Spring, pp. 232–41.

Williamson, George
1927. "The Talent of T. S. Eliot," *Sweeney Review* July, pp. 284–95. Reprinted as *The Talent of T. S. Eliot*. Seattle: Univ. of Washington Book Store, 1929.

Wilson, Edmund
1931. *Axel's Castle*, pp. 93–131. New York: Scribner's.

Worth, Katharine
1970. "Eliot and the Living Theatre," in *Eliot in Perspective*, ed. Graham Martin, pp. 148–66. New York: Humanities Pr.
1973. *Revolutions in Modern English Drama*, pp. 55–66. London: G. Bell.

Wright, George T.
1976. "Eliot Written in a Country Churchyard: The Elegy and *Four Quartets*," *ELH* Summer, pp. 227–43.

Yoklavich, John M.
1951. "Eliot's 'Cocktail Party' and Plato's 'Symposium,'" *Notes and Queries* Dec. 8, pp. 541–42.

Selected Additional Readings

Arrowsmith, William
1977. "Daedal Harmonies: A Dialogue on Eliot and the Classics," *Southern Review* Jan., pp. 1–47.

Bateson, F. W.
1951. "Contributions to a Dictionary of Critical Terms, II: Dissociation of Sensibility," *Essays in Criticism* July, pp. 302–12.

Collins, Michael
1976. "Formal Allusions in Modern Poetry," *Concerning Poetry*, pp. 5–12.

Donker, Marjorie
1974. "*The Waste Land* and the *Aeneid*," *PMLA* Jan., pp. 164–73.

Everett, Barbara
1980. "Eliot's Marianne: *The Waste Land* and Its Poetry of Europe," *Review of English Studies* Feb., pp. 41–53.

Heywood, Christopher
1977. "Francis Hodgson Burnett's *The Secret Garden:* A Possible Source for T. S. Eliot's 'Rose Garden,'" *Yearbook of English Studies*, pp. 166–71.

Knight, W. F. Jackson
1958. "T. S. Eliot as a Classical Scholar" in *T. S. Eliot: A Symposium*, ed. Neville Braybrooke, pp. 119–28. New York: Farrar, Straus and Cudahy.

Mendel, Sydney
1971. "Dissociation of Sensibility," *Dalhousie Review* Summer, pp. 218–27.

Misra, K. S.
1977. *The Plays of T. S. Eliot.* New Delhi: Sana's Univ.

Monod, Sylvere
1976. "Entre l'argre et l'écorce: T. S. Eliot chez les Victoriens," in *De Shakespeare à T. S. Eliot*, ed. Marie Jeanne Durry et al., pp. 263–73. Paris: Bouvier.

Morrissette, Bruce A.
1953. "T. S. Eliot and Guillaume Apollinaire," *Comparative Literature* Summer, pp. 262–68.

Morse, J. I.
1976. "T. S. Eliot in 1921: Toward the Dissociation of Sensibility," *Western Humanities Review* Winter, pp. 31–40.

Mudford, P. G.
1969. "Sweeney among the Nightingales," *Essays in Criticism* July, pp. 285–91.

Paul, David
1952. "Euripides and Mr. Eliot," *Twentieth Century* Aug., pp. 174–80.

Schluter, Kurt
1966. *Der Mensch als Schausspieler.* Bonn: H. Bouvier.

Shanahan, C. M.
1955. "Irony in Laforgue, Corbière, and Eliot," *Modern Philology* Nov., pp. 117–28.

Unger, Leonard
1981. *Eliot's Compound Ghost: Influence and Confluence.* University Park: Pennsylvania State Univ. Pr.

Zulli, Floyd, Jr.
1966. "T. S. Eliot and Paul Bourget," *Notes and Queries* Nov., pp. 415–16.

CHAPTER 6

The Modern Poet

Eliot may have proclaimed himself a Classicist, a royalist, and Anglo-Catholic, but many, perhaps most, of his admirers have not shared those commitments. In recent years we have come to see more clearly his links with the English poetic tradition, even with his Romantic and Victorian predecessors, but he made his mark as a poetic revolutionary. *The Waste Land* is a classic modern poem rather as *Ulysses* is a classic modern novel—an impressive *tour de force* and something of a dead end. The years which transformed Eliot from an unknown young American into a pillar of the British literary Establishment also made the difficulties of his poetry less shocking. But increased familiarity and understanding has not made the poetry less difficult, even by comparison with much contemporary verse. Eliot has more in common with the great Victorians than he conceded, but when we read his poems there is no question but that we are reading a modern poet.

What makes Eliot's poetry distinctively modern is more a matter of poetic technique than sensibility, if such distinctions are at all valid. Unfortunately, Eliot criticism has devoted far less time to analysis of technique than to interpretation. The availability of drafts of *The Waste Land* and *Four Quartets* allows us to see Eliot at work, but critical analysis of these drafts has so far been limited. We do not seem to have a generally accepted critical vocabulary for discussing the techniques of modern poetry.

It is possible, of course, that one should speak of Eliot as a "modernist" rather than a "modern." The great modern classics have been with us for over fifty years, and their authors have passed from the scene. The Age of the Modern may be over; our contemporary poets do not write like Eliot, any more than our contemporary novelists write like Joyce. Eliot is a part of our history, along with the other great modernists, despite his considerable influence on younger writers. The "New Criticism" Eliot is sometimes credited with inspiring is no longer fashionable. Looking at the course of Eliot criticism over the years, one cannot escape the impression that it has grown more knowledgeable but less sensitive. This may simply reflect the general state of contemporary literary criticism, which seems excessively mechanical and excessively theoretical by turns, faults which may be the price of having attained academic respectability. This trend is nevertheless far more serious than the ups and downs one can expect to find in the reputation of a recently deceased poet like Eliot. If Eliot criticism is to have anything but academic interest, it must help us recover those aspects of his work which remain fresh and which continue to challenge our preconceptions about the nature of poetry—those qualities, in other words, which make him a modern poet.

The Craftsman

Eliot's criticism of individual writers is at its best when it is concerned with matters of craft; interpretation, as such, is relatively rare in his essays, and ideological essays like those in *After Strange Gods* are among his weakest efforts. His method in dealing with craftsmanship leans heavily on selective and comparative quotation. Such comparisons often lead Eliot to generalizations; for example, he quotes William Morris and then Andrew Marvell. After the latter quotation, he remarks that "these verses have the suggestiveness of true poetry; and the verses of Morris, which are nothing if not an attempt to suggest, really suggest nothing; and we are inclined to infer that the suggestiveness is the aura around a bright clear centre, that you cannot have the aura alone" ("Andrew Marvell"). The immediate object of such remarks is to illuminate the qualities and merits of a particular poet, though the generalizations have often influenced other critics in dealing with other poems. Although F. R. Leavis and others follow a similar critical method, criticism of Eliot's craftsmanship has been more affected by his generalizations than by his method. Eliot criticism seems determined to find some more systematic approach, but this honorable purpose has not yet resulted in many great successes.

One might, of course, hope to find the key in Eliot's generalizations. Something like this hope animates Ann P. Brady's

Lyricism in the Poetry of T. S. Eliot (1978). Brady's insistence on the lyric character of Eliot's poetry is very sound, but she begins by setting impossible conditions for generic definition and goes on to maintain that Eliot meets them. Brady insists that critics discussing literary genres must work only within the categories honored by tradition, no matter how vague in outline these may be; such restraints apply, if at all, to literary historians only, and the looseness with which "lyric" has been used through the years means that any inclusive definition on these terms is likely to lack all heuristic value. Brady rejects as insufficiently inclusive both Elder Olson's neo-Aristotelian description of the characteristic objects and manner of lyric poetry and the common definition of lyrics as poems meant to be sung; her resistance to the notion that lyrics have characteristic subject matters is more consistent than Eliot's, and she retains the relationship to music as no more than an analogy. Brady claims that "Eliot nevertheless has something which approximates a theory on lyric poetry" (p. 8), but what she quotes in support of this are remarks suggesting that, in reading poetry in general, we should attend to clarity of expression, rhythm, diction, imagery, and syntax. This does not constitute a theory of lyric poetry in particular, and it leads Brady to no new insights into Eliot's craft. Her best passages are interpretive in ways which have little to do with either theory or technique.

A much more acute account of Eliot's efforts to describe the distinctive features of poetry is *Between Fixity and Flux* (1947) by Sister Mary Cleophas (Costello), a monograph which deserves more recognition than it has received. Cleophas finds Eliot relatively consistent in his generalizations, but she does not claim that they add up to a fully developed theory, much less an adequate one. Her approach is Aristotelian, a critical stance that is at least systematic enough to be able to describe Eliot's positions in a broader intellectual context. His criticism is seen as couched "in a romantic vocabulary and riding in the territory of expressionism" but somehow eluding "romantic capture" (p. 110). Writing without the benefit of later studies of Bradley's influence and in the belief that Eliot's criticism lacks "a metaphysical center" (p. 109), Cleophas cannot explain why Eliot did not become a Romantic subjectivist. Nevertheless, her study is worth consulting.

The most frequently discussed aspect of Eliot's craftsmanship is probably his imagery, perhaps because it is most clearly linked to interpretation. A number of such studies have been cited in earlier chapters, and among those remaining we might note several which touch on imagery which serves a structural function in *Four Quartets:* Sister Marie Virginia, "Some Symbols of Death and Destiny in *Four Quartets*" (1958); John Bradbury, "*Four Quartets:* The Structural Symbolism" (1951), which explores the use of the four classical elements of air, earth, water, and fire; George A. Knox, "Quest for the Word in Eliot's *Four Quartets*" (1951), which discusses those passages in which Eliot debates the power of words to convey the Word; and R. V. Lancaster, "Symbols of the Journey in T. S. Eliot's 'Four Quartets' " (1972). More general in scope is Paul Fussell's "The Gestic Symbolism of T. S. Eliot" (1955), which is also of interest, once one gets past its pretentious Jungianism.

Partly because of the interpretive bias of such studies, they say little about what makes Eliot's imagery distinctively Eliotic or distinctively modern. More technically oriented is Krishna Rayan's essay "Suggestiveness and Suggestion" (1969). Influenced by Eliot's remarks like those on Marvell (cited above), Rayan argues that Eliot employs a form of "controlled suggestion," with more exact images suggesting more precise associations (though not allegorical) than some of the fuzzier Romantics. The images are certainly precise (Eliot's "bright, clear centre"), but reading Eliot criticism would suggest that Rayan exaggerates the amount of control Eliot exercises over the associations he raised (Eliot's "aura of suggestiveness"). The paucity of controlling context is, in fact, one of the unsettling features of some images in the early poetry—for example, "Madame de Tornquist, in the dark room / shifting the candles" ("Gerontion").

The sharp contrast between such images and more context-bound images in the same poem has been seen as an important feature of Eliot's early poetry in Sherna S. Vinograd's "The Accidental: A Clue to Structure in Eliot's Early Poetry" (1949). The figures in "Gerontion," writes Vinograd, are isolated, "pure" images, but they "appear in a poem saturated with meaning"; the irony of the poem as a whole "tends to make symbols of images," as the reader struggles to make arbitrary images cohere with "the more strictly symbolic 'old man in a dry month' " (p. 234). The poems move from level to level; Prufrock's meditations move us from simple images (e.g., "arms that lie along a table") to mysterious symbols (e.g., "a pair of ragged claws"), as the poem oscillates between lyric and dramatic manners.

Vinograd points out that such pure images were cultivated as well by the Imagists; and one might add that investing such images with the evocative power of symbols is an important feature of Symbolism and, perhaps, of the Romantic movement in general.

Vinograd's essay is an unusually useful account of the way that effect is achieved in Eliot's early poetry. Many critical interpretations of Eliot try too hard to make such "accidental" images seem necessary, while critics who stress Eliot's Symbolist background provide a valuable corrective but sometimes neglect the context of meaning in which such images appear. To neglect either is to distort the character of his poetry.

Vinograd's "accidentals" probably lie behind the phenomenon which G. Rostrevor Hamilton discusses in the title essay of *The Tell-Tale Article* (1949). Hamilton is concerned with the increasing use of the definite article in modern poetry, an increase which he offers some statistics to document. Some of the more obtrusive examples may well be due to Eliot's influence—W. H. Auden's "the simple act of the confused will" certainly seems to echo Eliot's "the infirm glory of the positive hour." The definite article suggests particularity and recognition, but many of its uses work to make arbitrary images claim the general significance of symbols. Hamilton sees Eliot's use of "the" as related to the Imagist emphasis on particular images, the fragmentary character of Eliot's individual vision, and the peculiarities of his syntax: "its inactive verbs, its restricted interplay of the parts of speech, its avoidance of subordinate clauses, and its reliance on the adjectival phrase" (p. 58). Hamilton is not entirely comfortable with this phenomenon in Eliot, and deplores its use in Auden and others. Hamilton is stronger in description than analysis, but his discussion of Eliot is one of the most specific discussions of Eliot's diction and syntax.

The most obvious and remarked-upon aspects of Eliot's diction are connected with his conscious efforts to reform poetic diction by bringing it closer to everyday speech and the reality of everyday life. The importance of this is more often assumed than discussed in detail. The approach followed in A. C. Partridge's discussion of Eliot in *The Language of Modern Poetry* (1976) is primarily, perhaps excessively, rhetorical. Kirsti Kivimaa's "Aspects of Style in T. S. Eliot's *Murder in the Cathedral*" (1969) provides an unusually detailed account of a single work. Kivimaa's conclusions are sometimes intolerably banal—"Eliot's vocabulary is characterized on the one hand by the concrete, on the other by the abstract" (p. 87)—but he provides a useful description of the diction of this play and some comparisons with other works. One of Eliot's most characteristic devices is discussed in some detail by Keith Wright in two useful essays: "Rhetorical Repetition in T. S. Eliot's Early Verse" (1965) and "Word Repetition in T. S. Eliot's Early Verse" (1966). Peter Reinau has also contributed a study on these devices: *Recurring Patterns in T. S. Eliot's Prose and Poetry: A Stylistic Analysis* (1978).

Traditional rhetoric is still our only fully developed vocabulary for such analysis; and of the studies just mentioned, only Reinau takes us far into the newer stylistics. We hope, of course, that developments in linguistics will ultimately produce a more securely based methodology for stylistic analysis. M. H. Short's " 'Prelude I' to a Literary Linguistic Stylistics" (1972) offers some observations on Eliot's poem and on the appropriate role of linguistics in such efforts. Short's analysis is based on Halliday's grammatical work, while Chomsky's is the ultimate source for Nina Nowakowska's *Language of Poetry and Generative Grammar* (1977), which offers analyses of a number of Eliot poems. Nowakowska's monograph is ambitious and interesting, but does not take us very far. Written in the dense jargon of apprentice linguists, it suffers from the syntactical and sentence-level biases of the linguistic grammars it relies on. Linguistic analyses may someday help us analyze Eliot's style, but the case is not yet proved.

Although traditional rhetorical terms can be useful in classifying Eliot's figures of speech, traditional metrical terms do not always help us understand his rhythms, and traditional stanza patterns are even less applicable to his verse. Eliot, of course, used traditional forms on occasion, with a virtuosity that is, perhaps, a bit obtrusive. Outside the early quatrains, the clearest example is probably the "sestina" which opens "Dry Salvages II." Critics have generally noted, sometimes with disapproval, that this is not a classic sestina. Stephen J. Adams has probably put an end to criticisms of its technique by his demonstration that the form employed is a *coblas estrampas* with *rimas cars*, a form employed by Arnaut Daniel and known to Eliot through Pound ("T. S. Eliot's So-called Sestina: A Note on 'The Dry Salvages,' " 1978), though one may continue to find it unsuccessful in other ways. More unusual is William M. Gibson's discovery, "Sonnets in T. S. Eliot's *The Waste Land*" (1961): a regular Shakespearean sonnet begins at line 236 in the typist sequence of the Fire Sermon and a less regular one follows immediately. Gibson argues that the irony of the passage is enhanced by recognition of the sonnet form and its associations. That is possible, although most of the irony is probably already present in the more readily recognizable iambic pentameter base of the lines.

Except for the occasional use of standard stanza forms, the usual object of Eliot's verse is to establish a rhythm regular enough to affect the ear but too varied to impress itself on the casual reader. The most thorough account of Eliot's metrical manipulations is Thomas R. Rees's *The Technique of T. S. Eliot* (1974). Rees is at his best in working with the early verse, which he finds dominated by variations on iambic pentameter, with which Eliot took increasing liberty. After the tetrameter quatrains of the 1920 volume, " 'Gerontion' marks a return to the repetitive patterns, the longer lines, and blank verse variations of Eliot's earlier poetry" (p. 158). The heroic line also dominates *The Waste Land*, where it is sometimes syllabic and sometimes accentual, and subject to even greater variation. After *Ash Wednesday*, Eliot's verse is primarily accentual, with syllabic sequences as occasional variants. As it becomes more difficult to analyze Eliot's verse in terms of an underlying traditional English metric, Rees's touch seems less sure, but in this he is no worse than most critics.

Metrical variation is not simply a matter of variations within the measures of traditional scansion, but of playing the natural rhythms of speech off against the conventional stress pattern of the metrical line employed. Even when accentual, traditional English metrics is based on a simple opposition of stressed versus unstressed syllables, while the spoken language has more than one level of stress. In *An Analysis of the Prosodic Structure of Selected Poems of T. S. Eliot* (1948), Sister Mary Martin Barry recognizes two kinds of stresses, primary and secondary. Much of her analysis is based on "groups" of syllables, each with a primary stress as a "centroid." A group will have its own distinctive cadence, based on the placement of the primary stress, and groups of cadences may form a recurring "phrasal cadence." Discussion of the patterns these form in Eliot's verse is kept largely separate from discussion of the pattern of stresses across the line; the latter reveals Eliot's use of a metrical base and his variations on it. This separation has the unfortunate effect of obscuring the interplay of the two patterns. Since Barry's discussion of groups and their cadences is not very productive, her failure to relate it more closely to traditional metrics seems a pity.

Many linguists would prefer to see English treated as having four significant (phonemic) levels of stress (unstressed, tertiary, secondary, and primary), as proposed in the 1957 Trager-Smith analysis of English stress, pitch, and juncture (*An Outline of English Structure*). Pitch and juncture are also relevant to the rhythms of natural speech, for they affect our perception of stress. Few prosodic discussions of any poet are that sophisticated, and Elizabeth K. Hewitt's analysis, "Structure and Meaning in T. S. Eliot's *Ash Wednesday*" (1965), is a rare example among Eliot criticism. Hewitt tries to relate traditional metric analysis, cadences created by the alternation of primary stresses with other syllables, and the Trager-Smith phonemic analysis. Pitch and juncture are marked where relevant, and the analysis is based on Eliot's recording of *Ash Wednesday*. The resulting essay is rather technical, but far superior to Rees or Barry as a guide to Eliot's rhythmic manipulations. The most interesting finding is probably that metrically regular lines are often irregular at other levels of analysis, while metrically irregular lines often "contain a regular rising or falling movement on the measure or cadence level" (p. 434). The most important service of Hewitt's essay, however, is as a model for prosodic analysis of Eliot.

More traditional in its approach but still worth consulting is Jiri Levy's essay, "Rhythmical Ambivalence in the Poetry of T. S. Eliot" (1959). Levy is particularly concerned with "the incongruence of line division and clause division, resulting in the surprising frequency of enjambement" (p. 54). Of special interest is her reconstruction of lines 11 through 19 of *Ash Wednesday V*, where a rhythmically regular rhymed sequence may have been rearranged by the poet into a passage heavy with enjambement. Also of interest is John Chalker's "Aspects of Rhythm and Rhyme in Eliot's Early Poems" (1966). This is a rather miscellaneous essay, but it makes a number of useful observations, particularly about the ways in which Eliot sets up and defeats our expectations. There is room for more essays along the lines explored by Hewitt, Levy, and Chalker, as there is for work on other aspects of Eliot's craftsmanship.

Eliot in the Arts and Drafts

Contemporary criticism is not at its best in dealing with lyric sequences and the problems of form they present. Eliot's longer poems present similar problems of structure, *The Waste Land* most of all. One symptom of these difficulties is the tendency to discuss Eliot's work in terms of analogies with other art forms, and it may be a sign of the state of contemporary criticism that such symptoms are sometimes mistaken for solutions. We now have draft versions of both *The Waste Land* and *Four Quartets*, but so far these have done more to cast doubt on earlier accounts of the poems' structures than to encourage more adequate ones.

There are, of course, some real connections between Eliot's work and contemporary developments in other arts. Jacob Korg has a valid point to make about the development of Modernist sensibility when he says that "the fragmentation and re-integration observable in *The Waste Land* can be regarded as the same process as that used by the Cubists and Futurists, springing from a similar intention, and having a comparable effect" ("Modern Art Techniques in *The Waste Land*," 1960, p. 457). Supporting details about Eliot's interest in contemporary art movements can be found in works like David Tomlinson's "T. S. Eliot and the Cubists" (1980) and Timothy Materer's *Vortex: Pound, Eliot, and Lewis* (1979). But Materer's "Vorticists" are a very diverse group; Eliot's links to contemporary art say more about the *Zeitgeist* than about Eliot's craftsmanship. To speak of the "spatial form" of works like *The Waste Land*, as Joseph Frank does ("Spatial Form in Modern Literature," 1945), may be to mistake a metaphor for an analysis. B. H. Fussell's "Structural Methods in *Four Quartets*" (1955) is less troublesome, since Fussell recognizes that the "spatial" elements which pattern the poem are balanced by the way in which, through "repeated use of such symbols as fire and rose in varied contexts throughout the poem, each symbol accumulates a load of rich associations" (p. 239). But even here one feels that Fussell has more faith in poetry's ability to halt and reverse the flow of time than Eliot displays in the *Quartets*.

Eliot was also interested in the dance. Like other modern poets, he sometimes used the dance as a symbol, uses well covered by Audrey T. Rodgers in "Dance Imagery in the Poetry of T. S. Eliot" (1974) and *The Universal Drum* (1979). But it is hard to agree with M. Gilbert Porter that "by envisioning the Quartets as planned and improvised commentary on a taped performance of a serious ballet, and by imagining Eliot as the commentator offering the descriptions, interpretations, and personal reflections that make up the commentary, the reader can see in the poetry and in the narrative stance a rationale that would otherwise be difficult to discern" ("Narrative Stance in *Four Quartets:* Choreography and Commentary," 1969, p. 66). Porter's "reading" of the *Quartets* in this fashion is, however, amusing.

Analogies with music are even more common in Eliot criticism. Encouraged by Eliot's titling his last poems "quartets," critics have pursued the analogy between them and string quartets far past the point of usefulness. There has been less written about the role of music in his early verse, though there are many musical references in it. The most famous are the Wagner references in *The Waste Land.* These serve no structural function, though Herbert Knust has made large claims for the role of Wagner and mad King Ludwig of Bavaria in the poem and has found more references to them than one would have believed possible—far more, in fact, than it is possible to believe ("Wagner, the King, and *The Waste Land,*" 1967). Another operatic reference (to Puccini) has been suggested by George E. Dorris, but it has little significance ("Two Allusions in the Poetry of T. S. Eliot," 1964). In music as in painting, Eliot's real place is with the Modernists of his time, a likeness manifest in his late-blooming friendship with Igor Stravinsky (described in Robert Craft, "Stravinsky and Eliot," 1978).

Eliot also displayed continuing interest in less serious music, including a special fondness for music hall songs and performers. Bawdy songs lie behind Mrs. Porter and her daughter in *The Waste Land* and the one-eyed Riley song in *The Cocktail Party*. Such tastes give some point to Charles Sanders' essay "*The Waste Land:* The Last Minstrel Show?" (1980). The ubiquitous Tiresias seems less objectionable when presented as "Mr. Interlocutor," and the analogy points to a real vein of humor in Eliot. Bruce R. McElderry, Jr., has identified a ragtime tune which provides *The Waste Land* with "Eliot's 'Shakespeherian Rag' " (1957). Eliot's interest in the heavy rhythms and other effects of jazz has been noted in studies like Morris Freedman's "Jazz Rhythms and T. S. Eliot" (1952) and W. E. Yeomans' "T. S. Eliot, Ragtime, and the Blues" (1968). Freedman's essay concentrates on *Sweeney Agonistes,* Eliot's most interesting experiment with jazz rhythms. Both Freedman and Yeomans find influences in *Old Possum's Book of Practical*

Cats, though both are aware of the resemblance between Eliot's nonsense poetry and the stress-heavy verse of Edward Lear and W. S. Gilbert. Yeomans is more inclined than Freedman to find jazz and blues sounds in the later poetry; his most convincing examples come from *Murder in the Cathedral*.

The jazz rhythms used in *Sweeney Agonistes* can be found in jazz lyrics; their presence is quite clear, and they bring to *Sweeney Agonistes* many of their original associations. The common analogy between the form of the *Quartets* and music like that of Beethoven's late string quartets is a simple analogy. The analogy is hardly original with Eliot, but he certainly endorses it in "The Music of Poetry" (1942): "There are possibilities for verse which bear some analogy to the development of a theme by different groups of instruments; there are possibilities of transitions in a poem comparable to the different movements of a symphony or a quartet; there are possibilities of contrapuntal arrangement of subject-matter." It seems likely that this reflects Eliot's thinking in working on the *Quartets* and that this passage may even have been meant as a gentle hint to his critics.

The usefulness of this analogy can be seen in Helen Gardner's chapter "The Music of 'Four Quartets' " in her *The Art of T. S. Eliot* (1949). She notes that the form of the *Quartets* is "essentially the same as the structure of *The Waste Land*" but "far more highly developed" (pp. 37, 43). One is tempted to say that the difference is between a form discovered and a form imposed. Gardner also suggests that the form provides an English equivalent for the Pindaric ode, and she calls attention to the great freedom Eliot allows himself within the constraints of the overall form. The virtue of such observations is that Gardner makes it quite clear that Eliot used the musical analogy to help himself work out a literary solution to an essentially literary problem. Gardner's treatment of the "music of imagery" in the *Quartets* points to another merit of the analogy, in that it calls one's attention to variations and development, which "should prevent any reader from trying to fix the symbols in *Four Quartets*" (p. 54). Gardner's treatment of this topic, like other chapters in her book, has influenced many later commentators.

The danger in such analogies, of course, is when one begins to look for one-to-one correspondences. Herbert Howarth's "Eliot, Beethoven, and J. W. N. Sullivan" (1957) proposes that Eliot based all the *Quartets* on Beethoven's *A Minor Quartet*

Opus 132, a work earlier suggested as an analogue for *Ash Wednesday* by Stephen Spender (*The Destructive Element*, 1935). Howarth also proposes Sullivan's biography of Beethoven as a source for the *Quartets*. Few, if any, of the examples are convincing. Harvey Gross's "Music and the Analogues of Feeling: Notes on Eliot and Beethoven" (1959) at least recognizes the futility of picking out particular quartets, but presses the analogy further than is justified.

Another danger inherent in the quartet analogy can be seen at work in Keith Aldritt's *Eliot's Four Quartets: Poetry as Chamber Music* (1978), where the analogy becomes an excuse for reading the poem as four interwoven monologues. Aldritt identifies the four voices as "the lecturer, the prophet, the conversationalist, and the conjurer" (p. 39), and finds several of these voices in each section of the poem. As a heuristic device for talking about the shifting tones of the poem, this sometimes pays off, but Aldritt's insistence that the voices he hears are a real part of the poem is wholly unpersuasive. As a whole, this procedure does more to dissolve the unity of the *Quartets* than to explain it. One cannot help observing that in a true string quartet, more than one voice would be heard at a single moment, an effect hard to achieve in poetry. Although Aldritt has some scattered insights to offer, few have any legitimate connection to chamber music; his most interesting pages deal with Eliot's connection to the French Symbolist tradition.

So long as Eliot's drafts were unavaible, it was possible to hope that, buried in them, would be irrefutable evidence of some elaborate form, concealed in the published version by poetic transformation and condensation. Aware that Pound had made heavy cuts in *The Waste Land*, some thought that the drafts would reveal a more clearly structured form. If the primary effect of publication of *The Waste Land* manuscript was to accentuate the personal sources of the poem, almost equally important was the revelation that the original manuscript was even more fragmentary in form than the finished poem.

The Waste Land manuscript is the main topic of three of the essays in *Eliot in His Time* (1973), a collection edited by A. Walton Litz in honor of the poem's fiftieth anniversary. Richard Ellman's essay, mainly concerned with biographical implications, sees Pound's revisions as tightening the form of the poem, but this comes to little more than reducing the variety of fragments included. Helen Gardner speaks of Eliot as having "invented a form that allowed him to compose in the jets and spurts of inspiration that came naturally to him, and, like a worker in mosaic, to find a place in his pattern for lines and even passages that had been composed at very different times" (p. 92). This is very just, and it applies to all of Eliot's longer poems, but it does not help us understand what that form is. Hugh Kenner speaks of the final poem as "the first exemplar of a category that still has no name" and of Eliot's repetition of the form in "Burnt Norton" as done "on the principle that a form is anything done twice" (pp. 24, 47). Kenner argues that the central portion of the poem began as a Drydenesque London satire, but this is not entirely convincing; in any case, Kenner sees the final poem as very different. His negative conclusions are much more persuasive: "It is difficult to believe that anyone who saw only the first four parts in their original form would believe that 'the plan and a good deal of the incidental symbolism' were suggested by Jessie Weston's book on the Grail Legend, or that *The Golden Bough* (Frazer's, not Vergil's) had much pertinence" (p. 43). Such reflections need not imply that the Grail legend, for example, is unrelated to the form of the final version; what is clear is that such form as *The Waste Land* exhibits in its final version is not the result of any initial plan but of Eliot's attempts to organize his fragments.

Given sufficient ingenuity, it is possible to give deceptive traditional labels to the formal structure of both the drafts and the final poem. Marshall McLuhan, for example, says that Pound's intervention transformed the poem from "meditational four-level exegesis" to "a five-division pattern of classical oratory" ("Pound, Eliot, and the Rhetoric of *The Waste Land*," 1979), but McLuhan's learned numerology is defensible only as an analogy which allows one to talk about the differences between Eliot and Pound. Although the drafts make Tiresias-as-unifying-persona look even more like a not very appropriate afterthought, Glauco Cambon's rambling consideration, "*The Waste Land* as Work in Progress" (1972), shows that it is possible to see the poem as evolving naturally toward such a central prophetic persona.

On the whole, however, publication of the drafts has made it more difficult to see such patterns or personae as keys to the poem's structure. One might still argue that they have been successfully imposed by the final arrangement, but the effect of the drafts has been to reinforce doubts about the significance of such traditional guideposts to the poem. One possible response is to denigrate the poem for failing to meet the formal criteria held by the critic, but such responses seem pointless. *The Waste Land* remains a powerful poem; despite the fragmentary character of its surface, it has far more unity of effect than, say, Tennyson's lyric sequences. Criticism must be able to explain such qualities before attempting to evaluate them. The object, not yet achieved, is to explore the implications of what M. L. Rosenthal has called "*The Waste Land* as Open Structure" (1972). Rosenthal's essay emphasizes both the tentativeness of any closure achieved in the poem, including the final passages, and the undeveloped possibilities glimpsed in the draft.

The form of *Four Quartets* is open as well, at least in the sense that the closure achieved at the end of "Burnt Norton" left room for Eliot to build on this model the structure of the *Quartets* as a whole. The imagery of seasons and elements which binds the poems together was devised after "Burnt Norton" was written. The "Burnt Norton" model and the pattern of imagery constitute, in any case, a very minimal scaffolding for a poetry still composed in fragments. Helen Gardner's book, *The Composition of Four Quartets* (1978), gives us the drafts and associated correspondence, along with invaluable commentary by Gardner. It is, perhaps, less exciting than the rediscovery and publication of *The Waste Land* manuscript, but it is far more complete. The friends Eliot relied on for criticism of these drafts—notably John Hayward—lack the independent stature of Pound, but their criticisms and Eliot's responses are often detailed at some length in correspondence. There is material here for a great deal of discussion of Eliot's craftsmanship—one notes his great concern for rhythm, his self-awareness in the use of sources, and his interest in establishing links with his earlier work.

At this writing, critics have only begun to respond to the *Four Quartets* drafts. One would expect that the material in the Gardner volume would suggest the *ex post facto* character of their structure as a whole. It appears, for example, that Eliot at one point planned no more than three poems in this group. A letter to Hayward would appear to set limits to the musical analogy implied by the term "quartets": "I am aware of general objections to these musical analogies: there was a period when people were writing long poems and calling them, with no excuse, 'symphonies' (J. Gould Fletcher even did a 'Symphony in Blue,' I think, thus achieving a greater *confusion des genres*). But I should like to indicate that these poems are all in a particular set form which I have elaborated, and the word 'quartet' does seem to me to start people on the right tack for understanding them ('sonata' in any case is *too* musical). It suggests to me the notion of making a poem by weaving in together three or four superficially unrelated themes: the 'poem' being the degree of success in making a new whole out of them" (p. 26). The musical analogy thus points more to Eliot's aims than to his literary means.

Gertrude Patterson's *T. S. Eliot: Poems in the Making* (1971) is a full-length study of Eliot's process of revision, based on manuscripts then available, including access to *The Waste Land* manuscript before its publication. Patterson makes interesting use of the analogy with Modernist art, and her book contains some particularly acute observations of interest, but it can only be considered a preliminary effort. Robert L. Beare's "Notes on the Text of T. S. Eliot: Variants from Russell Square" (1957) is based on published volumes. These variants pose a variety of problems; many appear to be errors, but some may represent the author's intentions. We might note that Gardner's book on the *Quartets* drafts raises some further problems with the published text. These are matters which are bound to complicate any study of Eliot's craftsmanship; only in the plays are there variations of substantial significance, except for isolated lyrics later included as part of poems like *Ash Wednesday*. More work remains to be done in the textual bibliography of Eliot's work, in his process of revision, and in the larger formal issues raised by his major poems.

The Modernist

If there is reason to see Eliot's work in the context of Modernist movements in the other arts, it is even more appropriate to see his poetry as part of the Modernist movement in literature. Whether or not "Modernism" proves, in the end, to be a useful term to describe Eliot's era, his relations with his literary contemporaries remain of great interest. It must be admitted that no other figure looms as large as Pound, whose influence on the younger Eliot was so large that it belongs as much to Eliot's biography as to any account of his purely literary relationships. As authors go, Eliot shows an unusual amount of self-doubt, a relatively rare striving after humility, and even a fair amount of generosity of spirit; even so, his relations with the other major literary figures of his time are characterized by a certain wariness on his side (often more than reciprocated).

Among the great Modernists, James Joyce is, after Pound, the most closely linked with Eliot, for *Ulysses* and *The Waste Land*, both published in 1922, remain among the major landmarks of Modernism. Through Pound, Eliot had seen much of Joyce's work in advance, and he echoed Pound's praise of it. His response to *Finnegans Wake* was somewhat more ambivalent (see Jack P. Dalton, "A Letter from T. S. Eliot" 1968), but he helped arrange for its publication by Faber and Faber and generally spoke well of it in public. By then, Eliot's and Joyce's work had taken different directions, Eliot's poetry becoming more traditional and Joyce's prose less so. In 1922, however, they seemed to share what Eliot called "the mythical method" in his 1923 *Criterion* essay "*Ulysses*, Order, and Myth."

In this essay Eliot wrote that "in manipulating a continuous parallel between contemporaneity and antiquity, Mr. Joyce is pursuing a method which others must pursue after him. They will not be imitators, any more than the scientist who uses the discoveries of an Einstein. . . . It is simply a method of controlling, of ordering, of giving a shape and a significance to the immense panorama of futility and anarchy which is contemporary history." Since that is what Eliot hoped the Grail motif would do for *The Waste Land* and since Eliot had seen much of *Ulysses* before writing his own work, one is bound to wonder whether the imposition of the Grail quest on *The Waste Land* was due to the example of Joyce. Joyce may have thought so, and seems to have resented the prestige and prizes that came to Eliot while *Ulysses* was banned. Joyce's feelings can be seen in the references to Eliot in the *Wake*, which have been summarized by Nathan Halper ("Joyce and Eliot," 1965).

For some critics, Eliot's debt goes much further than the mythic method. The earliest of such source studies seems to have been Giorgio Melchiori's "*The Waste Land* and *Ulysses*" (1954a). The fullest is probably Robert Adams Day's "Joyce's Waste Land and Eliot's Unknown God" (in *Literary Monographs*, ed. Rothstein, 1971). More recent and limited is Peter Barry's "Some Further Correspondences between the 'Proteus' Section of James Joyce's *Ulysses* and *The Waste Land*" (1976). The most cautious of such efforts is probably Thomas Lorch's "The Relationship between *Ulysses* and *The Waste Land*" (1964), which concludes that the influence was largely unconscious. Many of the parallels adduced in these studies are unconvincing; manipulation of literary allusions, pastiche, and even an interest in myth were features of Eliot's poetry before his acquaintance with Joyce's work.

Stanley Sultan's monograph, "*Ulysses,*" "*The Waste Land*" *and Modernism* (1977), reviews some of the alleged cases of influence. Although he accepts some as genuine borrowings, his concentration is on the mythic method. He sees the influence of Joyce as most significant in part V of *The Waste Land*, which retrospectively established the framework for the parts written earlier. Even more important, in Sultan's view, is the existence of important similarities in method between two works of very different men. This confluence of theme and approach, he suggests, demonstrates that "Modernism" has some legitimacy as a term, despite the diversity it must cover.

Sultan's monograph is well argued, though whether Joyce was the particular influence leading to the presence of the Grail quest in *The Waste Land* (or at least in its notes) remains uncertain. A. Walton Litz's essay, "Pound and Eliot on *Ulysses:* The Critical Tradition" (1972), suggests that Eliot did not fully understand the "mythical method" of *Ulysses* until he read Valery Larbaud's 1922 essay on the book. Pound praised it for realism in the tradition of Flaubert, but Eliot was uneasy with Joyce's work until he managed to see it in a more congenial frame. Litz takes Pound and Eliot as early exemplars of permanent poles in criticism of *Ulysses*, the long conflict between those who praise its novelistic qualities and those fascinated by its archetypal structure. This is an important point, for the same split exists in criticism of *The Waste Land.* If one believes that the structure of *The Waste Land* derives from Jessie Weston, and if one follows faithfully all the charts Joyce passed on to critics like Stuart Gilbert and Larbaud, the mythical method is very important to both works. But one may see either or both works as less determined by such mythic themes than their authors led early readers to believe. Perhaps it is the playfulness and ambiguity of their relationship to such imposed forms which most links the authors of *The Waste Land* and *Ulysses.*

In "The Lotus and the Rose: D. H. Lawrence and Eliot's *Four Quartets*" (1954b), Giorgio Melchiori suggested a debt that would be surprising if it rested on sounder grounds. The *Four Quartets* is also where C. E. Baron finds "Lawrence's Influence on Eliot" (1971). Melchiori's case rests on shared images with a much longer history; Baron's on trivial verbal echoes. Although Baron's essay is not persuasive as a source study, its review of Eliot's attitude toward Lawrence is interesting in other ways. Eliot's critical animadversions on Lawrence, especially in *After Strange Gods*, are sufficiently notorious. Critics who regard Lawrence as a major figure, notably F. R. Leavis, have tended to reduce the relationship between them to a contrast between the life-affirming Lawrence and the life-denying Eliot. Baron's essay reminds us that Eliot's attitude was not consistently negative and that it always rested on a willingness to take Lawrence's ideas seriously.

When one looks at contemporary figures who may have influenced Eliot, it seems that minor figures are as apt to have provided sources as major ones. An early Thomas Mann novella shows some interesting parallels with *The Waste Land*, demonstrated in Heinz Wetzel's "The Seer in the Spring: On *Tonio Kroger* and *The Waste Land*" (1970), but the two works do not suggest a direct link. *The Cocktail Party*, where Edward says that "hell is oneself," may somehow be meant to respond to Jean Paul Sartre's *No Exit*. Bernard F. Dick's suggestion that the same passage may echo Sartre's *Nausea* is plausible, but no more than that ("Sartre and *The Cocktail Party*," 1978). At least as convincing are suggestions that *The Cocktail Party* may take its theme from a novel by Charles Williams, Eliot's saintly friend. Unfortunately, we have two candidates here–*Descent into Hell*, proposed by R. H. Robbins (in an essay mentioned in Chapter 3, above), and *The Greater Trumps*, proposed by Lois G. Thrash ("A Source for the Redemption Theme in *The Cocktail Party*," 1968). Among little-known poetic sources, one might cite Madison Cawein, who published a poem about a desolate landscape called "The Waste Land" in *Poetry* in 1913. Richard F. Patteson thinks this cannot be coincidental ("An Additional Source for 'The Waste Land,' " 1976), but it could.

In his essay on *Ulysses*, Eliot mentions Yeats, in passing, as an employer of myth; and certainly, if the mythical method is a feature of Modernism, Yeats had his own way of practicing it. Eliot can be linked to Yeats, as to Joyce, through Pound; but Eliot was never comfortable with Yeats' unabashed Romanticism. His remarks on Yeats in *After Strange Gods* are less harsh than those on Lawrence but equally notorious. Like Lawrence, Yeats can be seen as an anti-Eliot, warm blooded where Eliot is cold; like Lawrence, Yeats seems to have seen the difference in that way. Because Yeats and Eliot are two of the major poets of our time, their differences are important, seeming to force upon us a choice we are unwilling to make. Considering their contrasting views, G. S. Fraser concludes "the two great poets are complementary because we sense obscurely that there is some point at which the way of acceptance and the way of rejection of the world's bright images meet" ("W. B. Yeats and T. S. Eliot," 1958).

Although Eliot usually treated Yeats' work with wary respect, Yeats does not become a living presence in Eliot's verse until Eliot himself concluded that "the way up" and "the way down" are the same. Even then, it is a partial Yeats who appears as part of the compound ghost in "Little Gidding." Richard Ellmann provides a graceful account of Eliot's attitudes toward Yeats in his survey of Yeats in the work of other great Modernists, *Eminent Domain* (1967). Ellmann concludes that "true friendship was only possible after Yeats was dead, and could be sifted down to those elements which Eliot found congenial. That he found, at last, so many, is a measure of Yeats's continued sway over the mind" (p. 95). Eliot seems to have intended the "Little Gidding" passage as a tribute; Christopher Brown reads it in a more negative way, and finds another "attack" on Yeats' style in "Eliot on Yeats: 'East Coker, II' " (1976). Brown may be right in seeing a Yeats echo in the lyric of "East Coker II," but it does not follow that the subsequent comment on "a worn-out poetical fashion" is intended for Yeats.

Yeats as a source appears to be rare in Eliot. Ellmann's book certainly suggests little mutual influence, though a more positive account is given in Kristian Smidt's "T. S. Eliot and W. B. Yeats" (1965). Among more specific articles, Donna Gerstenberger's suggestion that Yeats' *Calvary* influenced Eliot's *Murder in the Cathedral* is very tentatively put, and is less likely than her observation that Eliot's play, in its turn, influenced Stephen Spender's *Trial of a Judge* ("The Saint and the Circle: The Dramatic Potential of an Image," 1960). Phillip L. Marcus' comparison of Yeats' "The Tower" with "Gerontion" has some interest, but it does not seem likely that Yeats wrote his poem with Eliot's in mind (" 'I Declare My Faith': Eliot's 'Gerontion' and Yeats's 'The Tower,' " 1978). An alternative suggestion of Marcus, that Yeats later saw his poem as an appropriate response to Eliot's, is more plausible. Perhaps the most likely case of influence, mentioned by a number of critics of Eliot's plays, is the influence of the metrics of Yeats' *Purgatory* on Eliot's adoption of a three-stress norm for his later plays: In "Poetry and Drama" (1951), Eliot says that Yeats "solved his problem of speech in verse" in *Purgatory* "and laid all his successors under obligation to him."

As Frank Wood points out in "Rilke and Eliot: Tradition and Poetry" (1952), 1922 was the year of Rainer Rilke's *Duino Elegies* and *Sonnets to Orpheus*, as well as *The Waste Land* and *Ulysses.* Although Margaret Church has suggested the influence of *Sonnets to Orpheus* in "Eliot's 'Journey of the Magi' " (1960), most essays on Rilke and Eliot are, like Wood's, comparative. Both, notes Wood, can be seen as Alexandrian poets, and there are some shared thematic concerns as well. Wood's essay concentrates on their common concern for tradition, which they approached in very different ways. H. P. Rickman compares the two poets in "Poetry and the Ephemeral: Rilke's and Eliot's Conceptions of the Poet's Task" (1959). The similarities found by Rickman and Wood are very general in character; whatever affinity they suggest between the two poets seems more temperamental than distinctively Modernist. A common interest in experiences that go beyond words is apparent in the *Duino Elegies* and the *Four Quartets.* Elsie Weigand makes a sensitive comparison of the eighth elegy and "Burnt Norton" in "Rilke and Eliot: The Articulation of the Mystic Experience" (1955). Even in Weigand's analysis, the differences bulk as large as the similarities. Stephen Spender, who has been influenced by both poets, writes of their contrasting visions in "Rilke and the Angels, Eliot and the Shrines" (1953).

In 1930 Eliot published a translation of St. John Perse's *Anabase*, helping to spread Perse's influence among poets writing in English. Eliot has admitted to influence by particular lines and rhythms of Perse in his poems of the late twenties and early thirties, but Perse does not seem to be a significant source for Eliot, however, and the affinity between them is less than may be suggested by the translation of *Anabase*. Eliot's translation may in fact distort some of Perse's qualities, as is held by C. E. Nelson ("Saint-John Perse and T. S. Eliot," 1963) and Roger Little ("T. S. Eliot and Saint-John Perse," 1969). Little's study is the better of the two, noting the changes made in the translation through the years, generally in a direction closer to the simplicity of the original and away from the archaisms and biblical tone of Eliot's first version.

The natural relationship between Eliot and other poets writing in English was rivalry, exacerbated by Eliot's established position. Jeffrey Hart's review, "Frost and Eliot" (1976), speaks of Frost's having "conducted a kind of private war with Eliot"

(p. 425), though Hart goes on to discern some resemblances. Robert Graves' early collaboration with Laura Riding, *A Survey of Modernist Poetry* (1927), treats Eliot's work with considerable respect and acuity; but Graves later attacked Eliot as Muse-less, notably in "These Be Your Gods, O Israel" (1955), an essay included in Graves' *The Crowning Privilege* (1955). William Carlos Williams came to feel that Eliot's and Pound's great error was in going to Europe; and Paul Mariani cites a number of Williams' comments, public and private, in "The Poem as Field of Action: Guerilla Tactics in *Paterson*" (1976).

In Graves and Williams, as in Frost, one can find resemblances to Eliot—both, for example, have their own "mythical method"—but their reactions remind us that poets are, in Graves' terms, natural competitors for the favors of the Muse. All three poets demonstrate, as well, that concern for poetic independence which marks our age as Romantic and suggests how little Eliot's "Tradition and the Individual Talent" affected that Romanticism. Poets less strong minded than these had yet another reason for rejecting Eliot: his lines and rhythms have a way of sticking in one's ear and reappearing in one's verse; and those who seek their own voice may need, first, to reject his influence.

The Influence

Measuring Eliot's influence on others is, of course, not much easier than measuring their influence on him, particularly when one is dealing with poets, who may feel bound to resist the influence even of poets who have served them as early models. With critics, one is perhaps on firmer ground, since they are apt to flourish their sources as authorities. The case is somewhat easier for novelists or poets working in another language, where potentially dangerous influences become less threatening by operating in another medium or another language. Eliot's poetry has found echoes in a number of novels and in a multitude of tongues. Even so, it seems likely that most would find him most important as an influence on poets and critics writing in English, though examining the works of those he is said to have influenced may suggest that it was his criticism that influenced the poets and his poetry that influenced the critics.

One of the clearer cases of Eliot's influence, and one of the earliest, is the debt owed to Eliot's "The Love Song of J. Alfred

Prufrock" by Conrad Aiken's "The Jig of Forslin," as noted in Joseph Warren Beach's "Conrad Aiken and T. S. Eliot: Echoes and Overtones" (1954); Beach also notes possible echoes of Aiken's poem in *The Waste Land*. The verbal echoes are close in each case. Whether, as Beach seems to suggest, Eliot is responsible for the new direction "Forslin" marks in Aiken's verse is much less clear. Here, as in many other cases, it is not easy to disentangle Eliot's influence from that of others, particularly Pound.

Another fairly clear case of influence by Eliot is W. H. Auden, whose verse, early and late, contains echoes of Eliot. Eliot also influenced other members of the "Auden group," including Stephen Spender and, to some extent, C. Day Lewis, who discusses Eliot's influence in his own *A Hope for Poetry* (1934). Eliot's influence on Auden and Spender has been discussed by Morton Seif ("The Impact of T. S. Eliot on Auden and Spender," 1954) and by most critics who have dealt with either of the younger poets. In Spender's verse, Eliot's influence appears as an alien presence; Auden, on the other hand, is a magpie poet, with great powers of assimilation, always Audenesque and always echoing someone. Much of Eliot's influence on Auden may have come through directing his attention to other poets.

In such American poets as Hart Crane and Allen Tate, Eliot's critical essays also seem to have been as influential as his poetry. Critical essays on both poets often cite Eliot as a poetic influence, and it is generally conceded that Crane's *The Bridge* was written in emulation of and rivalry with *The Waste Land*. Some of Eliot's allusive manner may have communicated itself to both poets, Crane in particular, but the critical revolution Eliot (and Pound) helped bring about was at least as important. Where one finds in such poets the influence of the Metaphysicals or the later Elizabethans, one is bound to suspect the presence of Eliot.

If Eliot's early influence is hard to disentangle from that of Pound, it is hard to separate his later influence from that of Auden or Tate. Only biographical or autobiographical works can settle such questions. Among the latter, one of particular interest is Donald Davie's essay "Eliot in One Poet's Life" (1972), which deals with Eliot's influence on a poet of a younger generation. Of his early, apprentice poetry, Davie says that his first efforts "had nothing to do with Eliot's practice as a poet but had everything to do with what he was taken to have recommended in theory" (p. 231), particularly the "unified" sensibility of the Metaphysical poets. The earlier poems of Eliot had already been closed off as possible living influences for Davie by the well-meaning explications of schoolmasters. *Four Quartets* he could discover and explore for himself, but their verse was too loose to suit Davie's needs; what he learned from Eliot was diction and carefulness in the use thereof.

Davie speaks of having deliberately avoided reading Eliot for several years, in an effort to "root out of my own style the Eliotic cadences which were making it not mine at all" (p. 236), a reminder at once of the strength of Eliot's influence and of a poet's natural resistance to it. Although ours is increasingly an age of Romanticism in criticism as well, celebrating originality and inclined toward subjective Idealism, our critics seem far more comfortable than our poets in echoing the ideas of their masters. Eliot is generally recognized as one of those masters. In particular, he is usually given credit for fathering the American "New Criticism." Eliot's influence on the New Critics is enshrined as conventional wisdom in such surveys as Walter Sutton's *Modern American Criticism* (1963) and Arnold Goldsmith's *American Literary Criticism, 1905–1965* (1979), and Eliot is discussed at length in John Crowe Ransom's *The New Criticism* (1941), a book which gave its name to the movement. But Ransom, presumably a New Critic himself, is very critical of Eliot's views, although an admirer of Eliot's early poetry. Eliot also assumes a fairly prominent part in Murray Krieger's *The New Apologists for Poetry* (1956), one of the earliest attempts to draw a coherent theory out of New Critical practice, though Krieger, too, is not uncritical of Eliot. Most of the major New Critics have written about Eliot's poetry and cited his criticism at some point—respectfully—unless one includes Yvor Winters as a New Critic.

The association of Eliot with New Criticism is, however, puzzling in a number of ways. Eliot's critical theories, if one may call them that, do not seem closely aligned with the New Critical practice, and his critical practice is quite unlike theirs. It is likely that he had some effect on their critical tastes, but it is hard to decide whether this was because his essays persuaded others to appreciate the Metaphysicals or because his poetry affected their sensibility in ways which made the Metaphysicals seem newly relevant. As usual, it is hard to distinguish in some cases between Eliot's influence and Pound's. It is certain that phrases from his criticism, though sometimes rather obscure, became watchwords in some circles. In poetry, one takes such verbal echoes as signs of influence; in criticism, one attends to ideas, and Eliot's ideas have not always remained attached to Eliot's words. As an intellectual source for the New Criticism, I. A. Richards may well be more important; as an example, William Empson may be more important.

One of the most interesting recent examinations of Eliot's relation to the New Criticism is Grant Webster's *The Republic of Letters* (1979). Webster's is one of those humanistic applications (or misapplications) of Thomas Kuhn's *The Structure of Scientific Revolutions* (1962) to other facets of intellectual history. Eliot's *The Sacred Wood* is seen as a "charter," a source of intellectual authority which allows subsequent generations to develop its implications and work under its umbrella, rather as Kuhn's "paradigms" are said to do in science.

As is perhaps inevitable when one turns from science to a more subjective field, literary charters turn out to have social determinants. Webster's term for the New Criticism is "Tory Formalism," and he stresses its conservative social implications. Whether this is fair to the New Criticism is a moot point. Webster's treatment almost certainly has the effect of overstating the congruence between Eliot and the New Critics. It is probably not unfair to term Eliot a Tory (though Davie suggests he is more like a Whig), but neither his views nor his practice have much in common with the "formalism" eventually developed by the New Critics. Webster's book is, however, excellent of its kind, and stimulating as well. Other Kuhnian parallels occur to one, for example. One could see Eliot's poetry as one of those "anomalies" which prove the old paradigm inefficient and force a new approach; what Webster calls "the Age of Explicators" has little to do with Eliot's theory or practice but a great deal to do with the critical problems posed by his poetry. Much of the prestige of Eliot's criticism derives from the prestige of his poetry; some of the appeal of his criticism must have been that it offered clues to reading his poetry and examples of other poetry which might respond to the same approach.

We do not reprove novelists for borrowing images from poets or insist that they understand them; this is just as well, as critics have found images from Eliot's poetry, particularly *The Waste Land*, in a number of American novelists. Such references appear as incidental touches in the novels, though it is customary to exaggerate their importance in critical articles. In F. Scott Fitzgerald's *The Great Gatsby*, for example, the billboard eyes of Dr. T. J. Eckleburg gaze on a "valley of ashes," at one point described as a "waste land." Critics have noted this and found a number of less convincing parallels. One of the first such efforts was Philip Young's "Scott Fitzgerald's Waste Land" (1956), in which Young is concerned with the possibility of influence. More purely comparative in approach and based on more tenuous links are such later essays as those by Dale B. J. Randall ("The 'Seer' and 'Seen' Themes in *Gatsby* and Some of Their Parallels in Eliot and Wright," 1964) and Michael Pottorf ("*The Great Gatsby:* Myrtle's Dog and Its Relation to the Dog-God of Pound and Eliot," 1976).

The thematic parallels between *The Waste Land* and Ernest Hemingway's *The Sun Also Rises* are more striking, particularly in Hemingway's use of water symbolism, as discussed in George D. Murphy's "Hemingway's *Waste Land:* The Controlling Water Symbolism of *The Sun Also Rises*" (1971). Richard P. Adams, in fact, has claimed that Hemingway's novel is based on the same myth and method as Eliot's poem, and that this was probably due to direct influence ("Sunrise Out of *The Waste Land*," 1959). Nicholas Joost and Alan Brown provide a useful, though overly appreciative, survey of the various parallels that have been seen between Eliot and Hemingway in their "T. S. Eliot and Ernest Hemingway: A Literary Relationship" (1978). Despite Hemingway's professed aversion to *The Waste Land*, it is possible that he picked up certain tricks of style from Eliot. The larger claims made by Adams and generally endorsed by Joost and Brown are, at best, unproved. Even if one accepts a "mythic" reading of *The Sun Also Rises*, interest in myth was common enough in the period that the direct influence of Eliot need not be hypothesized; the parallels between the novel and *The Waste Land* need reflect no more than common sources of imagery. Shared temperament seems a sufficient explanation for the parallels which lead Joost and Brown to conclude that "Eliot's attitude toward sex approximated Hemingway's so closely that he imitated Eliot's depiction of sexual relationships" (p. 449).

Frederick L. Gwynn has noted echoes of Eliot's early poetry in William Faulkner's *Mosquitoes* ("Faulkner's Prufrock–And Other Observations," 1953), but it is far more usual to make comparisons between a Faulkner novel and *The Waste Land*. Critics have found parallels between Eliot's poem and most of Faulkner's early novels. The most convincing parallels are with *Pylon*, but those most often cited are with *The Sound and the Fury*, resemblances probably doomed to frequent rediscovery as teachers of modern literature find themselves teaching the two works in close succession. The resemblances are not, however, terribly striking. Faulkner's use of April, for example, may serve the same function as Eliot's, but Faulkner's dating is presumably tied to Easter, while Eliot's April represents a more general springtime. In most of Faulkner's novels, in fact, the "mythic" imagery is much more specifically Christian than Eliot's in *The Waste Land*. The parallels between *The Sound and the Fury* and *The Waste Land*, drawn in Ida Fasel's "A 'Conversation' between Faulkner and Eliot" (1967), sometimes seem ludicrous, as when "maternal lamentation" is paralleled with "Mother Compson's repeated 'I'll be gone soon' " (p. 205), a very different kind of lamentation.

Eliot's high prestige makes it seem likely that many novelists have been familiar with his work. To the extent that the "mythical method" is common in modern works—as opposed to being common only to critical discussions of them—Eliot is certainly one possible source, but hard to separate from others. Such reservations apply to most of the articles just discussed. Anthony R. Kilgallen's "Eliot, Joyce, and Lowry" (1965) has at least the virtue of recognizing such multiple sources. In other cases, one may have the author's confession of a debt as supporting evidence, as Leonard Deutsch does in "*The Waste Land* in Ellison's *Invisible Man*" (1977). Minor verbal echoes aside, however, what Ralph Ellison may admit owing to Eliot are technical devices that are part of the common currency of Modernism—discontinuity, allusiveness, and the mythical method.

Eliot's influence in other literatures is also frequently more as a representative of Modernism than as a poet with unique characteristics. The most distinguished of the foreign poets Eliot may be said to have influenced is probably George Seferis, who translated *The Waste Land* and who himself received the Nobel Prize for Literature in 1963. In his 1956 essay "T. S. Eliot and the Poetry of George Seferis," Edmund Keeley cites a number of verbal parallels but gives special stress to the influence of *The Waste Land* on Seferis' "Mythical Story" (or "Myth of History"), a long poem undertaken a couple of years after Seferis first read Eliot's. Even in this essay, Keeley notes that myth plays some role in Seferis' poetry *before* Seferis read *The Waste Land*. Writing in 1969, Keeley finds even less influence by Eliot in "Seferis and the 'Mythical Method.' " Keeley now stresses the differences between Eliot's and Seferis' use of myth, while continuing to believe that reading Eliot may have encouraged

Seferis "to move from the rather vague symbolizing of *The Cistern* to the much more dramatic mode of expression in *Mythistorema*" (p. 117). Our understanding of the nature and limitations of Eliot's influence on Seferis is also improved by Rowena Fowler's article "'Η Ἔρημη Χώρα: Seferis' Translation of *The Waste Land*" (1972). Fowler suggests that this was a case of a poet's recognizing in "another's work the poem which he himself feels both the need and the power to write" (p. 444). What struck Seferis, and what survives in his translation, are the images of sterility and the introduction of modern men and colloquial speech. The metrical distinctions of Eliot's verse are flattened out, and even the diction is more regular in tone. What Seferis found in Eliot was a way of dealing in poetry with the life around him.

In non-Western cultures, Eliot's influence is partly that of a prestigious Modernist and partly that of a representative Western culture. A number of studies have testified to Eliot's impact on consciously "modern" Arabic poets. That Eliot was held in particular regard seems evident, but the qualities and techniques cited as influencing Arabic poets are shared with other modern poets. This is reasonably clear in Shmuel Moreh's "The Influence of Western Poetry and Particularly T. S. Eliot on Modern Arabic Poetry (1947–1964)" (1969). The qualities Moreh dwells upon are sometimes not very important in Eliot, and actually clearer in, say, the Imagists—and Moreh quotes the verse of Amy Lowell several times. Even more striking is the linking of Eliot's influence with that of Edith Sitwell in the poetry of al-Sayyab—noted in studies by Nazeer El-Azma ("The Tammuzi Movement and the Influence of T. S. Eliot on Badr Shakir al-Sayyab," 1968) and Arieh Laya ("Al-Sayyab and the Influence of T. S. Eliot," 1971). Besides allusions to traditional myths, what is stressed in these studies is Eliot's influence on al-Sayyab's efforts to break out of traditional Arabic verse patterns—a bit surprising when one remembers Eliot's famous dictum that there is no such thing as "free" verse.

Free verse is also seen as the product of Eliot's influence in Khalil I. H. Semaan's "T. S. Eliot's Influence on Arabic Poetry and Theater" (1969). To be fair, the cited examples sound, in technique, more like Eliot than like true free verse. Semaan's essay, after a few preliminary generalities, is devoted to the work of al-Sabur and, especially, to comparison of the Egyptian poet's play *Tragedy of Hallaj* with Eliot's *Murder in the Cathedral*. Semaan recognizes that much is individual and distinctively Arabic in the former play; even so, Louis Tremaine has argued that the parallels with Eliot have been exaggerated by Semaan and the contrasts understated ("Witnesses to the Event in *Ma'sat al-Hallaj* and *Murder in the Cathedral*," 1977).

If Eliot influenced al-Sabur's play, this would be an exception to the rule that non-European writers have been most influenced by Eliot's early poetry, especially *The Waste Land*. That rule is borne out in such general surveys as Yoko Sugiyama's "*The Waste Land* and Contemporary Japanese Poetry" (1961) and Kim Jong Gil's "T. S. Eliot's Influence on Modern Korean Poetry" (1969). The same is true, of course, of European poets like Seferis and novelists like Faulkner.

If *The Waste Land* was not intended to express the disillusionment of a generation, it came to do so; the apocalyptic images which appealed to American novelists in the twenties may seem understandably relevant to some Japanese poets living in the age of Hiroshima. Eliot's early poetry also incarnates a sense of vanishing tradition and urban fragmentation which may be relevant to other societies undergoing rapid, sometimes forced, "modernization." To a lesser extent, we may also say that Eliot's influence on Anglo-American poetry and criticism has often been as a leading exemplar of Modernist trends. That does not mean that his influence has not been real and important. It suggests, rather, that Eliot was right in maintaining (in "Tradition and the Individual Talent") that the most important features of a poet's work need not be the most individual ones.

The Culture Hero

In 1945, Delmore Schwartz wrote "T. S. Eliot as the International Hero"; in 1949, Schwartz wrote "The Literary Dictatorship of T. S. Eliot." The titles of these essays suggest the stature Eliot had acquired in Anglo-American literary circles since the publication of *The Waste Land* in 1922. The first of Schwartz's essays goes even further than its title suggests, for it celebrates Eliot as one of those Promethean "culture heroes" who make "possible a new range of experience" (1945, p. 199). The second article, however, despite the respect it shows for much of Eliot's criticism, shows a certain restiveness about his "dictatorship." Eliot's reputation was probably at its height in those years, when the achievement of the *Four Quartets* was still fresh. In the years between World War II and his death,

Eliot gained a wider audience with his plays, but he did little to enhance his reputation as a poet and critic in literary circles. His importance was generally acknowledged, but the battle to establish that importance was over, and Eliot no longer seemed a fresh discovery; in the same period, Eliot criticism lost some of its freshness, though articles and books on his work proliferated.

To follow the progress of Eliot's reputation in those years, the handiest aid is Mildred Martin's *A Half Century of Eliot Criticism: An Annotated Bibliography of Books and Articles in English, 1916–1965* (1972). Martin's annotations are brief but they are useful and sometimes evaluative; items she considers especially valuable are asterisked in the bibliography and its subject index. Martin's book contains nearly 2,700 items; even so, it did not exhaust the possibilities, and a supplementary volume, covering the same period, has since been issued by the *Yeats-Eliot Review* (formerly the *T. S. Eliot Review*), which also annotates current Eliot criticism on a regular basis. Martin's knowledge of the body of that criticism is also displayed in an earlier review article, "T. S. Eliot: The Still Point and the Turning Wheel" (1953). Much of this article concentrates on the ideological sources of critics' responses to Eliot's work.

The best of the other available guides to the mass of Eliot criticism is probably Richard Ludwig's chapter on Eliot in *Sixteen Modern American Authors* (rev. ed., 1973), a bibliographical volume edited by Jackson R. Bryer. Ludwig and others have also contributed comments on current Eliot criticism to the annual volumes of *American Literary Scholarship.* Two earlier review essays are still of interest for their comments on issues raised by the criticism: E. K. Brown's "Mr. Eliot and Some Enemies" (1938) and Peter Monro Jack's "Review of Reviews: T. S. Eliot's *Four Quartets*" (1944). The tremendous volume of Eliot criticism has led some recent critics to be rigidly selective in their notes and bibliography, at the cost of obscuring some of their debts. Authors who attempt to relate their interpretations to those of their predecessors risk having their own work submerged in a flood of bibliographical comment. Something like that happens in Marianne Thormählen's "*The Waste Land*": *A Fragmentary Wholeness* (1978), giving her book a rather fragmentary character, but making it especially valuable as a guide to the views of various Eliot critics on particular passages of *The Waste Land.*

Although later critics usually note their predecessors as a

prelude to correcting their errors, Eliot's admittedly difficult poetry received perceptive criticism well before the postwar boom in Eliot criticism. George Watson's essay "The Triumph of T. S. Eliot" (1965) reviews the early criticism and concludes that "Eliot's success was not only profoundly merited, but was total and instantaneous within the terms it set for itself: the capture of young intellectuals of creative energy in England and the United States in the 1920's" (p. 337). Watson argues that most of the opposition was from an older generation and its adherents, as one might expect in any literary revolution; even so, he notes, establishment organs, like the *Times Literary Supplement,* recognized Eliot's distinction quickly, and Cambridge was awash with Eliot's influence well before F. R. Leavis began to advocate his cause.

Watson suggests that Leavis and others are inclined to exaggerate their own daring in championing Eliot. Watson probably underestimates the power of older generations in academic circles; there is reason to believe that Leavis has suffered for his opinions at times, though he has hardly been a passive victim. But Watson's principal points seem well taken. Even the early attacks on Eliot's work usually confirm, by their complaints, that Eliot had rapidly become an accepted leader of the avant-garde young. Some of the early critical response was also remarkably perceptive, for example, Edmund Wilson's 1922 essay on *The Waste Land* as "The Poetry of Drouth."

By the 1930s, Edith Sitwell could describe the publication of "Prufrock" as having begun "a new reign in poetry" (*Aspects of Modern Poetry*, 1934, p. 99). In England, a number of works of lasting significance in Eliot criticism were published early in the decade, including the sections on Eliot in Leavis's *New Bearings in English Poetry* (1932), I. A. Richards' *Principles of Literary Criticism* (1930), and an excellent short book on Eliot, Hugh Ross Williamson's *The Poetry of T. S. Eliot* (1932). Richards' and Leavis's essays were to influence a number of later critics, an influence multiplied in Leavis's case by his editorship of *Scrutiny*. Leavis's essay is still a worthwhile exploration of what is new in Eliot's poetry and what makes it valuable. Williamson's book is one of the first to take up the detailed explication of Eliot's poetry; as such, it still seems sensible and sensitive.

In America, the early thirties saw the publication of the chapters on Eliot in Wilson's *Axel's Castle* (1931) and of valuable essays by critics like Allen Tate and R. P. Blackmur. The burden of more detailed explication was taken up in America by F. O. Matthiessen in *The Achievement of T. S. Eliot* (1935). Matthiessen's book was revised with chapters on later work in 1947, and the 1958 edition includes a chapter by C. L. Barber on the later plays. It has helped shape the reading of Eliot by two generations of American academics. Part of its interest, and even its influence, may come from Matthiessen's open efforts to reconcile his wholehearted acceptance of Eliot's poetry and aesthetic principles with his distaste for Eliot's political and religious tendencies. Matthiessen's solution to this "problem" helped provide a model for many later critics. His interpretations have largely been absorbed into the received wisdom about Eliot. Today, his book's most unusual feature may well be its efforts to relate Eliot to the American literary tradition, since this is an aspect of his approach which has not seemed especially useful to later critics.

Although most of what is valuable in Matthiessen no longer seems surprising, his book remains one of the better one-volume treatments of Eliot's work. Matthiessen is able to deal with Eliot as a major poet without losing sight of his limitations and to deal with Eliot's limitations without abandoning the critic's natural humility in the face of art. Matthiessen is personally engaged with Eliot's poetry and his own task of interpretation, but one feels that his goal is to understand the poetry and convey that understanding, rather than impress the reader with his sensibility. These are qualities which Matthiessen shares with many of Eliot's early critics–Leavis being a notable exception–which one misses in many later critics.

Much of the best early criticism of Eliot is collected in Leonard Unger's *T. S. Eliot: A Selected Critique* (1948). Included, along with a few negative estimates, are many of the essays which helped consolidate the interpretation of Eliot's poetry in the years of his most creative work. (Many of these essays have been noted in earlier chapters.) What is worth noting is the personal and undogmatic tone of most of these pieces. It may be significant that those items not extracted from books generally derive from literary quarterlies; five, for example, come from the *Southern Review*. The rhetorical model of such essays, one feels, is the personal essay rather than the scholarly article.

By 1950, Eliot had published all of his significant poetry and the best of his plays. Much of the basic work of Eliot criticism had also been done. Readers could turn to Matthiessen, the

Unger volume, and the contributions to B. Rajan's *T. S. Eliot: A Study of His Writings by Several Hands* (1947), which included a number of important essays. As a basic one-volume introduction to Eliot's work, Matthiessen's had been matched in importance by Helen Gardner's *The Art of T. S. Eliot* (1949). Gardner's book gave special attention to the *Four Quartets*, and remains one of the best introductions to them. To this basic library some would add Elizabeth Drew's *T. S. Eliot: The Design of His Poetry* (1949); a rather uneven collection of essays edited by Tambimuttu and Richard March (*T. S. Eliot: A Symposium*, 1948); or other works. In any case, readers were reasonably well served by the criticism then available.

In the 1950s and early 1960s, good essays and books on Eliot's work continued to appear, but it seems fair to say that little new ground was broken in discussion of his poetry. Hugh Kenner's *The Invisible Poet* (1959) deserves credit for drawing attention to the importance of Bradley, and Eliot's plays began to receive detailed scrutiny. Grover Smith's book on Eliot's use of sources, first published in 1956 (discussed earlier), was certainly important, but all of Smith's careful exploration of sources adds little to our understanding of Eliot's work. Source hunting became a characteristic feature of Eliot criticism in these years, and the customary exaggeration of the importance of the sources (found or alleged) contributes to one's impression that Eliot criticism had become the "Eliot industry," characterized by routine production, often shoddy workmanship, and overselling. The focus seems to shift from the originality of the poet to the originality of the critic, in essays more distinguished for ingenuity than for plausibility. In other essays, neither the poet nor the critic seems to have any original ideas, the essay serving as a simple act of piety toward an established idol; some of the religiously minded journals seemed to publish several such pieces each year. Eliot himself has sometimes been blamed for the deficiencies of such Eliot criticism, on the dubious basis of his alleged responsibility for the New Criticism; but even if Eliot is held responsible for the New Criticism, neither he nor its pioneers can fairly be held accountable for what its epigones made of it. Eliot was fated to be a figure of indisputable prominence in a period in which there were more and more professors, under more and more pressure to publish, with more and more journals in which to publish.

The major lines of attack on Eliot's reputation were arrived at fairly early. We have already seen this in the case of ideological objections to the political and religious assumptions and implications of his work, and it is true of more strictly literary approaches as well. Some of the early attacks on Eliot, to be sure, were based on simple, almost willful misunderstanding. Suggestions that *The Waste Land* was some kind of hoax probably come under that heading. One of the best, though hardly the first, is Herbert Palmer's "The Hoax and the Earnest of *The Waste Land*" (1933). This line of attack has been largely abandoned, though as late as 1973 one can find Sisirkumar Ghose pondering the question "hoax or masterpiece–if only one could be sure!" ("*The Waste Land* Revisited," p. 7). Criticism of Eliot as overintellectual, narrow in range, and lacking in respect for Life began early, encouraged by early interpretations which refused to see any kind of hope in the ending of *The Waste Land*.

At least some of the objections to Eliot were objections to qualities he shared with other Modernist writers, but that is not to say that the objections lack force or value. One of the most forceful and articulate attacks on Eliot is Yvor Winters' "T. S. Eliot: The Illusion of Reaction," which appeared in the *Kenyon Review* in 1941 and whose editor, John Crowe Ransom, had his own reservations about Eliot's poetry and criticism. Winters' literary judgments have always been based on consistent literary principles much at variance with the modern consensus, and their resulting "eccentricity" has deprived him of much of the influence that might otherwise have come from his merits as a poet and intelligence as a critic. Even so, admirers of Eliot should try to come to terms with Winters' essay, which is also available in the Unger collection and two of Winters' collections. Winters complains that Eliot's poetic practice and influence exhibit a subjective Romanticism out of keeping with his alleged Classicism and traditionalism. Winters links the alleged defects of Eliot's poetry with Eliot's praise of Pound. Winters may well be more Classical and traditional than Eliot, and, given his assumptions, his denigration of Eliot may be justified.

In the late 1950s, one begins to hear more of an alternative complaint against Eliot; he is not a modern at all, but a representative of the dead hand of tradition. As an ideological line of attack on Eliot, this goes back to the thirties. There is a poetic version of this complaint, too, though the two sometimes are conflated. It is based on what seems to some a return to traditional poetic diction in parts of Eliot's later poetry; even more important is the disagreement over metrics. Eliot's reservations about *vers libre* set him somewhat apart from the Imagists from the beginning, and continued to divide him from poets like William Carlos Williams, the heirs to the Whitman tradition in American poetry. Some of these poets were influenced by Pound, but they took different principles from him than Eliot had. In the postwar period, Williams and Pound were more important influences on young poets in America than Eliot. Eliot was often identified with the rival influence of Auden, a poet of wide range, impressive facility, and traditional meters; and Eliot's reputation was certainly affected by the emerging struggle between the followers of Whitman and Williams and the followers of Auden. In some cases, the struggle over metrics is part of a larger struggle between Classical and Romantic principles; but metrics had little to do with the revival of Blake's reputation and influence in the sixties.

Perhaps the most widely read attack on Eliot produced by this struggle was Karl Shapiro's "T. S. Eliot: The Death of Literary Judgment" (1960), which pronounced Eliot "the chief obstacle to poetry today" (p. 12). The essay appeared in a journal with traditionalist and liberal political biases against Eliot, but Shapiro's position is closer to that of William Carlos Williams, though his all-out attack takes advantage of most possible arguments against Eliot—even the suggestion that *The Waste Land* "was originally a hoax" (p. 35). Shapiro decides that Eliot's "problem" was a fruitless and frustrating search for mystical experience, and his "failure" seems to be traced to reluctance to take the road of excess trod by Blake, Whitman, and D. H. Lawrence.

The violence of Shapiro's attack on Eliot is partly that of a convert, for Shapiro had praised Eliot in his 1945 *Essay on Rime*, a long poem about poetry. Even in 1945, we might note, Shapiro expressed doubts about the prosody of *Four Quartets* and implied that Eliot's poetry was not much used as a model. By 1960, Shapiro's earlier admiration for *The Waste Land* had largely vanished, though he had some good words for the earlier poetry and for *Ash Wednesday*. The real secret of Shapiro's *animus* would seem to be that "literary dictatorship" of Eliot's which Delmore Schwartz had written about with ambivalence in 1949. Eliot and Pound are attacked precisely because they are said to be the sacred cows of a bland, formalist orthodoxy which threatened to strangle the development of American poetry. Returning to the attack in 1962 (in "The Three Hockey Games of T. S. Eliot"), Shapiro again appealed to the values of Whitman and Williams and denounced the Eliot-Pound "sell-out of American poetry" (p. 285). But his essay is primarily an attack on the New Criticism of the American academic establishment, for which Eliot is blamed. As one of the idols of that establishment, Eliot was the natural enemy of those for whom Modernism meant permanent revolution.

There is no alternative Modernist tradition in Britain quite like the Whitman tradition in America. D. H. Lawrence, however, has sometimes been used as a counterweight to Eliot, a way of pointing up Eliot's failure to affirm the Life Force and other good things. Lawrence's greatest British champion, F. R. Leavis, was also an early advocate of Eliot's poetry, but, as we have noted, he came to have increasing reservations about Eliot's work, particularly the later poetry. In a 1958 essay, "T. S. Eliot's Stature as Critic," Eliot was praised as a poet but damned for his failure to recognize Lawrence, and labeled an intellectual pawn of a literary-social coterie. Leavis's remarkably good ear makes him worth reading when he discusses poetry, but his remarkably inflexible mind makes him less useful as a critic of other men's ideas. For all of Leavis's moral seriousness, much of this essay has the ring of personal resentment, and its point sometimes seems to be that Eliot's *Criterion* was not as good a journal as Leavis's *Scrutiny*. One pictures a heavyweight contender talking with sullen respect of a champion who will not fight him.

Very different temperaments are involved here. Leavis believes that the "essential function of an important critic" is "value-judgment" (1958, p. 403), and his prose is chock full of them; so one can understand his distaste for Eliot's moral squeamishness and manifold qualifications. The temperamental differences can lead to misreadings. Eliot does not, for example, take the positions in "Tradition and the Individual Talent" that Leavis believes he is refuting by telling us that "without the distinguished individual, distinguished by reason of his potency as a conduit of urgent life and by the profound and sensitive responsibility he gives proof of toward his living experience, there is no art that matters" (p. 400). But Leavis's language points to the Romantic individualism of Lawrence as part of those modern sensibilities which were stirred by *The Waste Land* and troubled by *Four Quartets*.

Eliot and Posterity

In the years since Eliot's death in 1965, no single figure has won the kind of preeminence that was his, and Eliot's reputation remains high. Although negative estimates of his enduring value are becoming more common, they generally reflect old lines of attacks. Although one hears that we are moving into a "postmodern" age, it is possible that we are still too close to the great Moderns in sensibility to permit any serious reassessment. Such assessments, after all, depend in part on whether works prove to be sufficiently independent of their time to survive periodic changes in sensibility; but there is reason to believe that Eliot's work is rich enough to appeal to readers who look for qualities other than those which won him fame in his time. But the jury is certainly not yet in. In the meantime, Eliot criticism displays both gains and losses.

The two most obvious gains in understanding in this period have been in understanding the philosophical background of Eliot's criticism and the personal sources of his poetry, stimulated by the republication of Eliot's dissertation in 1964 and the publication of *The Waste Land* manuscripts in 1971. One might also say that there has been a renewed recognition of the fragmentary character of Eliot's poetry, though few of his better critics have been without that recognition, and some who now call attention to it seem unable to deal with what they find. Finally, despite the mediocre quality of much of the work in the field, the cumulative process of scholarship has added a good deal to our knowledge of Eliot's literary and intellectual sources.

The chief losses over this period are a continuation of trends that were visible as early as the fifties: Eliot criticism is too often "academic," in ways which have made that term pejorative. Too many essays seem written out of duty or self-aggrandizement rather than inner need; too few communicate any sense of intellectual excitement. And there has been a quite unnecessary proliferation of one-volume introductions to Eliot for the general reader, a need quite adequately filled by earlier works, by Matthiessen, Drew, Gardner, Kenner, George Williamson, and Hugh Ross Williamson. One of the first such books, Northrop Frye's *T. S. Eliot* (1963) is particularly suggestive, but it is rather slight for the serious reader and rather advanced for the inexperienced reader. Philip Headings's Twayne Series book, *T. S. Eliot* (1964), justifies itself by its special sensitivity to the influence of Dante, and Stephen Spender's *T. S. Eliot*

(1976), for the Modern Masters series, benefits from insights which reflect both Spender's acquaintance with Eliot and his own poetic career in the English literary world. It is hard to see any special justification, though, for T. S. Pearce's *T. S. Eliot* (1969), part of a series of Arco Literary Critiques. Nor can one see why English translations should be required for introductory volumes originally intended for French- and German-speaking readers by Georges Cattaui (*T. S. Eliot*, 1969) and Joachim Seyppel (*T. S. Eliot*, 1972). Specific guides to particular poems, aimed at students, have also proliferated.

In the 1970s, some of the book-length treatments of Eliot with greater pretensions seem scarcely more original than those intended as basic introductions to his work. Besides those already mentioned, one may cite Balachandra Rajan's *The Overwhelming Question* (1976), Derek Traversi's *T. S. Eliot: The Longer Poems* (1976), and David Ward's *T. S. Eliot: Between Two Worlds* (1973). None of these works has many original insights to offer, and none of them is very complete in recording its debts. None of them, of course, is without merit, for all three authors are sensitive and knowledgeable readers of Eliot. Rajan has a rather "poetic" prose style which sometimes seems overwrought but sometimes suceeds in capturing the movement of feeling in the poems. Although over half of Traversi's book is devoted to *Four Quartets*, its most valuable feature may be its reading of *Ash Wednesday*, probably the least thoroughly explored of Eliot's major poems. Ward's opening chapter offers some interesting observations on the relation between Eliot's poetry and his philosophical studies. Even so, all three books give one a feeling of *déjà vu*. The new data from the scholarship of the sixties and early seventies have been absorbed, but their effect on the interpretations is largely a matter of nuances.

Although Eliot is still regarded as a major modern poet, there are certainly signs pointing to a decline in his reputation. In America, this is mainly a matter of his ceasing to attract the attention of the best young critics. In England, debate over Eliot's meaning and importance remains more lively, and critics like Barbara Everett continue to find fresh approaches to his work. One is tempted to believe that the merits of "Modernism" remain moot in Britain. Accepting the argument that "Modernism" is an American invention, A. Alvarez has suggested that "it has affected English poetry peculiarly little. Instead, the most significant and powerful British geniuses, Lawrence and Yeats, were merely extending into modern terms what has always been there in the most vital of our tradition" (*Stewards of Excellence*, 1958, p. 9; published in England as *The Shaping Spirit*). One certainly hears the accents of a revived traditionalism in recent British critics who have renewed the old attacks on the "incoherence" of *The Waste Land*. But one wonders if national origins are really the key to transatlantic figures like Auden and Eliot, and one notes that Yeats and Lawrence bulk fairly large in Monroe K. Spears' *Dionysus and the City: Modernism in Twentieth Century Poetry* (1970). Such differences make one sympathize with those who ban the term Modernism, though it is no more ambiguous than most of our terms for literary periods and movements. Both Alvarez and Spears help one see Eliot in the context of fellow moderns, despite their differing definitions.

Less seriously, one might suggest that American and British critics differ in the kinds of Romanticism they are apt to embrace. In America, for a while at least, it was customary to regret Eliot's lack of Blakean excess; in Britain, his lack of Lawrentian healthy mindedness. At any rate, this line of argument, encouraged by the example of F. R. Leavis, seems to have conditioned much of the British response to the revelations of *The Waste Land* manuscript, so that discussions of the personal sources of Eliot's poetry sometimes give the impression that he would have been a better poet if he had been a better man. Americans, one sometimes feels, rather like their poets to be aberrant.

The British approach can be seen in A. D. Moody's *Thomas Stearns Eliot, Poet* (1979). In many ways, this is one of the best of recent book-length studies of Eliot. Moody is well versed in Eliot's work and Eliot criticism, and he has consulted what manuscript material is available. He is a sensitive reader of the poetry, and his critical style is personal rather than dogmatic. He reads the poetry in terms of its personal sources but without reducing it to them. At the same time, he seems drawn to the poetry rather against his will. Moody's way of dealing with this ambivalence is to suggest that the deficiences of Eliot are those of our time. "The rite of *The Waste Land*," for example, "is one to save the self alone from an alien world. . . . In such a world as ours to save even oneself takes courage, even heroism, and Eliot's poetry shows him to have had enough for that. But the heroism of *The Waste Land* is of the kind which would end the human world, not give new life to it" (p. 111). This line of argument takes over (and gets out of hand) in Moody's closing pages, where we learn that Eliot's "life-work had gone against nature and against human love" (p. 288), that Eliot's is a "neurosis which is like a dominant gene in our culture" (p. 290), and that Eliot is "a true voice of our Western world" (p. 298). This seems unnecessarily hard on both Eliot and Western civilization; it also suggests that even our evaluation of Eliot's poetry as personal poetry may be somehow tied to our judgment of his age.

The essays occasioned by Eliot's death in 1965 were, in general, reaffirmations rather than reassessments. In the volume edited by Allen Tate (*T. S. Eliot: The Man and His Work*, 1967), the only critic to make a noticeable change from previous positions is John Crowe Ransom, who recants some of his earlier reservations about Eliot's prosody and dramatic method. The Eliot spoken of in these essays is, by and large, the Classicist and formalist Eliot. Even those essays of the late sixties which make some stab at reassessment tend to express themselves in terms of such critical ideals. One of the best short essays to appear in 1965, John Wain's "T. S. Eliot," praises Eliot for having seen the need for new conventions in the twenties and then having turned to exploring the possibilities of those conventions, rather than engaging in revolution for revolution's sake.

There is obviously considerable truth in this view of Eliot's poetry and his career. At the same time, it fails to do justice to the extent to which Eliot's poetry has always been a poetry of emotions and feelings, and to the extent to which his poetry makes a deliberate effort to continue exploring ways of containing that material within some kind of form. Moreover, judging Eliot in this framework can lead to problems in dealing with the very loose character of the forms achieved in his major poems.

As the editor, Graham Martin, observes in his introduction, few of the essays in *Eliot in Perspective* (1970) offer grounds for a full-scale reassessment of Eliot and his career. Martin seems most sympathetic to his contributors whose essays on specific topics suggest some general devaluation of Eliot. In some cases, as in Ian Hamilton's essay on *The Waste Land*, the negative case depends on demonstrating that his poetry is not as impersonal, mythic, and coherently ordered as previous commentators have sometimes alleged. In other cases, the critique is essentially ideological—and even Hamilton's essay has an ideological bias. Martin's introductory remarks appear to see post-World War II conservative revival as a factor in Eliot's continued reputation, and he takes polite issue with his contributors who attempt to disentangle *Four Quartets* and Eliot's dramas from the ideological interpretations offered by admirers and detractors alike. One cannot help feeling, however, that the latter, Katharine Worth and Donald Davie among them, are on the right track. Eliot's poetry was able to speak to many left-wing readers in the 1930s despite Eliot's conservatism, probably because he is, in many ways, a personal and experiential poet rather than an intellectual one. If a new generation is to appreciate this poetry, it may have to begin by rejecting the didactic terms in which it was praised by the previous generation.

Several collections of original essays were published in response to the fiftieth anniversary of *The Waste Land*'s publication, including a fine special issue of *Mosaic* (Fall 1972), A. Walton Litz's *Eliot in His Time* (1973), and A. D. Moody's *The Waste Land in Different Voices* (1974). Some of these essays have been dealt with earlier; all reflect the new emphasis on the personal sources of Eliot's poetry. As a group, they offer very mixed signals on the likely future of Eliot's reputation. David Newton DeMolina's collection of essays, *The Literary Criticism of T. S. Eliot* (1977), on the other hand, seems predominantly negative in tone, and F. W. Bateson's title, "Criticism's Lost Leader," is symptomatic. Even the earlier criticism, generally seen as at least historically important, now seems to many less theoretically significant than it once did. Since such "doctrines" as the "objective correlative" have been under attack for decades, and since Eliot's later criticism was lukewarmly received even at the height of his reputation, these judgments are not really new, but one finds them more forcefully expressed in this collection and other recent studies.

Given such collections and the recent publications covered in earlier chapters, what can one predict about the future of Eliot criticism and Eliot's reputation? One would expect the next few decades to see continued interest in the personal character of Eliot's poetry, because it is intrinsically justified and because new biographical sources may become available. One would expect continued interest in the specifically American character of his work, less because this approach is particularly fruitful than because such an approach is useful, in different ways, to both American and British critics. At least, one can hope for a gradual reduction in the number of source studies and religious interpretations of Eliot's poetry, both of which have long since reached the point of diminishing returns. One would expect that Eliot's criticism will be increasingly of interest only to those concerned with the history of criticism or Eliot's creative work, partly because one of its most distinctive features, early and late, is a suspicion of interpretation, which appeals to critics only when accompanied, as it is not in Eliot, by a high estimation of the creative possibilities of criticism.

Such predictions depend, of course, more on the social conditions that determine criticism than on evaluative factors. Although social and political trends may have had some effect on Eliot's reputation in his lifetime, one would be loath to predict that they will determine posterity's verdict on his poetry. There will, no doubt, always be readers who find the religious character of *Ash Wednesday* or *Four Quartets* a bar to their enjoyment of those poems, and there will probably be periods in which such considerations are considered determinants of poetic value, especially since one can attach political significance to them. But even in his own time, Eliot's poetry has given pleasure to many who do not share his religious or political commitments, and it is hard to believe that his poetry is time bound in that respect.

A more serious question, one may believe, is whether the future reputation of Eliot's poetry is bound to the historical fate of the Modernism it helped foster. Eliot's respect for Classicism and tradition is based on a sense of how difficult it is to achieve balance and certainty, and a sense of how hard it is to remain in living contact with our past. Those who assume that form is easy to achieve may find, as some critics do even now, that Eliot is "formless"; one may find such attacks ill founded if one shares Eliot's vision of the world; but a new Augustan Age might well reject Eliot as Dr. Johnson rejected the Metaphysicals. Such an age might well prefer his criticism to his poetry. Still, in our own time, Eliot has appealed to some whose principles seem more in tune with his critical ideals than his poetic practice. It is possible that Eliot comes close enough to the bone of experience to satisfy at least some in the most Romantic of periods and that his efforts to impose order on that experience will satisfy at least some in the most Classical of periods.

But it is probably a condition of any really dramatic shift in literary sensibility that it changes the very terms in which one talks about literary works and their value. Words like Romantic and Classical, to be sure, may remain in use, but the meanings attached to them shift and change. The real test of Eliot's likely place in posterity is whether, over a series of such changes, new kinds of poetry provide new ways of reading Eliot, ways that give his poetry new life. In his time, Eliot gave us poetry which helped alter our sense of the literary tradition and criticism which helped register the changes. Whatever the future of Eliot criticism, it is likely to give him credit for that.

References

Adams, Richard P.
1959. "Sunrise Out of *The Waste Land*," *Tulane Studies in English*, pp. 119–31.

Adams, Stephen J.
1978. "T. S. Eliot's So-called Sestina: A Note on 'The Dry Salvages,'" *English Language Notes* Mar., pp. 203–8.

Aldritt, Keith
1978. *Eliot's Four Quartets: Poetry as Chamber Music*. London: Hogarth Pr.

Alvarez, A.
1958. *Stewards of Excellence*, pp. 9–47. New York: Scribner's. Published in England as *The Shaping Spirit*. London: Chatto and Windus.

Baron, C. E.
1971. "Lawrence's Influence on Eliot," *Cambridge Quarterly* Spring, pp. 205–48.

Barry, Sister Mary Martin
1948. *An Analysis of the Prosodic Structure of Selected Poems of T. S. Eliot*. Washington: Catholic Univ. of America Pr.

Barry, Peter
1976. "Some Further Correspondences between the 'Proteus' Section of James Joyce's *Ulysses* and *The Waste Land*," *English Studies* June, pp. 227–38.

Beach, Joseph Warren
1954. "Conrad Aiken and T. S. Eliot: Echoes and Overtones," *PMLA* Sept., pp. 753–62.

Beare, Robert L.
1957. "Notes on the Text of T. S. Eliot: Variants from Russell Square," *Studies in Bibliography*, pp. 21–49.

Bradbury, John
1951. "*Four Quartets:* The Structural Symbolism," *Sewanee Review* Spring, pp. 254–70.

Brady, Ann P.
1978. *Lyricism in the Poetry of T. S. Eliot*. Port Washington, New York: Kennikat Pr.

Brown, Christopher
1976. "Eliot on Yeats: 'East Coker, II,' " *T. S. Eliot Review*, pp. 22–24.

Brown, E. K.
1938. "Mr. Eliot and Some Enemies," *University of Toronto Quarterly* Oct., pp. 69–84.

Cambon, Glauco
1972. "*The Waste Land* as Work in Progress," *Mosaic*, pp. 191–200.

Cattaui, Georges
1969. *T. S. Eliot*, trans. Claire Pace and Jean Stewart. New York: Minerva Pr.

Chalker, John
1966. "Aspects of Rhythm and Rhyme in Eliot's Early Poems," *English* Autumn, pp. 84–88.

Church, Margaret
1960. "Eliot's 'Journey of the Magi,' " *Explicator* June, item 55.

Cleophas (Costello), Sister Mary
1947. *Between Fixity and Flux: A Study of the Concept of Poetry in the Criticism of T. S. Eliot*. Washington: Catholic University of America Pr.

Craft, Robert
1978. "Stravinsky and Eliot," *Encounter* Jan., pp. 46–57.

Dalton, Jack P.
1968. "A Letter from T. S. Eliot," *James Joyce Quarterly* Fall, pp. 79–81.

Davie, Donald
1972. "Eliot in One Poet's Life," *Mosaic* Fall, pp. 229–41.

Day, Robert Adams
1971. "Joyce's Waste Land and Eliot's Unknown God," in *Literary Monographs*, ed. Eric Rothstein, pp. 137–210. Madison: Univ. of Wisconsin Pr.

Day-Lewis, C.
1934. *A Hope for Poetry*. Oxford: Basil Bunting.

DeMolina, David Newton
1977. (editor) *The Literary Criticism of T. S. Eliot*. London: Athlone Pr.

Deutsch, Leonard J.
1977. "*The Waste Land* in Ellison's *Invisible Man*," *Notes on Contemporary Literature*, no. 6, pp. 5–6.

Dick, Bernard
1978. "Sartre and *The Cocktail Party*," *Yeats-Eliot Review*, pp. 25–26.

Dorris, George E.
1964. "Two Allusions in the Poetry of T. S. Eliot," *English Language Notes* Sept., pp. 54–57.

El-Azma, Nazeer

1968. "The Tammuzi Movement and the Influence of T. S. Eliot on Badr Shakir al-Sayyab," *Journal of the American Oriental Society* Oct.–Dec., pp. 671–78.

Ellmann, Richard

1967. *Eminent Domain*, pp. 89–95. New York: Oxford Univ. Pr.

Fasel, Ida

1967. "A 'Conversation' between Faulkner and Eliot," *Mississippi Quarterly* Autumn, pp. 195–206.

Fowler, Rowena

1972. "῾Η Ἔρημη Χώρα : Seferis' Translation of *The Waste Land*," *Comparative Literature Studies* Dec., pp. 443–54.

Frank, Joseph

1945. "Spatial Form in Modern Literature," *Sewanee Review* Apr.–June, pp. 221–40; July–Sept., pp. 433–56; Oct.–Dec., pp. 643–53.

Fraser, G. S.

1958. "W. B. Yeats and T. S. Eliot," in *T. S. Eliot: A Symposium*, ed. Neville Braybrook, pp. 196–216. New York: Farrar, Straus and Cudahy.

Freedman, Morris

1952. "Jazz Rhythms and T. S. Eliot," *South Atlantic Quarterly* July, pp. 419–35.

Frye, Northrop

1963. *T. S. Eliot.* Edinburgh: Oliver and Boyd.

Fussell, B. H.

1955. "Structural Methods in *Four Quartets*," *ELH* Sept., pp. 212-41.

Fussell, Paul, Jr.

1955. "The Gestic Symbolism of T. S. Eliot," *ELH* Sept., pp. 194–211.

Gardner, Helen

1949. *The Art of T. S. Eliot.* London: Cresset Pr.

1978. *The Composition of "Four Quartets."* New York: Oxford Univ. Pr.

Gerstenberger, Donna

1960. "The Saint and the Circle: The Dramatic Potential of an Image," *Criticism* Fall, pp. 336–41.

Ghose, Sisirkumar

1973. "*The Waste Land* Revisited," in *Literary Studies: Homage to Dr. A. Sivaramasubramonia Aiyer*, ed. K. P. K. Menon et al., pp. 4–7, Trivandrum, India: Dr. A. Sivaramasubramonia Aiyer Memorial Committee.

Gibson, William M.

1961. "Sonnets in T. S. Eliot's *The Waste Land*," *American Literature* Jan., pp. 465–66.

Gil, Kim Jong
1969. "T. S. Eliot's Influence on Modern Korean Poetry," *Literature East and West*, pp. 359–76.
Goldsmith, Arnold L.
1979. *American Literary Criticism, 1905–1968*, pp. 102–7. Boston: G. K. Hall/Twayne.
Graves, Robert
1955. "These Be Your Gods, O Israel," *Essays in Criticism* Apr., pp. 140–45. Reprinted in *The Crowning Privilege*, pp. 112–35. London: Cassell, 1955.
Gross, Harvey
1959. "Music and the Analogues of Feeling: Notes on Eliot and Beethoven," *Centennial Review* Summer, pp. 269–88.
Gwynn, Frederick L.
1953. "Faulkner's Prufrock–And Other Observations," *Journal of English and Germanic Philology*, pp. 63–70.
Halper, Nathan
1965. "Joyce and Eliot," *A Wake Newsletter* June, pp. 3–10; Aug., pp. 17–21; Dec., pp. 22–26.
Hamilton, G. Rostrevor
1949. *The Tell-Tale Article*. London: William Heinemann.
Hart, Jeffrey
1976. "Frost and Eliot," *Sewanee Review* Summer, pp. 425–47.
Hewitt, Elizabeth K.
1965. "Structure and Meaning in T. S. Eliot's *Ash Wednesday*," *Anglia*, pp. 426–50.
Howarth, Herbert
1957. "Eliot, Beethoven, and J. W. N. Sullivan," *Comparative Literature* Fall, pp. 322–32.
Jack, Peter Monro
1944. "A Review of Reviews: T. S. Eliot's *Four Quartets*," *American Bookman* Winter, pp. 91–99.
Joost, Nicholas, and Alan Brown
1978. "T. S. Eliot and Ernest Hemingway: A Literary Relationship," *Papers in Language and Literature* Fall, pp. 425–49.
Keeley, Edmund
1956. "T. S. Eliot and the Poetry of George Seferis," *Comparative Literature* Summer, pp. 214–26.
1969. "Seferis and the 'Mythical Method,'" *Comparative Literature Studies* June, pp. 109–25.
Kenner, Hugh
1959. *The Invisible Poet*. New York: McDowell, McDowell.
Kilgallen, Anthony R.
1965. "Eliot, Joyce, and Lowry," *Canadian Author and Bookman* Winter, pp. 3–6.
Kivimaa, Kirsti
1969. "Aspects of Style in T. S. Eliot's *Murder in the Cathedral*,"

Turun Yliopiston Julkaisuja, Annales Universitatis Turkensis, series B, pp. 1–96.

Knox, George A.

1951. "Quest for the Word in Eliot's *Four Quartets*," *ELH* Dec., pp. 310–21.

Knust, Herbert

1967. "Wagner, the King, and *The Waste Land*," *Pennsylvania State University Studies*, pp. 1–87.

Korg, Jacob

1960. "Modern Art Techniques in *The Waste Land*," *Journal of Aesthetics and Art Criticism* June, pp. 456–63.

Krieger, Murray

1956. *The New Apologists for Poetry*, pp. 46–56. Minneapolis: Univ. of Minnesota Pr.

Lancaster, R.V.

1972. "Symbols of the Journey in T. S. Eliot's 'Four Quartets,'" *Philobiblon*, pp. 32–39.

Laya, Arieh

1971. "Al-Sayyab and the Influence of T. S. Eliot," *Muslim World* July, pp. 197–201.

Leavis, F. R.

1932. *New Bearings in English Poetry*, pp. 75–132. London: Chatto and Windus.

1958. "T. S. Eliot's Stature as Critic," *Commentary* Nov., pp. 399–410.

Levy, Jiri

1959. "Rhythmical Ambivalence in the Poetry of T. S. Eliot," *Anglia*, pp. 54–64.

Little, Roger

1969. "T. S. Eliot and Saint-John Perse," *Arlington Quarterly* Autumn, pp. 5–17.

Litz, A. Walton

1972. "Pound and Eliot on *Ulysses:* The Critical Tradition," *James Joyce Quarterly* Fall, pp. 5–18.

1973. (editor) *Eliot in His Time*. Princeton: Princeton Univ. Pr.

Lorch, Thomas M.

1964. "The Relationship between *Ulysses* and *The Waste Land*," *Texas Studies in Literature and Language* Summer, pp. 123–33.

Ludwig, Richard

1973. "T. S. Eliot," in *Sixteen Modern American Authors*, ed. Jackson R. Bryer, rev. ed., pp. 181–222. New York: Norton.

Marcus, Phillip L.

1978. "'I Declare My Faith': Eliot's 'Gerontion' and Yeat's 'The Tower,'" *Papers in Language and Literature* Winter, pp. 74–82.

Mariani, Paul

1976. "The Poem as Field of Action: Guerilla Tactics in *Paterson*," *Iowa Review* Fall, pp. 94–117.

Martin, Graham
1970. (editor) *Eliot in Perspective*. London: Macmillan.
Martin, Mildred
1953. "T. S. Eliot: The Still Point and the Turning Wheel," *Bucknell Review*, pp. 51–68.
1972. *A Half Century of Eliot Criticism: An Annotated Bibliography of Books and Articles in English, 1916–1965*. Lewisburg, Pa.: Bucknell Univ. Pr.
Materer, Timothy
1979. *Vortex: Pound, Eliot, and Lewis*. Ithaca: Cornell Univ. Pr.
Matthiessen, F. O.
1935. *The Achievement of T. S. Eliot*. New York: Houghton Mifflin. Rev. 1947. Rev. by C. L. Barber, 1958.
McElderry, Bruce R., Jr.
1957. "Eliot's 'Shakespeherian Rag,'" *American Quarterly* Summer, pp. 185–86.
McLuhan, Marshall
1979. "Pound, Eliot, and the Rhetoric of *The Waste Land*," *New Literary History* Spring, pp. 557–80.
Melchiori, Giorgio
1954a. "*The Waste Land* and *Ulysses*," *English Studies* Apr., pp. 56–58.
1954b. "The Lotus and the Rose: D. H. Lawrence and Eliot's *Four Quartets*," *English Miscellany*, pp. 203–16.
Moody, A. D.
1974. (editor) *The Waste Land in Different Voices*. London: Edward Arnold.
1979. *Thomas Stearns Eliot, Poet*. Toronto: Univ. of Toronto Pr.
Moreh, Shmuel
1969. "The Influence of Western Poetry and Particularly T. S. Eliot on Modern Arabic Poetry (1947–1964)," *Asian and African Studies*, pp. 1–50.
Murphy, George D.
1971. "Hemingway's *Waste Land:* The Controlling Water Symbolism of *The Sun Also Rises*," *Hemingway Notes* Spring, pp. 20–26.
Nelson, C. E.
1963. "Saint-John Perse and T. S. Eliot," *Western Humanities Review* Spring, pp. 163–71.
Nowakowska, Nina
1977. *Language of Poetry and Generative Grammar: Toward Generative Poetics? (With Sample Analyses of T. S. Eliot's Poems)*. Poznan: Uniwersytet im Adama Michiewicza w Pozniau.
Palmer, Herbert E.
1933. "The Hoax and the Earnest of *The Waste Land*," *Dublin Magazine* Apr., pp. 11–19.

Partridge, A. C.
1976. *The Language of Modern Poetry: Yeats, Eliot, Auden.* London: Andre Deutsch.
Patterson, Gertrude
1971. *T. S. Eliot: Poems in the Making.* Manchester: Manchester United Pr.
Patteson, Richard
1976. "An Additional Source for 'The Waste Land,'" *Notes and Queries* July, pp. 300–301.
Pearce, T. S.
1969. *T. S. Eliot.* New York: Arco.
Porter, M. Gilbert
1969. "Narrative Stance in *Four Quartets:* Choreography and Commentary," *University Review*, pp. 57–66.
Pottorf, Michael
1976. "*The Great Gatsby:* Myrtle's Dog and Its Relation to the Dog-God of Pound and Eliot," *American Notes and Queries* Jan., pp. 88–90.
Rajan, Balachandra
1947. (editor) *T. S. Eliot: A Study of His Writings by Several Hands.* London. Dennis Dobson.
1976. *The Overwhelming Question: A Study of the Poetry of T. S. Eliot.* Toronto: Univ. of Toronto Pr.
Randall, Dale B. J.
1964. "The 'Seer' and 'Seen' Themes in *Gatsby* and Some of Their Parallels in Eliot and Wright," *Twentieth Century Literature* July, pp. 51–63.
Ransom, John Crowe
1941. *The New Criticism*, pp. 135–208. Norfolk, Conn.: New Directions.
Rayan, Krishna
1969. "Suggestiveness and Suggestion," *Essays in Criticism* July, pp. 309–19.
Rees, Thomas
1974. *The Technique of T. S. Eliot.* The Hague: Mouton.
Reinau, Peter
1978. *Recurring Patterns in T. S. Eliot's Prose and Poetry.* Berne: Francke.
Richards, I. A.
1930. *Principles of Literary Criticism*, pp. 289–94. New York: Harcourt Brace Jovanovich.
Rickman, H. P.
1959. "Poetry and the Ephemeral: Rilke's and Eliot's Conceptions of the Poet's Task," *German Life and Letters* Apr., pp. 174–85.
Riding, Laura, and Robert Graves
1927. *A Survey of Modernist Poetry.* London: W. Heinemann.

Rodgers, Audrey T.

1974. "Dance Imagery in the Poetry of T. S. Eliot," *Criticism* Winter, pp. 23–28.

1979. *The Universal Drum.* University Park: Pennsylvania State Univ. Pr.

Rosenthal, M. L.

1972. "*The Waste Land* as Open Structure," *Mosaic* Fall, pp. 181–89.

Sanders, Charles

1980. "*The Waste Land:* The Last Minstrel Show?" *Journal of Modern Literature* Feb., pp. 23–28.

Schwartz, Delmore

1945. "T. S. Eliot as International Hero," *Partisan Review* Spring, pp. 199–206.

1949. "The Literary Dictatorship of T. S. Eliot," *Partisan Review* Feb., pp. 119–37.

Seif, Morton

1954. "The Impact of T. S. Eliot on Auden and Spender," *South Atlantic Quarterly* Jan., pp. 61–69.

Semaan, Khalil I. H.

1969. "T. S. Eliot's Influence on Arabic Poetry and Theater," *Comparative Literature Studies* Dec., pp. 472–89.

Seyppel, Joachim

1972. *T. S. Eliot.* New York: F. Unger.

Shapiro, Karl

1960. "T. S. Eliot: The Death of Literary Judgment," *Saturday Review* Feb. 27, pp. 12–17, 34–36.

1962. "The Three Hockey Games of T. S. Eliot," *Antioch Review* Fall, pp. 284–86.

Short, M. H.

1972. " 'Prelude I' to a Literary Linguistic Stylistics," *Style* Spring pp. 149–58.

Sitwell, Edith

1934. *Aspects of Modern Poetry*, pp. 99–140. London: Duckworth.

Smidt, Kristian

1965. "T. S. Eliot and W. B. Yeats," *Revue des Langues Vivantes,* pp. 555–67.

Spears, Monroe K.

1970. *Dionysus and the City: Modernism in Twentieth Century Poetry*. New York: Oxford Univ. Pr.

Spender, Stephen

1935. *The Destructive Element*, pp. 132–75. London: Jonathan Cape.

1953. "Rilke and the Angels, Eliot and the Shrines," *Sewanee Review* Autumn, pp. 557–81.

1976. *T. S. Eliot.* New York: Viking Pr.
Sugiyama, Yoko
1961. "*The Waste Land* and Contemporary Japanese Poetry," *Comparative Literature* Summer, pp. 254–62.
Sultan, Stanley
1977. *Ulysses, The Waste Land, and Modernism.* Port Washington, N.Y.: Kennikat Pr.
Sutton, Walter
1963. *Modern American Criticism*, pp. 98–106. Englewood Cliffs, N.J.: Prentice-Hall.
Tate, Allen
1967. (editor) *T. S. Eliot: The Man and His Work.* New York: Delacorte Pr.
Thormählen, Marianne
1978. "*The Waste Land*": *A Fragmentary Wholeness.* Lund: C. W. K. Gleerup.
Thrash, Lois G.
1968. "A Source for the Redemption Theme in *The Cocktail Party*," *Texas Studies in Literature and Language* Winter, pp. 547–53.
Tomlinson, David
1980. "T. S. Eliot and the Cubists," *Twentieth Century Literature* Spring, pp. 64–81.
Traversi, Derek
1976. *T. S. Eliot: The Longer Poems.* New York: Harcourt Brace Jovanovich.
Tremaine, Louis
1977. "Witnesses to the Event in *Ma' sat al-Hallaj* and *Murder in the Cathedral*," *Muslim World* Jan., pp. 33–46.
Unger, Leonard
1948. (editor) *T. S. Eliot: A Selected Critique.* New York: Rinehart.
Vinograd, Sherna
1949. "The Accidental: A Clue to Structure in Eliot's Early Poetry," *Accent* Summer, pp. 231–38.
Virginia, Sister Marie
1958. "Some Symbols of Death and Destiny in *Four Quartets*," *Renascence* Summer, pp. 187–91.
Wain, John
1965. "T. S. Eliot," *Encounter* Mar., pp. 51–53.
Ward, David
1973. *T. S. Eliot: Between Two Worlds.* London: Routledge and Kegan Paul.
Watson, George
1965. "The Triumph of T. S. Eliot," *Critical Quarterly* Winter, pp. 328–37.

Webster, Grant
1979. *The Republic of Letters*, pp. 63–206. Baltimore: Johns Hopkins Univ. Pr.
Weigand, Elsie
1955. "Rilke and Eliot: The Articulation of the Mystic Experience," *Germanic Review* Oct., pp. 198–210.
Wetzel, Heinz
1970. "The Seer in the Spring: On *Tonio Kroger* and *The Waste Land*," *Revue de Litterature Comparée* July–Sept., pp. 322–32.
Williamson, Hugh Ross
1932. *The Poetry of T. S. Eliot*. London: Hodder and Stoughton.
Wilson, Edmund
1922. "The Poetry of Drouth," *Dial* Dec., pp. 611–16.
Winters, Yvor
1941. "T. S. Eliot: The Illusion of Reaction," *Kenyon Review* Winter, pp. 7–30.
Wood, Frank
1952. "Rilke and Eliot: Tradition and Poetry," *Germanic Review* Dec., pp. 246–59.
Wright, Keith
1965. "Rhetorical Repetition in T. S. Eliot's Early Verse," *Review of English Literature* Apr., pp. 93–100.
1966. "Word Repetition in T. S. Eliot's Early Verse," *Essays in Criticism* Apr., pp. 201–6.
Yeomans, W. E.
1968. "T. S. Eliot, Ragtime, and the Blues," *University Review*, pp. 267–77.
Young, Philip
1956. "Scott Fitzgerald's Waste Land," *Kansas Magazine*, pp. 53–57.

Selected Additional Readings

Birje-Patil, J.
1977. *Beneath the Axle-Tree: An Introduction to Eliot's Poems, Plays and Criticism*. Delhi: Macmillan Co. of India.
Bose, Amalendu
1948. "T. S. Eliot and Bengali Poetry," in *T. S. Eliot: A Symposium*, ed. Tambimuttu and Richard March, pp. 225–30. London: Editions Poetry.
Brotman, D. Bosley
1948. "T. S. Eliot: The Music of Ideas," *University of Toronto Quarterly* Oct., pp. 20–29.
Brown, Lloyd W.
1971. "The Historical Sense: T. S. Eliot and Two African Writers," *Conch* Mar., pp. 59–70.

Dallas, Elizabeth
1965. "Canon Cancrizans and the *Four Quartets*," *Comparative Literature* Summer, pp. 193–208.
Davison, Richard Allen
1972. "Hart Crane, Louis Untermeyer, and T. S. Eliot," *American Literature* Mar., pp. 143–46.
Gallivan, Patricia
1975. " 'The Comic Spirit' and *The Waste Land*," *University of Toronto Quarterly* Fall, pp. 35–49.
Geraldine, Sister M.
1967. "The Rhetoric of Repetition in *Murder in the Cathedral*," *Renascence* Spring, pp. 132–41.
Hoover, Judith Myers
1978. "The Urban Nightmare: Alienation Imagery in the Poetry of T. S. Eliot and Octavio Paz," *Journal of Spanish Studies: Twentieth Century* Spring, pp. 13–28.
Johnson, Anthony L.
1976. *Sign and Structure in the Poetry of T. S. Eliot.* Pisa: Editrice Technico Scientifica.
McGann, Mary E.
1976. "*The Waste Land* and *The Sound and the Fury:* To Apprehend the Human Process Moving in Time," *Southern Literary Journal* Fall, pp. 13–21.
Ransom, John Crowe
1968. "T. S. Eliot: A Postscript," *Southern Review* Autumn, pp. 579–97.
Wilson, Frank
1948. *Six Essays in the Development of T. S. Eliot.* London: Fortune Pr.
Woodward, Kathleen
1980. *At Last, the Real Distinguished Thing: The Late Poems of Eliot, Pound, Stevens, and Williams.* Columbus: Ohio State Univ. Pr.

Index

Note: Prefatory material and chapter references are not indexed.

PROSE